BARTÓK'S CHAMBER MUSIC

BARTÓK'S CHAMBER MUSIC

JÁNOS KÁRPÁTI

PENDRAGON PRESS
STUYVESANT, NY

Title of the Hungarian original: Bartók kamarazenéje (Budapest: Zeneműkiadó, 1976).
Translated by Fred Macnicol and Mária Steiner
Translation revised by Paul Merrick

Library of Congress Cataloging-in-Publication Data

Kárpáti, János
    [Bartók kamarazenéje. English]
    Bartók's chamber music / János Kárpáti; [translated by Fred Macnicol and Mária Steiner
    p. cm.
    Includes bibliographical references and index.
    ISBN 0-945193-19-X
    1. Bartók, Béla, 1881–1945. Chamber music. 2. Chamber music—20th century—History and criticism. I. Title.
    ML410.B26K413   1994
    785'.0092—dc20   93-45813
                                                                          CIP
                                                                          MN

CONTENTS

PREFACE

This book is an enlarged version of my earlier work, *Bartók's String Quartets* (Corvina Press, 1975). The possiblity of further amplification was in fact inherent in the first version itself, since the six quartets, though quite self-contained as a formal group, are linked by countless threads to other Bartók pieces, particularly his chamber works. That I attached importance to this relationship in the first version of the work could be seen in Part One: "Musical Idiom and Style," where I examined the style of the string quartets in virtually every respect against the background of Bartók's complete output, and have thus transferred this part to the present volume without any essential change. The enlargement and revision concerns mainly Part Two: "Analyses," to which a chapter on the early chamber works has been added, as well as analyses of the two Sonatas for Violin and Piano, the Sonata for Two Pianos and Percussion, and the trio Contrasts for Violin, Clarinet and Piano.

As becomes clear from this list, chamber works in my interpretation are compositions scored for small instrumental ensembles with the parts assuming completely equal roles and the structure being a complex large form. This consideration explains why the two Rhapsodies for Violin and the 44 Duos for Violins have not been included in the series of the works analyzed individually, though they are several times referred to in both parts of the book.

I would like to add that although the young Bartók composed ten chamber works between 1895 and 1904, the same number he wrote between 1908 and 1939, the first chapter includes only the most significant ones, and even those only in a summary discussion, as it is my firm belief that only the mature works (i.e., composed after 1908), which Bartók himself considered to be his very own, can offer an authentic picture of the composer.

In compiling the two parts of the work, I wished to avoid redundancy as much as possible, so in Part Two I left out phenomena already discussed in Part One. That is why to obtain detailed knowledge of an individual work both parts have to be consulted.

I wish to express my gratitude to all those who with their opinions, criticism and advice on the first version of my work, have helped the birth of the present revised and enlarged edition—the late Lajos Bárdos and Zoltán Gárdonyi as well as Peter Evans, György Kroó, György Kurtág, Ernő Lendvai, Jim Samson, Halsey Stevens, András Szőllősy and József Ujfalussy.

Special thanks are due to László Somfai for lending essential assistance in placing the material of the Budapest Bartók Archives at my disposal, and for his strictly analytical and at the same time constructive criticism, which gave me the greatest incentive towards completing my first work in 1976. The same should be said about Elliott Antikoletz whose help and criticism more recently played the most important role in this rather late English publication.

I am also indebted to the translators of my book: Fred Macnicol and Mária Steiner, and particularly to Paul Merrick who undertook the difficult work of its revision.

Budapest, August 1991
János Kárpáti

INTRODUCTION

The Place of Chamber Music in Bartók's Oeuvre

At first sight, a work devoted to Bartók's chamber music looks as though it were simply concerned with a genre division, attempting an exposition of no more than a single aspect of the whole oeuvre. But in Bartók's case the chamber music is not simply a matter of grouping according to genre: it is really the framework for his whole oeuvre. This applies especially to the string quartets, which accompany Bartók through his creative life from the very earliest youthful efforts to the last and unfulfilled plan of his life, the "seventh" String Quartet (Szabolcsi 1961:120).

We shall, therefore, be chiefly concerned with the string quartets, since they occupy a central position in Bartók's oeuvre. It would, nevertheless, be a great mistake to cut off these works from their connections with the other chamber works. For these, like shrubs, stand around the towering trees of the string quartets; among them there are characteristic "accompanying" or supplementary works, and there are others which rise to equal the level of the string quartets themselves, and can almost be considered along with this imposing series of six works.

When the string quartet originated as a genre, in Haydn's period, six compositions were required to be considered a work—an opus. This unwritten law of European music's golden age bears witness to true richness: these works appearing by the dozen or by the half-dozen were not at all the result of "mass production," at least not with the great masters. The opuses of Haydn, Mozart and Beethoven, consisting of groups of six string quartets, are the greatest masterpieces of the literature within the genre. This creative method was a legacy from the preceding period, when it was only by being arranged into groups like this that sonatas and concertos would be published. Publication practice does, however, reveal much in connection with the

contemporary practices of, and social respect (or disrespect) for, creative work in music: a single sonata, chamber work, or concerto did not
carry enough weight to be regarded as a work. Only in Beethoven's
lifetime is a change visible: string quartets and sonatas arranged into
groups of six and three gradually become rarer. One sonata or one
string quartet by the elderly Beethoven stands on its own: it carries as
much weight as a symphony or orchestral work.

The individual nature of musical creation and this transformation of its social function, beginning in Beethoven's lifetime and lasting right up to the present day, led to the "intensive" aspect of artistic
creation—its inner weight, density of content—becoming more important than the "extensive." Only in this way can the proportion shift
be explained, in which, as compared with the approximately one
hundred symphonies produced by Haydn and the approximately fifty
symphonies produced by Mozart, Beethoven composed only nine
symphonies, yet these nine works not only occupy a central position in
his own output but in the music of the whole period as well.

In the same sense, Bartók's string quartets are also central;
through their inner weight and concentration they are characteristically representative of his art as a whole, and at the same time—by
virtue of Bartók's importance—they compress within themselves the
most characteristic musical achievements of the first half of the twentieth century. Related features in the art of Beethoven and Bartók
have been noted for a long time now in the Bartók literature. As early
as 1929, for example, after the Budapest première of the Third and
Fourth Quartets, Aladár Tóth drew attention to the presence in
Bartók's work of a kind of periodicity also to be found in Beethoven,
who generally experimented with the new in his piano works, let it
mature in the symphonies, and finally sublimated it to its most refined
forms in his string quartets.[1] Being familiar with the complete oeuvre,
and now looking back with a certain perspective, we should be inclined to modify Aladár Tóth's statement in that with Bartók the
string quartets stand at the heart of individual creative periods; they

---

[1]Aladár Tóth, "Bartók új vonósnégyesei" [Bartók's New String Quartets], *Zenei
Szemle* XIII (1929): 63.

do not so much refine the new as compress within themselves every element of its message and form (Perle 1967:196). Before discussing the subject more deeply in a general critical examination of the style and analysis of the works, we should attempt to form a comprehensive picture of the relationship between his oeuvre as a whole and the chamber works.

Among the first compositions of the young Bartók, the Piano Quintet dating from 1904 stands out in particular. It appeared on the programme at the 1910 première of the First String Quartet, along with the Fourteen Bagatelles for piano—so that Bartók considered it worthy of performance even *after* writing the First Quartet. Yet, strictly speaking, a sharp dividing line can be drawn between the Piano Quintet and the First String Quartet. The Piano Quintet is a significant composition only in that it summarizes on a mature level the young Bartók's Romantic national tone carried on from Liszt. Indeed a similar role is played by the *Kossuth* Symphonic Poem, the Rhapsody op. 1 and the Suite No. 1. But whereas the influence of Richard Strauss dominates in the orchestration of the *Kossuth* Symphonic Poem and the First Suite, it is the Liszt inheritance that freely manifests itself in the piano chamber music. After the Piano Quintet almost four years passed before Bartók set about writing a chamber work again. These four years constitute an important period in his lifetime: it was the period of true maturing when the young artist pondered his aims and took stock of his possibilities with ruthless frankness. It is clear from his correspondence that it was these years that formed his personality—under the combined influence of several failures, loss of his illusions, and possibly an unrequited love. But the crisis period, as these few years are called by the biographical literature, also gathered together reserves of strength to extricate him from the crisis. After his visit to Paris in 1905, it was not only the unjust defeat suffered at the Rubinstein competition that affected him, but the life-influencing experience of the French capital itself. The unrequited love for Stefi Geyer was likewise compensated for artistically by the Violin Concerto and particularly the fourteenth Bagatelle (*Ma mie qui dance*). Yet most important of all, as a result of the first folk music-collecting journeys, the new creative ideal took shape which he was to follow throughout his whole life.

The First String Quartet, dating from 1908, bears witness to the crisis, but at the same time contains all the new features coming to life in Bartók at around that time. In the slow, measured music of the polyphonically unfolding first movement we find an explanation for virtually everything. And this is not the only movement of its kind; it has a kinship with the first of the *Two Portraits*, the "Ideal," which is the first movement of the Violin Concerto written for Stefi Geyer. Its yearning and resigned character more or less faithfully reflects Bartók's world of thought, which was struggling with the philosophy of Nietzsche and Schopenhauer. And as József Ujfalussy points out, the "Painful Wrestling" from the Ten Easy Piano Pieces, bearing a relation to the sorrowful cor anglais solo in Wagner's *Tristan*, also belongs here (Ujfalussy 1971:89).

For Bartók it appears that only in these years did the Wagner influence of his student days—manifesting itself as mere enthusiasm—come to full realization. Certainly the opening movement of the First Quartet could scarcely be imagined without the Wagner background, not just because of its melodiousness, going back on itself and resembling the "Painful Wrestling," but because of the harmony as well. Even the parallel thirds, which Stevens considers a Brahmsian influence, point rather to Wagner, and particularly to the Prelude to Act 3 of *Tristan* (Stevens 1964:173–76). In these parallel thirds it is not Brahms's kind of strong tonality which appears, but the veiled tonality characteristic of Wagner. At the same time the movement bears evidence of other influences: free counterpoint used for a string quartet follows the example of the late Beethoven works; in the same movement the influence of French music, mainly Debussy and Ravel, makes its first appearance in Bartók's art; and finally, the fresh folk music experience appears here as well.

It is almost unbelievable that these diverse, sometimes opposing elements—Beethovenian fugue, Wagnerian harmony, the third and sixth mixtures of Ravel and Debussy, and lastly the melodiousness of folk music—can meet in a single work, indeed in a single movement, without destroying one another. On the basis of the most recent results it can be assumed that the less heterogeneous, yet also less inspired, second and third movements of the First String Quartet were finished before the first movement, and so the qualitative leap forward in creative development really came within the period (we do not know exactly whether it is a period of weeks or several months) when Bartók composed the first movement.[2] In any case, there is certainly a remarkable interrelationship between different works dating from roughly the same time. In tone and technique the first movement of this quartet relates to the first movement of the Stefi Geyer Violin Concerto, and at the same time—as pointed out by Denijs Dille—its theme is akin to the theme of the Violin Concerto's second movement.[3] The Violin Concerto, however, is connected by other threads to the Fourteen Bagatelles, since the final form of the *Two Portraits* came into being later by making use of the last of the Bagatelles.

This inverted compositional order of the movements apparently contradicts Kodály's remark that the third movement is a *retour à la vie*.[4] The chronological order of composition does not, however, result unconditionally from the events of life. This whole creative period is characterized by a *retour à la vie*, for the fact that Bartók added a distorted, grotesque variation to the "Ideal" portrait likewise indicates that having succeeded in getting beyond the love crisis, he was capable of turning the idealized portrait of woman into its own antithesis, in this way writing it out of himself, so to speak. The First Quartet is a much more pioneering work, a successful experiment, than a summary. Viewed from a distance, this is also indicated by its position in the creative period as a whole: the year 1908 does not finish, but starts, a development which later achieves consummation in 1911 in the opera *Bluebeard's Castle*; by then the folk music elements, appearing only sporadically in the string quartet, have matured. There is almost a complete decade between the composition of the First String Quartet and

[2]Denijs Dille, "Angaben zum Violinkonzert 1907, den Deux Portraits, dem Quartett Op.7 und den Zwei rumänischen Tänzen," *Documenta Bartókiana* (1965), 92.

[3]Bartók himself also refers to this in a letter to Stefi Geyer. See note 2.

[4]Zoltán Kodály, "Bartók Béla II. vonósnégyese" [Bartók's Second String Quartet], *Nyugat* XI (1918).

the completion of the Second Quartet in 1917. Of all his string quartets, the second was conceived, matured, and took shape over the longest period of time in Bartók's creative imagination. He himself indicated 1915 as the date when he began the work—that is, he worked on it, even if not continuously, over three, or at least two years. During the same period he wrote *The Wooden Prince* and the Suite for Piano, not to mention several smaller works as well.

The fertile creative work of the war years is preceded by a period of "silence" in 1913. If we look for biographical reasons for this pause, we are struck by the increasingly far-reaching folk song-collecting journeys. After the Hungarian, Slovakian, and Rumanian collections, a more distant journey was undertaken that year as well: Bartók went to North Africa and, as long as his health permitted him, worked for two weeks in the oases of the Biskra district. Although scientific publication of the material found there came later, traces of the creative digestion of this musical experience are to be observed as early as the compositions dating from around 1915–17.

The appearance of an Arab folk music influence in Bartók's art does not mean merely a new colour in the palette of Hungarian, Rumanian, and Slovakian elements; it also facilitates a certain summarizing and reinterpretation. In one of his later works, the 1923 Dance Suite, he shows how it is possible to combine the characteristic elements of Hungarian, Rumanian and Arab folk music. Even preceding this, the Second String Quartet, the Suite for Piano, and *The Miraculous Mandarin* are examples of how this summarizing can be realized not only "horizontally," but also "vertically" in Bartók's style, which merges the various elements into a unified idiom. The first prerequisite for this merging was—and this refers back to an earlier creative phase—that the Hungarian (or mother-tongue) elements should mature and find their own natural leading role. As has previously stated, this was not yet the case in the First Quartet: only later, after numerous folk song arrangements, did it come about in the opera *Bluebeard's Castle*, the melodic world of which is pervaded in a unified and homogeneous way by the most ancient layer of pentatony in Hungarian folk music. This, therefore, was the basis which made possible the incorporation of the other folk music elements. Between

Bluebeard and the Second Quartet stands an individual Janus-faced work: the Four Pieces for Orchestra whose original conception dates from 1912, but which only came to be orchestrated once there were clear prospects for the première in 1921. The French-style natural poesy of its first movement points back to the *Two Pictures*, while its painfully passionate declamation points to *Bluebeard*. At the same time, quite surprisingly, the tone of the second piece (scherzo) anticipates the cruel, inhuman tone of *The Wooden Prince* and *The Miraculous Mandarin*.

It is here, in the Four Pieces, that the structural conception of the Second String Quartet, ending with a slow movement, first appears, and—as pointed out by József Ujfalussy—becomes the most typical formal plan of this period: we find it in the Suite for piano, the Five Songs, and, strictly speaking, in *The Miraculous Mandarin* as well (Ujfalussy 1971:142). This "tragic dramaturgy" is the achievement of Bartók's wartime and post-war art, showing that he had freed himself from illusions and gained a more profound and more moving vision of reality. The swelling lines of the First Quartet, beginning in the Wagner-Nietzsche tone, are here almost exactly reversed. The romantic voice of what was a personal hopelessness and death-wish is here replaced by the voice of an artist lamenting the Hungarian fate and that of humanity, a tone stemming not from individual awareness of life, but from identification with the social problems of the nation and of the age.

In all certainty, this is why the Second String Quartet represents an opening towards the external world, not only as regards the folk music elements: contemporary European art also makes itself conspicuous here for the first time (Perle 1967). The harsh motion, dolefully soliloquizing tone, and free tonality of Schoenberg's Three Piano Pieces, opus 11—though in a filtered form—appear unmistakably in Bartók's Suite for Piano and the Second String Quartet, and later command an increasingly important role in the op. 18 Studies, the Improvisations, and the two Sonatas for Violin and Piano. From the Four Pieces to the Dance Suite—that is, from 1912 to 1923—we see a unified and uninterrupted development; the works refer to each other, and although each is an independent, separate world, numerous common features are evident. The most striking transformation is found in the structural conception. After *The Miraculous Mandarin* the series of slow finales ending in a tragic gesture suddenly stops and the reverse begins to evolve: the tragic, sorrowful tone appears in the opening movements and the closing movements assume a fast, or at least faster, robust folk-dance character. Once more it is necessary to refer to József Ujfalussy's observation that, in Bartók, it is in the First and Second Violin-Piano Sonatas that the struggling tone, free tonality, and harsh expressive melody of the Viennese style first meets the closing movements of folk music conception (Ujfalussy 1971:200–201). This is one of many reasons for us to see the two Violin-Piano sonatas as "key compositions" similar to the string quartets.

The Third String Quartet, written in 1927, is again separated from the second by ten years. The two Sonatas for Violin and Piano, however, form a bridge between them. Like the Second Sonata, the Third Quartet is a two-part structure, and a large part is played in it by the characteristic "micro-melodic" quality present in the Violin-Piano Sonatas and perfected in the piano piece *The Night's Music*. The Third String Quartet is really the fruit of a period reflecting new aspirations. The turning point was the year 1926, which, as in 1913, was preceded by a period of "silence." This time, however, the productivity is quite imposing: within a single year Bartók writes the Sonata, the cycle *Out of Doors*, the Nine Little Piano Pieces, and the First Piano Concerto. And the Third String Quartet, written in 1927, is immediately followed in 1928 by the Fourth Quartet and the two Violin Rhapsodies.

The two string quartets, written in such close proximity, together form a central point for the works composed around them. The third is connected by strong threads not only to the two-movement Violin-Piano Sonata, but the Rhapsodies as well. The Fourth String Quartet seemingly represents a great turning point, for here a symmetrical five-section structure appears openly, a marked contrast to the two-part structure. The idiomatic-stylistic connection binding the Fourth Quartet to the Third is more important than the structural opposition. That is, in both works the thematic material can be traced back to one or two fundamental melodic germs or basic formulas. Apart from this, the two works are related to each other by a similar conception of tonality. In the Fourth Quartet Bartók further develops with strict regularity and consistency the complementary twelve-note system evolved in the Third Quartet. We might also say that after the preparatory experiments of the Third, it is in the Fourth that Bartók comes closest to the Schoenberg technique without actually adopting it in its complete, original form.

In the Fourth String Quartet it is not just this formal crystallization which appears: the individual types of tone also take on a more final form. The best example is the second movement, the sweeping, glittering scherzo mood of which can be found in earlier works as well—at the end of the Second Quartet's middle movement, for example, or the second part of the Third Quartet. What in the earlier works was merely a detail, an episode, single transitional patches in the dynamic variation or development processes, becomes in the Fourth Quartet a complete movement, an independent unit. In a similar way the so-called "night-music" tone also evolves. What Bartók developed into a complete work in the 1926 piano piece had already emerged earlier in an isolated way in the Violin Piano Sonatas; it then appeared in an equally isolated way in the first part of the Third Quartet. In the Fourth Quartet, however, it gains greater emphasis by virtue of its position: it forms the symmetry-axis of the whole work as its central third movement. It is curious, though demonstrating all the more clearly the complexity of Bartók's creative development, that in the Third and Fourth Quartets, which come closer to twelve-note technique, the folk music elements are appreciably more tangible than in the First and Second Quartets. This is not a step backwards but unites folk music and art music on a higher level. The two Violin Rhapsodies written during the same period also bear witness to this, as well as the latest large-scale series of folk-song arrangements, the Twenty Hungarian Folksongs.

Although, as far as the external plan is concerned, the Fifth String Quartet stands nearest to the Fourth Quartet, numerous factors do nevertheless distinguish the two compositions from one another. Between them—and at the same time between the two crea-

tive periods they represent—stands the watershed of the two great
works of the years 1930 and 1931, *Cantata Profana* and the Second
Piano Concerto. The latter still shows a strong bond with the 1926
neo-Baroque-style piano pieces; indeed, the Stravinsky influence is
even more thematically unambiguous. The *Cantata*, on the other
hand, prefaces the great works of the thirties.

In the five-movement structure of the Fifth Quartet the function
of the outer pillar movements has not changed in comparison with the
Fourth Quartet, but the transformation in the three inner movements
is all the more apparent. It is not a slow movement in the center here
but a scherzo in Bulgarian rhythm, and on each side of it a slow movement. Arranged so, the five-movement structure is even more
balanced than that of the Fourth Quartet since, by means of their fast
tempi, the first, third, and fifth movements form a unified arrangement into which the connecting chain of the two slow movements fits
more naturally. Beyond this, the Second Piano Concerto provides a
direct example of this formal construction, for the central movement
contains similar slow–fast–slow periodicity. That more or less similar
symmetrical organization obtains even within the individual movements also belongs to the symmetrical arrangement of the string quartet.

The Fifth String Quartet also is central within the creative
period concerned. On the one hand it begins the series of great works
dating from the thirties, continuing with the *Music for Strings, Percussion and Celesta* and the Sonata for Two Pianos and Percussion, on
the other hand it quite perceptibly retains a connection with the "border compositions," the Second Piano Concerto and *Cantata Profana*.
The thirties also saw a large-scale maturing and summarizing in the 44
Duos for Two Violins, finished in 1931, and the *Mikrokosmos*, completed in 1937. Detailed analyses will clearly show how what appears
in these series broken up into its parts, in the Fifth Quartet forms a
closed, complete, and complex world. How curious an order is also
displayed in the fact that these three compositions represent three
different structures at the peak of Bartók's creative career (1934,
1936, 1937): whereas the Fifth Quartet is constructed in a five-section
bridge-form (palindrome form) structure symmetrical in its every par-

ticle, the *Music for Strings, Percussion and Celesta* and the Sonata for Two Pianos and Percussion illustrate two fundamental (four-movement and three-movement) types of the classical sonata structure.

The slow–fast–slow–fast structure of the *Music* further builds a bridge in the direction of the Baroque sonata, and through this anticipates, as it were, formal endeavours of the final creative period, showing two-section divisions. It is true that three-part and five-part structures are present here, too (Violin Concerto, the Third Piano Concerto, Contrasts, the Concerto), but structurally greater novelty is represented by the Baroque four-movement Sonata for Solo Violin, and above all by the Sixth String Quartet.

Here we have moved into the last creative period. Although the course of Bartók's life can be divided into different periods, it was not in the first unproductive years of emigration that the creative turning point took place, but during the last years in Europe. This curving backwards, romantic in content, and already begun in the Violin Concerto (finished in 1938), and the Divertimento (dating from 1939), has its two most obvious representatives in the Sixth String Quartet and the Third Piano Concerto. There is absolutely no decrease in creativity here, or a diminishing of demands as regards concentration of expression, as certain aestheticians have interpreted this period. The transformation is of a qualitative nature, evidence of a change in aims and a whole new way of looking at things. Bartók is stimulated to a more "public" expression by the war and the danger threatening humanity; abstractness is replaced by the desire for concreteness, the innovative attitude by the idea of preservation and protection.

At this time Bartók turns back towards his own youth: once again Beethoven, the one-time model, assumes greater importance, and once again the *Leitmotiv* and the broken four-note chords reminiscent of Romanticism appear. The Sixth Quartet, composed in 1939, surprisingly harkens back, in its cyclical monothematicism, to the First Quartet. At the same time we are reminded of the Second Quartet by its slow ending. It would appear that in Bartók this construction consistently accompanies the "in tempora belli" works; the earlier work was written in the very midst of the First World War, and the later work at the time of the outbreak of the Second World War.

So—like its predecessors—the Sixth Quartet is also a central work, the problems of the war years are best concentrated in it, and it, too, has its hidden or open connecting threads branching out towards the other works.

To seek a direct reflection of the events of life and the world in the works would be to grossly simplify the mechanism of Bartók's creative art. Here, in the case of the Sixth String Quartet, however, it is impossible to disregard these interrelationships, if only because during the process of its composition, a change took place in the conception of the work which reveals a great deal about Bartók's inner world. Originally he had planned a quick finale for the work, yet instead he chose a sorrowful, resigned farewell. The transformation—as will be shown later in the analysis—was demanded by the inner nature of the musical material, but it is still impossible to separate from external events, for at that time Bartók was urgently concerned with the dilemma of whether to emigrate or remain at home.

If the Sixth Quartet is par excellence the work of the wartime creative period, and something of a foreboding of the tragedies which actually did come to pass, the Third Piano Concerto (which still really belongs here stylistically) with its relaxing tone and devout attitude, heralds a new creative period. Nevertheless, it has no continuation. In the last days Bartók still talked of compositional plans, among them mentioned a string quartet, but this "seventh" quartet was not to materialize.

I have attempted to give a general survey of Bartók's oeuvre by way of examining the place occupied by the chamber music, and I have attempted to divide it into periods. Such a division into periods is naturally not the only method towards the understanding of a genius, nor does it create an artificial "tidiness" out of the "untidiness" of spontaneous development. Development—even its most spontaneous form—always has its own inner laws, especially in the case of geniuses. I have tried to divide Bartók's oeuvre into periods on the basis of these inner laws, and it is precisely in the central position of the string quartets that one of these inner laws presents itself. It is very difficult to draw sharp demarcation lines between the periods, and it is purely in the interest of lucidity that I sought individual years as turning points.

The following table is another attempt at a summary and to make the survey clearly comprehensible. The reader should, however, consider all this as no more than greatly simplified guiding lines.

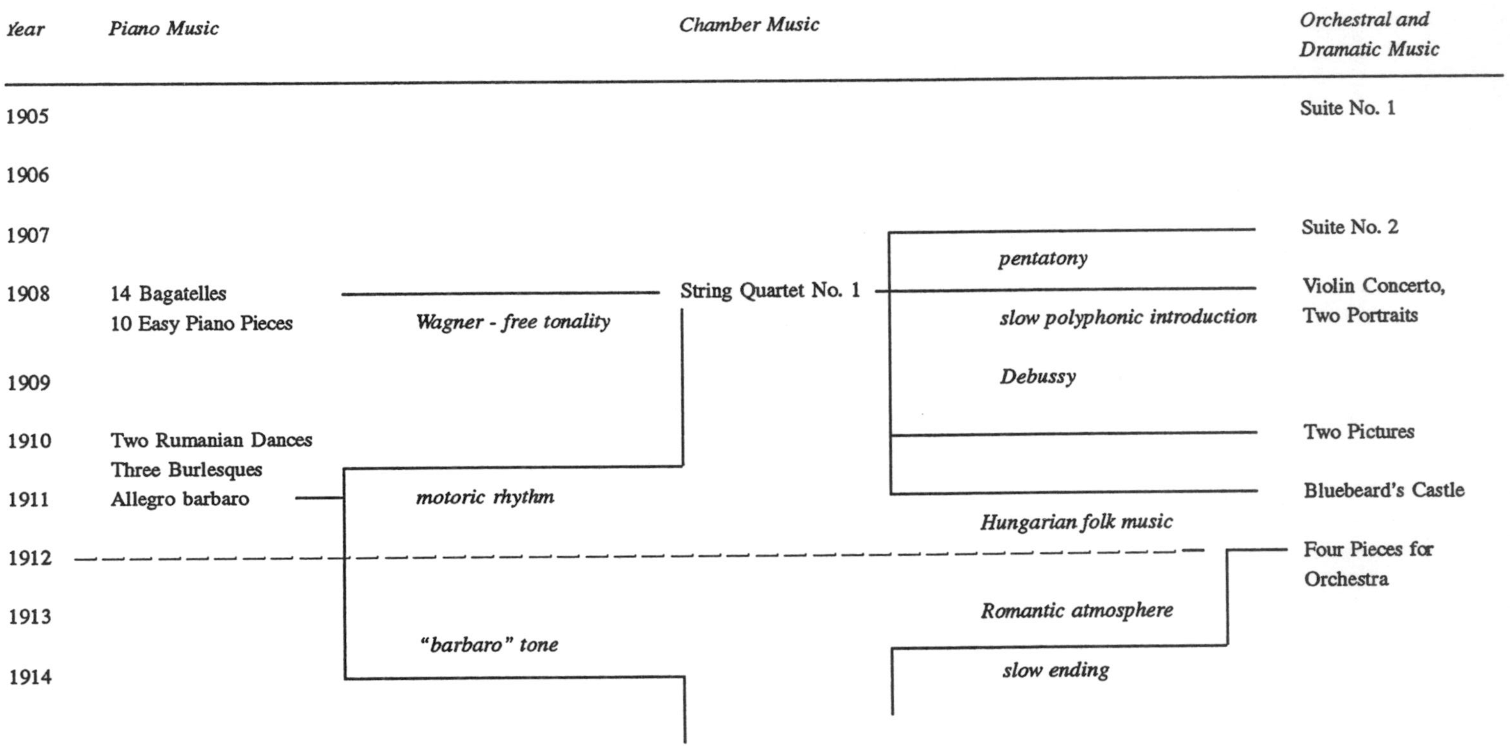

Year	Piano Music	Chamber Music	Orchestral and Dramatic Music
1905			Suite No. 1
1906			
1907			Suite No. 2
1908	14 Bagatelles 10 Easy Piano Pieces	String Quartet No. 1	Violin Concerto, Two Portraits
1909			
1910	Two Rumanian Dances Three Burlesques		Two Pictures
1911	Allegro barbaro		Bluebeard's Castle
1912			Four Pieces for Orchestra
1913			
1914			

Wagner - free tonality

motoric rhythm

"barbaro" tone

pentatony

slow polyphonic introduction

Debussy

Hungarian folk music

Romantic atmosphere

slow ending

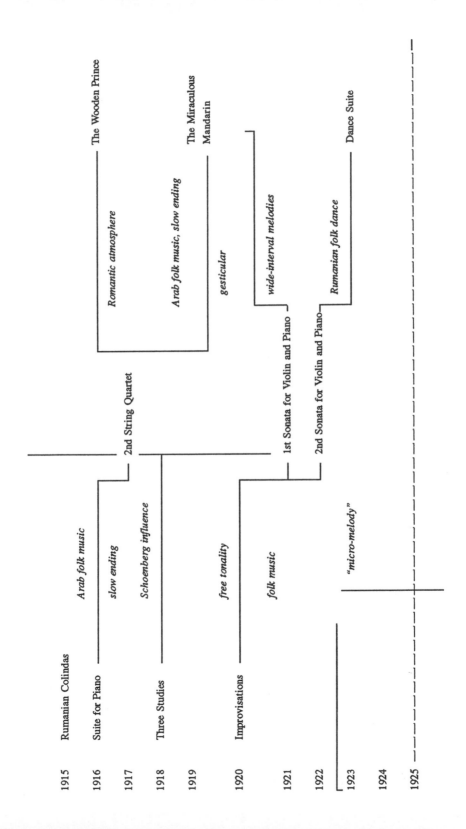

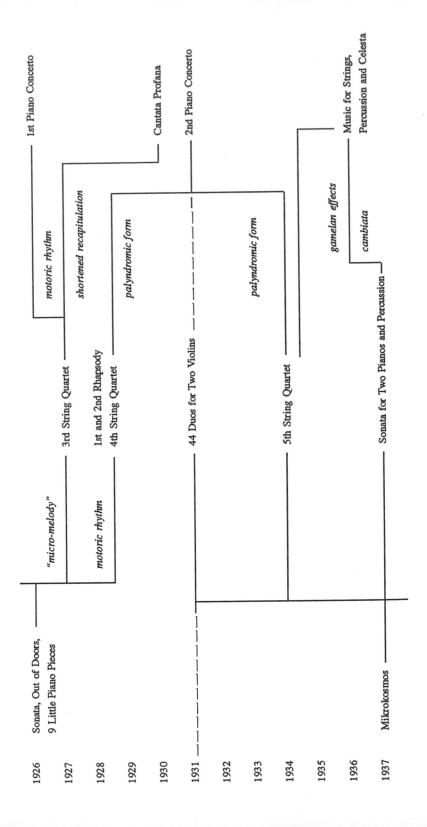

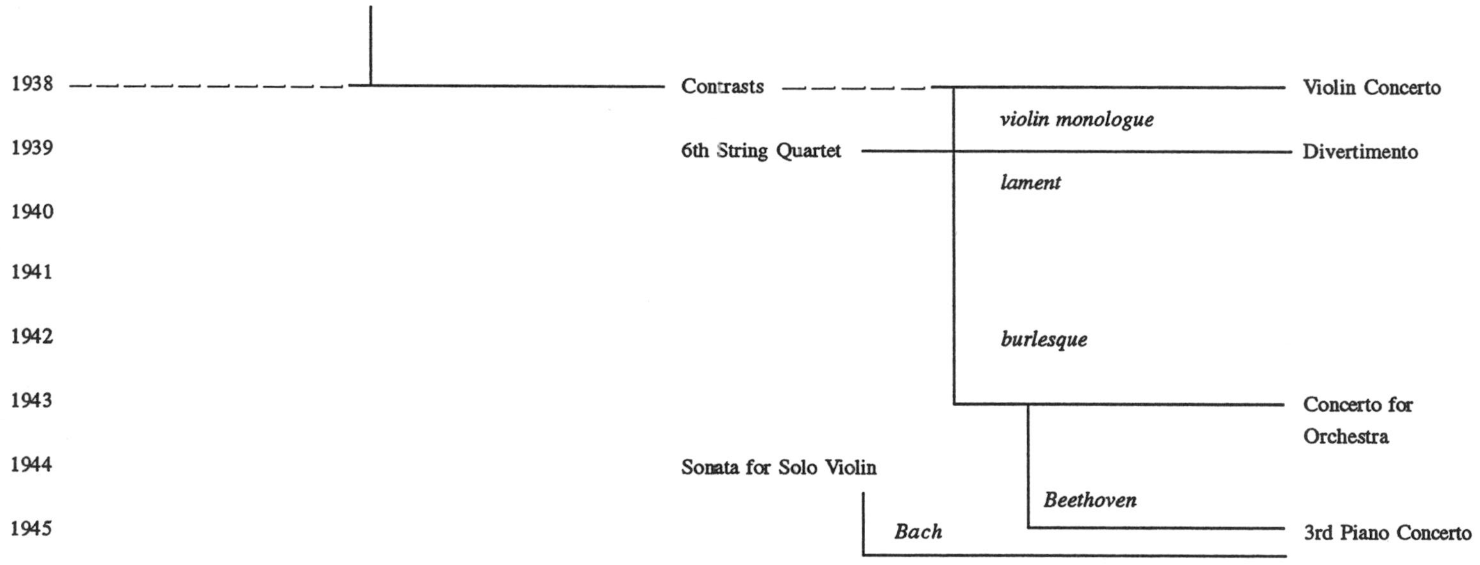

1938

1939

1940

1941

1942

1943

1944

1945

Contrasts

6th String Quartet

Sonata for Solo Violin

violin monologue

lament

burlesque

Beethoven

Bach

Violin Concerto

Divertimento

Concerto for
Orchestra

3rd Piano Concerto

PART ONE

MUSICAL IDIOM AND STYLE

CHAPTER ONE

THE LEGACY OF BEETHOVEN

Nineteenth-century developments did not favour chamber music, particularly not the string quartet. The revolutionary branch of Romanticism was drawn rather towards new, larger and more programme-like forms. From the so-called conservative romantics, engaged in the active continuation of classical traditions and forms, chamber music scarcely obtained any new meaning or new light to stimulate it to further development. It became the middle-class home genre par excellence, the indoor, small-circle art, which in this way lost not only its earlier dimensions in externals, but also in its inner conception. Thus, however faithfully the quartets of Schumann and Brahms preserve the classical form, in essence they became estranged from the Beethoven legacy.

It was the twentieth century which brought the chamber music renaissance. This renaissance showed itself not only in terms of quantity, on increased interest in the genre and in the number of works produced, but together with an inner, essential rebirth, a broadening of the possibilities of the genre. At the turn of the century itself there was still no such tendency: both the Debussy string quartet (1893) and the Ravel (1903) are characteristically isolated works. Their themes and their harmonic world do indeed reflect the principal features and stylistic elements of the new French school, although characteristically, they do not receive chamber music treatment. The position occupied by these works in the oeuvre is very revealing: it is as if the genre were alien to the composers, for whom the two quartets appear as just an experiment in a territory strange to them, not to be continued later. Ravel's other chamber works have even less to do with the classical tradition, rather representing an important step forward in the direction of new colour effects.

Among the great masters of the turn of the century, it is only Reger who places the quartet genre once more in a central position. True, in Reger this is rooted principally in his artistic attitude which reflects upon the past. The intention to regenerate is there indeed, but behind it lies a thwarted attempt at resurrection. His influence on Bartók was nevertheless beneficial: in the extravagantly chromatic, verbose musical thinking of late Romanticism, which loosened everything, he assisted the recognition of the binding force in Classical and Baroque tradition.

The new Viennese school which grew out of the late Romantic world initially followed the path of Romantic quartet art. This is borne out by Schoenberg's sextet (*Verklärte Nacht*), which employs the idiom of Wagner and the technique of Brahms, and also to a certain extent by his first two string quartets. Yet at the same time it becomes clear that with this new kind of polyphonic structural method, much more variegated than what preceded it, Schoenberg seeks to rely more on the laws of the genre's classical period—and mainly on Beethoven.

What kinds of models can have been before Bartók when he composed his First String Quartet in 1908 ? The great paragons in his artistic development—Wagner, Liszt and Richard Strauss—were able to offer him nothing in this area. Brahms is the only composer who could have provided a more immediate example, but in the F Major String Quartet composed in 1898, the young Bartók had already moved essentially beyond this influence. In this way, he was 'obliged' to jump back almost a century to the classical summit of quartet music, the works of Beethoven.

In this connection a few statements by him are well known. In 1929 he wrote to Edwin von der Null : "In my youth Bach and Mozart were not my ideals of the beautiful, but rather Beethoven" (Null 1930:108). And in his 1939 discussion with Serge Moreux he mentions as his highest creative ideal a synthesis of the art of Bach, Beethoven and Debussy (Moreux 1949). In any event, his personal attraction to Beethoven is evidenced by a very revealing quotation-like detail in the slow movement of the Third Piano Concerto. Although there can be no question of a note-for- note literal quotation, Bartók does unmistakably refer here to the ethereal chorale of Beethoven's A Minor String Quartet op. 132, and also builds up the whole movement in a similar manner.

This gesture of homage is to be found in another of his works as well, this time within the string quartet genre. In the two slow movements of the Fifth String Quartet, connected via a variational relationship, there also crops up a chorale-like detail in which the archaic character of the plagal chord progressions similarly reminds us of the atmosphere of the Heiliger Dankgesang in lydischer Tonart.

The Beethovenian features in Bartók's art, however, can hardly be appraised by mentioning a few quotations or references. Deeper relationships are manifest in a coincidence of creative principles and compositional methods. Straight away in the First String Quartet there is evidence of such coincidence: the slow opening movement of the first movement of Beethoven's C-sharp Minor Quartet op. 131.

Is this simply a question of the resurrection of counterpoint? One of the most important characteristics of twentieth-century music is the revival of counterpoint, preceding neo-Classicism and more deeply rooted, trying not merely to bring the past to life but to develop a guiding principle of a fundamental concept of musical creation that extends over a whole period. This counterpoint plays a vital role in Bartók's art, from the important piano pieces of 1926 and the Third String Quartet right up to the Sonata for two pianos.

A more appropriate expression than counterpoint would be "linear structure," which can exist quite independently of certain rigid rules belonging to the old counterpoint. It is in this way that a texture deriving from the combination of several structural methods evolves—and this is what Bartók learns from Beethoven. It is one of the main characteristics of the late Beethoven quartets, and it explains their peculiar significance in the history of the genre. This type of structure secures real equality of status between the parts even where there is no question of a strictly contrapuntal texture.

It must not be forgotten that Beethoven approached Bach's technique from the musical direction of his own period, unequivocally chordal in principles, and that in the technique—in contrast with that of his own period—it was the linear energies which attracted him. The Beethoven fugue is therefore inevitably different from the Bach fugue, and this difference indicates most importantly that for Beethoven a certain amount of effort was necessary for dealing with a consistent linearity. This effort, however, is not a sign of weakness, but one of the fundamental characteristics of Beethoven's creative work and his whole attitude. We should consider, above all, the Great Fugue op. 133.

The individuality in texture of the Great Fugue does not lie merely in the strict construction of the parts. The contrapuntal technique of the later sections is much more unusual than the opening double fugue. Nor is "free counterpoint" a fitting description, for the way the individual sections are fully worked out within themselves can scarcely be regarded as free. Rather, it is in the sense of form that there is freedom: numerous sections (for example, the Meno mosso e moderato) are not constructed in accordance with the customary fugal entry method, but on the basis of a different freely evolved contrapuntal plan. In some

Example 1.

Beethoven: Great Fugue op.133

parts (for example, in the Allegro molto e con brio section) contrapuntal structure becomes paired with an open, chordal structure.

This rather individual contrapuntal plan and structural combination is virtually an everyday matter in Bartók's quartets. An immediate example is offered by the Lento movement of the First Quartet. In Bartók's fugal exposition two pairs of parts progress as if following a double fugue pattern, but differ from this pattern in that the two simultaneously unfolding themes are almost identical note for note, each pair operating as a canon at the fourth. But much more frequent than this—a texture generally applied by Bartók, it might be said—is the free contrapuntal structure, either in its pure form or in combination with other types of structure.

Finally, still another very typical structural means must be recalled, which is likewise rooted in the late Beethoven quartets. It is a peculiar paradox: pure homophony dressed in a polyphonic cloak. We are faced with two types of it. First, where parts playing a harmonic role take on independent life by means of rich figuration and dense, active part-movement, creating the impression of a plastically prominent contrapuntal part (e.g. op. 127, Adagio; op. 130, Andante; op. 131, Andante ma non troppo e molto cantabile; op. 132, Heiliger Dankgesang . . .). The other frequent form of this "pseudo-polyphonic homophony" is the staggered, quasi-imitative sounding of a held chord. This technique, which often turns up in Beethoven (op. 18, C minor, Finale; op. 127, Adagio; op. 131, Allegretto; op. 132, Molto adagio, and the first movement Assai sostenuto; op. 135, Lento assai), also acquires a significant role in Bartók, naturally based on different harmonic laws (Third Quartet, Prima parte; Fourth Quartet, first and third movements).

The immediate models for the inner differentiation and dynamics of Bartók's melody writing are also to be found in the late quartets of Beethoven. The inner variating force unfolding the theme steps into action straight away in the exposition and makes the formal section, previously of a static nature, dynamic and development-like. Think, for example, of the first movement's first subject in the op. 132 Quartet in A minor. Even more "Bartókian" (the word is deliberately used since this is typical in Bartók, whereas with Beethoven it is still an exception) is the theme that is so dynamic that no one of its appearances can be regarded as a "basic form": that is, there is no theme with which the others are comparative variations.

The best example of this in Beethoven can be found in the Great Fugue. Though the introduction with the inscription "overtura" does indeed serve as the introduction of theme, there is no so-called basic form here, for the theme continuously accelerates: at the first cadence the rhythmic values of the extended, slowly moving form are shortened by half, and there is further acceleration in the following bars. In a similar way, it does not become clear from what follows which of the four kinds of thematic appearance is essentially the basic form. It is typical that after the three forms are presented in the introductory section, a form in yet another rhythm appears as the theme in the first double fugue.

The first movement of Bartók's Sixth Quartet runs a similar course. As in the Great Fugue, the theme is first presented in augmented form. (József Ujfalussy points out that not only the treatment but the theme itself bears some relationship to that of Beethoven (Ujfalussy 1971:350).

The increasingly dynamic themes or melodies are characterized not only by continual transformation of these themes and motifs, but also by the organic breaking up and putting together of the thematic units. The technique of division and disintegration set forth in the literature on Beethoven once more attains an important place in the works of Bartók. Several parts of the Great Fugue using this kind of structure combined with counterpoint really do have the effect of a Bartók piece (e.g., the first Allegro molto e con brio, A-flat section). In the same way, a very "Bartókian" impression is made by the closing part of the second Allegro molto e con brio, interrupted by pauses, immediately before the shortened returns of the theme, or the trill motif segmented before the coda. While in Beethoven this was still an exceptional treatment, in Bartók it becomes a familiar, everyday feature, a fundamental principle of technique. The motive behind this is not a decompositional tendency (just as it is not so with Beethoven), but the necessity to penetrate to the essence, the almost scholarly passion to display inner interrelationships.

Bartók is the follower of Beethoven in the area of formal construction, too. It is characteristic that the influential form-reformers of Romanticism, Liszt and Franck, also set out from the Beethoven sonata type, transforming this into something new in the fantasia-style, programme-style spirit. Bartók by no means remained untouched by the influence of the Liszt and Franck conception, though his own revolution in form relates more directly to Beethoven, at times almost conspicuously dispensing with the intermediary masters. On the other hand, Bartók resorts to sonata form not with a mind to disintegrate but to reconstruct. Naturally this does not mean a revival of the classical scheme, for it was never the complete forms as such that he took over, it was the principles behind them. The key to his sonata form is therefore not the pre-determined order of themes and modulations; it is the sonata principle stripped to its roots, in the free yet regular sense in which Beethoven used it.

How frequently Bartók employs development-like dynamism in the exposition can be demonstrated through virtually any sonata movement by him. For now I shall refer only to the Second Quartet's opening movement, which apart from this might be considered a regular sonata movement in its formal elements. It is, however, not in the least "regular" that the seven-bar first subject forces open its original range of a seventh with three-octave leaps through the next ten bars, and then immediately switches over to imitation. After this, what more can the development offer in the way of dynamism? Here Bartók's genius displays its strength, nourished on Beethoven, for after this tense exposition the climax of the development radiates even more titanic straining.

Incorporating the fugue form into the sonata is once more an achievement of Beethoven—from complete fugue movements (op. 106, op. 110, op. 131, and op. 133) to more isolated use of fugatos (the Third, Fifth and Seventh Symphonies). This sonata-principle application of the fugue does, incidentally, indicate that separating the Great Fugue from the B-flat Major Quartet, although it may be justified from a practical point of view, is misguided as far as the original conception of the work is concerned—even though the source is Beethoven himself.[1]

The fugue and fugato play a similar role in Bartók's oeuvre. In a few works it appears as an independent movement (First String Quartet, the *Music for Strings*, etc.) yet much more frequently the fugato is built into a movement, used as a constructional element (third movement of the First String Quartet, Third Quartet, Fifth Quartet, *The Miraculous Mandarin* and the Concerto). Thus Bartók unequivocally follows the example of Beethoven. And it is also Beethoven, rather than Bach, who is the model for the inner structure of a complete fugue movement. Beethoven's string quartet fugue in the C-sharp Minor Quartet is still a relatively strictly constructed form, and yet an attempt towards a new kind of articulation is quite perceptible in it, coming into full play in the fugue of the "Hammerklavier" Sonata and the free recapitulatory sonata conception of the Great Fugue. Bartók transplanted this new kind of fugue form into his own works; with him, however, it is not so much sonata-like planning that dominates, but rather trio form.

The positioning of the fugue movement is also very characteristic: with Bach the fugue generally has a finishing function, summarizing and forcing into a strict arrangement all that was given free rein in the preceding, more loosely structured movements (Prelude, Toccata, Fantasia). This completing, crowning character remains valid in Beethoven, too; only in the C-sharp Minor Quartet does he reverse this order. If not so long ago the fugue had been a weighty completion, now let it be a prelude, a birth from nothing, the clothing of "creation" in music! There can be no doubt that this example inspired Bartók even after the First Quartet—above all in composing the

---

[1]György Sólyom points out that the Great Fugue is also to be considered as an independent work on the basis of its structure, since it comprises a complete sonata. It can, however, scarcely be claimed that the work in question is a four-movement string quartet; on the other hand it is true that in its structure the elements of the sonata movement are to be found. (Cf. György Sólyom, "Beethoven utolsó vonósnégyesei és a klasszikus tételrend" ["Beethoven's Last String Quartets and the Classical Order of Movements"], *Magyar Zene* XII (1971), 194.

Music for Strings, Percussion and Celesta, where the first movement is really a structure gradually appearing out of a sort of swirling primeval mist.

The opening fugue is not the only Beethoven movement type which rises to new life in Bartók. The innermost nocturnal monologue of the lonely man, looking both himself and the infinite secrets of nature full in the face—this kind of content connects the two men's mature slow movements. In the same way, it is easy to find connecting threads between Beethoven's demonic scherzos and Bartók's rustling, reverberating, glittering movements.

All this, however, finds its own counterpole. Because of this Beethoven is *still* classical, while Bartók is *again* classical. It is curious how the Romantic tendency becomes its own antithesis : the expansion of the cycle and the almost violent transformation of the classical formal framework do not upset the balance of the relationships.

In this instance it is Bartók who explains Beethoven, rather than Beethoven Bartók. The extension of the sonata cycle—looking at it now from the Bartók angle—is obviously none other than the satisfaction of a specific desire for symmetry. The number of movements increases so conspicuously in the op. 130 and op. 131 Quartets, not to finally break up the laws of classical forms, but—just the opposite—to create a new formal conception more closed and complete than anything preceding it. If we examine the original order of movements in the op. 130 B-flat Major Quartet, ending in a fugue, we will see that by means of tempo identity and thematic or character interrelationships a particular structure begins to take shape.

1. Introduction – Allegro
2. Presto
3. Andante con moto
4. Danza tedesca
5. Cavatina
6. Fugue

Thus, under the great arch of the outer movements, the inner movements are interconnected as two overlapping pairs: the Presto, in a popular spirit, relates to the even more popular Danza tedesca, and the intimate Andante con moto to the ethereally singing Cavatina.

And here is to be found the root of the Bartókian bridge-form. Even closer to it stands the op. 131 C-sharp Minor Quartet, in which behind the seven indicated movements there lie in reality five large units:

1. Fugue
2. Allegro
3. (Allegro moderato) – Andante
4. Presto
5. (Adagio) – Allegro

Here, too, the most obvious interconnection is seen in the extreme movements. The work's third pillar is the variation movement in the centre, on each side of which comes a quick movement, scherzo-like in tone. Here we already find the symmetrically constructed bridge-form in virtually its final form, and which appears in the Fourth Quartet.

Thus, starting out from the purely technical aspect of structure, and moving through the very smallest musical motifs, we have arrived at connections between movements, tone, cycle and complete conception. At every point we have witnessed the common ground between the two great masters. But it is not just that Bartók has approached Beethoven, nor leaned so heavily on the classical tradition. We have also seen at times that Beethoven—in advance of his period—"ran forward to meet" Bartók and the twentieth century, which continuously claimed him as its own.

CHAPTER TWO

FORERUNNERS AND CONTEMPORARIES

One of the principal methods of style analysis is the demonstration of conscious relationships and unconscious parallels, at the same time making fine distinctions between them. In examining Bartók's art this is especially important since it has at once both a pioneering and a summarizing role in twentieth-century music. It is pioneering because in many respects Bartók moved invincibly in the vanguard of artistic progress, and summarizing because in his music he replaces the obsolete individuality cult by setting up the ideal of a new synthesis as an example to be followed. Thus, when we investigate the inner significance of Bartók's oeuvre, and the logic of its development, through analysis of the various influences, borrowings and parallels, we are in no way degrading him. József Ujfalussy pointed this out in connection with the *Kossuth* symphonic poem, relating it to the complete oeuvre, and put into words the thought what might well be the motto for this whole chapter: "Even in these early compositions it is possible to detect the characteristic feature of Bartók's creative imagination that was to remain one of its most striking traits, the influence of contemporary music did not merely manifest itself in easily recognizable outward similarities. The music was rather a source of inspiration in the formation of his own creative work, a means to the release of his own genius so that he could make his unique contribution to music" (Ujfalussy 1971:39).

Demarcation of genre goes hand in hand with a certain personal demarcation as well. In the evolution of Bartók as an artist the influence of a good number of his predecessors and contemporaries has to be taken into consideration. There is, for example, Richard Strauss, who was perhaps Bartók's chief ideal in his youth, but who counts little all as concerns the chamber music. The influence of Liszt also makes itself felt mainly in the orchestral works and, apart from that, possibly the piano chamber music—for example, the Piano Quintet dating from 1904. The case of Wagner is more complicated; Bartók was not presented with any particular genre model by him, but in harmony and melody writing he had a strong influence on the young Bartók, especially around 1907–1908. In the slowly rolling texture of the First Quartet's Lento movement, its four-note chords, its ascents, climaxes and descents, the great German master's orchestral style unmistakably lives on in a chamber music transposition.

The curious thing is that this first "Wagnerian" period is followed by another wave at around the time of the composition of The Wooden Prince and the Second String Quartet. In the quartet's first movement, Wagner's technique can again be discovered in the intertwining textures of the section leading to the second subject, an influence that echoes in the movement's closing chord, coloured with an augmented triad.

We must also consider another figure from the German Romantic tradition, for his influence in the First String Quartet—principally in connection with tonality—is very significant. This is Max Reger, characteristically representative of late Romanticism, who endeavoured to build his art on the firm foundations of times long past, above all on the architectonics of the Baroque. Bartók knew the art of Reger well, proved, if nothing else, by his buying in 1907 the following Reger works: Aus meinem Tagebuch op. 82; the D Minor String Quartet op. 74; the C Major Violin-Piano Sonata op. 72; the F Major Cello-Piano Sonata op. 78 ; Variations and Fugue op. 81 ; Aeolslharp op. 75 no. 11.[1]

Bartók was mainly attracted to the peculiarly floating tonality in Reger's works, which the German master achieved not so much through increased Wagnerian chromaticism as by an individual atomization of tonal interrelationships. That is, whereas in Wagner tonality is ambiguous *all the way* through long stretches—unsteady,

[1]Documents in the possession of the Budapest Bartók Archives.

virtually undefinable—with Reger, tonally unambiguous patches appear, but instead of the tonality becoming stabilized, more and more new modulations carry the musical progression still further onward.

This method is first used by Bartók in the Two Portraits, and then appears in the First String Quartet, not only in the Lento movement but in the Allegretto as well. A good example is the snaking line of the frame-theme moving in parallel thirds and spanning the two movements. It is scarcely possible to determine its tonality, even though individual phrases may still have tonal significance. We are faced with a process in the course of which the organically connected theme breaks up, in a tonal sense, into parts.

Example 2.

It is also here, in the First String Quartet, that we are first faced with the influence of the French masters. It was not during his visit to Paris in 1905, but through Kodály in 1907 that Bartók came to know the art of Debussy and Ravel. Much later, in his study written in 1938, he himself put into words the significance of having become acquainted with this art. "From the political and cultural viewpoint, Hungary for four centuries has suffered the proximity of Germany; this fact cannot be ignored. Nevertheless, our intelligentsia always rebelled against this abnormal situation and acknowledged that the Latin spirit— above all the French spirit—is infinitely nearer to the Hungarian genius than the German; and that is why this élite was always oriented toward the French culture. . . . Regarding the field of music is no less evident and, moreover, entirely understandable that this trend collided with the absolute hegemony of German music which prevailed for three centuries, until the end of the nineteenth century. It was then that a turn occurred: Debussy appeared and, from that time on, the hegemony of France was substituted for that of Germany. From the beginning of this century the young Hungarian musicians, among whom I belonged, already oriented themselves in other domains toward the French culture. One can easily imagine the significance with which they beheld Debussy's appearance. . . . The situation stabilized and took on all its significance when we became acquainted with the music of Maurice Ravel."[2]

In this study, Bartók slightly exaggerates the importance of French music as far as his own art is concerned. But there can be no doubt that the first impressions really did have an inspiring effect on him and helped him in discarding the "dead weight" of post-romanticism. In any event, it is curious how well the "battle" between the German and French influences can be observed in a single work, the first movement of the First String Quartet. While traces of Wagner and Reger can be found in the fugally structured parts, the third and sixth mixture chords of the movement's trio evoke Debussy's G Minor String Quartet or Ravel's *Ma mère l'Oye* (Stevens 1964:174; Pütz 1968:77).

The pastel orchestral tone, otherwise alien to chamber music as a genre, later plays an important role in Bartók in such works as the first piece in the *Two Pictures*, "In full flower," and the first and third of the Four Pieces for Orchestra. In the chamber music nourished on the Beethoven tradition there is absolutely no room for this, and when a colour effect makes an occasional appearance here and there in Bartók's later quartets, by then it has nothing to do with the Debussy sonority ideal, but rather the discovery of the possibilities of clusters and note-bunches.

There is, however, another instance in Bartók's quartet art where the influence of Debussy is unmistakable. In the Second Quartet's tragic closing movement there appears, almost as a quotation, a detail from *Pelléas*: the heart-rending depiction of the death of Melisande.[3] All this might be considered complete coincidence, but

[2]Béla Bartók, "Hommages de l'étranger: Hongrie-Hommage à Maurice Ravel," *La Revue Musicale* XIX (1938), 436. *Bartók Essays* No. 86, 518.

[3]Dénes Bartha, "L'influence de Debussy: Hongrie," in *Debussy et l'évolution de la musique au XXème siècle—Colloques internationaux du CNRS* (Paris, 1962). Further: Ferenc Bónis, "Quotations in Bartók's Music," *Studia Musicologica* Vol. V (1963).

why should we consider it so in the case of Bartók, who explicitly wished to bring about in his art a synthesis of Bach, Beethoven and Debussy? Even though comparatively few places can be found in his oeuvre which refer so obviously to the French master, this does not mean an abandonment of the idea (for this, in retrospect, Bartók himself said to Serge Moreux in 1939) (Moreux 1949:), but that the stimuli gained from Debussy are metastatically merged into his musical style.

In a critical stylistic examination of the First String Quartet the investigator is led to two other contemporaries whose influence, if not lifelong, was nevertheless important for Bartók at that period. One is Ernő Dohnányi, basically a Brahmsian, who interweaved this feature with his Hungarian melody writing, and his chamber music style presented Bartók with a direct, immediate example.[4] The other is Zoltán Kodály, who not only passed the way for Bartók's acquaintanceship with the French masters, but with Hungarian folk music as well.[5] There are a few parts in the First Quartet in which the tone resembles that of the later chamber works of Kodály—the unusually lyrical interpretation of Hungarian folk music melody. True, at this time these works of Kodály—string quartets, string trio, solo sonata for cello—had not yet been written and thus they could not have exercised any influence on Bartók. It is rather a question of Bartók striking in one or two places the peculiar lyrical note which was later to become so characteristic of Kodály's music (see ex. 3). In the later compositions, too, a melody or melodic phrase similar to this occasionally crops up; for example, in the Second Quartet's first movement or the Fourth Quartet's central movement. In the case of the latter, we can begin to discuss direct influence, for the friendly relationship between the two musicians justifies the assertion of such an artistic interaction and conscious or unconscious borrowings (see ex. 4).

[4]Vázsonyi Bálint, *Dohnányi Ernő* (Budapest: Zenemukiadó, 1971), 222–29.

[5]This question is dealt with in detail in József Ujfalussy's lecture "Gemeinsame Stylshicht in Bartóks und Kodálys Kunst" which appeared in *International Musicological Conference in Commemoration of Béla Bartók 1971* (Budapest: Editio Musica, 1972).

Example 3.

Example 4.

Just as Bartók hinted in advance at certain elements of Kodály's later style, he encountered several idiomatic and expression-technique discoveries of his two greatest contemporaries, Schoenberg and Stravinsky, before he actually came to know these masters. Bartók's first mature works, the Fourteen Bagatelles and the First String Quartet, are, as regards both the time of their composition and the function they fulfill in his oeuvre as a whole, parallel with Schoenberg's Three Piano Pieces op. 11, and his Second String Quartet. Yet in 1908, when he composed the works in question, Bartók did not know the music of Schoenberg, as he himself states in an article which appeared in 1920.[6] In 1911 Schoenberg knew Bartók's works—in his *Harmonielehre* he quotes a few bars from Bartók's tenth Bagatelle,[7] but he did not know Bartók's piano pieces when he composed his own in 1909.

It is mainly in their conception that the piano pieces of the two composers are related: both men wrote study-like pieces of a rather free structure, exhibited to a certain extent even by their titles. The works of both are equally characterized by a certain experimental harshness, a frank and eruptive tone. The peculiar and unconscious connection, however, is most manifest in the means of expression employed in the pieces: the solitary declaiming melodies developed like a monologue, the ostinatos, and the free treatment of dissonant harmonies. Of the latter it is the fourth chord which is prominent—a completely familiar feature in Schoenberg from the First Chamber Symphony (1906) onwards, but discovered by Bartók only in 1908. In a similar way, consistently used parallel major sevenths and melodies progressing in sevenths also testify to a common aspiration, and there is further a kind of loosening of tonality such as in Bartók's thirteenth Bagatelle, where the polar divergence between E-flat minor and A-minor triads results in tonal ambiguity.

The two string quartets are even more alike; almost going as far as thematic similarities. In the second movement of both quartets there appears a repeated-note rhythm motif in the cello, which can incidentally be traced back to a common source—the scherzo of Beethoven's F Major String Quartet op. 59. Apart from that, this movement of the Schoenberg quartet uses a series of melodic fourths in unisono instrumentation in a manner very similar to the finale of the Bartók quartet. In the closing movement of the Schoenberg work the rolling bass ostinato before the entrance of the melodic part comes very close to Bartók's "Painful Wrestling," in which the in-

---

[6]According to Denijs Dille, Bartók was mistaken here because, going by the documents found in his estate, he had already ordered the Schoenberg Op. 11 through the Rózsavölgyi company before 1912. Cf. Denijs Dille, "Die Beziehungen zeischen Bartók und Schoenberg," in *Documenta Bartókiana* II, p. 54.

[7]Arnold Schönberg, *Harmonielehre* (Wien: Universal, 1911).

fluence of Wagner has already been mentioned. So this encounter also takes place by way of a common inspiration. The glorious high chords of the movement's coda appear in Bartók in the Lento movement of the quartet—a similar "post-Wagnerian" yearning tone and attitude characterize both.

It has to be emphasized that all this similarity and coincidence is not the result of direct influence. Nor can it be regarded as accidental. Schoenberg and Bartók arrived at these procedures quite independently of one another, the common root being the common tradition. We know what kind of influence was exerted on the young Bartók by Richard Strauss and Wagner. Brahms, too, was a model for him, first during his years in Pozsony, but also later during his studies in Budapest. His composition teacher was Hans Koessler, who was well known as an admirer of Brahms. It was these same composers who were the early influences on Schoenberg, too. He also came to chamber music through the works of Brahms, and in the spheres of idiom and harmony he learned a great deal from Wagner. It was in 1899 that Schoenberg wrote the composition which of all his works stands closest to Wagner, the D Minor String Sextet (*Verklärte Nacht*). As has been said, Bartók also went through this, but with him the Wagner tone arrives in the First String Quartet with a host of other influences.

One of the most important "common" achievements of Bartók's and Schoenberg's early, still unconscious, progress together was the breaking up of tonality. In the opening bars of the First Quartet, for example, there is already a decidedly recognizable attempt, possibly instinctive, at using all the notes of the twelve-note chromatic scale. There would be no sense in trying to force the analytical method of the twelve note technique onto this work as well, but from this it becomes quite clear how closely tonal floating or indefiniteness is connected in Bartók with the fullest possible use of the twelve-note range. With this, strictly speaking, Bartók moves further forward on the road leading to twelve note technique than Schoenberg, for in the Viennese master's Second Quartet, apart from a certain freedom in the tonal harmonic sphere, there is no evidence of such consistent anticipation of the consequent technique. With this in mind it is scarcely surprising to find the eleven notes of the chromatic scale reeled off well within the first three bars at the opening of Bartók's Second String Quartet (Babbit 1949:382). And at the opening of the third movement ten chromatic notes are heard within four bars.

Example 5.

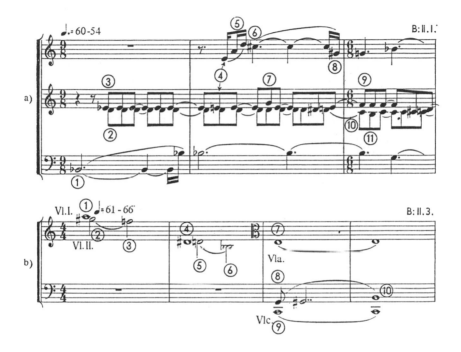

In the interval between the First and Second String Quartets, however, there was an important change of direction: becoming familiar with several of Schoenberg's works, Bartók began quite consciously to borrow elements from the Viennese master. His 1920 study which appeared in the Viennese *Musikblätter des Anbruch* is an important document concerning this change. Under the title "Schoenberg's Music in Hungary" he writes among other things: "In 1912 one of my pupils brought me home from Vienna a copy of Schoenberg's Three Piano Pieces op. 11, which at that time had still not been published; this was the first Schoenberg music I came to

know. Presumably until then, as far as I can remember, hardly anything by Schoenberg was known in Budapest, and even his name was
unfamiliar to the majority of musicians. And yet from then on there
were a few young musicians, scarcely out of college, who plunged
themselves with great enthusiasm into the study of the Schoenberg
works. It is understandable that the new possibilities of technique and
expression resulting from the suspension of the principle of tonality in
his works exercised a greater or lesser influence on those of our young
composers (and indeed also on those more mature composers) who
were already striving towards similar goals. I use the word 'influence'
in its best sense: in this there is no question of slavish imitation; I am
thinking of a similar process to that noticeable in Stravinsky's work
(from approximately 1913, i.e., in 'Rossignol'): under the influence of
Schoenberg he did not lose his individuality; on the contrary, in this
way he unfolded, as it were, even more freely; the direction indicated
by Schoenberg led him in a similar direction, but further, and on a different path . . ." It is not difficult to read between the lines here that
the phrase "more mature composers" refers first and foremost to
Bartók himself.

In 1920 when Bartók wrote this article, and also subsequently, he
was very much in touch with the journal of the Viennese avant garde,
the *Musikblätter des Anbruch*, and likewise with the very progressive
Berlin periodical *Melos*. Bartók's connection with the Viennese
school extended in these same years to the personal sphere, too;
whether he actually met Schoenberg is not known for certain, but
through correspondence they were unquestionably in contact with
each other, as is proved by letters from Schoenberg addressed to
Bartók, now in the Bartók Archives in Budapest. The main theme of
these letters is the work of Schoenberg's Viennese society, the *Verein
für musikalische Privataufführungen*, and the Bartók works played
there. It is well known that at these exclusive meetings Schoenberg
and his pupils introduced in turn the works of their most significant
contemporaries. Bartók's works were also performed on several occasions.[8]

[8]See note 6.

On the other hand, Bartók, as shown by the above quote, was very dissatisfied that Schoenberg's works were not played in Budapest. He also complains of this in 1921 in a letter to Cecil Gray in London: "It is true you have no Opera House but at least you do have some good concerts and from time to time you can hear even the music of Schoenberg, whereas here there is absolutely nothing" (Bartók Letters No. 387). Clearly, at this time Schoenberg symbolized the new aspirations in music for Bartók, and the criterion for musical life was whether Schoenberg's music was performed or not. He also wrote a study in 1920 on "the problems of the new music" in which, although wishing to give a general picture of the musical aspirations of the age, he discusses most exhaustively the tonality problem posed by the Schoenberg school.[9] It is in this study that a picture of Bartók emerges—searching and investigating without the slightest trace of prejudice the paths of the new music and who, with a truly scientific attitude, does not make any statement on anything in a prejudiced or apodictic way. At the same time his tone is personal and shows that he discusses these matters not as a scientist viewing them from the outside, but as one who has already tried them out in his own creative work, and who has his own opinion in the matter. His study is a summary of *his own opinion* and not an interpretation of the various others of period.

It can thus be attributed to the influence of Schoenberg and the dissolution of functional tonality that from the years of the First World War onwards Bartók, without any departure from folk music, increasingly moved towards the chromaticism of European art music. In this a large role was played by the so-called "distance phenomena"—that is, the division of the octave into equal intervals. Construction based on distance principles, although it has historical precedents, is a typically twentieth-century method, and stands in a natural relationship with the break-up of diatony and functional tonality because, as a contrast to the asymmetric structure of the latter, it evolves a new kind of symmetrical scale. Strictly speaking, the

[9]"Das Problem der neuen Musik," *Melos* I/5 (16 April 1920).

chromatic system itself is a distance principle system for it consists of equal semitones, and as a natural consequence it follows that within the possibilities of the twelve notes it produces further distance systems made up of larger intervals of two, three, four, and six semitones.

Distance principle combinations[10] appeared very early in Bartók's art, as has been largely demonstrated by Elliott Antokoletz, who devoted an entire work to this phenomenon. (Antokoletz 1984) The most striking example, however, is the Suite for piano, the four movements of which—even if in different forms—have the distance principle as their dominant element. Simple distance methods are represented by the whole-tone scales of the first movement and the augmented triads of the second. Alongside these is a rich flow of combined distance scales, in which the octave is filled out by an alternation between a larger and a smaller distance interval. An example is the minor third and minor second scale (3+1), or the fourth and minor second scale (5+1).[11]

How this distance principle construction became naturalized in Bartók's music is still a much-debated question. He may certainly have gained some inspiration in that direction from Liszt's works, where virtually every distance scale appears, and from Debussy, who was one of the pioneers of the whole-tone scale. George Perle's statement, however, is very appropriate and convincing when he says: "The impressionists employed symmetrical formations in order to suspend temporarily the effect of key-centre, to neutralize any tendency towards motion, and to de-emphasize motival characteristics and

---

[10]This term is mainly used by Hungarian scholars as Lajos Bárdos, Zoltán Gárdonyi and Ernő Lendvai while American scholars, as George Perle and Elliott Antokoletz, use the terms "symmetrical formation" or "symmetrical pitch construction" (see: Perle 1955:300 and Antokoletz 1984:67).

[11]Ernő Lendvai calls these 1:3 and 1:5 models (See: Lendvai 1971:51) Elliott Antokoletz's interpretation is much larger, and a whole system of interval cycles is created upon these symmetrical pitch constructions. Starting from Gerge Perle's discussion of symmetrical formations, he extends the symmetrical sets of intervals called *cell X* and *cell Y*, (having initiative from Leo Treitler's study "Harmonic Procedure in the Fourth Quartet of Béla Bartók," *Journal of Music Theory* III (1959) to *cell Z*. (See: Antokoletz 1984:68–77.)

developmental procedures; Bartók's intentions are precisely the opposite in every respect, and his symmetrical formations are one of the
compositional means through which he realizes his purposes" (Perle
1955:302).

Bartók arrived at twelve-note chromaticism as an inevitable consequence of late Romantic development, and quite independently of
Schoenberg, he may also have discovered the distance scales which go
with it in the same way. It is very probable, however, that after the
first unconscious effort and having come to know Schoenberg's music,
he took more decisive steps towards these new implements of musical
language. The fourth+minor second combination is already present
in Schoenberg's Second String Quartet and can also be found here
and there in the Five Orchestral Pieces. In Bartók it plays an especially important part in the Four Pieces for orchestra and in the Second
String Quartet. Some characteristic examples are quoted below.

Example 6.

Of the minor third+minor second combination there is likewise an
abundance of examples in the works of both masters. With Schoenberg this usually stems from consistent major third parallels; that is, in
the case of minor third displacement of major thirds there arises a
chord-change having a false relation effect which together give the
3+1 distance system.

Example 7.

In Bartók, too, we often encounter these kinds of phrases, but it is
much more frequently a case of the minor third+minor second combination arising from simultaneous use of major and minor thirds.

Example 8.

Example 8 (continued)

Schoenberg: op.11 no.1

Schoenberg: op.11 no.3

Also belonging to the sphere of structures based on the distance principle are the chord types which use equal intervals piled one on top of the other. Two such types had already appeared in tonal-functional music, too—the diminished seventh chord containing minor thirds, and the augmented triad containing major thirds—but both demanded resolution as a dissonance. Of these two, the diminished seventh chord is so forcefully tonal in content that it did not attract composers heading in the direction of atonality. Much more potential lay hidden in the augmented triad, neutral as far as tonality is concerned. Liszt had great preference for it, even lending it philosophical significance ("Faust" Symphony).

To the model of distance chords based on a structure of thirds, Schoenberg created in his work the fourth-chord and the second-pile. The appearance of the fourth-chord represented an important qualitative leap in the history of European music since it really declared war on the acoustic overtone laws of tonal music. For the heaping up of fourths emphasizes that this interval is *not* the inversion of the fifth and not insertable into the series of overtones. On the other hand, it breaks the bounds of the perfect octave and in this way also weakens the foundations of tonality. It is no accident that the fourth-chord of Schoenberg's First Chamber Symphony became a symbol for the avant-garde artistic movement.

In his theoretical works Bartók stressed that he came to the fourth-chord by way of folk music examples. "The characteristic ac-

cumulations of fourth intervals in our ancient melodies have initiated
the formation of fourth-chords : horizontal succession has here . . .
been projected into vertical simultaneity."[12] It is extremely doubtful,
however, whether Bartók's first fourth-chords in the Fourteen
Bagatelles came about on the basis of this reasoning. It is more likely
that the folk music example, together with the knowledge of his own
art music experiences and Schoenberg's similar aspirations, encouraged him. Here are a few characteristic examples from Bartók.

Example 9.

[12]"The Influence of Peasant Music on the More Recent Art Music," *Új Idők* (1931).
In English see *Bartók Essays* No. 43.

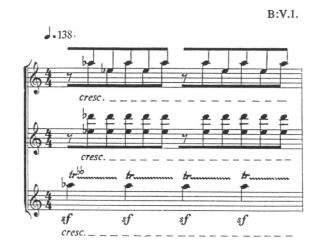

In Bartók's Second String Quartet the fourth is, so to speak, the "parent cell"—the two fundamental possibilities of distance principle melodics built from fourths are concisely exposed in the theme: the perfect fourth-chord (conjoint fourths) and the fourth+minor second model (disjoint fourths).

Example 10.

The basic motif of the theme, consisting of two perfect fourths, is extended in the course of the movement's thematic work: in this way a

possibly even more characteristic figure is crystallized in which the
perfect fourth becomes paired with an augmented fourth.

Example 11.

This sort of formation—it may be called a heterogeneous fourth
group—plays perhaps an even greater role in Bartók's style than the
"homogeneous" fourth-chord made up of perfect fourths. Schoenberg, too, has a preference for it.

Example 12.

This chord almost certainly comes to the fore because, in contrast with the homogeneous fourth-chord, it has a tense major seventh framework and thus its function is more dynamic. With some degree of freedom it is possible to draw a parallel between this kind of chord with a heterogeneous make-up and the triads of the other diatonic-tonal harmonic world. Just as, according to the Rameau principle whereby a major and minor third together form "harmonie parfaite,"[13] a common chord, so the typical chord, the "perfect harmony," of the beginning of the twentieth century arises from two intervals of different size.

The heterogeneous fourth-chord, moreover, is closely related to another distance phenomenon, the fourth+minor second model, which likewise has a major seventh framework. The heterogeneous fourth-chord can thus be regarded as an incomplete fourth model and vice versa: the fourth model can be regarded as an augmented heterogeneous fourth chord.

Example 13.

From the melodic aspect, too, there are numerous elements in Bartók's musical idiom which hint at Schoenberg—either as a consequence of direct influence or indirectly as a companion of other elements. Melody—or, as a larger generalization, melodic action—has great significance in this style where linearity once more becomes a leading structural principle. At the same time, the harmonic phenomena are also characterized in a certain sense by the melodic phenomena, for the handling of the vertical and the horizontal elements is in principle identical. This identity is asserted by Schoenberg in practice as well, in the technique of serial composition, and Bartók likewise builds his fundamental harmonic principles on this, as is clear from the above quotation in connection with the fourth-chord. This is

[13]Jean-Philippe Rameau, *Traité de l'harmonie réduite à ses principes naturels* (Paris, 1722).

why, in the course of discussing the distance phenomena, their melodic and chordal forms can be treated as equivalents.

One common feature in the melody writing of the two masters is "complementary melody writing." This technique, which with Schoenberg played a great role mainly in the creative period before the establishment of serial composition, is present in Bartók throughout his whole life-work. The reason for its being discontinued in Schoenberg's serial period is not hard to find: the Reihe itself ensures exhaustion of the twelve-note range of notes—either in melodic or chordal form. On the other hand, in pieces which are not serial but nevertheless twelve note, it is precisely this complementary technique which makes full use of the tonal system possible.

Melody building based on the complementary principle can take two forms. One solution is for melody and harmony together to create a closed system; the melody is dependent on the harmony insofar as it consistently avoids the component parts of the latter. The other solution is purely linear: the melody is formed so that there will be no repetition of any note and larger leaps will be filled out by the melodic line turning back on itself. These principles of melodic creation can be traced back in music history as far as Palestrina, the difference being merely in the range of notes employed. The following are some typical examples from the works of Schoenberg, Alban Berg, and Bartók.

Example 14.

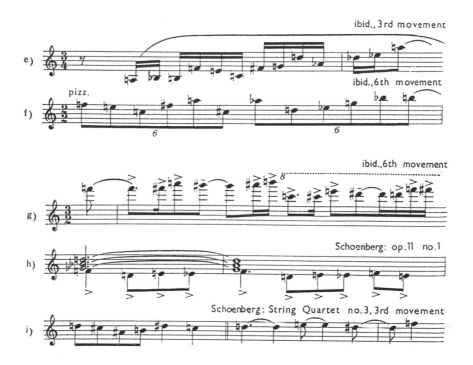

Another important feature of melodic creation which is equally characteristic of the art of Schoenberg, Berg, and Bartók is a certain geometrical construction in the melodic line. The geometric-graphic element was always of some significance in linear thinking, usually organically related to the emotional-conceptual content of the work. Albert Schweitzer elaborated on this vividly in connection with Bach's melodic art, attributing great importance to the symbolism of these melody patterns.[14] It is virtually natural that in a musical conception which affords such significance to a linearity resembling that of Bach, structured melodies of this kind assume great importance. In this way are born the various kinds of straightforward melodies—horizontal, rising, and falling—expanding and contracting themes, circle-melodies in a wave line or turning back on themselves, and melodic lines which are, like a spring, stretched out tensely or pushed in close together. In Bartók's first mature compositions these kinds of graphic-geometric

[14]Albert Schweitzer, *J. S. Bach* (Leipzig, 1907).

melody formations are already present: the two-directional chromatic expansion in the second of the Fourteen Bagatelles; and the "Painful Wrestling" of the *Ten Easy Pieces* is characterized by circular motion. Later, obviously under the influence of Schoenberg—but also a further development of his own individual experience—these types of melodic patterns become condensed, especially in the compositions dating from the years after the First World War.

Example 15.

Together with geometrically arranged, hence symmetrical-regular, melodiousness goes its corresponding disarrangement and decomposition. It has emerged in the case of melodic patterns opening up into great width that although the principle demands "order," the result arising from it has the effect of being disorderly, confused, and frighteningly broken up and dislocated.

Schoenberg's expressionistic ambitions found a useful implement in these confused, gesticulating melodies devoid of shape. The harsh melodic movement, the exaggeration, the gesticulating character do, indeed, serve well the purposes of increased expressiveness, willing to abandon "beauty" for the sake of the goal—expression, impact, suggestiveness, agitation. Melody using wide intervals, however, does have another function: for one thing it loosens up in a healthy way the close, small- interval chromaticism inherited from Wagner. In one of Schoenberg's Stefan George Songs we find the following melodic unit:

Example 16.

Schoenberg: 15 Stefan George Songs

Here it is easy to see that wide-interval melody is not used exclusively in the service of expressing a confused frame of mind: it is in a certain sense one concomitant of the chromatic, atonal tendency. Schoenberg might easily have formed the melody in the following way:

Example 17.

Nevertheless, he needed the upward octave transposition of the last two notes not only because of the heightening of emotion, but to avoid the monotony of chromaticism. The climbing, swelling melodiousness of Tristan is replaced by intricate, sparkling melody evoking a shock effect. A second point is that the large intervals help to loosen up the feeling of tonality since they extend the sonic sphere and resist the naturalness of leading-note-like attraction relationships.

The vertical break-up of the melody is also accompanied by its horizontal break-up; that is, the occasional interruption of melodic continuity by pauses. The pause does not necessarily mean disintegration or fragmentation; however, classical melody offers good examples of this, where the pause is in reality built into the melody, giving it inner division and articulation. But now it is a different matter. The broken quality of the melody springs from the same inner decompositional tendency as the vertical confusion of the melody. This, too, is a typically avant-garde attitude, fitting in well with Busoni's revolutionary ideas about making music entirely "free."[15] This tendency is clearly observed in Schoenberg as early as the works from around 1909–10. The breakdown of melodies, and the reconstruction of melodies made up of smaller parts into a larger whole, appear perhaps most characteristically in the Five Pieces for Orchestra. Many elements from this Schoenberg work are to be heard again in Bartók's *Miraculous Mandarin*, above all the use of melodic fragments, fragment melodies, and ostinato technique. Thus the broadly arching melodic ideal of romanticism turns into its own antithesis—occasionally even in late romantic music itself—the differentiation and dissolution of melodic processes, initially simple but later becoming more and more extreme. This process is very interesting within Schoenberg's own output: even

[15]Ferruccio Busoni, *Entwurf einer neuen Aesthetik der Tonkunst* (Triest, 1907).

Verklärte Nacht, though written mainly under the influence of Wagner, betrays a tendency towards breaking up the broadly arching melodies. The process was also accelerated by the effect of Richard Strauss's characteristic short motif technique. It attains its fullest development in Schoenberg's expressionistic period, above all in *Erwartung* and the Five Pieces for Orchestra.

In Bartók the process is not so conspicuous. This is doubtless largely due to the influence that folk music had on him, preventing the extreme breaking up of melodies. That the tendency did not leave Bartók's melody untouched, however, is a consequence of his life's path and his attitude, which frankly and openly confronted reality. Typically it is Bartók's most illusion-free work, *The Miraculous Mandarin*, that best shows the influence of Schoenberg in this direction. The distorted figures, alienated from humanity, of the dance- play's dramatic world and its emotions, inevitably produced this system of expression and the linear break-up of the melodies.

Example 18.

Yet in the settling down which followed *The Miraculous Mandarin*
something of this tendency remained, shown principally by the two
violin-piano sonatas, then became transformed, giving birth to a completely new form of musical-melodic expression. I have in mind those
musical pictures where Bartók brings to life a completely new kind of
"micro-melodics" through the transference into music of nocturnal
sounds, natural noises, and movements.

It may appear incorrect to apply the term "melody" to these
melodic snatches and fragments, these musical stirrings of one or two
notes, but in the last analysis they do belong to the sphere of melody,
for they are linear phenomena, even if they are the borderline cases
of linearity. This decomposition of melody beginning around the turn
of the century which enabled the representatives of the Viennese
school to musically formulate an individual view of the world, led
Bartók—and also Webern—to the discovery of a new tonal world.
Quotation of only a few examples from Bartók's works will be sufficient to prove what fundamental areas of expression were conquered
by this conception of melody and how that conception remained
central to Bartók's most personal articulations.

Example 19.

From here it is only one step to the system of special colour effects
which Bartók evolved in parallel with the Viennese school, and the
expressive function which is related to that melodic phenomena. In
both, the intensification of expressiveness leads the composer to the
conquest of certain "extra-musical" territories, or at least to the extension of the "existing boundaries" of music. From the earliest mature piano works onwards, Bartók favours the use of grating semitone
dissonance as a colouring function. Edwin von der Nüll's 1930 study
contains numerous interesting statements in this regard (Nüll 1930:10,
68). The real terrain of these colouring pursuits, however, proves to
be the string quartets, in which, from the third onwards, a completely
sovereign colour-world evolves more decisively, alongside the encouragement derived from the Vienna school's free use of chords and
dissonances. By means of frequent use of the fourth-chord and the
four-note chord with a major seventh, new tonal values become established, the major seventh loses its dissonant character which demands
resolution, and it becomes possible for a new chord to come into existence by building one on top of another. The minor second, the inversion of the major seventh and equal in value to it, also begins to
play a more sovereign role, and by accumulation the first note bundles
and clusters in music history evolve, the new colour effects which
were to be raised to the level of basic implements in the period following the Second World War. Bartók was one of the first to evolve
new kinds of colour effects from the different parts, supplementing
them in a complementary way and in various rhythms, a type of note
bundle also anticipating those means offered by aleatory.

Example 20.

Example 20 (continued)

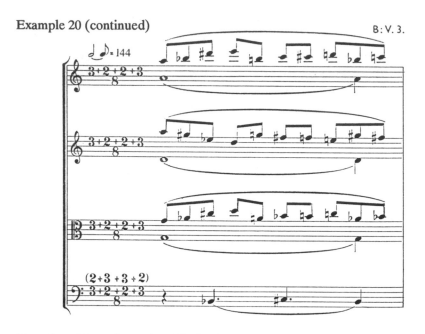

Bartók achieved another kind of extension of the string quartet world of colour through special use of the instruments. Unique ways of playing string instruments which until then had been used only rarely (such as pizzicato, sul tasto, sul ponticello, etc.) he now used more frequently and richly, apart from which new effects became naturalized—for example, the hard pizzicato obtained by slapping the string on the fingerboard, which has since become known throughout the world as the "Bartók pizzicato." Good examples of this kind of innovation in quartet sound are particularly evident in the Fourth Quartet and in part in the Sixth.

Further common ground between the styles of Bartók and Schoenberg—and beyond that the achievements whereby they made musical history—can be found in the qualitative transformation of the century's harmonic world so that the efficiency and significance of individual chords are determined not merely by the structure of the intervals sounded but also by the way they are distributed. So-called "distribution" always played an important role in polyphonic music, determining the sonority of the texture and in many respects its function as regards meaning. In tonal-functional harmonics, however, the distribution of the notes in a chord was of secondary importance as compared to the intervals which went into its make-up. The essential nature and structure of the chord was unequivocally determined by its closest form—and possibly an abstraction of it. After the new harmonic principle became valid the analyst no longer "had the right" to carry out any such abstraction. In the definition of a chord the closest distribution offers no help—indeed, it is rather inclined to obscure the nature of the chord. Thus, here it is always necessary to consider the intervals actually sounding, taking the differences in register fully into account.

In this tonal system the colouring of the individual parts of a chord assumes great significance; the colour constitution is perhaps just as important and decisive as interval structure. In Schoenberg this first materialized in a concentrated form in the third movement of the Five Orchestral Pieces. Bartók also experimented with it, though not in such an extreme form. We need only think of the central—slow— movement of the Fourth String Quartet, where different structuring and colour distributions of a single chord essentially determine the character of the whole movement. (Apart from this, in his 1920 *Melos* study Bartók also declared himself strongly theoretically in favour of this sort of interpretation and application of harmony.[16])

Example 21.

In the sphere of more traditional types of chord, too, there are characteristic points of contact between the styles of Bartók and Schoenberg. Both masters use the four-note chords inherited from romantic music, and of these preference is given to those in which the tense major seventh interval is present, most in accordance with the demands of tonal freedom. We know that this chord type very frequently appeared as a melodic leitmotif in Bartók's first mature

[16]See note 9.

period. It is also encountered on numerous occasions in the works of Schoenberg dating from this time.

Example 22.

In addition to third structuring, however, an essentially new element was introduced in fourth-structure chords. The historical events leading to this have already been outlined in the course of discussing distance phenomena; the principal thing to be examined now is how this original means is related to the former. It has been mentioned that beside the chord consisting of perfect fourths, the so-called heterogeneous fourth-chord, composed of perfect and augmented fourths, is more prevalent. When the augmented fourth is placed underneath, the chord comes very close to that type of traditional third-structure four-note chord which contains a major seventh above a diminished triad. Thus a natural summary is achieved by the heterogeneous type of fourth-chord in which the remains of traditional third-structuring, the new principle of distance structure and the seventh tension of free tonality can assert themselves simultaneously.

The harmonic world of Bartók and Schoenberg between 1910 and 1925 is most faithfully characterized by these two chord types: the four-note chord composed of thirds, and the fourth-chord. Yet the way in which the individual chords are more freely structured, and the way in which they are strung together, both reflect the complete freedom of the disintegrating tonal system. With this freedom in chord progression, however, new regularities come into being, above all the law of tension in the chords. Since an important role is played in both basic types by the major seventh, this gives the chords a common framework—in more or less the same sense that, in the functional-tonal style, the perfect fifth contained the two basic types of triad —major and minor. In chord progressions major-seventh tension is a nearly permanent factor without parallel sevenths actually occurring (just as parallel fifths were "forbidden" in the earlier style). This harmonic supremacy of the major seventh does not in the least signify monotony or deterioration in the harmony. The significance and the aesthetic content of individual chords depend on their inner structure and on their relationship to each other. Thus, not even this style renounces the life-like rhythm of arsis-thesis, tension and resolution.

Example 23.   Schoenberg: op. 11 no. 2

B: Suite, 4th movement

After digesting the direct Schoenberg influence—observable from the Suite for piano to the First and Second Sonatas for violin and piano— Bartók briefly turned his attention in the direction of Stravinsky's neo-baroque style in the year 1926. But already in the following year, chiefly in the string quartet genre, he once more returned to his own path, which was closer to the Viennese school. Perhaps it was no accident that it was when he had the opportunity of hearing Alban Berg's *Lyric Suite* for string quartet during the concert in which his own Piano Sonata received its first performance in Baden-Baden, 16 July 1927, that this genre made a renewed appearance after such a long period of neglect—for the preceding string quartet had been completed in 1917.[17] In any event, it is quite striking that he began composing a string quartet as the first work after this summer concert tour, and the work was already finished in September. No great significance would be attached to these external circumstances if the influence of Berg's work were not be felt in the Third String Quartet.

Without the slightest doubt, Berg's *Lyric Suite* belongs among the greatest masterpieces of this century. This six-movement composition, in which each single movement intensifies the contrast of lyric characters to a polarization level—the Presto delirando and the Largo desolato—is quite unique. It might be imagined that it was as a "counter piece" to this six-movement work of such enormous proportions that Bartók wrote his shortest string quartet. But shortly afterwards he again turned to this genre, and in the following year composed his Fourth Quartet. In this he succeeded in realizing a conception related to that of Berg but which is at the same time completely different: the cycle of five movements does not travel the road of polarization expressing reality, rather it attains the harmony of classical balance. As indicated in the preceding chapter, Bartók may have taken the model for his five-section structure from Beethoven. Indeed, a further possibility is that in the twenties, when he was in such close contact with the musical world of Western Europe, and with the I.S.C.M., he also came to know Hindemith's Third String Quartet,

---

[17]The two works heard at a *Deutsches Kammermusikfest* concert. Cf. Demény 1962, p. 219.

dating from 1922, which likewise uses a five-movement bridge- or palindrome form.

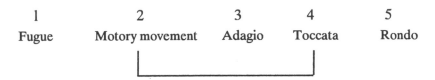

1	2	3	4	5
Fugue	Motory movement	Adagio	Toccata	Rondo

Within this the central movement is also in palindrome-form. Bartók was thus in a position to become acquainted with two different types in the course of his visits to Germany; though common to both is the increased number of movements. Apart from this, the Alban Berg work was an inspirational influence on Schoenberg, too: in the same year as Bartók he also composed his Third String Quartet. And with Schoenberg an even greater lapse in time separates the Second and Third Quartets—almost twenty years. These four string quartets dating from almost the same time—Berg's *Lyric Suite*, Schoenberg's Third Quartet and Bartók's Third and Fourth Quartets—are related to each other by numerous connecting threads. The Schoenberg and Berg works are characteristic products of progressive bourgeois art, blossoming for an additional decade in the Weimar Republic. A few of the larger towns in Germany were at that time the principal stage for avant-garde movements: in Berlin musical life flourished, Klemperer and Zemlinsky worked in the Kroll-Oper, and Berg's *Wozzeck* was given its premiere in the great Unter den Linden Opera. Until 1925, Busoni taught in the composers' master class of the Prussian Academy of Fine Arts; he was followed by Schoenberg, who there trained several generations of young musicians. This short period was favourable to more than music, however: in Weimar the Bauhaus became a great attraction, in Berlin Piscator revolutionized theatrical art, and the two outstanding writers Leonhard Frank and Robert Musil were working there, their works appearing in wide circulation through the progressive publishing house Rowohlt Verlag.

This atmosphere favoured Bartók as well, and it is not surprising that his first journey after the war should lead him precisely to Berlin, where he wrote his two important articles for the periodical *Melos*. In 1923 the Melos Society organized a series of three concerts consisting entirely of his works. Among other pieces, the first two string quartets were performed and the Second Sonata for violin and piano was given its premiere. From this time onwards, his works had a permanent place in the I.S.C.M. festivals and concerts in Frankfurt and Baden-Baden, as well as in Berlin. At one I.S.C.M. concert Berg's *Lyric Suite*, together with Schoenberg's Third Quartet and Bartók's Third Quartet were performed by the Kolisch Quartet. Through this concert it was discernible—as was indeed observed by a few critics and progressive musical opinion—that although each of the three composers represented a different path in the application of atonality and twelve note technique, yet in their conception and world of expression and attitude they come close to one another.

Bartók and Berg are particularly interrelated by novel types of tone. The *Lyric Suite*'s Allegro misterioso (third movement) and Presto delirando (fifth movement) resemble in many respects the mysteriously fleeting prestos and scherzos of Bartók (Second Quartet, second movement, Coda; Third Quartet, Seconda parte, fugato; Fourth Quartet, Prestissimo, con sordino, and Allegretto pizzicato). Bartók and Berg's musical pictures of this nature are also related to each other in that the colour effects—in contrast with the impressionistic method—are associated with linear-polyphonic structure worked out in minute detail. These are not patches, not mood pictures, but the condensation of expressive experiences into a strict musical form.

In connection with Schoenberg's Third Quartet other kinds of relationships can be observed. This work is, in the strict sense of the term, a serial composition, in which every melodic and harmonic event is determined by the twelve-note-row present in the background of the work. At the same time, it represents a turning-point in the composer's creative career: since developing strict serial technique it is here that Schoenberg first uses the few loosening-relaxing methods which make it possible for the purely logical-speculative elements not to reign supreme, to assume too great an emphasis in the composition. Repetition of a note is therefore not avoided, and the inner order of an occasional section of the note-row is used freely. This last assumes particular importance in the first movement of the quartet, where the basis of the musical texture is provided by an eight-note ostinato motif almost throughout. It is indicative of the unified process of Schoenberg's creative development that the Third Quartet's note-row is composed of internally related smaller units, each of which also played a part in the so-called "freely atonal" period. And this is the point at which kinship can be seen with Bartók's technique. In the first four-note section of the row lie concealed both the incomplete four-note chord with major-seventh tension and the heterogeneous fourth-chord. The following four notes form a fourth+minor second pattern. And finally, the closing section is none other than the inversion of the first four-note unit—that is, once again an incomplete seventh-chord and a heterogeneous fourth-chord.

Example 24.

It is also worth briefly mentioning the rhythmic relationships. It is more or less common knowledge that a considerably large role is played in Bartók's work by the rhythmic influence of the folk music of various peoples. Of the different polymetric and asymmetric phenomena, the so-called "Bulgarian rhythm" is the most important. Yet the early appearance of asymmetric rhythm draws our attention to the fact that Bartók was already experimenting with these kinds of rhythm and metre even before he came to know folk music—and Bulgarian folk music in particular.[18] It is therefore possible to approach

[18]In the scherzos of the early F Major String Quartet (1899) and the Piano Quintet (1904) there had already appeared a rhythm pattern which metrically actually comes in the ordinary $\frac{3}{4}$ framework but is in reality a hemiola-like alternation of triple and duple units.

such asymmetrical kinds of rhythm and metre from another direction as well. Brăiloiu, the great pioneer in ethnomusicology, also made claims for the view that this rhythmic phenomenon must not be considered restricted to the metres peculiar to Bulgarian folk music; that it is much more general and widespread in the folk music of various peoples. Brăiloiu uses the term *aksak* (which is Turkish for "lame") and shows theoretically—that is, independently of the existing types already found—all of its forms that are possible in principle.[19] That this rhythm is not exclusively a folk music phenomenon is proved by ancient Greek rhythm theory and prosody, which takes numerous such asymmetric formulas into account (hemiolia, paion, etc.). On this basis it is by no means surprising that even in Schoenberg, who had such an antagonistic attitude toward folk music, this aksak rhythm crops up in, among other works, his Third Quartet. The essence of Schoenberg's idea is to make a certain special order in the asymmetry: the $\frac{2}{8}, \frac{3}{8}$, and $\frac{4}{8}$ groups within the metre are placed alongside each other in increasing or decreasing order of size.

Example 25.

> ' = stressed
> ᴗ = unstressed

One of Bartók's favourite Bulgarian metres is also made up of these same basic elements, but with him the quaver groups come in the order 4+2+3 (see, for example, the third movement of the Fifth Quartet). In Bartók, too, it is possible to find metric changes based on the principle of logically arranged gradual augmentation. If we take a

[19]Constantin Brăiloiu, *Le rythme aksak* (Abbeville: F. Paillart, 1952).

closer look at the pizzicato scherzo movement of the Fourth Quartet, we will find hiding behind the $\frac{3}{4}$ time signature an actual metrical division in which—in logically increasing order of size—5, 6, 7, and 8 crotchets are placed beside one another.[20]

Example 26.

There is a similar phenomenon in the Burletta movement of the Sixth Quartet.

From all these phenomena it becomes possible to draw the conclusion that in the sphere of rhythmic innovation and refreshment Bartók and Schoenberg moved very close to each other, even if unique motives were operational in their individual efforts. In comparing the creative paths of the two masters, it is possible to claim that in Bartók's attitude two distinct phases began to take shape. In the first, as a consequence of the common tradition and numerous other factors, they set out, quite independently of each other, to break up tonality, and through a whole series of idiomatic-stylistic means they arrived at the same or similar results. In the second phase Bartók, in acquainting himself with Schoenberg's works, came under the in-

[20]My attention was drawn to this by András Mihály.

fluence of more than one achievement of the Viennese master, and even consciously attempted to merge these into his own works. This period extended from the years of the First World War roughly to the end of the twenties. He did not follow Schoenberg along the path of serial composition, for it was basically alien to him to force his art within the limits of a single, all-embracing compositional system. He made chromaticism his own, too, as the material and tonal range of his music, but retained tonality as a guarantee of structural unity and tonal stability in a work.

On the other hand—and this is not taken into consideration by most studies—Bartók also remained faithful, even after his path diverged from Schoenberg's, to those achievements which he had taken over from him during the twenties and, having filtered them thoroughly, built them organically into his own musical style-system (Forte 1960:233–45). One single example will suffice, and that is the twelve-note theme of the Violin Concerto which, with its multi-faceted nature and paradoxically tonal limitations, proves how much imagination and potential Bartók saw in the compositional principle of avoidance of note repetition.

Example 27.

Although in this study we are chiefly concerned with Bartók's side of the matter, it is nevertheless necessary to take a brief look at the other side. As is well known, Schoenberg, retiring within himself, proceeded through his life without paying much attention to external influences. He did, however, take notice of Bartók's music as early as 1911, and took the trouble to arrange performances within the framework of the *Privataufführung* meetings. However, precisely in the period when Bartók approached him, Schoenberg was occupied with the evolution of his system. What is even more peculiar is that in the thirties Schoenberg made an approach towards Bartók, at least insofar as his works showed assimilation of some typical Bartókian elements. And so in 1936, in the Fourth String Quartet, composed when he was already in the United States—in spite of the twelve-note technique, or "consecrated" by the note-row—there appear Bartók's typical three-note motifs, his major-minor chord and his distance models.

Example 28.

Example 28 (continued)

What appeared only in patches in Schoenberg's Fourth Quartet became extended to pervade a whole composition in the *Napoleon Ode* of approximately six years later. The note-row serving as the basis of the work is indeed no more than two interlocking minor third + minor second (3+1) scales, which Schoenberg uses in every possible form. Analysis of these late Schoenberg works leads to two notions in the nature of a summary. Firstly, from the end of the twenties onwards, Schoenberg endeavoured ever more decidedly to make the row, the preformed reference system providing the basis of the work, include those harmonic and melodic elements which, at the time of the

Example 29.

development of the atonal idiom, came into being before the development of serial composition. From this it follows that if there are
numerous points of contact between the art of Bartók and that of
Schoenberg in the earlier period, then it is not possible to contrast the
development of the two masters in the period following that either, at
least with regard to idiomatic expression. And secondly, even with his
observance of the theoretical foundations of twelve-note composition, Schoenberg did nevertheless make a definite approach towards
the "Bartókian route"—that is, the binding of the chromatic system to
distance patterns.

It is further characteristic of historical development that the
younger generation following the Viennese school—Mátyás Seiber,
Humphrey Searle, and others—likewise composed their serial works
on the basis of the "Bartókian" patterns.[21] This trend in development—it would seem—is a crystallization of the most logical and most
musical conception of the chromatic system.

The development of Bartók's style was further considerably influenced by his other great contemporary, Igor Stravinsky. The three
stages that have been marked in connection with his relationship with
Schoenberg can also be observed here. But if we take notice of the
time factor in the creative development, it will become clear that the
individual stages are consistently displaced, taking place later. Here it
is the years 1910–11 that can be regarded as an unconscious parallel
progress when, roughly coinciding with the Russian ballets of
Stravinsky, Bartók himself also discovered strongly rhythmic dance
music of a folk character ("Village Scene" from the Two Pictures) and
the barbaric ostinatos of primitive folk music (Allegro barbaro). Nor
had he any need for the example of the Russian master in the further
development of this last type of music since he studied the source itself in Rumanian and North African Arab folklore. That he found additional inspiration and encouragement in the Stravinsky music is
another matter. In the most important of his theoretical writings,
reference to Stravinsky is virtually indispensable—whether it is a

[21]Josef Rufer, Die Komposition mit zwölf Tönen (Berlin, 1952).

question of reconciling atonality and folk music, or the relationship between folk music and art music.

It is difficult to establish the beginning of a conscious parallel progress since we do not know exactly what Bartók became acquainted with from the Russian master's works, and when. In *The Wooden Prince* there crops up an occasional detail which can scarcely be imagined without the model of *The Firebird* (Wolff 1952). And the use of the trumpet in the Scherzo of the Four Pieces for Orchestra also decidedly evokes the Stravinsky ballet, but it is possible that these characters only took shape in Bartók's creative imagination at the time of orchestration (that is, in 1921), by which time there can be no doubt that he was familiar with the Stravinsky works which had by then appeared.

In his first study to be published in the Berlin *Melos* ("Das Problem der neuen Musik") Bartók refers to the *Pribaoutki Songs* composed in 1914. As far as our present investigation is concerned, this is an important document, partly because it touches on the technical problems of compositional craft, and partly because it uses the sphere of chamber music as an example and not orchestral works employing virtuosic orchestration. The effect of the Stravinsky works *Pribaoutki* and the later *Les Noces* is unmistakably apparent in Bartók's compositions dating from the twenties. The Slovakian folksong arrangement *Falun (Village Scenes)*—in either its solo or female chamber chorus versions—is, with its hard, almost harsh tone and dryly knocking instrumental accompaniment, a direct sister piece to Stravinsky's Russian wedding ceremony, *Les Noces*. On the other hand, it is chiefly in the Third String Quartet, written in 1927, that we can feel the influence of *Pribaoutki* becoming fruitful; here Bartók takes over a great deal from the idiom of the Russian master's work— the frequent metre changes, many-sided variation of small-scale motifs, the technique of roughly grating, colouring dissonances. During these same years, neo-baroque aspirations make themselves felt in Bartók's art: the hard concerto rhythm, the filled chord playing and the even, musical motor-movement in toccata- prelude style. This, too, can certainly be considered a Stravinsky influence, for of the various European composers aspiring towards a neo-baroque and neo-classical direction, it was he who gave voice to this tone in its most characteristic form. Traces of it are to be felt less in the chamber genres, but are found all the more active in the piano compositions: the Sonata, and the First and Second Piano Concertos. Here are a few very typical quotations from the works mentioned, and from the Third and Fourth String Quartets, in which, although not so general as in the orchestral works, the influence of Stravinsky does appear.

Example 30.

Example 30 (continued)

Example 30 (continued)

Then, in the creative period of the thirties, the elements referring openly to Stravinsky disappear from Bartók's style, or at least they become so organic that their origins are untraceable. And it is peculiar that when baroque-like phrases once more make their appearance in Bartók's last creative period, they no longer have anything in common with the baroque tone which characterized the works of the twenties. The reason for the difference, no doubt, is that in the twenties it was in the same sense as Stravinsky that Bartók turned towards the baroque masters, whereas in the period of the Third Piano Concerto and the Solo Sonata he turned directly to the source, principally to the art of J. S. Bach.

      Yet even in this last period there is also a composition, one detail of which is as if the grotesque Stravinsky tone were appearing for a moment: the violin's syncopated double stopping in the Burletta movement of the Sixth String Quartet reminds us of the folk violin music of *The Soldier's Tale*. This is the same sort of "waving goodbye" to Stravinsky as the twelve-note theme of the Violin Concerto was a "farewell" to Schoenberg.

Example 31.

In Bartók's artistic development, in the evolution and consolidation of his style, the problem of reconciling folk music sources and modern means of expression is always present, almost like an *idée fixe*. In this, even though he had definite ideas of his own from the very outset, Bartók gained effective conceptual help from the art of Stravinsky. In one of his American lectures he claimed atonality was an unnavigable route for art nurtured on folk music, but in his study written in 1920—a much more serious conceptual study—he offers a contrary opinion. "How can this influence of folk music, tonal to its very roots, be reconciled with the atonal trend? It will suffice to make reference to one very typical example: Stravinsky's *Pribaoutki*. The vocal part of this consists of motifs which—even though they have not been borrowed directly from Russian folk music—have taken shape completely in accordance with Russian folk music motifs. The characteristically short nature of these motifs, in themselves without exception completely tonal, provides an opportunity for a kind of instrumental accompaniment consisting of a series of more or less atonal patches quite characteristic of the atmosphere of the motifs. The total effect at all events comes closer to atonality than to tonality."[22]

[22]"Der Einfluss der Volksmusik auf die heutige Kunstmusik," *Melos* I/17 (16 October 1920).

In the reconciliation of folk music influence and atonality, moreover, lies the conceptual antithesis which evolved on a larger scale in the European music of the twenties between neo-classicism and the Schoenberg school. It is well known that Schoenberg vigorously condemned both folk music inspiration and the neo-classical style because he saw in them avoidance of the real problems. Bartók and Stravinsky committed both "crimes," and there is also some inevitability in this. In a certain sense both aspirations were actually of a defensive nature: one appealed to the great impersonal community, and the other to the great tradition, after the experience of the terrifying crisis of the age. There is also, however, an essential difference between the two: whereas the influx of fresh air brought by folk music did indeed exert a beneficial influence on European art music—and this is best proved by the example of Bartók or the early works of Stravinsky—neo-classicism brought with it the danger of an unproductive stylistic game. Without going into a discussion of this antithesis in aesthetics and ethics, which is beyond the limits of the present study, we do have to consider one question. How was it possible for Bartók to take in the influences of both Schoenberg and Stravinsky at one and the same time and unite them in his own art? The stage-displacement outlined above does not really offer an explanation since some of the works of the twenties display a distinct combination of the two influences.

This question is posed even more pointedly by Theodor W. Adorno, who sees in the art of Schoenberg and Stravinsky not only two different creative attitudes, but two absolutely basic and fundamentally opposed conceptions of art.[23] If we think of this as a basis, it becomes perfectly understandable that, of all his contemporaries, it is to the influence of these two that Bartók reacted most sensitively. It is scarcely possible to find a composer of any worth in that period who could have avoided the artistic pull of either one or the other. And Bartók shows his artistic greatness to be similar to theirs in that he submitted himself to the force of both of them but at the same time managed to retain a completely independent position. This was considered by René Leibowitz to be a compromise,(Leibowitz 1947) and

[23]Theodor Adorno, *Philosophie der neuen Musik* (Frankfurt/M, 1958).

Adorno also found fault with Bartók for this "middle" route. In his book *The Philosophy of the New Music* Adorno writes: "The best works of Béla Bartók, who in many respects attempted to reconcile Schoenberg and Stravinsky, are probably superior to those of Stravinsky in density and richness."[24]

Thus Adorno's interpretation, although his decision favours Bartók rather than Stravinsky, somewhere within itself conceals an element which in the last analysis pushes Bartók's oeuvre out to the periphery of the musical art of the age. It is in the conception of Schoenberg, of whom he was an absolute supporter, that he sees progress and the only possible way forward, and the way of Stravinsky being the precise antithesis of this, is regarded as retrogressive in tendency. And the way of Bartók—in his opinion—is not independent, sometimes following Schoenberg, and sometimes Stravinsky. In recognizing the polar positions of Schoenberg and Stravinsky, Adorno is unquestionably right, but the content of their positions cannot be fitted so simply into the progression-restoration antinomy. Most important of all: Bartók, standing between them, does not vacillate between progression and regression, but takes over and filters certain elements from the art of each in order to merge these in a sovereign way into his own art. Bartók therefore made no compromise: he brought about a synthesis. He had no wish to make peace between two tendencies which were really antithetic, but rather to select from them what was for him important and useful and enclose it in a dialectical unity. His success is not merely the result of his personal talent, but is also due to his starting point: he wanted to take care of both the preservation of traditions and also their further development. He was able to bring about this synthesis because he found the point of contact between the legacy of the past and the revolution of the present.

[24]Ibid., 111–12.

CHAPTER THREE

THE FOLK MUSIC INFLUENCE

"The melodic world of my string quartets does not differ essentially from that of folksongs; it is just that their setting is more strict," said Bartók to Denijs Dille in 1937.[1] At first sight this claim might well surprise the reader, as it did Denijs Dille, stimulating him to further questions. For the concentrated means of expression, the complicated quality of the structure, and the abstractness of the whole conception give the precise impression in Bartók's string quartets that here it is exclusively the laws of European art music which are followed, and that this refined genre, esoteric in function, is apparently irreconcilable with the simpler world and forms of folk music.

Bartók's statement, however, inspires the researcher to deeper and more thorough investigations. No matter how well known the attraction of folk music is for the Hungarian master, and the relationship between folk music and his creative work, the problem is in reality multi-layered, and in spite of numerous articles and studies dealing with the topic, it remains unsolved to this very day. As a starting point, the study by Bence Szabolcsi which appeared in 1950 should be mentioned in particular; because of its scope it was hardly able to exhaust the "horizontal" aspect of the question, but "vertically" it penetrated very deeply. (Szabolcsi 1950) It showed clearly the ways that this relationship changed, the kind of development it experienced from Bartók's first signs of interest in folk music on to his last period. "This aesthetics could most properly be introduced by a

---

[1] D. Dille's interview with Bartók, published in *La Sirène* (Brussels), March 1937.

separate musicological study: in this way it would become quite clear how interest from the purely artistic point of view is replaced by the desire for scientific clarification; how he was excited from the very outset by the political aspect which became more prominent from that moment—virtually immediately after the beginning of Hungarian folksong collecting—when Bartók, turning against the nationalistic slogans of Hungary in 1908, began Rumanian, Slovakian and Ruthenian collections as well; we should see how in the last analysis he extracts, quite beyond scientific problems, a historical, moral and social lesson from folk music: how he sees in it first the problems of the nation and the country, then those of the continent, and finally of all humanity."

In this light the classification of Bartók as a "national folklorist" becomes untenable: this notion, however, does occasionally crop up in a few handbooks that discuss modern music now in circulation.[2] The category of folklorism, while not in itself signifying a lack of esteem, takes second place in the aesthetic values of our age, following creative artists of so-called universal significance. Thus folklorism also means a certain kind of national limitation, since the driving force is generally national, and the material itself, folk music, belongs mainly to one people. Bartók's life began in an atmosphere of national aspiration, complete with national statement of aims: the first was the creation of an independent Hungarian music culture of European rank on the social-political basis of the nation then becoming independent. Late in life, however, he went considerably beyond this initial, merely national goal, and as a direct result of his folkloristic research journeys, he arrived at the idea of the brotherhood of man, and inevitably thereafter opposed Hitler's fascism. This widening course along which Bartók progressed in itself contradicts his being classified in any way as a mere folklorist.

The problem, however, is greatly complicated by two extreme aesthetic conceptions, directly opposed to one another on theoretical

[2]Hans Heinz Stuckenschmidt, *Neue Musik* (Berlin: Surhkamp, 1951); Claude Samuel, *Panorama de l'art musical contemporain* (Paris: Gallimard, 1962); Paul Collaer, *La musique moderne* (Brussels: Elsevier, 1958).

grounds, meeting on an essentially faulty platform in the judgment of Bartók's "folkiness." The aestheticians of the new Viennese school— above all René Leibowitz and Theodor W. Adorno—considered Bartók's attraction to folk music a mistake, particularly in that the popular movement and demagogy of fascism brought great discredit to the concept and practice of popular art.[3] They therefore divided Bartók's works into two groups according to the role played in individual works by folk music, and only that which came close in idiom and technique to the aspirations of the European avant-garde could be recognized as a masterpiece. On the other hand, the Marxist criticism of the fifties declared this more unambiguously popular branch of the oeuvre to be its own, and was quite prepared to hand over to the other side the very greatest masterpieces, having branded them as products of the "decadent bourgeois" avant-garde.[4]

Interestingly, both of these trends later developed a broader, more liberal branch. The one side became prepared to accept— though only with some pardoning criticism—Bartók's more "popular" works, and the other side was willing not to discard a significant section of the oeuvre, but at the same time classified it as "deviation" and considered Bartók a great master of the age inasmuch as he "was capable" of resisting the spirit of deviation and finding the "popular" way.[5]

In recent years a more sober and scientific approach has fortunately begun to surface in both Hungarian and international musicological literature, according to which Bartók's complete legacy is regarded as a unified whole, and instead of screening its aesthetics, the way of analytical criticism has been chosen. For if the elements of

[3]Adorno, op. cit.; Leibowitz, op. cit; Pierre Boulez, "Bartók Béla" entry in Vol. I of *Encyclopédie de la Musique* (Paris: Fasquelle, 1958).

[4]Mihály András, "Bartók Béla," foreword to the volume *Bartók Béla levelei (Az utolsó két év gyűjtése).* Összegyűjtötte és sajtó alá rendezte Demény János. [B. B. Letters (Collecting of the last two years)] (Budapest: Zeneműkiadó," 1951). Further from the same author: "Válasz egy Bartók-kritikára" ["Answer to a Criticism of Bartók"] cf. Leibowitz, op. cit. *j Zenei Szemle* I (1950).

[5]A characteristic example of the latter view is I. Nestiev's *Bartók-book* (Moscow: Isdatelstvo Musika, 1969).

folk music influence are also to be found in those works which to all appearances follow the European tradition, and make even the newest idiomatic aspirations their own, then there are not two Bartóks—one remaining close to folk music, a folklorist composer using the material as a source, and another who is a great master of universal influence. There is only *one* artist here, who on various levels and with a varying measure of concentration solved the problems he imposed upon himself. "It is necessary to know the melodies of the people as we know them," he said,[6] obviously referring to the fact that the idiom he used, comprehensible chiefly in a European context, has other dimensions of greater universality: apart from European culture, self-contained and limited by time and space alike, the great traditions of the East, with a background of thousands of years, are also built into his art. As Bartók himself stated, he strove for a "synthesis of East and West."[7]

This idea finds expression in the chamber music, and since, in its tradition and special texture, it is the string quartet that is related most closely to European art music, the folk music elements that appear are of even greater significance than those to be found in other genres.

In the works of Bartók's youth, the majority of which, incidentally, are chamber works, the only noticeable Hungarian tone is still that which had been born as a result of the Hungarian music aspirations of the nineteenth century, and which Bartók probably came to know through Liszt's Hungarian Rhapsodies and Brahms's Hungarian-style works. It is now well known that their origins lay in the *verbunkos* recruiting music and popular art songs—that is, they have nothing in common with the deeper layers of Hungarian peasant music discovered by Bartók and Kodály. It is the First String Quartet which represents the turning point in Bartók's output: here the experiences of the first folksong-collecting journeys produced their artistic fruit. The multi-faceted nature of the work is typical—within the framework of the late Romantic melodic and harmonic world, which

[6]See D. Dille's interview.
[7]Moreux, op. cit.

forms the basic tone of the quartet, two other characteristics are perfectly recognizable: romantically Hungarian elements recalling the past, and traces of peasant music reflecting new experience and pointing decidedly forward. A good example of the reminiscent Hungarian tone is the cello cadenza in the introduction preceding the third movement, behind its theme it is not difficult to recognize the model: Béni Egressy's setting of the *Szózat* (*Appeal*) or Szentirmay's well-known song beginning "Csak egy szép lány" ("Just one lovely girl").

Example 32.

In both the first and third movements we can also find examples of the other, new Hungarian tone. Pentatony is not in itself unequivocal proof of the influence of Hungarian folksongs, for Bartók might just as easily have found it in contemporary French music. Moreover, in the central section of the first movement—just where one of the pentatonic melodies appears—the influence of Debussy and Ravel is quite conspicuous. The descending melody characteristic of both places, however, unmistakably evokes a characteristic type of ancient Hungarian pentatonic melody. It is shown by Bartók's later publication that he noted a variation of this melody type in Csíkrákos (Transylvania) in 1907, with the text "Romlott testem a bokorba" ("My rotten body into the bush") (Bartók 1924: no. 24).

Example 33.

Example 33 (continued)

Hn   Rom - - lott testěm   a ᵃ bo - kor - ba,___

At this time it is characteristic how very uncertainly Bartók still uses this melodic material, which contains so many possibilities within it. True, he does develop a beautiful arching cello melody out of it in the first movement, but it remains an "island" in this impressionistic and late-romantic environment. Yet in the third movement he simply does not know "what to do" with the otherwise effectively prepared melody, and it is only its iambic cadence that he either weaves on further (after figure 11) or merely repeats it (6 bars before 35).

The influence of folk music shows itself in a more mature way in the rhythm of the third movement. The movement's most important thematic elements can without exception be traced back to one or two typical folk line patterns. It is necessary to note that the line type of seven syllables (see Ex. 34 b) is frequent in the folk music of West European countries as well, and it was used even by the classical Viennese masters (for example, by Haydn in his Symphony no. 88 in G major, first movement); but in all probability it was from the freshly discovered Hungarian folksong that Bartók took his inspiration.

Example 34.

Taken together, these elements are evidence that in Bartók's First String Quartet the influence of Hungarian folk music is just as conscious and appears in just as important a form as in his later works; it is simply not yet so organically incorporated.

Several writings, lectures, and studies bear witness to the consciousness and deliberateness of the use of folk music. In "Der Einfluss der Volksmusik auf die heutige Kunstmusik"[8] and in different words elsewhere, Bartók analyses with scholarly precision the three stages of incorporating folk music into art music. "We may, for instance, take over a peasant melody unchanged or slightly varied, write an accompaniment to it and possibly some opening and concluding phrases."[9] Thus Bartók describes the first and simplest stage, to which, in addition to folksong arrangements, simple folksong quotations also belong. Such methods are frequently encountered in the pre-Bartók literature as well—witness Beethoven's Rasumovsky Quartets—so as to remain within the framework of the genre. In the string quartets Bartók avoided this method, but it is to be found on several levels in the two Violin Rhapsodies and the Duos for two violins; the latter series of forty-four duets being, strictly speaking, folksong arrangements, absolutely in the style of the piano series *For Children*. Whereas in the piano pieces Bartók employs only Hungarian and Slovakian melodies, in the violin duos Slovakian, Rumanian, Ruthenian, Ukrainian, Serbian and Arab melodies find a place beside the Hungarian tunes. The two Violin Rhapsodies are a special case in the "first stage" of Bartók's folk music inspiration: all the themes of both works stem from actual folksongs, and the majority of these are Rumanian. There are also Hungarian and Ruthenian melodies. Bartók arranged the two rhapsodies into slow and fast movements based on the model of the Hungarian *verbunkos* (recruiting music) tradition and created a higher art music form from them; that is, he created a special high-level form of folksong arrangement which is really a borderline case between true folksong arrangements and pure art music creations. This sort of high-level folksong

[8]*Melos* no. 17 (1920): 384–86.
[9]"The Influence of Peasant Music on Modern Music," in *Bartók Essays* No. 43, p. 341.

arrangement is not unique in Bartók's work, but whereas in the *Improvisations* the art music intervention virtually covers the folksongs, in the two rhapsodies Bartók reconstructs even the folk manner of performance in the violin part.

In the string quartet genre it was the second mode of treatment that Bartók used; he said "the composer does not make use of a real peasant melody but invents his own imitation of such melodies" (*Bartók Essays*, 343). In reality, the folk music phrases already quoted from the First Quartet also belong here, for it is not the complete folksong that Bartók uses, merely a typical detail from it, and even that not as a quotation but as an independently expressed form. An array of "folksongs" invented by Bartók himself are to be found in his danceplay *The Wooden Prince*. In the string quartets and sonatas, however, this is rare, since a closed, folksong-like formal unit cannot be organically built into the higher-level forms. Solely in the trio of the Fifth Quartet's third movement do we have a complete melody which is folksong-like equally in melody, rhythm, and strophic structure: it comes in a section of the structure which is able to receive this static formal unit into itself without suffering disintegration. Immediately parallel with one of the bagpipe-type songs of *The Wooden Prince* may be placed (a) this song verse from the quartet (b) and a folk model for them (c):

Example 35.

The even crotchets of the bagpipe tunes, which in popular practice change according to the syllable values of the language, are modified by the familiar choriambic formula in the melody quoted from the Fifth Quartet. However, in comparison with the simpler popular solution, the rhythmic formula here is more unusual, for in place of the normal dotting in the proportion of 3 : 1, there is a Bulgarian metre using 3 : 2 dotting.

To the category of self-invented folksongs belong virtually all the themes whose structure resembles the strophic structure of a folksong. These themes differ from the above quoted four-line melodies in that reference to folksongs is more free, the formal and stylistic closedness of the folksong is at some point broken. The following quotation is from the Seconda parte of the Third Quartet: the cello's pizzicato mixtures outline a three-line folksong verse in the Dorian mode (a). Even though the three-line verse is fairly rare in Hungarian folk music, the theme is pervaded by a folksong character. A melody which may be placed beside it as model can be found in Bartók's own collection (b).

Example 36.

The two melodies have several features in common: tripartite division, a dome-shaped structure in the verse, considerable melodic emphasis of the Dorian sixth degree, and the tripodic closing line with an almost identical rhythmic pattern. Whether this song or any other song actually served as a model for Bartók is a secondary matter. What is essential is that this kinship with the less than typical Hungarian folksong is an indication of Bartók's attempts at individualization; that is, even in his folksong-like composing he usually sought what was unique, what was special. This same endeavour is further proved by the development of the melody four bars later. Here the verse is augmented to four lines, but the means employed for this augmentation is the sequential repetition of a variation form of the second line—again a method not typical of folk music. At the same time, by retaining the modality of the melody, the tonality is loose and the closing cadence of the tune moves over from D to A.

In the Bulgarian-rhythm Scherzo of the Fifth Quartet we meet the following theme, likewise divided into three phrases. From the obvious fifth relationship of the first two phrases it is easily recognizable that on this occasion it was the two-level melodic structure of ancient Hungarian folksongs that served as a model. The relationship between the two phrases is clear.

Example 37.

This double reference indicates the connection. At the same time Bartók breaks right through the folksong framework, first by placing the typical first and third phrases immediately adjacent to each other (as a consequence of which the verse is shortened to three phrases), and also by tonal displacement of the third and closing phrases. In this way an individual verse structure is produced which can scarcely be claimed as typical of Hungarian folksong: a fifth-answer variation of Bar form: A A₅ B. And beyond this, the Hungarian folk music character is further broken through by the asymmetrical rhythm of the whole melody. An example of the further combination of fifth-answer structure and a three-line verse is offered by two interrelated melodies of the Fourth Quartet. In both, the third line comes about through the addition of yet another fifth-level. In order that the third repetition of the phrase, essentially identical in content, should not become wearisome, the melody is also enriched by rhythmic variation. Besides this, an impression of novelty is given by tonal mistuning; this also ensures the continuation of the closed verse within the form. Here, too, the principle of Bar form can be discovered, for the third line—even if it is essentially a variation of the first—has a relatively *Abgesang* effect after the obviously identical *Stollen* of the first two.

Example 38.

A typical example of verse structure consisting of four lines is provided by the scherzo theme in the third movement of the Fifth Quartet. The four lines are separated from each other by a definite caesura, and the cadence of the individual lines, with the exception of

the third, is reinforced by a sustained note. Both the position of the
individual lines and the line cadences unambiguously demonstrate
that here we are faced with the typical dome-shaped structure of the
new-style Hungarian folksongs. Within this framework, the separate
lines themselves also form a dome-like outline. Alongside the fifth-
structure of the verse as a whole, each line shows a consistent third-
structure, and this is equally characteristic of this type of Hungarian
folksong.

Example 39.

A similar dome-shaped structure in four sections can be found in the
broad cello melody in the slow movement of the Fourth Quartet (bars
55–63). Compared to the earlier example, the structure is much more
free and relaxed here, the relative positions of the lines only approximately give the outline of the dome-arch familiar from folksongs.
The third and fourth lines, weaving in sequences, descend more than
two octaves and in this way even the fourth-cadence of the closing
line comes lower than the first line. Although the whole melody is a
much more complicated construction than the folksongs serving as
models, its character is nevertheless unambiguous as a result of the
rhythm and the individual fourth-melody. The above quotations have
given examples of the two basic verse-types of the Hungarian
folksong—the descending, two-level structure of the ancient songs,
and the architectonic structure of the more modern songs. In the
second movement of the Fifth Quartet, however, we find a four-line

melody which, as far as its structure is concerned, belongs to neither of these basic types. The lines of the melody, with the exception of the last, are of a considerably wide range, and their direction consistently changes: the first line is descending, the second ascending, the third descending and the fourth, in the nature of a summary, is ascending and descending. This strophic arrangement, not at all typical of folk music, is, however, completely pervaded by common folk music elements. In the melody the interval of a fourth plays the leading role. Moreover, the individual lines are consistently built on a fourth basis.

Example 40.

This fourth-structure skeleton of the melody displays three connecting methods. In the second and third lines the fourths are conjoint as in a chain, like the *synemmenon* tetrachords of ancient Greek music theory. The first line is an example of the other kind, disjoint (*diezeugmenon*) linking. And the last line is based on the fourths slipping into one another. Behind the disjoint linking of the first line, contracted into chromaticism, it is not difficult to recognize its diatonic origin, the outline of two-level Hungarian folksongs.[10] The three kinds of fourth connections are very frequently met with in both Hungarian folksongs and in the melodics of Bartók's music.

---

[10]The phenomenon of contraction into chromaticism will be further discussed in the chapter "Mistuning."

Example 41.

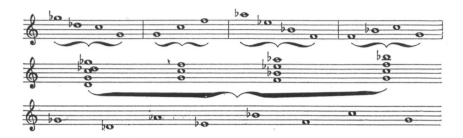

It is more than in a theoretical sense that this fourth-structure of the melody related it to the melodic world of Hungarian folk music. A verse built up in this way can scarcely be found among Hungarian folksongs, but of the individual lines it can easily be demonstrated that they are variations or condensations of certain folksong lines. The first, for example, can be traced back to the second line of the song beginning "Megállj, pajtás!" ("Stop, matey") from Vikár's collection (and notated by Bartók), or the first two lines of the song beginning "Kérették nénémet" ("They asked my sister in marriage")—which melody was collected by Bartók in 1910.

Example 42.

The fourth-skeleton of the second line can often be discovered in a descending form in Hungarian folksongs. It does occur in this kind of ascending form, but it is rare (Bartók notated this, too, from Vikár's collection).

Example 43.

The popular character is perfectly alive in the third line as well. It is, for example, a very familiar phenomenon in Hungarian folk music that the melodic line begins from the ninth above the final note. But a descent of three fourths does not occur in a single actual folksong line, so here it is a question of the condensation of the material of two lines. For example, in the song beginning "Mikor engem férjhez adtak" ("When they gave me away")—from Bartók's 1907 collection—this area is covered by the second and fourth lines together.

Example 44.

The folk music kinship of the last line is the most obvious: it is no more than a cadential commonplace.

Example 45.

After such relationships and agreements, it is very important to consider the phenomena which are atypical of folk music and are in direct contrast to it. Such is, above all, the already mentioned mistuning of the disjoint fourth-skeleton of the first line. And, further, such are the individual lines for even if they correspond in some degree to the melodic lines in folk music, they do not come in the same place as in folksongs. The first line of the Bartók melody, for example, is such a vigorous condensation that it already includes the second line of the folksongs, descending to the keynote. The rising second line, ending on the seventh degree, is practically absurd from the folk music aspect, since it originally has the function of a third line. The third line, as we have seen above, is the compression of the second and fourth lines of a folksong, and so here it is once more a question of a deviation in function. Only the final lines correspond in the Bartók melody and in the folksong patterns.

It is now time, in discussing structural imitation of Hungarian folk melodics, to mention Bartók's when he takes as a basis for his melody not a complete verse, but a single folksong line and develops it—though not according to the laws of folksong verse structure. In the string quartets, a typical example of this is to be found in the final movement of the Second Quartet. In this oppressive slow movement, radiating a deathly atmosphere, this melody appears with its descending line:

Example 46.

It is not difficult to recognize behind this that ancient type of Hungarian folksong quoted above as analogous with the melody analysed from the Fifth Quartet (Ex. 42). There is, however, an example which comes even closer than this: a Transdanubian lament melody from Kodály's collection:[11]

Example 47.

We feel this example is more closely related principally from the functional and tonal aspects. Indeed, here in the Second Quartet is born a type of tone which becomes very important in Bartók's later art: the lament. The Bartók lament is not merely an imitation of the folk lament. The folk lament melodies only supply one source for this melodic type, in which other elements are also condensed, such as the

[11]*A Magyar Népzene Tára* [*Corpus of the Hungarian Folk Music*] ed. by Béla Bartók and Zoltán Kodály, Vol. V: *Laments*. Arranged for publishing by Lajos Kiss and Benjamin Rajeczky, (Budapest: Akadémiai Kiadó, 1966).

tradition of art music *lamentos*, naturalistic sobbing, other sorrowful
sound effects, and the lonely monologue tone. We encountered this
kind of doleful, plaintive outburst at the end of the first movement of
the First Quartet (five bars before the end of the movement), but
whereas there the musical idiom of late Romanticism was the means
of expression, here in the Second Quartet the mournful, resigned
tone is pervaded by the melodics of folk music and the folk lament.
Similar reference, if in a different sense, is made to the folk lament by
the cello monologue in the slow movement of the Fourth Quartet,
and within it primarily by the repetitive, chromatic first part:

Example 48.

Relationship with folk music is here shown merely by the declamatory
note repetition and the rhythm. The rhythm of Bartók's laments is
generally characterized by the accented iambics originating from Hungarian folk music, together with considerably contrasting rhythmic
values. This can be readily observed in the very first bar of the example: in the iambic start there is a 1 :13.5 semiquaver proportion between the values of the first and second notes. And in the next motif,
in which the iambus is augmented to a fourth paeon (UUU-), a long
note with a value of 17 demisemiquavers is connected to the three
demisemiquavers. The lament in the second movement of the Sixth
Quartet is likewise characterized by this kind of rhythmic contrast.
Here it is the fourth-structure of the melody that indicates the
relationship with folk music.

Example 49.

The application of the structural elements of folk music—or, it might be said, the undisguised imitation of folk music—is not confined in Bartók to Hungarian folk music. As a combined result of his folkloristic research work and artistic beliefs, it is possible to recognize in his works the folk music influence of all the peoples that came within the scope of his research. As in the discussion of the "first stage," we can also refer here to Slovakian, Ruthenian and, above all, Rumanian examples. Among the forty-four duos, for example, we know with certainty that two of them are not actual folksongs: the Ruthenian *kolomeika*, no. 35, and the Rumanian bagpipe tune, no. 36, were written by the composer himself. In the First Violin-Piano Sonata and the last movement of Contrasts the sound of Rumanian instrumental folk music is also heard—although not utilizing any actual folk melody.

Besides the single Arab folksong arrangement (the forty-second violin duo) there are numerous Arab imitations in Bartók's music. These need to be discussed separately since after he became familiar with the music of the Hungarian and neighbouring peoples there was really only one other discovery which influenced him with similar intensity: the folk music of the North African Arabs. The folk music of East Europe, and particularly that of Rumania, "opened a window" for him towards the musical cultures of the East. Through this window he was able to look more profoundly into the musical world of the East than any of his western predecessors or contemporaries. He was thus given the opportunity of setting himself the aim of a synthesis of East and West.

Bartók's visit to the Biskra district of Algeria in 1913 remains to this day a virtually unsurpassed scientific feat. The results of his research were published in the German periodical *Zeitschrift für Musikwissenschaft.*[12] He was the first pioneer of modern ethnomusicology who collected on the spot. And he was also one of the first, insofar as

---

[12]"Die Volksmusik der Araber von Biskra und Umgebung," *Zeitschrift für Musikwissenschaft* (1920).

he strove in his investigation of Arab music, to make a scientific distinction between the musical styles of town and village.[13] The creative significance of his experience collecting in North Africa can only be fully understood when we reflect that Bartók composed *Allegro barbaro* as early as 1911, and thereby raised elemental ancient rhythms to the level of art music, together with ostinato melody composed of small units. It is thus almost symbolic that in the very year that Stravinsky introduced his *Sacre du Printemps* in Paris, an imaginary sacrificial festival of the Russian tribes of pagan times, Bartók was in Africa, getting to know real primitive folk music and its authentic environment.

Just as it was possible in the First String Quartet to hail the appearance of the influence of Hungarian folk music, so in the Second String Quartet we can hail as a novelty of similar significance the artistic reflection of the collecting experience among the Arabs, which can also be found in the Suite for piano dating from roughly the same time. Bartók himself speaks of the use of Arab folk music elements, but mentions only the Suite for piano and the Dance Suite.[14] The following examples may serve to supplement this, in an effort to prove that the influence of Arab music is also present in numerous other works, especially in the string quartets. The influence can be equally observed in melodies and in instrumentation—the same sort of conscious association as the simultaneous use of melodic and structural elements in connection with Hungarian folk music.

The quaver accompaniment and minor third repetition in the second movement of the second quartet is in fact a stylization of the drum effects of Arab folk music. This is borne out by the accompaniment part in the forty-second violin duo under the title "Arab Song." From this we may also conclude that we ought to seek the origin of other kinds of barbaric ostinato minor third motifs by Bartók primarily in primitive folk music, and not in popular art songs by Szentirmay, as

[13]For more detailed discussion of this theme see János Kárpáti, "Béla Bartók et la musique arabe," *Musique Hongroise*. Revue publiée sous la dir. de Maurice Fleuret, éditée par l'Association France-Hongrie (Paris, 1962).

[14]"The Folksongs of Hungary," *Pro Musica* (1928) 28–35. See further Bartók's letter to O. Beu in Bartók Letters No. 577.

Kodály attempted to assert in one of his lectures.[15] Below are quotations giving the original Arab melody (no. 15, Biskra collection), the violin duo which arose from it, and the beginning of the theme of the Second String Quartet.

Example 50.

+ = 1/4 higher pitch
o = 1/4 lower pitch

The continuation of the quartet's third-motif hints even more unmistakably at Arab folk music. In this way it becomes clear that the third-motif is really an augmented second, a typical Arab scale interval. The same can be established concerning the accompanying ostinato of the "Arab Song." The scale composed of the violin duo's two parts is none other than a transposition of the two disjoint tetrachords of the augmented second scale, transforming them into conjoint tetrachords.

[15]Zoltán Kodály, "Szentirmaytól Bartókig" ["From Szentirmay to Bartók"], lecture at the Hungarian Academy of Sciences in 1955. *J Zenei Szemle* VI (1955).

We meet this same scale in the fugato in *The Miraculous Mandarin*, the Arab character of which is determined by the scale and the melodic line winding upwards and downwards from the centre. Here is the melody, and beside it the no. 48 example from Bartók's Biskra collection, which has a similar melodic outline.

Example 51.

On the basis of the note range, the snaking melodic line and the peculiar rhythm, we notice Arab influence in a theme from the Fourth String Quartet, which plays an important role in both the first and last movements. Its tone in the first movement is soft and lyrical, which is not in the least alien to a certain kind of Arab folk music, and which type also appears in the Dance Suite.

Example 52.

In the last movement this same melody changes to a hard, robust dance theme with a drumming accompaniment.

Example 53.

In Bartók's music the presence of Arab folk music elements is frequently accompanied by drum effects. In North African Arab and Berber folk music—vocal and instrumental alike—drum accompaniment has an important function. The percussion instruments used in these areas (bandir, tabal) have one feature in common in that the player can produce sounds at two or three different pitch levels. The metrical character of the rhythmic patterns they produce is consequently influenced by the stress (dynamic) and the pitch (colour) together. Bartók's interest was attracted not merely by the primitive, barbaric ostinato rhythm of the percussion instruments, but by the frequent appearance of virtuosic polymetrics between melody and accompaniment, or even within the drum accompaniment itself. The previously mentioned second movement of the Second Quartet provides a good example of drum accompaniment imitation in a regular metre; the metrical beat of the parts imitating the drum is occasionally given emphasis by the instrumentation (pizzicato crotchets in the stressed part of the bar) and later the stressed notes are supported by melodic ornamentation (e.g., figures 8 and 15). Here the deliberately naturalistic drum accompaniment in the quoted detail from *The Miraculous Mandarin* may also be mentioned.

In the "Arab Song" violin duo the minor third repetititon is an imitation of the drum accompaniment. When the two-note accompaniment becomes three notes, a polymetric result is produced, which is similar to that found in the original Arab melody which served as its model: in the drum part the stresses bring out $\frac{3}{8}$ and $\frac{5}{8}$ units which form a consistent counterpoint to the $\frac{2}{4}$ beat of the melody (see Ex. 50). Similar metrical phenomena are to be found in nos. 58, 59, and 60 of Bartók's Arab publication. In the bandir accompaniment of no. 58, $\frac{2}{8}$ and $\frac{3}{8}$ units alternate in such a way that their total metrical value remains constant. That is, within the $\frac{6}{8}$ metre, a hemiola is produced: $3 \times \frac{2}{8}$ ($=\frac{3}{4}$) alternating with $2 \times \frac{3}{8}$ (= $\frac{6}{8}$). Besides North African music, this phenomenon is very common in Spanish folk music.

A different kind of alternation of duple and triple units is the basis for the drum accompaniment of melodies 59 and 60. Here two $\frac{3}{8}$ units are followed by one $\frac{2}{8}$, altogether $\frac{8}{8}$, in an asymmetrical distribution,[16] a typical Bulgarian rhythm in a non-Bulgarian environment! But the two metric types—the earlier symmetrical hemiola and this asymmetrical metre—are not in the end all that distant from each other: rhythmic theory in ancient Greece—as Curt Sachs demonstrates—included in one category under the name of *hemiolia* all those measures in which duple and triple units were connected.[17]

Example 54.

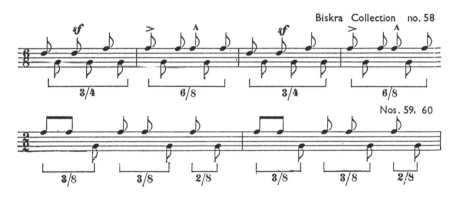

I do not wish to explain every similar metrical technique in Bartók's music through the influence of Arab music, but there can be no doubt that the drum imitation accompanying the Arab-like melody of the Fourth Quartet acquired its asymmetrical emphasis as a result of the

[16]Cf. no. 6 of *Six Dances in Bulgarian Rhythm* (no. 153 of *Mikrokosmos*).

[17]Curt Sachs, *The Rise of Music in the Ancient World, East and West* (New York: Norton, 1943), 261.

influence of the Arab metre type quoted above. A better example of
the pairing of characteristic Arab melody and rhythm can scarcely be
found in all Bartók's works. In addition to this example we can quote
the two-piano version of the "Ostinato" from *Mikrokosmos*. In this
the composer gives the initial even quaver ostinato an asymmetrical
stress in the second piano part, thus bringing about the same $\frac{3}{8} + \frac{3}{8} + \frac{2}{8}$
metric units as in the quartet. On the basis of its melody we feel the
"Ostinato" to more closely resemble Rumanian folk music, although
it does have something in common with the short motif units of the
quartet as well. There are, however, no data to indicate that the
metrical phenomenon already discussed occurs in Rumanian folk
music too. In his published pieces of Rumanian instrumental folk
music Bartók frequently makes a special point of the open fifths
played by the violin accompaniment, but he does not mark any asymmetrical displacement of accents. It may be presumed that in the two-
piano version of "Ostinato" he combined the effects of two different
kinds of folk music which nevertheless do come close to each other.

Example 55.

Example 55 (continued)

"There is yet a third way in which the influence of peasant music can be traced in a composer's work. Neither peasant melodies nor imitations of peasant melodies can be found in his music, but it is pervaded by the atmosphere of peasant music. In this case we may say he has completely absorbed the idiom of peasant music which has become his musical mother tongue" (*Bartók Essays*, 343–44). In the aforementioned study this is how Bartók describes the third, still higher degree of the use of folk music. At this level we can scarcely look for concrete parallels between art music and folk music as we have done up to this point. The relationships can only be demonstrated by a method of investigation which explores at two levels simultaneously: on the one hand, among the very smallest structural elements of the music, in the world of musical language's microstructures, and on the other hand in the area of generalized conceptual phenomena abstracted from the actual forms of music as it is heard. That is, in the first case analysis to the utmost possible degree, and in the second case abstraction in a greater measure than has been necessary thus far.

Let us first consider microanalysis. A very important role is played in Bartók's melodic world by single phrases and typical melodic germs from Hungarian folk music, quite separately from the other melodic and structural regularities of folksongs. It frequently occurs, for example, that some melody with a considerably chromatic, post-Romantic or twentieth-century harmonic background gradually—or quite suddenly—falls into a cadence of folk music simplicity. Both examples of this are taken from the Second Quartet. The first is a clarifying moment in the first movement's development section, animated and tense from every point of view (a). The second is the fourth-melody and fourth-harmony theme of the third movement, which in the mirror movement of its lower and upper parts comes very close to Schoenberg's style. The warm folksong phrase at the end of the theme forms a great contrast to the cold, mysterious fourth-chords. Here, too, is justification for one of Bartók's statements in which he traces fourth-chords back to the frequent fourth-phrases of Hungarian folk music: the pentatonic system of the melodic phrase is really only the extention of the continuous fourth-chain of the harmonies (b).

Example 56.

Example 56 (continued)

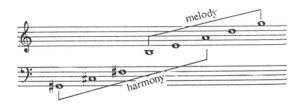

The cadence of the second example (b) is identical note for note with one of the most common cadence types in pentatonic Hungarian folksongs. This tiny melodic germ of three notes plays a large role in Bartók's melodic world, being, so to speak, one of the main means of reconciling art music and folk music melodics; or, to put it another way, a means of idiomatic use of folk music elements.

This three-note melodic nucleus is the meeting point of the traditions of folk music and art music. As a minute cell, nevertheless complete in itself, constructed with musical logic, it fits into musical processes. Multiplied and varied, a complete organism can develop from it. Its structure unequivocally relates it to the pentatonic system without semitone containing as it does the two basic intervals of that system, the major second and the minor third, and through a combination of these two a fourth is produced, which is the "proto-interval" of pentatonic systems. This three-note system may be considered, in both the historical and the logical senses, the bud, the root of pentatony. Although its use points principally to the ancient-style Hungarian folksongs, it is related by natural connecting threads to all anhemitone pentatonic folk music and is thus a real symbol of Bartók's aspirations towards universality. At the same time, this melodic germ, if only molecularly, contains within itself important elements of the European art music tradition: the melody-formation proportion and direction laws stemming from Palestrina, and the arsis-thesis pulse related to even the smallest musical organism. Finally, its asymmetrical structure makes it suitable for taking part in every kind of linear development process.

Example 57.

It fulfills an important, almost central, function in the Prima parte of the Third String Quartet. It often crops up elsewhere in Bartók's works, and everywhere—sometimes openly, sometimes more discreetly—it evokes the spirit of folk melody. It may also be pointed out that the above motif works to more or less the same effect in its inversions and rotations well.

Example 58.

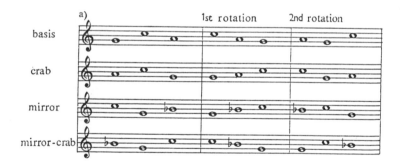

Example 58 (continued)

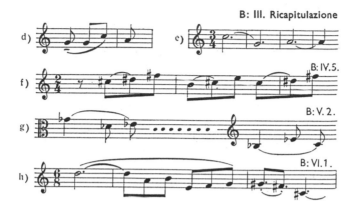

In the first part of the Third Quartet, where this melodic cell appears as the movement's basic motif, its monothematically elaborated "proto-motif," we also encounter a characteristic—we might say, inevitable—development of it. The three-note cell is enlarged by a fourth note. Its long chain appears in the fourth-sequences of the Fifth Quartet. The example from the Third Quartet, incidentally, draws attention to an important phenomenon: the four-note motif is really two three-note motifs fitted into one another, in which the major second-minor third structure is symmetrically enlarged by another major second.

Example 59.

The four-note system thus produced—we can call it tetratony[18]—exists, in the shape of two very characteristic phrases, in the older style of Hungarian folkscngs: one is a cadential type, composed of two fourth-leaps, and the second is a line-starting pattern in which the notes are placed as in a scale.

Example 60.

Working right through Bartók's chamber works we can find numerous examples of different uses of this tetratonic motif. The scale-like pattern appears straight away in the First Quartet—indeed in two places. A particularly important part is played by this motif in the first movement of the Fifth Quartet. The nearest relation of the Third Quartet's fourth-structure form is likewise contained in the Fifth Quartet. And another version of the fourth-structure method, which is identical with the folksong cadence type, occurs in the same manner in the Fourth and Fifth Quartets.

Example 61.

[18]"Tetratony" is the name given to the system of four notes which can be considered the forerunner of pentatony both from theoretical and historical points of view. Its principal characteristic is that its notes fit into a related fifth-chain, and in this it clearly differs from the scales called "tetrachord" which contains neighbouring degrees.

It is from development of these three-note and four-note motifs or melodic cells that Bartók's pentatony arises. But this is the point where the examination method reaches its borderline case: minute melodic analysis meets with the abstraction of tonal systems and scales. It is common, however, to find in Bartók's music that the actual musical material contains, purely and in exemplary fashion, the abstraction.

Pentatony can also come about through the simple complement and melodic development of the tetratonic melodic nucleus. Indeed, tetratony is really incomplete pentatony and wherever it occurs it suggests pentatony. The following example shows how Bartók develops the three-note basic motif of the Third Quartet (a, b), and the tetratonic thematic elements in the Fifth Quartet (c), into pentatony.

Example 62.

In the case of the Third Quartet it is very characteristic that the three-note motif is developed chromatically in the exposition and only takes on a pure pentatonic form in the calmer and more static recapitulation—that is, in the Ricapitulazione section, and even there only within a smaller range. The tetratonic theme becomes pentatonic in the development section of the movement—that is, in the most dynamic part, although in a relatively static section within that, when the motif becomes firmly fixed in the area of the tonality of E (bars 104–111). Both examples indicate, therefore, that in comparison with chromaticism pure pentatony is more static, usually having some concluding, rounding off function. (It is quite another matter that in the part quoted from the Fifth Quartet the "pure" pentatony has another pentatonic layer, displaced by a minor second, as a counterpoint. We shall return to this later.)

Every single appearance of pentatony is isolated. Thus, no example can be found where one pentatonic system reigns supreme for a whole movement or even the whole of a formal section. This would obviously mean some impoverishment i.e., the musical material, and it was precisely in the interests of enrichment that Bartók turned to folk music. Hence in Bartók's musical idiom pentatony evolves a special relationship with tonal systems possessing greater and richer possibilities—for example, diatony and the chromatic scale. In numerous places pentatony is hidden within a diatonic or chromatic texture and can only be discovered by analytic investigation. For example, in the unambiguously diatonic first subject of the Sixth Quartet, if we disregard the various passing and changing notes, a pentatonic melody is outlined. We are faced with similar hidden pentatony in the trio of the Burletta as well: the pentatonic skeleton of the melody is reminiscent of the mysterious introductory theme in *Bluebeard*.

Example 63.

Another kind of treatment involving hidden pentatony appears in the Bulgarian rhythm Scherzo of the Fifth Quartet. Behind the Dorian mode of the second theme in fifth-layers it is not difficult to recognize pentatonic origins, especially as the third and final melodic line does not contain one note outside the system. This third line, however, draws attention to another, no less important phenomenon: by a sudden turn the pentatonic system of the first two lines slides up to a level which is a major third higher (see Ex. 37). This points decidedly to Bartók's feeling that the pentatonic framework is limited from tonal and melodic aspects alike, and his seeking immediately to broaden it. In earlier examples it has been shown how he places the isolated pentatonic parts within the framework of a wider system. On the other hand, this last is an example of one pentatonic system being broken up by another pentatonic system. The simultaneous use of two different pentatonic systems results in a peculiar kind of bitonality. On this occasion, however, the concept has to be interpreted in a wider sense: for the pairing of systems is possible vertically and horizontally—that is, simultaneously and adjacently. Bartók usually combines vertical pairing with imitation. Good examples can be found of even the "pre-pentatonic" elements. In the Third Quartet, the three-note motif moves at a distance of a diminished fifth. And in the first movement of the Fifth Quartet two tetratonic levels come together separated by one semitone.

Example 64.

Bitonal superposition of complete pentatonic systems is encountered
in the Fourth and Fifth Quartets.

Example 65.

Horizontal pairing of two pentatonic systems counts as a very special
technique: on such occasions the two systems meet within one part—
exclusively in a melodic sense. The first example of this is taken from
the Scherzo of the Fifth Quartet discussed above. The three-line
folksong theme already belonged to two pentatonic systems as a result
of the upward displacement of the third line. The varied recapitulation of the theme is even more characteristic. Here it is enlarged to
four lines and the falling verse structure is replaced by a dome structure. Although the first two lines move in one related system, in the
third and fourth lines we witness displacement even within the lines.
It is scarcely necessary to emphasize how essential the difference between the two methods is: in the first case tonal displacement occurs
between lines forming a related, closed unity, and in the second case it
takes place *within* each line.

Example 66.

Example 66 (continued)

The most classic example of the horizontal pairing of two pentatonic systems is found in the last movement of the Fourth Quartet.[19] The movement's first subject of an Arab character is significantly enlarged at one point in the recapitulation (bar 285): it grows to ten bars in length and its range approaches two octaves. In the melody thus developed we can observe two different pentatonic layers: a lower one from A-sharp to F-sharp, and an upper one from G to G. So far we have been dealing only with the pentatonic system itself and have not taken its various modes into consideration. But since we have been looking for the characteristics of Hungarian folk music, our examples have been produced as evidence of the pentatonic quality of the ancient Hungarian melodies. The exception is the example in which the tetratonic motif develops into pentatony; for this detail of the Fifth Quartet's first movement does not demonstrate the characteristic Hungarian pentatony. Strictly speaking, it is a distance scale, for the octave is divided by the regular alternation of major seconds and minor thirds.

	2		3		2		3		2	
E		F♯		A		B		D		E

This warns us that in examining Bartók's music we have to deal with pentatony in a wider sense and move beyond the forms of it native to Hungarian folk music. In this respect the most significant new feature is that hemitonic pentatony also finds a place in Bartók, even if it does

[19]Incidentally, this will be discussed from another angle in the chapter on "Mistuning."

not appear as frequently as the non-hemitonic forms. In the late works, such as the Concerto and the Viola Concerto, we can hear these kinds of phrases, absolutely free of any *couleur locale*.

Example 67.

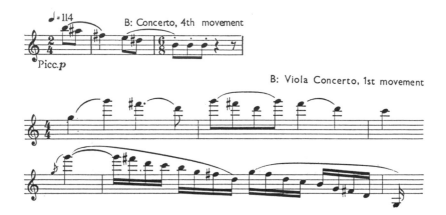

Hemitonic pentatony is, however, a very typical phenomenon in the Far East, occurring in Japan and the Balinesian Islands. Bartók was obviously quite aware of this when he used a composed fragment of the hemitonic pentatonic scale in his piano piece "From the Island of Bali":

Example 68.

The minor second–major third–minor second structure of the melody is really the other mode of the so-called *mèlog* pentatonic scale of the other two examples, which shows in virtually finished form the model scale consisting of alternating minor seconds and major thirds.[20]

[20]*Mèlog* is a special case of the so-called *pèlog* system. Cf. Jaap Kunst, *Music in Java* (3rd ed., The Hague: Martinus Nijhoff, 1973), 52–55.

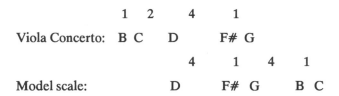

	1	2		4		1		
Viola Concerto:	B	C		D		F#	G	

		4		1		4		1
Model scale:		D		F#	G		B	C

With all this in mind, the principle itself stands clearly before us: using a stage of hemitonic pentatony which is originally periodic, we reach the same kind of model scale as the minor third–minor second or the fourth–minor second scales in the sphere of distance phenomena. Bartók knew this very well, for in the piano piece "From the Island of Bali" he places side by side, as though variations of each other, the fourth–minor second and the major third–minor second forms of the theme.

Example 69.

B: From the Island of Bali

In the course of the piece the fourth form is primary and only later does it become contracted to a major third. But in Balinesian musical practice, the *melog* major thirds are certainly typical, and the fourth form is only an art music abstraction. It is true that Jaap Kunst, for example, instances a Java *mèlog* with the following values.[21]

0.87 1.78 4.32 0.62 4.40

Here, too, there is a tendency towards expansion: the larger intervals spread at the expense of the smaller. The major third with the value 4.40 is almost a quarter-tone larger than the tempered form, thus approaching the fourth, while the semitones contract almost into quarter-tones (0.62).

In the *Mikrokosmos* piece in question Bartók was in no way striving after scientific precision, nor did he evolve the programme of the

[21]Ibid. Cf. page 395.

piece beforehand. In all probability the fourth model supplied the fundamental idea and he connected that on a musical basis with the character of the tropical hemitonic pentatony of the Far East. In any event, this much is certain: he considered the two forms of model scale to be one identical category.

Another manifestation of the fourth model, however, is related by Bartók to Arab folk music. Of the third movement of the Suite op. 14, he himself declared that he composed it under Arab inspiration.

Example 70.

The motor rhythm of the movement undoubtedly has much in common with the previously discussed drum effects of Arab folk music, but no example of the melodic element of the movement, the fourth model, is to be found in the Biskra collection. It is to be presumed that Bartók freely associated two elements here: the motor rhythmic world of Arab folk music and the vaguely oriental fourth model.

A Far East, tropical atmosphere becomes paired in two other places with the form of the fourth model expanded to an augmented fourth: in the third movement of the *Music for Strings, Percussion and Celesta*, and in the second movement of *Contrasts*. The instrumentation, with its imitation of gamelan colours, also makes the reference quite obvious.

Example 71.

Example 71 (continued)

In this augmented fourth form the model still remains close to the perfect fourth form, and yet simultaneously it is identical with the major third type as well.

Example 72.

In the quotation from *Contrasts*, incidentally, the minor third is also heard above the augmented fourth model. The minor third model, which has already been mentioned in another connection, is likewise a typical and unmistakable stylization of the various oriental scale types. In this case it is principally Arab folk music that must be considered, in which a scale consisting of alternating minor thirds and semitones is to be found in a natural form, too, and with no stylization whatsoever (see Ex. 51/b). The developmental tendency of the Second Quartet also points in this direction; the melodic pattern of the second movement's Arab theme consists of a minor third and a minor second, and from this the composer develops the larger melodic contours of the coda, among which there is, indeed, no exact minor third model scale, yet the peculiar melody-building intention is nevertheless evident.

Example 73.

If the stylization process were to be continued, the major second model could be produced from the contraction of the minor third model. But on this occasion the derivation, although permissible in theory, proves artificial in practice. That is, this new model scale does actually evolve in "From the Island of Bali"—before the listener's very ears—from a combination of two fourth models. This eight-degree tonal system, the roots of which reach back into European art music traditions as well, is also an indirect descendant of the Far East's periodic scales.

Example 74.

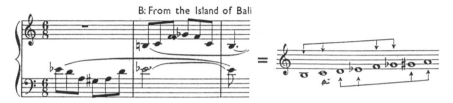

From this is clear the masterly and consistent way Bartók developed one or two popular and Eastern art music tonal systems (hemitonic pentatony and Arab minor third model) which served as examples. On this basis, to the three models indicated by Ernő Lendvai, which are indeed the most frequent, it is necessary to add the following in both number and interpretation:

major second model	$(2+1)$:	expanded *mèlog* combined
minor third model	$(3+1)$:	Arab scale or contracted *mèlog*
major third model	$(4+1)$:	Far Eastern *mèlog*
fourth model	$(5+1)$:	expanded *mèlog*
augmented fourth model	$(6+1)$:	expanded or inverted *mèlog*

These models and the scales evolved from them have a double role in Bartók's music: on the one hand, in association with other elements, they are apt to give a particular work or part of a work its folk character, or add colour to it; on the other hand, changing to an idiomatic element, they secure at virtually every point the communal background to Bartók's music, its natural and popular roots. Their purpose is not in the least to produce a certain *couleur locale*: they fit rather on the idiomatic level into Bartók's music and sometimes, his dramaturgy. To give one example: in the following detail from *The Miraculous Mandarin* the melody moves in the non-hemitonic pentatonic system. The chord mixture of two parallel diminished fifths, however, is essentially a fourth model. If we consider the latter's relationship with the hemitonic melody, we can claim that in this detail of the dance-play Bartók united the two basic types of Far East pentatony—the non-hemitonic Chinese and the hemitonic Javanese—in simultaneous horizontal and vertical movement.

Example 75.

B: The Miraculous Mandarin

And since we have already found Arab elements elsewhere in the dance-play (cf. Ex. 51/a), this means we have uncovered no less than three oriental interrelationships in the work. This mixture of characters and the veiling of the purely Chinese character has a dramaturgical function: Bartók obviously did not want the character of the Mandarin to degenerate into a mere stock Chinese figure.

This is of secondary importance in comparison with the idiomatic significance of the application of Eastern or popular tonal systems. For Bartók does not reserve either pentatony or the model scales for forming undisguisedly Eastern or popular content, moods or type depiction. As a result of his consistent forming and transforming work these models fit organically into his world of expression as a whole, leaning as it does on western art music tradition, and thus into the different diatonic and non-diatonic modes and finally into chromaticism. This, among other things, explains why only three of the above listed five models assumed a conspicuous role noticeable throughout Bartók's work. For the major second, minor third and fourth models fit exactly into the chromatically divided octave since their totals measured in semitones (2+1=3, 3+1=4, 5+1=6) provide numbers of which 12 is an integral common multiple (see also Antokoletz 1984: 68–71). In opposition to this, the value of the major third model is five semitones, which cannot be divided exactly into 12, and so it is only 60 semitones (5 octaves) higher or lower than it will reach the starting point of the scale again. And the scale of the tritone model (6+l) comes back to its starting point at an even greater distance (7 octaves)—the lowest common multiple being 84.

It is not only in the melodic and harmonic sense that Bartók uses the three most important model scales: as Elliott Antokoletz has demonstrated, he makes them the very pillars of his chromaticism and symmetrical organizations (Antokoletz 1984). In this way he approaches serial technique without completely adopting that system's organized quality, which extends to every element.

The important role and significance of these models are indicated by the fact that we have arrived at them as a conclusion in analysing the influence both of Bartók's contemporaries and of folk music. It is here that the creative method inherited from western music and that deliberately taken over from eastern music meet in Bartók's art. The question may suggest itself as to which factor—east or west, folk music or art music tradition—played the initiating role in the evolution of his compositional technique. To give an answer to this would be very difficult since it is probable that he was led by a complicated network of interrelationships in creative practice. And an answer is perhaps not even necessary as in this case it is the synthesis itself which is the essential point: the fact that Bartók's model scales fit just as well into the twelve note chromatic system of European music as into various characteristic scale types of eastern music. Thus when Bartók uses an expressly eastern method, the spirit of European music, nurtured on tonal tradition but now beyond tonality, is also present: and vice versa—the idiom of his compositions, the style of his music is at every point imbued with the influence of the tonal systems and modality of eastern music—folk music and art music alike.

For this reason it can justifiably be claimed that Bartók was the first composer in the history of European music in whose art the European principles of the West met in a true synthesis with the spirit of the East. His predecessors turned to the East to depict no more than an occasional mood, scene or atmosphere. For Bartók, however, the eastern experience seeped into his whole work. This is also closely related to the maturing of his artistic world: as the sphere extended for him from the melodic world of the Hungarian and neighbouring peoples to becoming acquainted with the music of the peoples beyond Europe, the significance of his use of folk music was likewise extended and enriched. The movement from the simple towards the complicated is expressed by the three degrees—as described by Bartók himself—of merging folk music into art music. And this was no mere theoretical statement: he himself carried it out. But to attempt to place these three stages into some sort of chronological order would be to misunderstand the essence of his creative development. The development of a creative artist is a much more complex phenomenon than can be depicted with a simple straight line. The return to an older method and re-composition on a higher level: it is thus that Bartók's development can be summarized. This applies to the development of the creative method stemming from folk music, as well. The creative period of the twenties is a good example of this: while Bartók was building folk music into his art on the very highest idiomatic level in the two Sonatas for violin and piano and the Third and Fourth String Quartets, he was at the same time composing "simple" folksong arrangements, which differ from the first folksong arrangements of 1906 only in their maturity and exigency.

Bartók's relationship with folk music can, however, be characteristically illuminated if differently categorized. This categorization is not completely independent of that outlined above, but perhaps shows the development on a more profound and less technical level. Here, too, it is Bartók's own words which serve as a starting point. Replying to his critics and opponents in connection with the creative method nourished on folk music, he writes in 1931: "It is fatal error to attribute so much importance to the subject, the theme of a composition. We know that Shakespeare borrowed the stories of his plays from all sources . . . Molière's case is even worse! He not only borrowed the themes for his plays, but also part of the construction, and

sometimes took over from his source expressions and whole lines unchanged . . . In music it is the thematic material that corresponds to
the story of a drama. And in music too, as in poetry and in painting, it
does not signify what themes we use. It is the form into which we
mould it that makes the essence of our work."[22]

The second quotation is taken from an American interview in
1941. "It is rather a matter of absorbing the means of musical expression hidden in them, just as the most subtle possibilities of any language may be assimilated. It is necessary for the composer to
command this musical language so completely that it becomes the
natural expression of his musical ideas."[23]

And the third quotation is from the second of Bartók's articles
published in the Berlin *Melos*. " . . . the pure folk music can be considered as a natural phenomenon influencing higher art music, as
bodily properties perceptible with the eye are the fine arts, or the
phenomena of life are for the poet. This influence is most effective
for the musician if he acquaints himself with folk music in the form in
which it lives, in unbridled strength, amidst lower people, and not by
means of inanimate collections . . . If he surrenders himself to the impact of this living folk music and to all circumstances which are the
conditions of this life, and if he reflects in his works the effects of
these impressions, then we might say of him that he has portrayed
therein *a part of life*."[24]

These three quotations, in connection with our analysis above
and in that order, show quite clearly what folk music meant to Bartók.
And the three levels are even less concerned with chronology here—
at most only in connection with how the three conceptions were
placed beside one another in parallel with his creative development
and artistic growth. The essence of the first is folk music as *theme*; the
common heritage, the basic type on which the composer builds his

---

[22]"On the Significance of Folk Music," *Bartók Essays* No. 44, p. 346.

[23]Friede F. Rothe, "The Language of the Composer—An Interview with Béla Bartók,
Eminent Hungarian Composer," *The Etude* (Philadelphia, 1941).

[24]"Der Einfluss der Volksmusik . . ., *Bartók Essays* No. 40, p. 318. Italics by the author.

own individual message. When Bartók treated folk music as a theme he was not behaving any differently than did those of his predecessors—including the very greatest—who similarly evolved their music from the melodic material in general circulation during the period. Thus the profoundly variational spirit of Bartók's art manifests itself not only through the fact that it continuously plays a part as a musical development technique, but also through his interpretation of the whole art as variation.

Interpreted according to the second conception, folk music represents for Bartók the possibility and means of communication: *idiom*. By this there is no intention of suggesting that Bartók's musical language and the language of folk music are one and the same thing. In art, idiom is more than the mere means of communication: it has numerous relations to content, and the language of the great creative artists emerges without exception from everyday language. Bartók, too, created by himself the language of his own art, and not from one source but from several. Among these various sources one of the most important was folk music, for this ensured democracy of communication for him, theoretical and practical connection with a communal tradition, powerful in space and time alike. But Bartók did not merely take over the folk music idiom: he also formed something new and universal. In his transforming intervention a large part was played by the association of the musical idioms of different peoples. It was not just a humanistic programme that lay behind this, "the idea of the brotherhood of peoples,"[25] but a sober statement of practical, musical aims towards the formation of an international musical standard language. Musical internationalism, that frequently occurring cliché, can scarcely be said to cover the whole truth; the language of music also has territorial limits, even if they cannot be defined as precisely as those of nations. This, however, does not matter. The healthy life of a language or a culture is assured by an interchange between its very separateness and its singularity. Among Bartók's greatest scientific distinctions belongs the demonstration of co-existence and mutual influence between the folk music of various peoples. In his study "Race Purity in Music" he came to consequential conclusions, among others

[25]Letter to O. Beu, 10 January 1931. BL No. 577.

the following: " . . . as a result of uninterrupted reciprocal influence upon the folk music of these peoples there is an immense variety and a wealth of melodies and melodic types . . . A complete separation from foreign influences means stagnation: well assimilated foreign impulses offer possibilities of enrichment."[26] Here is a concise description of the scientific experience which inspired him to the combination of various folk music languages and idioms in his own art, always alongside the priority of the development of the Hungarian musical language and continuous observation of it.

The third conception really contains the two preceding ones and can thus be regarded as Bartók's general attitude toward folk music, in the nature of his ideology. There is here no question of popularism, peasant-romanticism, though we know that in certain respects Bartók did come close to this. For him, the village and the peasantry represented closeness to nature, an unspoiled quality, that "pure source" from which he was able to drink—not only in connection with musical material, but also as regards knowledge of life. At the same time there are many documents to prove that he did not in the least idealize this way of life, which contained so much wretchedness and ignorance. The quotation is an indicator chiefly in that it shows that folk music meant more in Bartók's thinking than merely a theme or an idiom; in a certain sense it was to assure his immediate relationship with reality itself. This is an attitude of an ideological nature, a true, realistic *ars poetica*, which sets "the recording of a piece of life" as the task of art.

But how are these two systems related—the three levels described by Bartók and the other kind of tripartite division deduced from his oeuvre? I consider the second to be merely a broader projection of the first, and at the same time a kind of summary. This can be clearly seen if the two are placed beside each other:

I Folksong arrangement

                                     I Folk music as theme

II Folksong imitation

III Idiomatic assimilation of folk music   II Folk music as idiom

                                               III Folk music as ideology

[26]"Race Purity in Music," *Modern Music* (1942). See *Bartók Essays* No. 5, p. 30.

Thus the first two levels of the first system are merged into one in the second categorization, since as far as an individual work is concerned, it is absolutely a subsidiary matter whether its basis is formed by an original melody or an imitation. Folk music as an idiom is striking in both; whereas in the first system it is the final degree, in the second it is in the middle, a transition. And perhaps precisely because of this the second is more complete, more characteristic: the large role of folk music on the ideological, conceptual level—on the basis of a summary and synthesis of the categories mentioned—is the key to the aesthetic appreciation of Bartók. For in this way an essential qualitative difference separates his art from the work of other musicians of his time who were similarly inspired by folk music.

It was this interpretation of folk music and the great communal tradition on the conceptual level that enabled Bartók to carry out the great synthesis of his period. It was this that provided a broad and secure basis for a revival of the values of the European art music legacy, a worthy continuation of the great tradition, and at the same time for a genuine adoption of the newest aspirations and technical revolutions.

CHAPTER FOUR

MONOTHEMATICISM AND VARIATION

Monothematic structure is to be found in virtually every one of Bartók's composite musical constructions. The monothematicism of the stage works further demonstrates that it is also of dramaturgical significance: not only the structural unity of the composition is secured—the logic of the interrelationships in content is also revealed thereby.[1] "You have probably noticed that I lay great emphasis on the work of technical development, that I do not like to repeat a musical thought identically, and that I never bring back a single detail exactly as it was the first time. This treatment stems from my inclination towards variation and transformation of themes." This is how Bartók, in a statement quoted above, describes his attitude in connection with structure based on variation.[2] Here is an indication that variation in the art of Bartók is not a strictly observed formal category, but that it is permanently linked with the various musical processes. For this reason in this chapter the concept referring to development—that is, variation—is examined in relation to the structural concept of monothematicism.

Variation is one of the very oldest existing forms in music, being present throughout its whole development from the most primitive folk music to the highest consummation of European musical culture. In comparison, the phenomenon of monothematicism moves within

---

[1] The dramaturgical significance of monothematicism is analysed in György Kroó, *Bartók színpadi művei [Bartók's Stage Works]* (Budapest: Zeneműkiadó, 1962).

[2] D. Dille's interview with Bartók, published in *La Sirène* (Brussels), March 1937.

much narrower limits: within the framework of sonata form it is *one* formal principle of the so-called Viennese classics, the period of thematic principles. It first comes to light in the works of Haydn and blossoms more fully in Beethoven's late period. It is, however, characteristic of its significance that this so-called monothematic, single-theme sonata form also proved the most long-lived classical achievement in the following stage of music history: it was further developed by the nineteenth-century masters and has played a large part in the music of the twentieth century, as well.

As a result of the most recent research in the history of form it is generally accepted today that the sonata based on the monothematic principle is not really a separate branch of the form, but an inevitable consequence of its development, a fuller and more consistent realization of the form principle. Rudolph Reti has very convincingly shown that the so-called "inner unity" of the works by the classical masters using a sonata construction is the result of thematic-motivic relationships between the apparently different or even contrasting themes.[3] Thus Beethoven's monothematicism and the romantics' development of it, the cyclic sonata, differ only from the "normal" sonatas of the classical masters insofar as the monothematicism is more frank and emphasized.

In the development of the monothematic conception after Beethoven, two different tendencies become apparent. The first is romantic and typical of the nineteenth century: to counterbalance the enlargement of the dimensions and the weakening of the formal contours, the central theme demands open, easy perceptibility. The most characteristic type is the cyclic sonata of Franck, in which the work's monothematic system of interrelationships is secured by one or two basic motifs. Strictly speaking, Liszt's B Minor Sonata also belongs here, together with all his symphonic poems based on a single theme.

The other tendency in monothematic structure seems more conservative for, relying upon Beethoven and the other classical masters, it uses a method of thematic interrelationships which is more subtle

---

[3]Rudolph Reti, *The Thematic Process in Music* (London: Faber & Faber, 1964), 4.

and may only be discovered through close analysis (Schumann, for example). This is the point where the formal conception of monothematicism and the systematic conception of variation begin to approach each other. It can scarcely be mere coincidence that the greatest master of this monothematic principle—Beethoven—was at the same time the greatest master of variation form: the dynamism of the variational process, continuous change, the dialectic spirit of identity and difference of thought permeated his monothematicism.

So when Bartók made construction formed in the variational spirit and structure based on the monothematic principle the very centre of his art he was committing himself to the two greatest and most fundamental traditions in music: folk music, and the greatest products of European art music. The double variational conception represents two widely different levels of the artistic creative method; folk music is *still* variational in spirit since it does not know any means of recording or fixing a musical idea, or the possibility of a single form. Here variation is truly the music's form of existence, for every folksong is a single way of performing a melody based on an outline everywhere identical, a unique realization of an imaginary general form. As opposed to this, the classical tradition is *already* variational, inasmuch as it regards continuous and conscious transformation of the material to be the essence of musical creation. Here variation finds an explanation in conscious creative aspiration: to show some thought or other as richly as possible, from within and without, from every side and every angle, in every dynamic form. It is precisely this dynamism that is one of the greatest achievements of classicism: the shaping of the musical form in such a way that the material should not cohere arbitrarily but that as result of organic development all new material should be interrelated with what has preceded it.

In the twentieth-century development of form we can see a definite tendency to revive monothematicism in the classical sense. This process is characteristically visible, for example, in the art of Schoenberg; starting out from the cyclic method of romanticism, the Viennese master arrived at his own less perceptible, but inwardly more organized, monothematicism. His first and second quartets are good examples of the exaggerated organicism typical of late romantic music, where virtually every detail of the musical process is "bound up" with the complex system of thematic-motivic interrelationships: in Schoenberg's later style thematic relationships are replaced by the serial relationships. Yet it must never be forgotten that the twelve-note technique itself is the ultimate product of continued development of thematic-organic interrelationships.

The art of Bartók also sets out under largely similar circumstances. Like Schoenberg, he inherited the direct tradition of romanticism and followed its cyclical pattern in his early works. As early as the 1904 Piano Quintet a melody crops up which returns several times, and which bridges over the more important formal sections. The subtle thematic interconnections in the early two-movement Violin Concerto then change to an open, unambiguous monothematic conception in the later variation under the title *Two Portraits*; the two human portraits, developed from exactly the same material, follow a high-level, Lisztian method of monothematic structure.

The First String Quartet offers a beautiful example of cyclic, organic monothematicism. In the form of a four-note motif the work's central idea traces its way throughout the whole composition. In its complete form it first appears in the framework theme of the second movement (a), and then immediately afterwards the first subject's ostinato accompaniment (b) is formed from its mirror-inversion. Corresponding with the latter are the finale's sharp principal theme (c) and its scherzando-like transitional theme—that is, the fugato theme (d).

Example 76.

The melodic root common to all these themes is to be found in a four-note figure in which a "clinging" melodic step is followed by a leap over a larger interval and the motif is completed by another close step, in the opposite direction. In this it is not difficult to recognize the so-called "cambiata" figure of the Palestrina style, which became crystallized from the disjunctive changing note and its melodic resolution. It must be emphasized, however, that the Palestrina cambiata can be compared with the string quartet's four-note formula exclusively in a melodic sense, quite independently of the harmonic content concealed within it.

Example 77.

In the course of later development, particularly in the functional-tonal style, the changing note ornament, mainly harmonic in content in the modal style, became independent. Since it was built up from conjunctive and disjunctive melodic details it was especially suitable for the leading-note support of tonal nuclei. Its outline changed, too: along with its original form, as a result of the laws of linear style, its mirror, crab, and mirror crab forms also appeared. It is in Bach that the best examples are to be found.

Example 78.

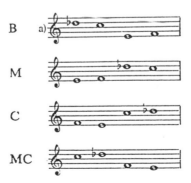

Example 78 (continued)

From the structure of the cambiata motif it follows that not only its in-version but also its permutational variations offer similar motifs. If the outer notes change places, the line of the melody does indeed change, but its symmetrical structure remains intact. The B-A-C-H- theme (B-flat–A–C–B-natural) also belongs here.

Example 79.

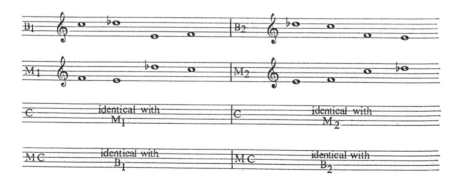

The tonal application of the motif meant almost inevitably that the two outer "clinging" intervals, depending on the position of the melodic formula, might equally be a minor- or a major second. Thus, for example, the version of it to be found in the "Jupiter" Symphony (the so-called Mozart calling-card) contains an upward major second and a downward minor second.

It is to be encountered on numerous occasions in Beethoven, as well: for example, the F Major String Quartet op. 59, and the Adagio of the A-flat Major Piano Sonata op. 110, or the orchestral Praeludium before the Benedictus in the Missa Solemnis. But it finds its most significant role in the last string quartets : this is what forms the common thematic root of the B-flat Major, op. 130, the C-sharp Minor, op. 131, and the A Minor, op. 132, Quartets and the Great Fugue op. 133.

Example 80.

It becomes quite obvious from the examples that in the majority of cases the cambiata motif comes on particular degrees of the scale—usually on the VII–I and VI–V degrees of the minor scale. Thus the "clinging" part of the cambiata coincides where possible with the leading note attractions given at the outset by the scale, and the "leaping" part is formed according to where the motif is positioned in the octave. The interchangeability of the two positions is also demonstrated by the C-sharp Minor and the A Minor Quartets. This type from among the various cambiata motifs enriches with tension-resolution content the dense, balanced musical event offered by the melody. The fundamental idea common to the last Beethoven quartets is, therefore, not merely one melodic idea among many but one of the tersest basic types of melody with a functional content.

However, the tonal-functional content of the cambiata motif began to disintegrate even within Beethoven's own output. In the introduction in the B-flat Major Quartet, for example, the clinging interval does not come about through the system, but by way of alteration. An even better example of this is the theme of the Great Fugue, obviously connected with the preceding example, the double cambiata of which, with the exception of the cadence, contains altered leading-notes not in the scale. The theme of the Great Fugue is therefore a purely melodic form of the cambiata motif, quite similar to the Bartókian cambiata. In this case the purpose of the chromatic changing notes is not to reinforce the tonal centres but the very opposite— to veil the tonality. This tendency can of course be found even in Bach's chromatic works; for example in the *Kleines harmonisches Labyrinth* or the A Minor Prelude from Book Two of the *Wohltemperiertes Klavier.*

It is characteristic of Bartók's endeavours that in the cambiata motifs of the First String Quartet the "clinging" parts do not reinforce the fifth basis of tonality but move around a diminished or augmented fifth —that is, a mistuned basis.

This brief survey of the harmonic and melodic content of the cambiata motif and its role in history paves the way for a more profound illumination of the monothematic construction of Bartók's First String Quartet. For in the above example only those occurrences of the cambiata motif were quoted in which it played a strikingly emphatic thematic or motivic role. The various versions of the cambiata motif can also be found in the contrapuntal texture of the first movement, although here the figuration does not stand out motivically, remaining hidden within the parts.

Example 81.

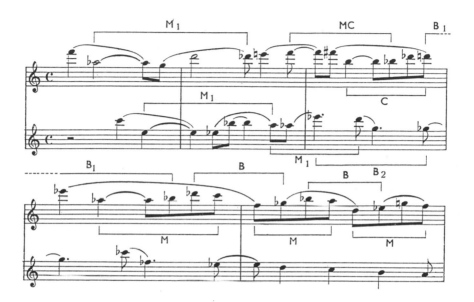

This last way of using the cambiata figure really represents a return to the original meaning it had in Palestrina: the four-note melody formula is a melodic structural element of harmonic function and without any motivic-thematic significance. This explains the peculiar intertwining character of the fugal parts of the movement; for the kind of melody which uses cambiatas so frequently creates the impression of a dense, complicated texture turning back on itself. Between the small intervals, tense larger intervals naturally make the complementary weaving of two pairs of parts possible: the melodic leaps of one part are consistently filled out by the other part.

Thus, the monothematic construction of Bartók's First Quartet is a unique example of the central thought being employed in two fundamentally different conceptions within a single work: in one part it is an organic, but not emphasized, structural element in the melodic processes; elsewhere it is a motif of thematic significance—that is, the theme itself.

At the same time this also represents a historical synthesis: the former method is characteristic of polyphonic music, and the latter of homophonic-thematic music. The cambiata motif also appears in several other compositions by Bartók—and indeed in both its functions: sometimes as a melodic structural element and sometimes within the closed framework of a theme or motif.

Example 82.

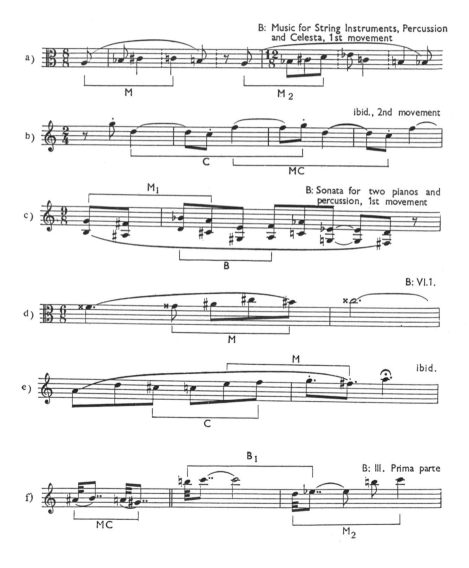

Example 82 (continued)

A very characteristic elaboration of the motif must also be mentioned: where the two outer "clinging" intervals of the motif are duplicated. This is how the gesticulatory motifs of *The Miraculous Mandarin* and the Divertimento come about.

Example 83.

Naturally it is not only in Bartók's music that the cambiata motif assumed importance: it was used as a classical principle of melody writing by several other composers of the period. Thus the famous B-A-C-H motif, for example, is to be found in two representative works of the new Viennese school: Schoenberg's Orchestral Variations and Webern's String Quartet.

The monothematic system of the Second String Quartet is partly more simple and partly more complicated. It is simpler in that there are obvious thematic interrelationships between the first and third movements. Yet at the same time it is more complicated since other interrelationships only come to light by way of very detailed analysis. The connections between the first and third movements can be followed along two lines, the first of which is kinship in the melodic line. The two themes, one rising in fourths and the other a descending fourth, are so close to each other that one can scarcely accept the story quoted by John Vinton in which Bartók was not even aware of the thematic connection.[4] The other connecting thread relates this same first movement theme to the lament theme of the last movement. Outwardly the two themes have a considerably different effect, the first being an arch-shaped melody, whereas the second follows the characteristic descending line of the Hungarian folksong. And yet the inner parts agree note for note, reminding one of César Franck's cyclic method.

Example 84.

The monothematic relationship between the two outer movements is therefore doubly founded, and this—also taking the tempo into consideration—indicates that on this occasion the monothematicism is of

[4]According to Christine Ahrendt, Bartók was supposedly unaware of this motivic interrelationship. Cf. her unpublished diploma thesis at the Eastman School of Music, 1946: "An Analysis of the Second Quartet of Béla Bartók," quoted by John Vinton, "New Light on Bartók's Sixth Quartet," *The Music Review* XXV (1964).

importance mainly in the structure of the form: it rounds the work into a finished whole. But monothematicism also has another function in the quartet. By means of the common melodic arch all the first movement themes are organically related to each other. Thus the second subject is born from the first subject and its development, and the development of the second subject prepares the way for the closing theme.

Example 85.

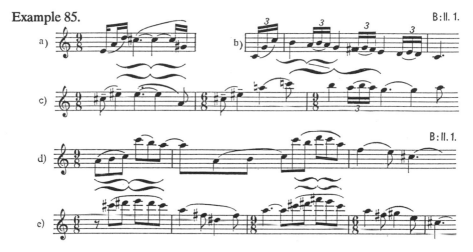

This gradual building up of the material, in which relatively remote forms are connected with the help of organic structure, is a typically late-romantic phenomenon, and again we are reminded of Franck's cyclic sonata and the Schoenberg method likewise coming close to it (First and Second Quartets). It is also part of this closed organism that the motif of the development section, which strikes us as being something new at first hearing, is strongly related to the cadential part of the first subject.

Example 86.

In the variational system resting on identity of melodic line it is mainly the consistently diminishing amplitude of the arch that appears regular: the line of the first subject consists of fourths, and accordingly its amplitude reaches a minor seventh; the second subject is made up of major thirds and so reaches only an augmented fifth. (A detail from the last movement "rhymes" with this major third version, where the arch-motif is compressed into a diminished fifth made up of two minor thirds.) And the closing theme, as compared with the seventh of the first subject, is squeezed within the framework of a minor third.

Example 87.

This second system of motivic interrelationships shows that the central movement of the work takes part—though only indirectly—in the process outlined above. In its first form the theme of the Allegro appears to have nothing in common with the arch-motif just analysed. In later versions, and especially in the melodic figures of the Coda, the arching quality is not so concealed. Here, too, the expansion and contraction of the arch-motif, originally extending to a third, is carried through in a consistent way. Virtually the whole movement is enclosed within the framework of the arch motif: the D–F–F-sharp opening gesture at the beginning of the movement is completed at the end of the movement by an F-sharp–F–D motif. The string quartet's system of cyclic interrelationships is therefore consistently complemented by this other system of relationships based on the dome-shaped melodic outline of the arch-motif.

Example 88.

In the Third Quartet there is but a single sign of cyclic monothematicism: in the development section of the Prima parte, as if in anticipation, one of the themes from the Seconda parte appears. And this makes it all the more conspicuous that each of the two parts—and especially the second—forms in itself a very closed monothematic system. The relationship in the Seconda parte thematic material is so obvious that it even leads the analyst astray in his judgment of the form; the sonata-like construction is almost obliterated by the conception of free variational development. The truth is that the three themes of this movement, which is built on the sonata principle, are evolved from the same melodic idea. Here, too, as in the second quartet, the dome-like melodic arch dominates, the essential difference being, however, that here the arch is of much larger proportions and both branches display scale-like straightforwardness in outline.

Example 89.

The variational character lying behind the movement is also reinforced by the fact that of the themes which may be regarded as variations of each other, two (b, c) are varied even within their own scope in the development section and in accordance with the norms of that section. So in this way there are really two variational processes of different dimensions progressing in close relationship with each other: firstly, ordinary theme-variation based on identity of melodic line, and secondly, development-like variation of themes, following the thematic-motivic development technique of the classical sonata tradition.

These two do not contradict each other—indeed in certain cases they rather reinforce each other. So, for example, the fugato version of the second theme (b) makes the dome-shaped structure of the theme even more obvious. And the completely chromaticized basis of the third theme (c) (at figure 40) proves the principle of "straight-lined" melody. At the end of the developmental process the themes— now stripped to their bare essentials, to their very skeletons as it were—appear in the glissandos which extend the stepwise quality of the scale to the very limits of absolute continuity.

The abstract melodic outline of the movement, the *maqam*, is therefore not just the dome arch but, in an even more emphasized form, the *straightly* rising and falling line. What is brought to the surface by the analytical process of the development section has *really* already been heard in nucleo in the movement's introduction. For at the beginning of the Seconda parte, against the background of the horizontal trill organ point, small melodic fragments anticipate the rising and falling straight lines.

The monothematic conception of the Prima parte is not so obvious, and for this reason I have left discussion of it until later. It is constructed on the sonata principle, but the thematic material is provided exclusively by motifs of small proportions. The interrelationships between these motifs are only to be found through penetrating analysis. The opening gesture of the first subject serves as a starting point, a small musical idea of three notes. Its profound folk music connections were demonstrated in the preceding chapter.

Example 90.

This three-note melodic germ is given its "proto-motif" character not only by its having the nature of a "pre-pentatonic root" as analysed in the preceding chapter, but also by the role it has played in European music. Just as with the cambiata motif, this has two interrelated, but essentially different musical aspects as well. The first is melodic: the feature characteristic of melody writing in polyphonic styles of linear structure, where a larger intervallic leap is followed and filled in by a smaller interval turning back in the opposite direction. This is perhaps the most classical example of the most concise melodic events of molecular proportions. As a thematic basis it can often be found in Bach, but it is quite at home in Beethoven's thematics as well. Here are a few typical examples.

Example 91.

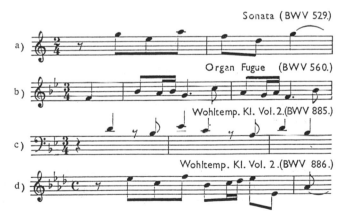

Example 91 (continued)

Thus this small motif from the first part of the Third Quartet, on which, strictly speaking, the material of the whole movement is based, is firmly rooted not only in folk music but also in the European art music tradition. Now let us look at how the motif is used. Just as with the cambiata motif, this is likewise equal in value with its inversions.

Example 92.

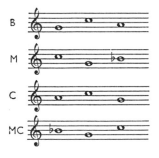

Apart from the inversions, the rotations of the motif have also to be taken into consideration. The first rotation produces a fairly open form, but it is also used less frequently. The second rotation, however, is a very important and recurrent version of the original pattern; the only difference being that it is not a third that stands opposed to the leap of a fourth, but a second. If we disregard the actual proportions of the intervals and depict the motif in abstract line form, the latter does not differ at all from the original form.

Example 93.

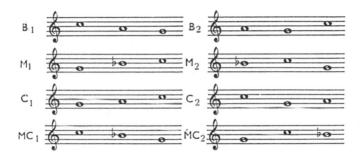

This theoretical generalization of the motif has to be supplemented by another generalization: retaining the outline, the three-note pattern has the same significance in wider and narrower forms. The metamorphosis of the motif can easily be observed in the movement: its framework consistently expands from the narrowest form of the introduction, through the "normal" form of the main theme, to the wide form in the closing theme. In each of its appearances it is the abstraction of the melodic event expressed in a line that is common: one larger and one smaller interval turning into each other combine to make a complete, closed unit.

Example 94.

Example 94 (continued)

It has already been mentioned in connection with the cambiata motif that its use as a melodic structural element produces the intertwining musical texture of the First Quartet's Lento movement. A similar result is also occasioned by applying the three-note motif in this way, for here, too, the curling back of the melodic line creates a rolling musical texture which revolves round itself.

Now it is possible to see the monothematic structure of the Third Quartet as a complete whole. There is no question of a single musical idea weaving its way through the whole composition: it is a case of two basic principles of melody writing which, in correlation with one another, create a unit. The monothematic axis of the Prima parte is the melodic *circular movement* produced by the texture of the three-note motif, and that of the Seconda parte is *straight movement* realized in the scale theme. Contrasting the two different movement conceptions with each other, their conditionality and complementary function here replace the monothematicism evident in the string quartets which precede this one.

The key to the Fourth Quartet's monothematic system is given by the small emblem-like motif of the first movement. It is functional on a considerable number of levels. After its first appearance in bar 7 it is given canonic treatment in a closed mass and is repeated in this way in the course of the movement, as if filling out the segments of the various formal sections. Its final appearance forms at the same time the end of the movement, and this returns almost note for note at the end of the fifth movement. This identity in the ends of the framing movements is a simple solution from the monothematic aspect; it fundamentally and exclusively fulfills a form-building function. When we take all the occurrences of the motif together, we can find the following forms of it: chromatic basic form (a), a larger chromatic form (b), and a quasi-diatonic closing form (c).

Example 95.

The way in which the second subject of the first movement (which Bartók calls a transitional theme) assumes the leading role in the final movement and is transformed is typical cyclic principle monothematic treatment: the almost rocking theme, at first lyrical and relaxed in rhythm, changes later into a hard, virtually barbaric dance theme, notwithstanding the note-for-note retention of its melodic structure. This is the same sort of contrasting monothematicism as that in the *Two Portraits*, where the same melodic outline, through use of different rhythms and being performed in different tempos, portrays two contrasting characters (see Exs. 52 and 53).

This free and richly imaginative renewed use of unchanging and slightly changing elements secures the relationship between the two outer movements and through this the foundation of the work's architectonic structure. This same architecture is served by the variational relationship between the two inner movements—that is, the second and the fourth. In the examples which follow almost all the themes of these four movements of the work (1, 2, 4, and 5) are placed beside one another, and from this it becomes unequivocally clear that on this occasion it is once again—similarly to the second part of the Third Quartet—a straight line arch-motif which provides the key to the monothematic structure. It is quite easy to see that the arch-shaped themes or theme-forming motifs, disregarding their rhythmic profile, differ from each other only in their spaciousness and—connected with this—in the basic unit of their scale progressions. (Mirror inversion, in this connection, cannot be considered as a separate variation, since from the point of view of the arch-motif principle rising and descending are of identical significance.) The basic motif is the most compressed form, and every other version is therefore produced by an expansion of it. The most immediate variants have already been shown. The closing theme of the first movement is similarly a close variation of the fundamental motif (b). In the Arab-like theme the chromatic arch expands into a mistuned tetratonic arch (c). In the first movement's second subject group the tight chromaticism of the basic motif is transformed into a whole-tone scale with a very spacious effect (d, e). And finally the theme of the two scherzo-like movements (f, g) is a chromatic and "quasi-diatonic" variation of the arch-motif, increasing it to fifth and octave amplitude respectively.

Example 96.

If along with all this we also consider that in the dynamic process of the composition these themes and motifs form further variations even within themselves, retaining the rising-descending or descending-rising line throughout, then it becomes obvious that the arch-motif condenses within itself the most basic melodic regularities of the whole composition.

The slow central movement is almost conspicuous by its absence from this closed and tightly constructed monothematic system of relationships. From the aspect of the symmetrical structure this is perfectly understandable, since this movement is an axis which almost inevitably differs in quality from the structure developed around and about it. But in spite of this the movement is part of—indeed the key to—a system of relationships extending throughout the whole work, one which is much more general than the monothematic structure hitherto discussed, and becomes manifest in an essentially different sphere.

Here it is a matter of a new conception of monothematic relationships which is rooted not in concrete melodic interconnections but in permanence of certain intervals and interval-complexes. It is Colin Mason that we have to thank for working out this peculiar system, and since it is the intention of this book to give the reader an indication of the most important research results as well, his thought sequence is given briefly below (Mason 1957:233). Incidentally, other interrelationships akin to this had already appeared in earlier works. For example, in the Second Quartet, fourth-structure formations and those built on the fourth model and the minor-third model dominated, in the melodic and harmonic sense alike. All this, however, did not determine the whole work in such a unified way as in the present case.

According to Colin Mason's analysis, all the melodic and harmonic formations of the Fourth Quartet can be traced back to a row which is actually heard at the beginning of the central movement, and which, radiating outwards from there as it were, fundamentally influences the structure of the whole work. Its upper and lower sections contain a three-note and a four-note whole-tone scale respectively (A, B). It is from this that the work's vertical major-second piles also come about. The part produced by the meeting of the two half rows gives a four-note chromatic row, from which scale chromaticism and complementary chromaticism can equally be deduced (C, CC). And finally, the outer notes of the two half rows explain the origin of the tritone and fourth model (D, DD).

Example 97.

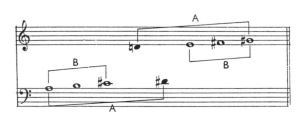

Example 97 (continued)

Example 97 (continued)

This Bartók method comes very close to the serial technique, at least insofar as the interrelationship between all the themes or motifs of a work—in the linear and vertical senses alike—is provided by the relationship system existing between certain intervals. There is, however, one essential difference in that with Bartók this "row", although it is applicable to almost every particle of the work, makes a more free order possible, and does not, in addition, serve the absolute application of the twelve-note range.

As a result of its similarly symmetrical construction, the Fifth Quartet offers us numerous monothematic methods which we have already encountered in the Fourth Quartet. Here, however, the first and last movements are not connected by such obvious theme identity as in the former case. Only one single quotation-like element is to be found: in the central section of the final movement—in a way closely resembling the corresponding part of the Fourth Quartet—a variant of the first movement's first subject appears. Another characteristic similarity is the "rhyming" between the two outer movements. Here there is no literal identity as there is in the Fourth Quartet, but the tetrachords and opening in mirror movement refer to one another directly enough. Before making further analysis of the other, and more profound, interrelationships between the two outer movements, it would be wise to examine the interrelationships which exist within the movements. It is possible to discover various kinds of relationships even within the first movement's thematic material, on so numerous levels as regards character. The movement's "leaping" second subject (B) is connected to the rising central part of the first subject by a cyclic principle relationship; the second subject, leaping over and over again back to the same support note, makes the same chromatic journey tensing outwards from a minor third to a tritone.

Example 98.

B: V.1.

And in the lyrical closing theme entering at C we can recognize the inversion of the first subject's rising melodic line.

The thematic relationships in the final movement are even more obvious. The two themes making up the first large formal unit are really a variation-inversion of each other. The composer makes immediate use of this ambiguity when he places adjacent to one another the literal note-for-note inversion (b) and the variated, free inversion (c).

Example 99.

Further, a very strict motivic connection can also be found between these two interrelated themes and the scale theme which has a rounding-off function; this last is no more than a special concentration of the two former.

Example 100.

This thematic interrelationship, on the other hand, draws attention to the tetrachord motifs which frequently appear in the work. In the final movement this is again obvious; apart from the themes already mentioned, they are to be found in the continuation of the contrast theme beginning in bar 202 and strictly speaking the framework motif itself also stems from them. Varied use of the tetrachord motif is also aided by rhythmic elements. Two basic types can be distinguished: one with an unstressed beginning and one with a stressed beginning. That with the unstressed beginning has a metrically rising character, its ending is stressed, and that in itself makes it have a finishing function. That with the stressed beginning, on the other hand, has an unstressed end, and its role thus has rather the nature of an opening. An interesting combination of the two tetrachords is to be found in the last phrase of the "second" first subject where the opening and closing tetrachords appear telescoped into one another (f).

Example 101.

After this the relationship between the two movements is even more obvious. The rising and descending melodic outline of the first movement's first subject and closing theme is related to the melodic outline of the fifth movement's two first subjects. (All the themes appear in inversion as well, and so the matter of direction is of subsidiary importance.) The first movement's closing theme, consisting of tetrachords built upon one another, comes very close to the fifth movement's scale motif which has a closing function. And finally, tetrachord filling out of the fourths can be observed in all the themes.

Example 102.

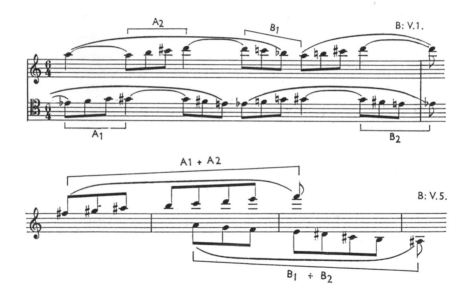

The close variational connection between the two slow movements will be discussed in detail in the course of the formal analyses. For the moment we have only to concern ourselves with the question of whether their relationship is valid merely with reference to each other or whether they form a part of the monothematic system of the whole work. Now, on this occasion the relationship is not completely self-evident. It is clear, however, that the tetrachord motif has a determining character in these movements, too. We have only to think of the scale theme, surrounded by static chord masses, after the introduction (second movement, from bar 10; fourth movement, from bar 31). Apart from this the accompanying melodic figures of the central folksong theme in the second movement also usually consist of small tetrachord motifs.

The most important relationships, however, are to be discovered in the folksong theme in the centre of each movement. Concerning this theme, it has already been demonstrated, in connection with its relationship to folk music, that it is based in its every detail on a fourth framework, using separate and interlinking fourth chains. The most important themes of the outer movements are also constructed on these fourth outlines, and so it becomes quite clear that this is where the inner thematic cohesion lies in the four movements of the work.

This system of interrelationships is considerably complex; it cannot be traced back to any single melodic basic pattern or fundamental motif. Here, too, we have to deal with the same sort of thing as in the Fourth Quartet: there is a surface system of relationships which more or less openly connects the material of the movements which can be put in pairs (1-5, 2-4). But behind this there is a deeper system of relationships which essentially reduces all the formations of the four movements to a single interval complex. Encouraged by the example of Colin Mason's "serial key," we have looked for the "row" which contains everything in the Fifth Quartet. In this case it is the fifth movement's scale motif, which has a closing function, that gives a "key" to the outlined thematic phenomena. It has been mentioned above that this theme has been produced by means of a combination of the tetrachord elements of the two first subjects. If, however, we interpret this scale in the sense of an abstract "seria," then it offers even more complex summations: virtually every melodic detail in the four movements of the work can be extracted from it.

Example 103.

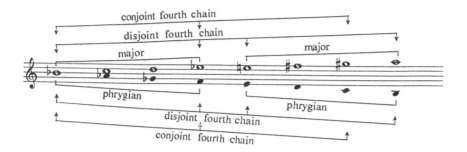

The "row" consists of two "disjoint" fourths built one on top of the other, filled out in an alternating way with tetrachords: if the movement is in an upward direction then they have a major nature, and if the movement is in a downward direction, they are Phrygian in character. In this way, incidentally, it becomes clear that in a system which has not a bottom keynote but a *central* note, major and Phrygian have exactly the same meaning, as each is the mirror of the other. The codas of the first and last movements also provide good examples in this connection. It should also be noted that the major and Phrygian are not just one of several possibilities, but the solitary possibility within the diatonic tetrachord system, since the other possible diatonic tetrachord structures are identical in mirror inversion (either symmetrical: 2-1-2; or distance: 2-2-2). At the same time the "row" contains the upward Phrygian tetrachord as well (an exceptional case), which in its mirror inversion naturally presents the major. Placing the major and Phrygian tetrachords on top of one another produces the complete chromatic range. Apart from this the "row" also contains the fourth framework of the themes mentioned from the work—that is, both the disjoint and the conjoint fourth chains.

On this occasion the third movement really does remain outside the work's monothematic network. It rises above the rest as a centrepiece, as an element of architectural completion, as a neutral foreign body. Its themes, as opposed to the fourth structure and scalelike melodics (seconds) of the outer movements, are characterized by third and fifth (= two thirds) structure, together with third melodics.

In comparison with the monothematicism of the preceding quartets, the Sixth brings a new method. The *ritornello* melody heard at the beginning of the first three movements and eventually growing into the final movement of the whole work, is not stronger than the earlier methods as regards its unifying effect, but from the "dramaturgical" point of view it is more open. The evolution of the *ritornello* theme, the course it travels, will be discussed in detail in the formal analysis. It is perfectly characteristic of Bartók's creative method, however, that this open monothematicism has another more complicated and more subtle system of relationships weaving its way behind it: the material of the individual movements is connected to the various elements of the *ritornello* theme by motivic threads. It is well known that Bartók worked on the *ritornello* theme for a long time, chiselling and polishing it, almost in parallel with the composition of the other movements. All this is no contradiction to the assertions made above—indeed, it rather bears them out. For we are not to take the *ritornello* which "includes everything" as being some sort of prefabricated material. It evolves together with the individual movements—it is rather a case of the possibility arising for the elements concealed within it to find the way towards variations of a different character.

The first subject of the first movement can be said to originate from the closing phrase of the *ritornello*—on the basis of the indication made by the gradual process composed by Bartók. Only a detailed motivic analysis of the movement would fully show what an important part is played by the three-note motif at the end of the *ritornello* theme in the whole course of the movement. Here, too, it is a question of the three-note motif which played such a large role in the first part of the Third Quartet. The principal theme of the Sixth Quartet's first movement is no more than the building into each other of three versions of this three-note motif.

Example 104.

This motivic interrelationship is reinforced by another kind of connection: in the rising phrase with the octave compass it is possible to recognize the second phrase of the *ritornello* which has an augmented octave compass. That is, from the chromatic mistuned melodics of the *ritornello* is born the pure diatonic melodics of the Allegro. (The *ritornello* extract is transposed here so that the relationship may become easier to see.)

Example 105.

Similar motivic and melodic outline connections can be found in the other movements, too. The characteristic opening motif of the Marcia stems from a motif from the second line of the *ritornello* just quoted. On this occasion it is as if the composer wished to "unmask" the relationship: at the end of the *ritornello* he inserts an intermediate chain link in anticipation of the opening motif.

Example 106.

The Burletta's "bear-dance" theme, coloured by quarter-tones, has some connection with the third phrase of the *ritornello*—likewise with the aid of interval expansion. Here, too, Bartók constructs the in-

termediate chain link when he forms the *ritornello*'s descending sequence motif so that it comes closer to the "bear-dance" theme.

Example 107.

When we consider that the Sixth Quartet's first movement was
formed from the fourth and second phrases of the *ritornello*, the
second movement from the second phrase of the *ritornello* and the
third movement from its third, being, as it were, the fuller development over a large area, then it would be logical and inevitable to expect the fourth movement to make use primarily of the *ritornello*'s
first phrase. In this way the individual balance of the piece is set up: in
the last analysis the four-movement composition is none other than a
many-sided unfolding of the principal idea embodied in the *ritornello*.

The various monothematic methods in the string quartets have
given a complete and graded picture of Bartók's compositional technique from this angle, from the aspect of consistency and variety of
monothematic structures and variational methods. In their survey the
outlines of certain new methods and individual creative endeavours
have been displayed before us. Bartók's romantic start was influenced
by a Lisztian and Brahmsian heritage. But all that did not prevent him
from going even further back—as early as in the First String Quartet—to draw inspiration and methods from Beethoven's monothematic technique. From then on, as we have seen, there are in all
the string quartets—in parallel with each other or in close relationship, and sometimes exercising organic mutual influence—three or
four different monothematic concepts lying behind the system of interrelationships unifying the work. We must now attempt to sort these
out and view them systematically.

In the art of Bartók, monothematicism based on cyclic principles is characterized by variation of one complete theme. The fundamental melodic structure of the theme remains unchanged or undergoes no more than the slightest alteration. It is, therefore, chiefly its character, its intonational nature or its presentation that changes. To this same type belong thematic interrelationships where some part of the theme appears in an unaltered form but is placed in a different setting, and in this way the meaning of the whole theme is transformed (a technique typical of César Franck). Fine examples of themes which change only in character are offered by the second and third movements of the First Quartet, the first and last movements of the Fourth Quartet (Arab theme), and the Sixth Quartet. And a good example of an unaltered section of melody placed in a different setting can be found in the first and third movements of the Second Quartet.

Bartók frequently uses this cyclic principle monothematicism for the expression of basic contrasts—combined almost without exception with dramaturgical significance. The best examples of this are supplied not by the string quartets but by such works as the *Two Portraits* or *The Wooden Prince*. Both of these compositions are an extension of th principle of Lisztian duality of the Faust-Mephisto variety, showing two contrasting sides of the same phenomenon. The "dramaturgy" of the string quartets is naturally more abstract; such concrete conflicts or elemental duality can scarcely be found in them, but a generalized aspiration in that direction can. In the thematic relations in the First Quartet, based on the cambiata motif, there also lies the same sort of ideal-grotesque, serious-ironic confrontation as in the *Two Portraits* or in the dance-play. In comparison with the romantic brightness and almost pathetic radiance of the second movement's framework theme, the first theme in the final movement is considerably wry and grotesque. In the Fourth Quartet the fine, subdued, almost lyrical theme of the first movement returns in the last with a hard dance-like intonation. And finally, the contrast-dramaturgy of the Sixth Quartet's monothematicism scarcely needs explanation: from different details of the lonely, contemplative resigned melody are surprisingly born a wry march and a mocking burlesque, as alternating contrasts to the central idea.

It is formally characteristic of cyclic principle monothematicism that themes confront themes, and for this reason, although dynamism is not at the outset excluded, this kind of monothematicism is relatively static. We might even say that the melody itself is virtually untouched by variation; setting and character may be altered but the *framework* is permanent.

A relatively more dynamic monothematic principle is in evidence in the first movement of the First Quartet. For here the cambiata motif, which forms the thematic basis of the second and third movements, is contracted into a melodic structural element. In this method, which afterwards assumes even greater significance in the later string quartets, we recognize one of the most important elements of Bartók's compositional technique: motivic monothematicism. Here it is no longer a case of whole themes standing in relation to one another, but merely small motifs consisting of three or four notes.

This motivic monothematicism is not by any means an absolute contrast to the cyclic method—it is rather partly a means within it or is complementary to it. This has already been referred to in connection with the First Quartet. In Bartók's creative development, however, this motivic technique frequently becomes independent: the composition or certain parts of the composition are completely pervaded by motif development; that is what directs, as it were, the whole musical process. Good examples of this are the first movement of the Second Quartet, the Prima parte of the Third Quartet, the greatly varied development of the Fourth Quartet's basic motif in the first and last movements, and the whole of the first movement in the Sixth Quartet.

The technical means of motivic monothematicism are supplied by those of contrapuntal variation—inversions, augmentation and diminution. At the same time there is another means of variation which had been used earlier but which became permanent only with Bartók: "spatial" expansion and contraction of the motif with retention of the original interval proportions. This spatial augmentation and diminution might also be called "projection variation," since the proportional enlargement or contraction of the interval structure can be thought of as being parallel to the phenomenon of projection.

Motivic monothematicism makes use of the most dynamic forms and possibilities of variation. The large role it plays in Bartók is also explained by the fact that development-like motivic-thematic work—as with the masters of the contemporary Viennese school—overflows into the other parts of the composition as well. Instead of the order of closed, complete themes and thematic units, free and non-thematic writing dominates in which cohesive strength is secured by the varied basic motif being built in many different ways. For this reason it can be said that in this conception of monothematic structure everything is dynamic and changeable; it is solely the *motif* that is permanent, as *a melodic structural element.*

Extension of the framework or motivic monothematicism, of which the Second Quartet is an example, leads to so-called *maqam-principle* monothematicism. Taking the basic melodic patterns and melodic outlines of Arab music as a basis, it was Bence Szabolcsi who first used this term to describe certain melodic variations in European music.[5] In the music of Bartók the *maqam* principle is found in the outline which can be abstracted from the melodic line and in the permanence of this outline. In analysing the Seconda parte of the Third Quartet we demonstrated that behind all the melodic movement lay the rising or descending straight line: this is the movement's melodic *maqam.* A similar system of interrelationships is used by the *maqam* of the Fourth and Fifth Quartets: in the former, from the proportional enlargement of a small arch-motif is born the dome *maqam* which stretches over the whole work; and in the latter it is the straight-line scale melodies, fourth-framework *maqam* structures that ensure the structural and conceptual unity of the work.

Maqam-principle monothematicism, like the motivic method, is a purely melodic phenomenon. The large part it plays in Bartók's music is at the same time one indication of his being a comprehensive master as regards melodic traditions; in spite of all tendencies to break things down to small units, he retains the original meaning of

---

[5]Bence Szabolcsi, "Makám-elv a népi és művészi zenében" ["Maqam Principle in Folk and Art Music," *Ethnographia* LX (1949): 81–87. Idem, *A History of Melody* (Budapest: Corvina Press, 1965).

the melody, its kinaesthetic significance. *Maqam principle* monothematicism secures the greatest rhythmic and melodic freedom for the composer; the quantitative relationships between the intervals forming the melody become of secondary importance, and the only fixed thing is the *abstract melodic line*, which may also be depicted graphically.

Finally we can see a fourth monothematic principle in Bartók's art in the shape of interval consistency, which is akin to certain simpler forms of *serial* technique. As we saw with the Fourth and Fifth Quartets, there is no question of serialism in the original sense. It is clearly apparent, however, that in these works of Bartók certain fixed interval relations have a differentiated role, providing, as it were, a key to the work's monothematic system of relationships. Thus the "seria" does not exist in Bartók as prefabricated compositional basic material, but as a monothematic principle which may be valid in a melodic and a harmonic sense—in other words, in a linear and a vertical sense. In this conception everything changes freely but the *relationship between certain intervals is fixed*.

These four different conceptions of monothematicism are characteristically present throughout Bartók's chamber music, and in this way throughout virtually his whole oeuvre. The various monothematic ideas and methods appeared and developed largely in the order outlined above. That is, the cyclic method presented itself as a natural starting point, but the demand to go beyond that arose from the very use of the classical heritage; it was for this reason that Bartók immediately turned to motivic monothematicism. From this, an abstraction of it, was born *maqam-principle* monothematicism, and finally, the last stage in the development appeared: serial principle monothematicism. This gradual appearance of more new monothematic methods, however—and here we can again grasp one of the important features of Bartók's art—never signified that Bartók gave up earlier principles and methods and moved over absolutely to using the new results. It becomes clear from analysis that the various new methods bring with them an enrichment of means, and they are organically built in alongside the earlier ones. This is the explanation for Bartók's monothematic richness, too: not one single work is to be encountered in which the monothematicism is limited by one kind of method, one kind of conception. In the First Quartet cyclic and motivic monothematicism appear together, and in the Second Quartet the *maqam* principle also appears in the company of cyclic and motivic monothematicism. The Third Quartet puts the cyclic principle in the background but there is rich development of motivic and *maqam* monothematicism. And in the Fourth and Fifth Quartets all four are present, and appear closely interrelated. In comparison, the Sixth Quartet is a "step backwards," for here only three mono-thematic methods are used together; the cyclic principle comes once again into the foreground accompanied by motivic and *maqam* phenomena.

This use of several monothematic methods alongside each other not only displays the ever present striving towards synthesis lying con-cealed in Bartók's work; it simultaneously indicates one of the most essential differences between the compositional methods of Bartók and the new Viennese school. It was by approaching from the angle of monothematic aspirations that Bartók came to an individual techni-que for the serial creative method, and this bears witness to a certain historical developmental inevitability in this creative method. Yet Bartók, in possession of this new serial technique, did not sacrifice everything else: on the contrary, he brought in the older elements to service the new. That he also used the *maqam* principle along with serial elements, for example, proves that in his music the intervals did not become absolute but retained their original melody-forming sig-nificance. Movement "up" and "down" primarily possesses melodic content with him, too—which nevertheless does not in the least mean that these directions are not interchangeable, for in Bartók's musical thinking, based on the centre principle, it is precisely mirror inver-sions that assume importance. His art is, however, characterized by preservation and new interpretation of the real, melody-forming con-tent of intervals.

CHAPTER FIVE

"POLYMODAL CHROMATICISM"

As a natural and direct consequence, the folk music basis of Bartók's art involves modality. Numerous examples have been mentioned—and more will be mentioned in the course of analysis—in connection with how an individual modal melody leaves its stamp on the whole of a movement or formal section. This is, however, only one side of the manifestation of modality. For the phenomenon of modality must not be restricted to the melodic use of church modes. It was modality, as a "pre-tonal" conception, that characterized a significant period in the development of European music, and it is virtually inseparably bound up with purely melodic kinds of music—from the folk music of different peoples, to Gregorian chant and the art music traditions of the East. It is not possible here to go into a discussion of modality in full historical and theoretical depth, and only its most typical features will be brought out—to support the train of thought which follows.

Modality in the wider sense is not to be thought of as limited to the use of the diatonic modes known under the name of "church modes," for, strictly speaking, it includes every possible division of the octave.[1] In European art music practice, it is chiefly the modes of the diatonic system we encounter, and this is why we automatically associate the concept of modality with these.

In Bartók's music, modality was the means of avoiding, expanding, or developing major-minor tonality. Bartók's modal attitude

---

[1] Edmond Costère, "Modes," entry in Vol. III of *Encyclopédie de la Musique* (Paris: Ed. Fasquelle, 1961).

would demand a separate study in itself; for the present we shall restrict ourselves to the few aspects which are the premise of the question posed. In this wider conception of modality all notes of the tonal system are equal—this, too, is a step towards free atonality—and the mode is chiefly determined by the relationship of the interval structure between the lowest and highest notes of the melody, and the prominence of repeated notes and final notes.

A phenomenon connected with the modal conception in Bartók is the diminishing of the role or importance of the keynote of tonal significance and closely related to the tonality system. The note determining tonality, the centre or "framework" note does not absolutely have to be positioned at the lowest point in the musical texture—it often comes in the middle or uppermost part. This indicates not only that Bartók broke with functional tonality in this respect as well, but also that in its place—though not exclusively—he set a method which is modal in spirit. For it is one of the fundamental features of modality that it recognizes no basic keynote and related to this is the fact that in this kind of musical thinking "below" and "above" do not have a decisive role as they do in the functional-tonal system built on overtones. The scales are recorded in a descending form by ancient Greek music theory and numerous eastern music theories.[2] That in Bartók modality transcends the limits of the diatonic modes is best shown precisely by his "ultra-diatonic" modes. Otherwise why should he have sought those special scales which sound foreign to the ear of the European musician, which appear to be combinations of different diatonic modes, in which special intervals—augmented second, diminished fifths and augmented fifths—make them different from accustomed tonal associations? In this way he arrived, among other things, at the scale of Máramaros Rumanian folk music which has "borrowed" its lower tetrachord from the Lydian mode and its upper tetrachord from the Mixolydian mode. He showed such a preference for this scale that for a while the analytical literature called it the "Bartók scale."[3] Ernő Lendvai, on the other hand, calls it the "acoustic

[2] Curt Sachs, *The Rise of Music in the Ancient World. East and West* (New York: Norton, 1943).

[3] György Kerényi, "Bartók hangeme" ["Bartók's Scale"], *Énekszó* IX (1941).

scale" on the basis of the emphasis placed on the characteristic degrees of the overtone series (Lendvai 1971:67). And the latest research by Lajos Bárdos has resulted in showing that this scale is none other than one mode of the tonal system called "second diatony" (*heptatonia secunda*).[4] That Bartók did indeed reach this "second diatony"—even if not on a theoretical basis—is proved by his numerous "ultra-diatonic" modes—for example, the opening melody of the *Cantata Profana*, which is not only the mirror of the closing Lydian-Mixolydian scale, as interpreted by Lendvai, but another "out-cut" of heptatonia secunda, another of its modes, as has been revealed by József Ujfalussy (Ujfalussy 1969).

Similar interrelationships can be observed—though not within one work, but certainly at the level of obviously related works—in the final movements of the First and Second Sonatas for violin and piano. The two dome-structure themes, both of a folk character, are two different hexachord-sections from heptatonia secunda.

Example 108.

Because of their structure, these scales, although they are from a seven-degree system, contrast even better with major-minor tonality than the diatonic modes do (with the exception of the rarely used Locrian), since they consistently avoid the perfect fifth. A similar result is produced by manipulation of the seven-degree scales in a way which, avoiding not only the perfect fifth but the perfect octave as well, expands the limits of modality in the direction of twelve-degree chromaticism.

[4]Lajos Bárdos, "Heptatonia secunda—Egy sajátságos hangrendszer Kodály műveiben" ["Heptatonia secunda—A Particular Tonal System in Kodály's Works"], *Magyar Zene* III–IV (1962-63).

Another kind of expansion of the seven-degree systems is represented in Bartók by the oscillation of the degrees within a single melody. To take a typical example, in the first subject of the Violin Concerto's first movement, the third and sixth degrees of the melody, which is unmistakably in the tonality of B, are not fixed: minor and major third and minor and major sixth appear equally. This wavering results in the latent presence of four different modes: namely minor third+minor sixth—the *Aeolian*; minor third+major sixth—the *Dorian*; major third+minor sixth—*one of the heptatonia secunda* modes; and finally major third+major sixth—the *Mixolydian*.

Another very characteristic example is to be found in the *Music's* last movement, where, in the closing phrase's melody, also static on account of its function, the lower, unambiguously Lydian octave section (y) is answered in the upper octave by a diminished fifth, minor third mode (x).

Example 109.

Before we draw any theoretical conclusions from this phenomenon, it is worth noticing that examples of this kind of degree-wavering are to be found in folk music as well. And here it is not chiefly the well-known third-fluctuation in Transdanubian folksongs I am referring to, but to Máramaros Rumanian instrumental folk music. The example quotes melody no. 42 of Bartók's publication.[5]

[5]Béla Bartók, *Volksmusik der Rumänen von Maramureş* (München: Drei Masken Verlag, 1923): 35.

Example 110.

The great Rumanian folklorist, Constantin Brăiloiu, draws attention to a similar phenomenon in his essay "Un problème de tonalité."[6] That Bartók on his own account was consciously aware of this phenomenon from the composer's point of view becomes clear from one of his "Harvard lectures." He writes: "It is very interesting to note that we can observe the simultaneous use of major and minor third even in the instrumental folk music. Folk music is generally music in unison; however, there are areas where two violins are used to perform dance music; one violin plays the melody, the other plays accompanying chords. And rather queer chords may appear in these pieces (*Bartók Essays* 1976:369–70).

This wavering of certain degrees is not, either in folk music or in Bartók's music, to be regarded as alteration, in the functional-tonal sense of the word, since here there is no question of some given primary scale, the individual notes of which become altered for this reason or that. The phenomenon is rather to be explained by the latent presence of several different modes. The mechanical placing of the notes of such melodies alongside each other leads to partial chromaticism, to systems of eight, nine or ten degrees, and the inner structure of Bartók methods shows that this partial chromaticism comes about through the insertion of different modes into each other.

Starting off with modality in the wider sense, we have therefore arrived at the phenomenon of simultaneity of various modes—that is,

---

[6]Constantin Brăiloiu, "Un problème de tonalité (La métabole pentatonique)," *Mélanges d'histoire et d'esthétique musicale offerts à Paul-Marie Masson* (Paris, 1955).

"polymodality," as it is called. This is no new observation nor a new term in literature connected with Bartók. As early as 1930 the pioneer analyst of Bartók's compositional technique, Edwin von der Null, pointed to the so-called "tonal neutrality" (*Geschlechtslosigkeit*) formed from simultaneous use of the major and minor third, and to the theoretical result of simultaneous use of the church modes, called "tonal mixing" (*Tongeschlechtervermischung*) (Null 1930:74). This trend in analysis was then pushed somewhat into the background and only in 1957 was this same thread again taken up by Colin Mason in connection with the analysis of the Fourth String Quartet (Mason 1957).

Although it does not belong to the Bartók literature, an important contribution to the theme is offered by the Rumanian Gheorghe Firca's work *The Modal Foundations of Diatonic Chromaticism*.[7] With an imposing critical apparatus Firca analyses the works of the East European composers—Bartók, Stravinsky, Enescu, Janáček and on this basis arrives at the conclusion that the chromaticism produced by them rests on foundations which are quite different from the chromaticism of the Romantic and post-Romantic music of West Europe. Firca's research broadly bears out the view expounded by Bartók in 1921, namely that . ". . .The genuine folk music of Eastern Europe is almost completely diatonic and in some parts, such as Hungary, even pentatonic. Curiously enough, at the same time an apparently opposite tendency became apparent, a tendency towards the emancipation of the twelve sounds comprised within our octave from any system of tonality. (This has nothing to do with the ultra-chromaticism referred to, for there chromatic notes are only chromatic in so far as they are based upon the underlying diatonic scale.) The diatonic element in Eastern European folk music does not in any way conflict with the tendency to equalize the value of semitones. This tendency can be realized in melody as well as in harmony; whether the foundation of the folk melodies is diatonic or even pen-

[7]Gheorghe Firca, *Bazele modale ale cromatismului diatonic* (Bucuresti: Editura Muzicala a Uniunii Compozitorilor, 1966).

tatonic, there is still plenty of room in the harmonization for equalizing the value of the semitones."[8]

The decisive word in the polymodality question was, however, pronounced by Bartók himself, in his famous posthumously published "Harvard lectures." It becomes perfectly clear from these that Bartók used the technique of "polymodality" quite consciously. "As the result of superimposing a Lydian and a Phrygian pentachord with a common fundamental tone, we get a diatonic pentachord filled out with all the possible flattened and sharpened degrees. These seemingly chromatic flat and sharp degrees, however, are totally different in their function from the altered chord degrees of the chromatic styles of the previous periods . . . In our polymodal chromaticism, however, the flat and sharp tones are not altered degrees at all; they are diatonic ingredients of a diatonic modal scale" (*Bartók Essays* 1976:367). Elsewhere, but in the same lecture, Bartók returns to this same subject. "I must recapitulate in regard to what results the superimposing of the various modes led us. First, a kind of restricted bi-modality or polymodality. Second, bi-modality led towards the use of diatonic scales or scale portions filled out with chromaticized degrees . . . This modal chromaticism (as we will call this phenomenon henceforward)... is a main characteristic of the new Hungarian art music" (*Bartók Essays* 1976:376).

As an illustration of Bartók's words, here are three quotations: an extract from the baritone solo from *Cantata Profana*, an extract from the first movement of the Sixth Quartet, and an extract from the second movement of the Third Piano Concerto. It is common to all three that the fifth or the octave is filled out by superimposition of the Lydian and Phrygian modes upon each other.[9]

---

[8]"The Relation of Folk-Song to the Development of Art Music in Our Time," in *Bartók Essays* 41 (1976): 323-24.

[9]A similar extract is quoted by József Ujfalussy from the second movement of *Contrasts*. See Ujfalussy 1968: p. 350.

Example 111.

To make the true meaning of polymodality quite clear, it is necessary to show counterexamples of the phenomenon. It is not possible to interpret every single one of Bartók's chromatic themes or twelve-degree structures as polymodality. In the rising melody of *Cantata Profana*, formed in a Bachian way, it is the spirit of functional leading-note attraction that is obtained, and here the chromatic degrees are indeed the products of alteration.

Example 112.

In Bartók's oeuvre it is also frequently possible to find examples of the musical fabric arriving at twelve-note chromaticism not by means

of polymodal treatment of diatonic cells, but—as with the representatives of the Viennese school—the musical fabric makes use of
the already given tonal range of the twelve-note chromatic system.
The fugue theme of the *Music*, or the introduction of the Sonata for
two pianos for example, can scarcely be analysed on the basis of
polymodality.

Although his endeavours are undoubtedly fine, Colin Mason follows an erroneous path in his analysis of the opening bars of the
Fourth String Quartet, because he attributes a modal significance to
individual isolated notes of the chromatic scale (Mason 1957). The
phenomenon of polymodality, however, in my opinion, is justified only
when connected melodies or at least melodic cells or closed structures
separately represent the individual modes.

In the lecture quoted above a statement was made by Bartók
himself against another mistaken interpretation of polymodality.
"You cannnot expect to find among our works one in which the upper
part continuously uses a certain mode and the lower part continuously
uses another mode. So if we say our art music is polymodal, this only
means that modality or bimodality appears in longer or shorter portions of our work, sometimes only in single bars" (*Bartók Essays*
1976:370).

There is yet a third misguided interpretation, which crops up
with Edwin von der Nüll and Colin Mason: the theory of simultaneous
presence of all the diatonic modes. The outstanding English
musicologist demonstrates each diatonic mode to be represented by at
least one degree in the first four bars of the Fourth Quartet, and from
Bartók's careful segregation of the use of the major third and the
minor sixth he draws the following, considerably adventurous conclusion: "There is no traditional mode with major third and minor
sixth, and this suggests that Bartók wished to make it clear that he was
not inventing new modes of his own but was simultaneously using all
the existing ones" (Mason 1957:196). Perhaps it is unnecessary to
stress the indefensibility of this argument. We should note, nevertheless, that the major third–minor sixth scale, "non-existent" according
to Colin Mason, is in one place referred to by Bartók himself, and this

is none other than one mode of heptatonia secunda (see, for example, the principal theme of the Violin Concerto mentioned above).

Simultaneous use of three or four different modes is naturally still a realistic possibility, as Erich Kapst has shown of the Bagatelles and the Fifth String Quartet.[10] But it is no accident that Bartók uses the term "bimodality" so often. For practice does indeed prove that even two appropriately chosen modes are sufficient to break up and develop further the old functional-tonal phenomena, and, in the last analysis, to form the complete twelve-note scale on natural foundations. Of the fair number of aspects involved in the complex of questions posed here I should like for the moment to deal with no more than two: superimposition of major and minor, and bimodality arising from mirror symmetry.

Bartók's creative development was accompanied from an early stage by simultaneous, sometimes even tonally ambiguous use of major and minor. This is present in the First String Quartet as ambiguity between relative keys. This same confrontation of relative keys is also to be found later in a considerably emphasized form in the Marcia movement of the Sixth Quartet. In the case of two pieces from Mikrokosmos even the title betrays the composer's intention: in no. 59 the F Lydian and F minor pentachords are used together, and in no. 103 the A minor and B major pentachords. In the latter, bimodality is apparently supplemented by bitonality, but in actual fact the B major pentachord does not represent an independent key level—it is reproduced on the A minor level, and as opposed to the minor, the major is in the end also represented here by the Lydian mode. Simultaneity of major and minor often appears in the melody and harmony relationship as well. Think of the closing theme in the first movement of the Second Quartet, or the first subject of the Violin Concerto.

Modal confrontation of major and minor in the chord named the alpha chord by Ernő Lendvai is one of the most frequently occurring phenomena in Bartók's music (Lendvai 1971:40). Edwin von der Null

---

[10]Erich Kapst, "Stilkriterien der polymodal-chromatischen Gestaltungsweise im Werk Béla Bartóks," *Beiträge zur Musikwissenschaft* VII (1970): 9, 15, 21.

was right when he described this chord with two thirds as being "tonally neutral" since the major and minor characters mutually extinguish or neutralize each other. But he was incorrect when he claimed that this neutrality of character deprives the chord of its expressive value (Null 1930:74). The chord has—on account of its actual structure—the special tension of the diminished octave, and depending on the different ways the notes may be distributed, it has a large expressive range.

Major-minor bimodality, however, became a permanent element in Bartók's musical language not only through one chord but also through an individual scale. What I have in mind is the scale consisting of periodic alternation of minor thirds and minor seconds, referred to by Lendvai as the 1:3 model. Without the slightest desire to refute Lendvai's theory in connection with the distance principle origin of this series, I should like to put forward the possibility of a different origin. In the centre of the first movement of the First Quartet (the end of the trio) a detail can be found in which an adjacent chromatic note is attached to each degree of the B-flat major triad. Thus the minor third model comes about not on an inter-key basis but with a definite B-flat basis. After this it can justifiably be concluded that the adjacent notes colouring the major degrees have also a minorizing function. And indeed the 3+1 model scale may be the most complete combination of the major and minor modes, since apart from the pillar notes (base-fifth-octave) the scale contains none other than two of the most typical degrees from both major and minor—or more precisely, the Ionic and Aeolian: the major third and major seventh of the Ionic, and the minor third and minor sixth of the Aeolian.

Example 113.

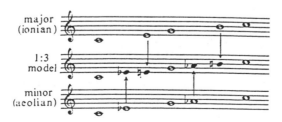

In this brief summary of polymodal phenomena, our last theme is the modal significance of mirror symmetry. As has been mentioned, the structuring in tonal thinking which takes place exclusively from below in an upward direction is joined in Bartók by the freedom of modal thinking. Indeed, musicality based on mirror inversions and centre notes in one sense stands opposed to the tonal conception, since the functional content of a given interval movement depends on whether it is directed upwards or downwards. Bartók's music, therefore, reflects a modal attitude in this respect as well.

This kind of thinking based on the symmetry principle already in-cludes polymodality concealed within it, for the exact mirror inversion of any melody produces in the majority of cases a change of mode as well. The diagram below shows clearly that, with the exception of the Dorian, the structure of which is identical upwards and downwards, all the diatonic modes are also mirror inversions of each other.

Example 114.

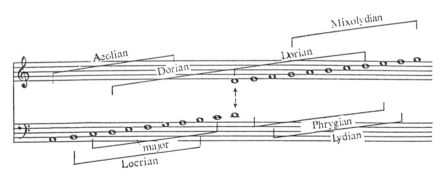

Since this change of mode arises from the non-distance structure of the scales, we can arrive at the same result through the mirror "reflec-tion" of the heptatonia secunda modes. (A good example of this is the two previously mentioned scales from *Cantata Profana*.)

Bartók was very much aware of this phenomenon, for the two pentachords put forward by him are also mirror inversions of each other. And he makes use of this possibility in numerous works : the best example is nevertheless to be found in the Fifth String Quartet, where the whole of the final movement, and partly the first movement, are based on virtuosic motivic development of major and Phrygian tetrachords corresponding to each other in a mirror-like way. In the closing episode of the first movement, in the nature of a summary—and on two occasions, as appropriate to sonata form—two superimposed layers of major and Phrygian tetrachords produce complete chromaticism. In the last movement there is a scale motif which corresponds to this same detail, where the major-Phrygian complementary filling out points similarly in the direction of chromaticism (see Example 102). This same phenomenon, related to a common centre, is found in the closing parts of the two movements.

Example 115.

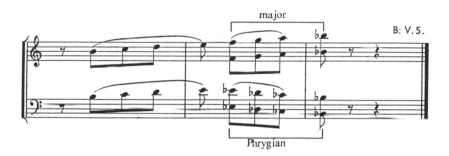

In the style of the modes fitting into each other in this way, like cogwheels, Bartók liked to join other complexes in the intcrest of bringing about chromaticism naturally. Traces of this can be discovered as early as in the whole-tone scale theme of the second movement of the First Quartet (after fig. 9): the six-degree whole-tone scalc is accompanied by a chord which is taken from the other whole-tone scale. The result is not yet twelve-degree, only nine-degree, but complementary aspirations are clearly evident in this. Later Bartók draws the final conclusion when he makes complete six-degree units confront each other (*Mikrokosmos* no. 136: "Whole-tone Scales").

Perhaps it is not accidental that it is precisely in the form of the whole-tone system that this treatment appears in Bartók; the distance systems are particularly suitable for producing complete chromaticism by being fitted together. The other six-degree system, the minor third model scale, is also such that two can be fitted exactly into each other.

Lastly, a classic example of complementary chromaticism can be found in the central movement of the Fourth Quartet, where pentatony and diatony—in the same way as the black and white keys of the piano—fit together precisely. As opposed to the earlier distance interlockings, where it was a question of absolutely identical structures, this technique likewise belongs in the last analysis to the sphere of polymodal phenomena, for the structures here confronted, pentatony and diatony, meet as "different modes" in the chromatic system.

Example 116.

Naturally it is not only modally that the two systems stand opposed to one another; to the notes of a diatony without key signature symbols is linked the pentatony of a system of six sharps (e.g., F-sharp major)

or a system of six flats (e.g., G-flat major). Modal superimposition is therefore supplemented by tonal superimposition. In a similar way the major-Phrygian bimodality of the Fifth Quartet only exhausts all twelve degrees because the two tetrachords are linked to each other by one semitone and in this way the unity of the tonality disintegrates. That is, both examples show that the phenomenon of polymodality does not give an answer to every question without being accompanied by a consideration of tonality.

CHAPTER SIX

TONALITY AND POLYTONALITY

The question of tonality in Bartók, although the literature has dealt at relative length with it, has so far received an answer only in part. The reason for the matter being so complicated is that on the one hand Bartók did not make such a radical break with tonal idiom as Schoenberg—to take an example from among his contemporaries; but, on the other hand, he did not retain such a firm relationship with it as, for example, the neo-Classical French composers. In his harmonic language the elements of the old world of harmony appear in abundance, while from the tonal point of view almost consistent identity of opening and closing notes is present virtually throughout the whole oeuvre of Bartók. Both phenomena create the impression of harmony and tonality in the older sense, although their real significance only develops fully within the framework of a new system of relationships. Bartók himself also referred to them in his aforementioned study: " . . . a deliberate (not too frequent) use of chords of older tonal phrasing within atonal music would not be in bad taste. An isolated triad of the diatonic scale, a third, a perfect fifth, or octave amidst atonal chords—certainly limited to quite special places which are suitable for the purpose—do not give an impression of tonality . . . Even whole sequences of such triads and intervals, if they do not have a tonal effect, might be perceived as quite in style. An unconditional elimination of these old sonorities would imply the disclaiming of a— not even considerable—part of the means of our art" (*Bartók Essays* No.68:457–58). And in connection with the other phenomenon, he writes: "The penultimate step toward atonality is demonstrated in those works which produce an atonal effect irrespective of their tonal point of departure and their return, at the end, to that very point (whereby the intention is—according to the old pattern—to obtain a homogeneous effect, create a solid framework)" (ibid., 455).

Both quotations definitely indicate that Bartók took into consideration all stages of the development of musical language, and he did not sever the contemporary phenomena at all from his own creative aspirations. Thus, when he wrote a study on the problem of tonality and atonality, he not only described the objective phenomena, but also—and this can be felt in the study—his own subjective attitude. Even the very first sentence betrays a great deal. "The music of our time strives decidedly toward atonality. Yet it does not seem to be right to interpret the principle of tonality as the absolute opposite to atonality . . . " (ibid. 455).

Thus, in the course of examining tonality in Bartók's works it would appear expedient to start from some ideas that make it possible for us to approach the problem in all its many aspects. The first such idea is that Bartók never considered atonality to be musical anarchy—rather he emphasized that it was precisely the inevitable result of historic development. Secondly, we must regard as a starting point that Bartók was not in the least reluctant to use the atonal way of expression. At the time when he wrote the study for *Melos*, a broader interpretation of the term atonal music was generally accepted: to this category belonged all expressive means which were based on equal use of the twelve chromatic degrees. From his first mature works onwards Bartók used this system augmented to twelve degrees, and—as was demonstrated in the comparison made between him and his contemporaries—in certain periods he did indeed come very close to using this chromatic system in a way which was free from all restrictions—so-called "free atonality." And finally, the third thought concerns the fact that, once he was able to make free use of the twelve-degree system, Bartók strove to re-establish the role of tonality, but the tonality which he brought about is essentially different from functional tonality in the old sense.

Here, too, it is necessary to emphasize, as in the other analyses so far, that Bartók's art cannot be contained conveniently by one single compositional technique system. An early and surprisingly good explanation in this respect can be read in Edwin von der Nüll's book which appeared in 1930; that he cannot, however, give an answer to everything is due chiefly to his effort to force the phenomena of Bartók's musical language, even though with praiseworthy freedom, into the Procrustean bed of earlier functional music (Nüll 1930). He accepts the new but explains it from the point of view of the old. I sense the danger of a likewise exaggeratedly unifying system in the works of Ernő Lendvai. The harmony system and axis-tonality theory discovered by Lendvai are undoubtedly one of the most significant products of Bartók research, and a scientific approach to the problem without taking this into consideration would be unimaginable today (Lendvai 1971:1–6, 35–66). The limitations of this theory, however, stimulate more recent investigators not to be satisfied with it. The approach is no longer exclusively analytical, precisely because it is not the recording of individual phenomena that is the expressed aim. There is rather an endeavour to seek out the lines of development and a striving in this respect towards synthesis and the demonstration of the interrelationships between different phenomena discoverable at various points. The main aim, therefore, is to give a more graded and authentic picture—by means of the genetics and dialectics of these phenomena—of this great, comprehensive genius of our own century.

There are a considerable number of aspects to the question of tonality. For this reason, before entering upon a discussion of tonality in the strict sense, we must touch on some phenomena which are indispensable for any investigation of the whole complex, and of which the lessons—directly or indirectly—contribute to a more profound clarification of the problem.

The Phenomenon of Mistuning

The term "mistuning" was first used in connection with Bartók's music by Bence Szabolcsi in his study on *The Miraculous Mandarin*.[1]

[1]Bence Szabolcsi, "A csodálatos mandarin" ["The Miraculous Mandarin"], *Zenetudományi Tanulmányok III*, ed. by Bence Szabolcsi and Dénes Bartha (Budapest: Akadémiai Kiadó, 1955).

This excellent observation supplied a new starting point for the deeper analysis of Bartók's compositional technique. It provided inspiration to examine this phenomenon methodically throughout his whole oeuvre, taking into consideration and—if possible—forming into a system the various ways in which it manifests itself and the inner relationships in its expressive function.

The phenomenon of mistuning can be traced back to string instrument practice. This is also indicated by the internationally known Italian term *scordatura*. While in the seventeenth and eighteenth century it was used primarily to extend the possibilities of the instrument (Biber, Strungk, J. S. Bach), in the nineteenth century one or two composers resorted to it to obtain special effects. For example, in his *Danse Macabre* Saint-Saëns tunes the solo violin's E string to E flat, thereby attaining a formidable, ghostly sound.

Bartók also used *scordatura* in its original sense. In *Contrasts*, the trio for violin, clarinet and piano, dating from 1938, he prescribes G-sharp–D–A–E -flat tuning for the violinist in the first thirty bars of the last movement. Bartók uses the sound of diminished fifths heard on open strings as an introduction, presumably on the basis of folk music examples.[2]

Example 117.

The original conception of the phenomenon makes the possibility of its expansion, its wider interpretation, very clear; since *scordatura* generally refers to one or two strings, it is only the pitch of notes played on these that is changed; thus it usually breaks the otherwise "level" plane of the tonal structure. Continuing the optical comparison, we come to the conclusion that we can regard as mistuning

[2]It is from this that József Ujfalussy deduces the tonal system employed in the work, too. See Ujfalussy 1968.

every phenomenon in which a certain distortion is produced as a result of partial alteration of some real or imaginary "musical picture" or tonal structure.

The word "distortion" draws our attention to the other root of the phenomenon, no longer practical, but having a figurative aesthetic meaning. In the music of the nineteenth century—chiefly in Liszt—one can observe the variational process, the essence of which is the expansion or contraction of the "spatial" range—the interval structure—of a theme or motif. This is a natural and logical extension of the augmentation and diminution of the temporal relations—the rhythmic values. In certain cases the expansion or contraction of the interval structure creates the impression that the structure is being distorted, especially if the alteration is partial—that is, if it only affects a part of the structure. Bartók's oeuvre starts off straight away with a Romantic character-variation—or, rather, caricature, when he quotes the melody of *Gott erhalte*, the imperial anthem, in the *Kossuth* symphonic poem, first of all in a minor form and then later further distorting this minor form.

Example 118.

Use of mistuning for distorting purposes of this kind in the works of Bartók's youth is still an expressly Romantic legacy which is bound up with a programme. But another trend also appears: displacing one or two notes of the melody presents a possibility to relax the framework of tonality. For example, when at the opening of the first of the *Two Pictures* the note G-sharp appears in the oboe melody, this is quite noticeably no more than the mistuning of one degree of the pentatonic melody which opens like a folksong. The G-sharp appearing in place of G suddenly tips the melody out of the expected pentatonic framework and fits it into the tonal system of the accompaniment, which moves in the whole-tone scale.

Example 119.

In the introduction in the last movement of the First Quartet the cello solo begins with the fourth motif characteristic of Szentirmai's "Csak egy szép lány" or Egressy's "Appeal." To move out of this folk atmosphere, the composer mistunes the second half of the melody and extends the expected octave framework to an augmented octave. Then when it is heard for the second time, the opening fourth is also mistuned into an augmented fourth so as to lead even more decisively into the tonally wavering cadence which follows.

Example 120.

This mistuning technique also appears later in Bartók's art—in the course of an occasional folksong quotation or development of a theme with an obvious folk character. In the Improvisations the line-end of the folksong beginning "Kályha vállán az ice . . . " suddenly slides upwards. And in no. 116 of *Mikrokosmos* ("Melody") the cadences at the ends of the phrases sometimes slide upwards and sometimes downwards.

In the last movement of the Fourth String Quartet we are presented with a classic example of the splitting in two of an imagined pure pentatonic system, of semitone mistuning. The lower section of the melody, developed from a four-note motif, is a pentatonic row extending from A-sharp to F-sharp, but the upper section is not the natural continuation of this but a mistuned variation extending from G to G.

Example 121.

This treatment of pentatonic systems points to Bartók's endeavours to make folk music elements fit into the higher order art music form, not "in the raw" but as the result of some transformation. Examples can also be found where it is precisely folk music that inspires Bartók to mistune the accustomed tonal structures.

It is one of the chief characteristics of the age of tonality that the foundations of its melody and theme formation—and indeed its tonal system too—are provided by the fifth-octave relations. Use of the diatonic modes did not represent any essential change in this area, since they, too—with the single exception of the Locrian—have this perfect fifth and octave structure. In Rumanian and Arab folk music, however, Bartók discovered numerous scales in which the melody is virtually completely independent of these acoustic-tonal limitations, and in which it may happen that the basic note has no perfect fifth or octave. Among the small-range Arab melodies the diminished or augmented fifth is almost an every-day phenomenon, and among the Máramaros Rumanian melodies there are some—Bartók himself refers to this in the foreword—in which, as a result of placing two pentachords one above the other, one finds within a single melody F below and F-sharp above (no. 42).

Since Bartók draws special attention to both these phenomena, this obviously means that he, too, was particularly sensitive to such irregular elements. He used the lessons to be learned from this in his own melody writing and evolved numerous new scales. Here are a few examples. In the last movement of the First Sonata for violin and piano the theme has a diminished fifth instead of a perfect fifth. In the Second Sonata for violin and piano we find an augmented fifth scale. Diminished and augmented fifth scales appear together in the exciting string crescendo of the finale of the Concerto. Likewise in the Second Sonata we find the sort of thematic development in which the scale-like melody avoids the perfect fifth and perfect octave alike.

Example 122.

This is also to be observed in one of the important scale themes in the First Piano Concerto.

Example 123.

The "revolving theme," centred on E-flat, in the Seconda parte of the Third String Quartet—which is, incidentally, the most important material in the movement—at first avoids the fifth altogether, and then in the fugato variation it touches the diminished fifth.

Example 124.

Viewed as tonal music, all these instances appear as mistuning since in that kind of musical thinking, no matter how much the melody may be enriched by alteration, the perfect fifth-octave framework is permanent and virtually impassable. Bartók also approaches the problem from this angle—as shown by the fact that perfect octave-fifth relations were by no means excluded from his theme writing, thus creating the specific meaning for the mistuned form.

As melodic outline and a structural factor, the fifth-octave framework plays an important part in Bartók's art, in two particular respects: (1) in folksong structures and (2) in contrapuntal structures. Let us therefore examine these two problems from the angle of the technique of mistuning.

It is more or less general knowledge that Bartók took over not only scales and typical melodic phrases from different kinds of folk music but also structural elements: the line and verse structures of folksongs. Hungarian folk music has different kinds of melody structure, but they are identical in so far as the octave-fifth structure plays a large role. So when Bartók built on the structural factors of Hungarian folk melody, he inevitably took over line formation with a fifth and fourth framework and its further development in an octave framework.

It is a more special but not at all unique phenomenon when Bartók constructs the melody on a mistuned fifth-octave framework—even though the folk origin may be perceptible. Behind the plaintive lament melody in the slow final movement of the Second Quartet, for example, it is not difficult to recognize the line structure of a Transdanubian lament melody from Kodály's collection.[3] Similarly it is possible to compare the first line of the Sixth Quartet's motto melody and the melody of no. 119 of "The Hungarian Folk-song."[4] In the first example, instead of the perfect octave structure consisting of two fourths there is an augmented octave structure. And in the second example, the perfect fifth framework of the folk melody line is retuned to a diminished fifth.

Example 125.

In these two examples we naturally only imagine or suppose the perfect structure source behind the mistuned melody. In numerous cases, however, the perfect structure form and the mistuned version appear

[3]Cf. chapter on *The Influence of Folk Music*.

[4]Gerald Abraham, "Bartók: String Quartet No. 6," *The Music Review* III (1942): 72; Benjamin Suchoff, "Structure and Concept in Bartók's Sixth Quartet," *Tempo* no. 83 (1967/68).

alongside one another in the same composition. A good example of this is also to be found in the Sixth Quartet. The first subject of the first movement is immediately mistuned in the course of thematic development, and this mistuned form remains in the inversion of the theme as well.

Example 126.

A good example of the mistuning of the fourth structure in folksongs is ordered by the central melody of the two slow movements in the Fifth Quartet. In the four-line melody, ending on G, the downward displacement of the upper G–D fourth by a semitone is readily noticeable. This theme from the second movement returns in a varied form in the fourth movement. Here the theory of the mistuning of the perfect octave framework is proved: the perfect and the mistuned forms appear alongside one another.

Example 127.

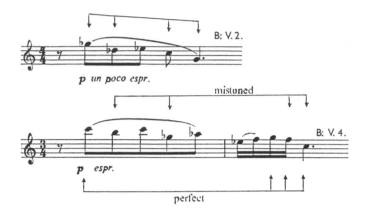

To follow the descending fourth structure, here is a fourth structure with a rising line taken from the last movement of the First Sonata for violin and piano. The gradual unfolding of the melody demonstrates very clearly that the composer first securely lays the foundations of the lower fourth of the melodic structure and then builds the upper layer upon this—sliding it down a semitone lower than the diatonic.

Example 128.

Mistuning of the division of the octave is to be discovered in the first subject in the first movement of the Fifth Quartet. One could imagine the melody, unfolding step by step and then ending with a pentatonic phrase, in a closed pentatonic system as well:

Example 129.

This perfect fifth–octave structure, however, would obviously have been flat and uninteresting for Bartók, so he actually shaped the melody so that the upper layer slides down a semitone, and in this way the augmented fourth-major seventh became the framework of the melody.

Example 130.

Bartók uses a similar method to transform—to mistune—the tetrachord structure of the diatonic modes, too. For the double fourth structure of the folksong lines—if the melody is not pentatonic—contains two tetrachords, namely so-called "disjoint tetrachords." Now Bartók, without laying a finger on the inner structure of the tetrachords, replaces the whole tone which separates them with a semitone—that is, he tunes either the upper tetrachord lower or the lower tetrachord higher. A classic example of this phenomenon is offered by the last movement of the Fifth Quartet where major and Phrygian tetrachords appear in this way within a diminished octave framework (a). And similar mistuning of major tetrachords occurs in the finale of *Contrasts* (b). It is as a result of this same kind of development that the version of the E-flat-centred revolving theme of the Seconda parte of the Third Quartet's Coda is produced, where it becomes straightened out into a scale (c). Here we are faced with the mistuning of tetrachords of a minor structure. It is to be noticed that in all three examples the "dramaturgical" function of the phenomenon is very similar: toward the end of a movement, as a result of some development work, like a summary, the part becomes arranged into a scale and in a stretto canon move in parallel or in mirror inversion.

Example 131.

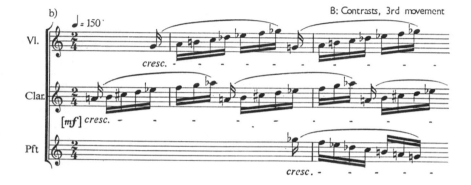

As regards structure, the three mistuned scales fit exactly into Bartók's favourite fourth-model.

Example 132.

Since two minor tetrachords of identical structure produce, within the framework of a perfect octave, a Dorian scale, we may consider their mistuned form to be a descendant of the Dorian. This mistuned Dorian scale, incidentally, is none other than the periodic scale consisting of alternating whole tones and semitones. It is not to be claimed that this scale can only have come into being by means of mistuning, for roots can be discovered for it elsewhere,[5] too, but here in the Third Quartet, where the Dorian mode plays such a large part, it is certainly this that provides the best explanation for the genesis of the phenomenon. In addition to this can be listed two further examples—no. 33 of the Violin Duos and no. 101 from *Mikrokosmos*. Each is a two-part contrapuntal texture, and apparently bitonal, for as opposed to one part moving within a tetrachord framework the other moves in a tonal plane which is displaced by a diminished fifth. To the *Mikrokosmos* piece Bartók himself gave the title "Diminished Fifth." But it is precisely the mistuning which creates the impression of bitonality. Let us try to prove it by a counter-effort! If, for example, we transpose the lower part of the duo a semitone down, the two parts move within a perfect octave framework; hearing this, no one would think of calling this "perfect fifth bitonality" since in a contrapuntal texture it is a perfectly normal occurrence that one part is imitated or "countered" by the other at a distance of a fifth.

[5] See interpretations by Lendvai 1983:277 and Antokoletz 1984:76.

Example 133.

For Bartók what is special is that he replaces the perfect fifth counter-part with diminished fifth counterpart, but this does not mean that here there are really two tonal planes confronting each other at a distance of a diminished fifth: the perfect octave framework has been contracted as a result of the mistuning of one tetrachord or the other.

Example 134.

Besides these two examples, unequivocal proof of the phenomenon is provided in the first movement of the Fifth Quartet. Two tetrachord layers move in a similar contrapuntal fabric, but that it is not a matter of diminished fifth bitonality is proved by Bartók's fitting the diminished octave movement in a D–A–D perfect octave compass (Ex. 135). The true contrapuntal forms, however, do indeed pose the problem of the perfect and mistuned fifths. And with this we have arrived at our second large group of questions.

One important permanent factor in the invention, fugue, and fugato structure of J. S. Bach is the tonal reconciliation of the *dux* and *comes* entering at a distance of a fifth. A natural consequence of the octave, it followed that, for example, if a theme with a fifth framework was transposed a fifth upwards it moved outside the framework of the

Example 135.

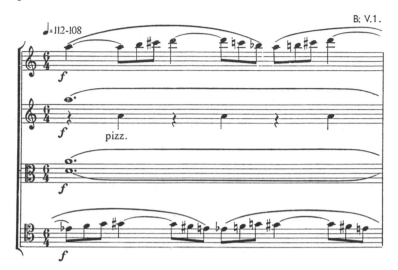

octave, and as a result outside that of tonality, and so in the interests of preserving the tonality the composer often transformed it into a fourth framework on the level of the dominant. How strongly Bartók preserved this Bach technique is clearly shown in the "hunter's fugue" in *Cantata Profana* where the B-flat–F incipit of the first and third voices (dux) is answered by the F–B-flat thematic motif of the second and fourth parts (comes). Bartók, however, not only preserved the tradition: he also transformed it. This sort of effort is shown by his introducing the technique of mistuning into counterpoint as well, when he replaces the perfect fifth answer in many of his fugally structured works by a mistuned fifth answer. As early as in the First Quartet's opening movement he works the imitation so that the major sixth leap of the thematic motif is answered by a minor sixth—that is, after starting perfectly regularly a fourth lower he puts the whole lower part at a distance of a diminished fourth (augmented fifth). He later uses this same diminished fourth canon technique in the first part of the Third Quartet.

Example 136.

In his later works it is another form of fifth mistuning that steps into the foreground. It will be enough to refer to no more than no. 145 of *Mikrokosmos* ("Chromatic Invention"), the "Chase" from *The Miraculous Mandarin*, the centre of the Fifth Quartet's final movement, or the slow introduction in the Sonata for two pianos and percussion.

Of these two kinds of mistuning the latter is obviously more refined, more classical, because it solves the problem of uneven (fifth-fourth) division of the octave by means of the distance principle, the diminished fifth-augmented fourth way of halving the octave, and—although it is built on the twelve-note chromatic system—it removes the danger of toppling tonality over.

The problem posed by contrapuntal forms leads back once again in one respect to folksong structures: namely, the two-layer structure of Hungarian folksongs. The most ancient pentatonic type of Hungarian folksongs, which displays a close relationship with the folksongs of other Asian related peoples, has an individual verse structure in which the material of the first two melodic lines is repeated a fifth lower. This fifth layering is naturally not a characteristic which is exclusively found in the folk music of these particular people; obviously it appears in the music of other peoples as well—as a result of the acoustic phenomenon of fifth relationship. In Bartók's melodic writing and also in his structuring of form it is possible to observe this peculiar fifth layering of folksong structures. For our present purposes it is those occasions when the basis of the structure is provided by the mistuned fifth instead of the perfect fifth that are interesting. A very characteristic example of this is the first theme in the last movement of the Fifth Quartet: it is constructed on descending levels in the style of the old Hungarian folksongs, but the material of the first two lines is repeated not a perfect fourth or fifth lower but a diminished fifth lower—that is, on a mistuned level.

Taking all these examples into consideration, therefore, it can be said that in Bartók's compositional technique there is a definite tendency towards the mistuning of perfect octave and fifth intervals, frameworks, structures—either by contraction or expansion. In the compositions of his youth, mistuning was still chiefly a means of character variation for producing distorted, grotesque, ironic moods. In the course of further creative development, however, mistuning assumes increasing importance, making a break with the distorted-ironic character and becoming one of the chief means of personal expression. This process, strictly speaking, begins in the First Quartet and reaches its full development in the works of the 1920s; by then it is by no means only an occasional episode in the musical fabric, but one of the fundamental components of Bartók's individual musical language.

Behind such a dominating role played by the phenomenon of mistuning lie two tendencies—each closely related to the other: one concerned with technique and one concerned with expression. The technical trend is closely bound up with the development of the musi cal idiom: with the breaking down of the framework of tonality and the expansion of the twelve-note chromatic system. In the first decade of this century there appears in the music of both Bartók and Schoenberg, in parallel with each other but quite independently, a denial of perfect fifth-octave structures. In this respect Schoenberg was more consistent than Bartók, for the Hungarian master was held back by folksong from drawing the complete range of conclusions. But that he, too, progressed in this direction has already been proved by numerous examples. Bartók was inspired towards a twofold method by his close relationship with folk music: first he sought out those places where *the various kinds of folk music themselves step outside the perfect fifth–octave limits*, and secondly he increasingly consistently sought a way in which to fit folk music elements with a perfect fifth–octave structure into the framework of the twelve-tone chromatic system by means of mistuning.

There follows just one example as evidence of this latter trend, but this is typical in every respect. In the preceding chapter we discussed how Bartók's chromaticism was formed chiefly by means of superimposition of different modes—that is, by bimodality or polymodality. One classic example of this bimodality is offered by the Fifth Quartet where two scales which mirror each other exactly—the major and the Phrygian—are superimposed. These two diatonic scales, however, add up to no more than eleven degrees. On the other hand, the mistuned form used by Bartók—referred to above—gives the full range of twelve degrees. Thus, in certain cases it is precisely mistuning which makes polymodality a suitable means for achieving complete chromaticism.

So far we have considered the phenomenon of mistuning on the level of scales, melodies, and complete structures. There is, however, a manifestation of this phenomenon which affects matters of harmony. An early example of chords which have been put "out of tune" in Bartók's art is the "Grotesque" portrait (the fourteenth Bagatelle). The interval structure of the melody does not in itself change in comparison with the "ideal" form; thus the composer has achieved the transformation into the distorted form by altering the rhythm and the harmony. The melody, transformed into a waltz rhythm, is accompanied by the stereotypical two-function chord alternation of waltzes—but in place of the dominant we get an "out of tune" chord: the most important components of the V7 chord are mistuned; they are replaced by adjacent chromatic notes.

Example 137.

Starting out on this track we also find the phenomenon of mistuning in Bartók's harmonic world. And as we saw to be the case with melodies and structures, the word "mistuning" loses its pejorative sense here, too, and the phenomenon, stepping outside the distorted intonation circle shown in the above example, directs attention to important, and indeed fundamental, regularities in the harmonic sphere. Before entering upon deeper discussion of the question, we must touch on Bartók's technique of using "adjacent chromatic notes," which became so characteristic in his style.

Edwin von der Nüll was the first to draw attention to this characteristic quality in Bartók's chords (Nüll 1930). Even in the world of chromatic harmony there appear chords in which some notes are sounded which are foreign to the theoretical structure of the given chord. One of the earliest types is the so-called *sixte ajoutée* which colours the triad in a characteristic way.

In Bartók's chords the adjacent notes also have this kind of colouring function. At the same time, Nüll's analysis demonstrates that the friction of minor seconds, possibly minor second piles, is in many cases a substitute for noise or percussion instrument effects, above all in the piano works. Although this is simultaneous sound if we consider external appearances, it is still not a harmonic phenomenon. In a similar way, colouring notes also have significance which is beyond, or just on the border of, harmony: this extension of colouring notes over a larger area is strictly an early form of cluster which is likewise not to be classified as a chord but as an effect.

It is, however, of essential importance that in Bartók's compositional technique adjacent notes have yet a third function, and this is a characteristically individual phenomenon in Bartók's musical idiom: the colouring note which becomes a chord note. In the central part of the opening movement of the First Quartet we have the following considerably impressionistic sound:

Example 138.

B: I.1.

Each component of the B-flat major triad is coloured by one adjacent note—the root and the third by the lower adjacent chromatic note and the fifth by its upper chromatic neighbour. Here there can be no question of doubting the colouring function of the adjacent notes, although the fact that the structure which is thus produced is none other than a minor third model cannot be considered to be of merely secondary importance either.

Later there is another example, incidentally in the same tonality, where the colouring function of the adjacent notes is considerably diminished. In the closing chord of the Suite for piano—taking the whole work into account—the tonality of B-flat can scarcely be doubted. But here the notes are not arranged unambiguously round the major triad as they were in the example taken from the string quartet, since the B-flat–C-sharp–G-flat–A chord (in Lendvai's terms, the G-flat alpha chord) is heard equally with the B-flat–D major third. Of these notes, the C-sharp is the chromatic neighbour of the major third and the A is the chromatic neighbour of the root; and the G-flat would be the chromatic neighbour of the fifth if the fifth of the chord were heard at all. From this, too, it can be seen that it is not in the least colouring notes that this second level of the chord contains but degrees which are equal in rank with the basic level, their function being to make the harmony complementary. Thus the C-sharp really means D-flat and is none other than the minor third placed alongside the major and equal in value to it; the A is complementary to the root and the G-flat to the imaginary fifth. Then these two basic levels of the chords are joined by two more notes forming a third level—F-flat and C-flat. The third level has an unambiguously colouring function but this follows rather from their positioning, since, as pitch values, these are also neighbouring notes of the root and the missing fifth.

Example 139.

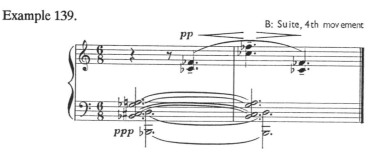

The closing chord of the Suite for piano encourages one to draw a further conclusion. For a long time we have been interpreting the alpha chord as a double third chord in which the major third is underneath and the minor third up above. But in the closing chord we have just been considering, where there can be no doubt as to the B-flat tonality, the notes B-flat and A cannot be the thirds of some chord with a G-flat (F-sharp) root. Is it thus possible for an alpha-type chord to be a root position and not a first inversion? It would appear so, particularly if we take into consideration the substitution technique just discussed. On this occasion, therefore, in the chord B-flat–C-sharp–G flat–A, the B-flat is the root, the C-sharp (D-flat) is the minor third substitute for the major third, the G-flat (F-sharp) is the minor sixth (mistuned fifth) substitute for the fifth, and the A is the chromatic note adjacent to the root, or its complementary note (a mistuned octave).

In the example taken from the Suite for piano, substitution was present only in the case of the missing fifth, and apart from that the adjacent chromatic notes appeared together with their real main-note partners. But other examples can be found where the double third chord can be interpreted as having double roots. The following chord occurs in the First Sonata for violin and piano:

Example 140.

The chord's being supported by the held D shows unequivocally that the A-flat–D-flat–E level is a substitute for the A–D–F level: that is, it has been slipped down (mistuned) by a semitone.

In a similar way, in "The Chase" from *Out of Doors* the ostinato figure contains the tonality of F and not C sharp: the notes G-sharp–B–C-sharp are the adjacent chromatic notes (substitute or mistuned degrees) of the imaginary major third (A) and the perfect fifth (C); and the E is the complementary note of the root, or a mistuned octave.

Example 141.

Seen in this light it becomes clear that two important and characteristic structures in Bartók's compositional technique, the minor third model and the alpha chord, are not just a "distance scale" and a chord reflecting golden-section proportions (Lendvai 1971), but on the one hand, the complementing of the major triad by adjacent chromatic notes of equal rank, and on the other hand, substitution or mistuning of the triad. In one case the adjacent notes stand beside each other (minor third model), and in the other the new adjacent notes replace the old "main notes," or we might also say that they mistune the perfect octave-fifth (and major third) structure. And finally, the minor third model scale can be broken up into a major triad and its mistuned "minor" variation, which fits in with the spirit of polymodality just as with that of bitonality (for example, C major–A-flat minor).

Example 142.

With this we have come to one of the basic problems in Bartók's chordal world. Although chords which deviate from third-structure have an important role to play in his work—various kinds of minor and major second piles, fourth-chords and fifth-chords—third structure does not lose its significance and is not pushed into the background. This is a typical Bartók attitude in the area of compositional technique; by introducing new means he does not exclude the earlier means—for then the range of these means would not be enriched. In his treatment of third-structure chords an entirely new way of using the earlier methods manifests itself very characteristically.

Bartók's third-structure chords can really be traced back to two basic types, one being the four-note chord with a major third and the tension of a major seventh ("hyper-major," to use Lendvai's term), and the other being the Lendvai alpha chord ("golden section chord," according to Lendvai himself) (Lendvai 1971). The first of these is not in the least a new harmonic phenomenon, being a seventh-chord on the first degree, which had already won complete acceptance in Romantic and post-Romantic music, and which, typically, appears frequently in the works of Bartók's youth—an unambiguous reflection in Bartók's art of his affiliation with the Romantic harmonic world—especially the harmonic language of Wagner and Richard Strauss.

Although within the framework of the major seventh there may be some wavering as regards the third—and sometimes the fifth—this chord type is chiefly characterized by its major third and perfect fifth. Indeed, in its own inner structure both of these occur twice because the seventh is the perfect fifth of the third and also the major third of the perfect fifth.

The other chord type has chiefly been interpreted as a double third-chord by Bartók research, and there can be no desire to doubt the correctness of this interpretation—indeed this origin of the phenomenon has been even further emphasized in connection with the phenomenon of polymodality. The question is, however, whether the simultaneous presence of the two tonal types is so dominating in the case of the already *evolved* chord type. Whether the inversion into a diminished octave (major seventh) of the major and minor third clash (semitone interval) does not decrease the contrast between the tonal types.

In the course of the analysis given above, as a result of Bartók's adjacent chromatic note technique and the substitution or mistuning technique related to it, we have reached a position where we also interpret this chord in a different way. Some help is also offered towards this new interpretation by the correlation of the major seventh major chord. For if an important role is played in Bartók's musical language by a chord which is major in its every particle (justifiably named "hyper-major" by Lendvai), the other basic type, which in a certain sense provides a contrast to the first, is not a chord "without tone species" (to use Nüll's expression) which mixes major and minor, but a chord which is minor in its every particle—we might say "hyper-minor."[6]

We can repeat the claim—with the insertion of a new viewpoint—that in the chord in question the major third is replaced by the minor third and the perfect fifth by the augmented fifth (and together with this, the diminished fifth). The diminished octave may be interpreted in two way: it may signify the mistuning of the perfect octave, but taken from the major seventh major chord angle it may be the same kind of permanent framework in Bartók chords as the perfect fifth was in the earlier period. That is, within this interval framework of eleven semitones (major seventh or diminished octave), chord structures of varied meaning appear: there is one which has an emphatically acoustic, major character dominated by the major third and perfect fifth, and another which has an emphatically minor character dominated by those intervals which differ from the acoustic and indeed stand directly opposed to it—the minor third and the diminished and augmented fifths. And we have already noticed that Bartók formed fourth-chords so that an augmented fourth should if possible be connected to a perfect fourth and so that in this way this chord, too, should fit within the major seventh framework.

Example 143.

What comes even more clearly into the foreground in the course of investigating these chord types is the function and meaning of in-

[6]Lendvai uses this nomenclature for another type of chord, with a minor thirds, perfect fifth and major seventh. Cf. Lendvai 1971:68

dividual intervals. Naturally it is not a matter of examining isolated intervals on their own; it is merely that it is necessary to devote some attention to those intervals, and their use, which have a distinctly differentiated significance in the various melodic and harmonic structures.

In the structures which have been examined so far it has become evident that there are perfect, acoustic intervals which are in a certain sense static, and opposed to these there are tense, dynamic intervals. The relationship between these two groups can be assessed according to the natural phenomenon of the overtone series: the tense dynamic intervals come about through the *mistuning by plus or minus one semitone* of the acoustic "perfect" intervals which come at the beginning of the overtone series. The intervals of the first part of the overtone series (discounting octave identity) and the mistuned intervals clearly demonstrate this peculiar relationship if they are placed alongside one another. (Again, here the intervals are shown in the customary scale of values where one semitone=1.)

Overtone number	Acoustic interval	Mistuned interval (+1 or -1)
2	octave	12 ⎡ 13 minor ninth ⎣ 11 diminished octave
3	fifth	7 ⎡ 8 augmented fifth ⎣ 6 diminished fifth
4	octave of no. 2	
5	major third	4 ⎡ 5 fourth ⎣ 3 minor third
6	octave of no. 3	
7	minor seventh	10 ⎡ 11 major seventh ⎣ 9 major sixth
8	octave of no. 4	
9	major second	2 ⎡ 3 minor third ⎣ 1 minor second
10	octave of no. 5	
11	augmented fourth	6 ⎡ 7 fifth ⎣ 5 fourth

The upper section of the table is perfectly clear and only the fourth as a mistuned interval with the value 5, requires explanation. Now it is easy to observe in the music of the twentieth century that the fourth is far from identical in value to the fifth; it cannot be regarded as simply the inversion of the fifth. We reach the same result if we examine this from the acoustic side as well, for we only meet with the perfect fourth of the fundamental note in a distant and virtually indistinguishable section of the overtone series.

The lower part of the table, beginning from the sixth overtone, displays some secondary interrelationships. The higher the individual overtones come in the series, the more their purely acoustic content decreases. In numerous cases, intervals which were produced earlier are produced once more (11, 3, 1); and the double role of the interval with the value 6 is very characteristic. This is the meeting point of acoustic and mistuned structures, but only in theory, for in practice in Bartók's music its acoustic use (cf. *The Wooden Prince*, Lydian-type scales) is well differentiated from the form produced by means of mistuning (cf. fugue structure, etc.).

It must be stressed that it is not as consonance and dissonance that these two kinds of interval types contrast with one another. This would lead in a mistaken direction, for consonance-dissonance is dependent upon convention determined by the period. Here, on the other hand, it is categories of an objective physical nature that confront one another; they naturally can—and do—appear in the form of a contrast between consonance and dissonance, but their classification is relative. The minor third, for example, which is the mistuned form of the acoustic major third, has now been present for a long time in European music as a consonant interval. But think of Bartók's characteristic minor third motifs (the Second String Quartet, the Dance Suite, the Second Piano Concerto, etc.). Pregnant with tension, their function, expressing barbaric primeval strength, is very far from creating an impression of consonance.

The phenomenon of mistuning the major third is extended in Bartók's music; alongside the natural acoustic intervals come their "artificially" mistuned partners. Thus it becomes evident from yet another angle that the fourth, as soon as it becomes independent and suitable for forming chords, is not merely the inversion of the fifth but an individual anti-acoustic interval loaded with tension. In the same way, the minor sixth is in this connection no longer the inversion of the major third, but an independent and tense interval, really an augmented fifth (or "diminished" major sixth). There is no need to offer explanations for the other primary mistuned intervals, their "anti-acoustic" nature being self-evident.

If we now examine the basic chord types anew in the light of all this, the lesson to be learned is clear: the structure of the major seventh chord is 4-7-11 semitones, that of the alpha chord 3-6-8-11 semitones, and that of the chord composed of two different fourths 5-11 or 6-11 semitones. If we disregard the framework which has a fixed nature and consists of 11 semitones, the structure of the first type is characterized by acoustic intervals and that of the second and third types by mistuned intervals.

Yet another brilliant proof of Bartók's comprehensive genius: he does not throw away tradition but retains it, and, transforming it, builds the new upon it. Unlike the twelve-note doctrine, he does not exclude from his system the acoustic intervals offered by earlier music, but brings about new relations through them. Thus he continues and reinterprets the major-minor duality of the tonal age. After the analysis given above it will scarcely seem exaggerated or contrived to draw an analogy between major-minor duality and Bartók's acoustic-anti-acoustic duality. Bartók developed major-minor duality by taking all the acoustic intervals to be major and then placing their mistuned versions alongside them as their minor counterparts. On this basis we can indeed speak of a "Bartók major" and a "Bartók minor." Ernő Lendvai also arrived at a kind of duality theory when he contrasted Bartók's diatony and chromaticism, or the corresponding "acoustic types" and the "golden section types" (Lendvai 1971:87). One may, however, argue with this contrast in several respects. In the course of the analyses made so far it has been proved by an abundance of examples—particularly in connection with polymodal technique—that in Bartók diatony and chromaticism do not oppose one another. Moreover, the so-called acoustic scale, although it consists of diatonic tetrachords, is not diatony but "heptatonia secunda," and so it cannot, even in a figurative sense, be the representative par excellence of diatony.

A further question presents itself as to why pentatony becomes excluded by Lendvai from the order of the acoustic musical world and why it fits unambiguously into the "chromatic or golden section system." If we examine not only an arbitrarily selected section of the pentatonic scales, as Lendvai does, it becomes clear that a major third is also present and a perfect fifth, and a major sixth and a minor seventh. It is obvious that in the case of pentatony, too—as with almost every means—its character depends on the way it is used and so also on which side of the duality it is placed. Bartók rarely uses pentatony in its original form; usually—as we have seen—he mistunes it in some way or other. For this reason Lendvai is partly right; in Bartók, pentatony belongs rather to the "chromatic world," not because of its original nature, but because Bartók has transformed it in a particular way.

Similarly the golden section system does not provide an explanation in the case of alpha type chords, for the structure of these is actually not shown by the series of golden section proportions 3-5-8-13, but by the following interval structures: 3-6-8-11, 3-5-8-11 and 3-6-9-11. Of these it is only the lower part of the second that can really be fitted into Lendvai's golden section proportions.

Thus Bartók's major-minor duality cannot be expressed by the contrasting sides of the diatonic-chromatic system or the acoustic-golden section system. The real duality behind Bartók's music is the dialectics of the acceptance and denial of the acoustic world.

This duality includes the preservation and mistuning of the perfect octave-fifth structure of scales, melodies and form, and also the preservation and mistuning of third structure chords inherited from European art music. This extension and reinterpretation of major-minor duality has more than technical-idiomatic significance; it provides possibilities for double development of processes, for tension and resolution undulation, and for lifelike breathing in the organism of the music. And the analogy of the major-minor system of meaning presents itself as an aesthetic component. On the other hand, the problem cannot be simplified to contain no more than this contrast. By their being constructed on natural extra-human phenomena, acoustic elements and modes of expression are identified with the objective, the natural in their aesthetic significance as well. And as a contrast to this, more human and more subjective content is given to the musical system of symbols which transforms what is given by nature, what is acoustically satisfying, and artificially reshapes it into something else.

What is characteristic of the very greatest masters is precisely that the two activities involved in accepting and transforming, or the two conceptions behind the natural and the artificial, are in classical balance with each other. Here is yet another point where the difference between Bartók and the majority of his contemporaries becomes apparent and with the aid of which it becomes possible to demonstrate Bartók's place among the great men of music history. There have been and continue to be trends in which imitation of the given natural world and striving in the direction of acoustic euphony reigned. Such was the discovery of the major third and its virtually immoderate use during the Renaissance and later in the so-called *galant* period (Johann Christian Bach). Another example was the discovery of the euphony of pentatony at the turn of the century, primarily with Debussy. On the other hand, there are also past and present trends which are dominated by rebellion against the natural and dominated by artificial, logical elements. One example of this was the polyphony of the Dutch masters, refined to a complex game at the end of the fifteenth century, and another is the trend represented by "orthodox" twelve-note music in the first third of the twentieth century; its aim was to exclude every natural, acoustic element from the sphere of musical expression. It is typical of both these one-sided aspirations that each places in the foreground one or the other part of the process of artistic recognition and expression. This major-minor duality in Bartók's music, however, which grows beyond the technical framework of mere tonality and manifests itself on an aesthetic level as well, bears witness to the kind of dialectical relationship and classical balance between those elements naturally given and those transformed by man that are characteristic of the work of only the greatest artists.

Thus for Bartók, when he got beyond the first Romantic period, mistuning did not stand for distortion and the ironic but signified rather rebellion, pain, suffering, the deeply personal. This is once again a point of contact with the expressionism of Schoenberg; the denial of perfect fifth and octave structures was the denial of the customary, banal, petty bourgeois melodics. Structures which mistuned the perfect fifth–octave—that is exclusive use of the most crudely dissonant intervals—meant intransigency for Schoenberg, and in Bartók dialectical rebellion. A parallel can obviously be drawn between this and the visual art of the period, not yet abstract but tending towards abstraction, in which the misdrawing of forms for purposes of expression represents more or less the same artistic attitude as the mistuning of perfect interval structures in music.

In this rebellious period in the arts—and, it might be added, at the time of the evolution of abstraction—the distorted and the amorphous lost their nineteenth-century meaning. What was alien then now became the innermost subject of the artist; forms and chords offered by nature could no longer be put to canvas or paper in their own original, unaltered form; these raw, natural forms and harmonies were made suitable for artistic expression by the activity of transformation—misdrawing and mistuning.

And so followed the great change around, the great change in meaning: the misdrawn and mistuned form became normal, personal and fine, while natural drawing or pure, banal consonance signified what was unacceptable, to be ridiculed, what was alien to man. Just as the little naturalistic landscape set up on the easel in one of Magritte's fiery landscapes seems laughable, the banal little melody which appears before the Coda in Bartók's Fifth Quartet is also odious and to be dismissed.

This enigmatic, quotation-like episode in Bartók's quartet can indeed be explained only by the mistuning phenomenon. The banal major melody is not a variation of the movement's second first subject, but its non-mistuned form. If we compare the two melodies we can see that the downward displacement—mistuning—by a semitone of the upper tetrachord of the major scale was enough for the banal theme to become Bartók's personal, demonic theme. This episode before the end is therefore the same sort of gesture on the composer's part as when the magician reveals the secret of his trick to the public at the end of his display. And at the same time it is a quotation, a reminder, the suggestion of a tone which the composer immediately thrusts angrily away.

Example 144.

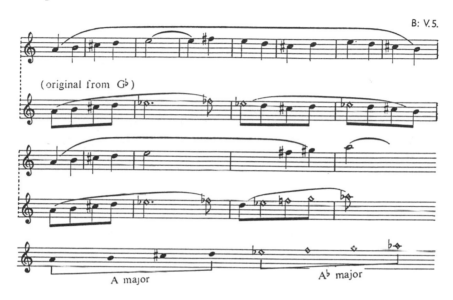

Does this mean that everything which is not mistuned or everything which belongs to the sphere of perfect fifth-octave structure is inimical and odious for Bartók? Not in the least. And this is where Bartók's path moves away from Schoenberg's. The art of the mature Bartók does not on principle refute perfect fifth-octave structures and does not replace them exclusively with mistuned forms: he uses the two together towards the enrichment of his artistic universe.

Polytonality

The *Allegretto con indifferenza* episode provides what amounts to a spectral analysis of the theme just discussed and, at the same time, of the mistuned tonality of the whole movement. For what was built into the theme in an organic way here becomes separated into an unambiguous A-major melody, and onto the A major as a separate key the composer sets the same melody in B-flat major (Perle 1967:206). But the end of the A-major melody and the beginning of the B-flat major melody are connected to each other precisely like the real theme and its scale-motif, which has a closing function.

Example 145.

This also proves that these kinds of structural mistuning usually have bitonality concealed somewhere within them. A melody clearly of tetrachord structure which—to return to its original position—starts off in G-flat major and ends in F major is in the last analysis bitonal, in a special, linear-projection kind of bitonality. In the same way the mistuned pentatony of the Fourth Quartet also contains a linear manifestation of bitonality. Even these few examples indicate that at certain points Bartók's bitonality comes into contact with the phenomenon of mistuning.

It is almost symbolic that even at the beginning of Bartók's career, in the first of the Fourteen Bagatelles, a seeming bitonality is present; the right hand's key signature is four sharps and the left hand's is four flats. Here, too, there is immediate evidence of polymodal thinking. In a late publcation Bartók himself gives a clear explanation: "The tonality of the first Bagatelle is, of course, not a mixture of C-sharp minor and F minor but simply a Phrygian coloured C major."[7]

From this relatively early starting point the development of the various key relationships and key associations can be followed quite clearly. For the present only a few typical examples will be given. Not long after the bagatelle mentioned above came the second of the *Three Burlesques*, the wry, ironic tone of which is secured by

[7]"Introduction to *Béla Bartók Masterpieces for the Piano*," Manuscript drafted in January 1945. Published in *Bartók Essays* No. 61, 432–33.

chromatic adjacent note relations. To the triads which give the melodic line are attached unstressed *Vorschlag* chords, and so each chord note is provided with its own chromatic neighbour.

If we examine the connections between the chords in more detail, however, our attention is drawn to something important: the *Vorschlag* chord before the E-minor triad is enharmonically identical with an A-flat major triad. The position is the same with the other chords, too. As a result, the notes of the minor triad are preceded not only by lower adjacent chromatic notes but by a chord of a different structure which reaches the root from below and the third and fifth from above. The effect created by these chromatic adjacent note connections is refreshed to a great extent by the fact that it is a major triad that is attached to a minor triad and the parts do not move mechanically.

Example 146.

In the quickly flitting chord connections in the second burlesque, another method appears which was later to become of great significance in Bartók's compositional technique: use of an extreme case of third-relationship triad connections, where every chord note moves on chromatically (for example, D major–A-flat minor). In this relationship the essential point is that in place of simple chromatic connection—that is B major or D-flat major related to C major (in other words chromatic approach of the root)—it is the chromatic neighbour of the triad's *fifth* that becomes the root of the triad. It should be noted that the minor third model is produced by this chord relationship, too—that is, in the last analysis the minor third model contains two tonalities, namely a major and the minor of its augmented (mistuned) fifth.

Thus, if we were able to regard the minor third model as a bimodal phenomenon—a compression of major and minor—based on a common root, in this new light we can see that bitonality also lies concealed within it, for it is scarcely possible to imagine simultaneous presence of these distant triads within one single tonality.

Although we are concerned with a third-relationship connection here, it must be emphasized that the essential point in the phenomenon—at least with Bartók—is the chromatic displacement of the fifth and the adjacent-note tension of the triad built upon it. Thus the major third distance appears as a diminished fourth (or augmented fifth). And this brings to light still further interrelationships.

It is really to this type of tonality pairing that the fugue technique of the Lento movement in the First String Quartet belongs. The first violin part is imitated by the second violin a fourth lower, which fits in perfectly with contrapuntal tradition, but from the second note onwards the imitation proceeds at a distance of a diminished fourth (major third). The same applies to the canon-like texture of the first part of the Third Quartet. From this parallel movement a minor third model is clearly outlined (see Ex. 169a).

These examples were mentioned when the phenomena involved in mistuning were being discussed in connection with the fact that we do not usually speak of bitonality when we are concerned with a fifth or fourth canon. Yet here it is precisely as a result of mistuning that we get the impression that the two parts in the contrapuntal fabric move in two different tonalities.

A good example of tonal levels separated by a diminished fourth (augmented fifth) being placed together can be found in the first movement of the Fourth Quartet where the canon of the "Arab theme" is accompanied by C major and G-sharp minor ostinatos. The minor sixth canon between two parts in the fifth quartet has a similarly bitonal character.

Example 147.

The other technique very characteristic of Bartók is the use of tonal levels separated by a diminished fifth. It has already been pointed out in connection with mistuning that this occurs most frequently in contrapuntal structures because it solves the problem of the asymmetrical fifth-fourth division of the octave. The literature refers to this relationship as a polar relationship since the two keys are placed at opposite points of the fifth circle, that is polar points, and for this reason it also leads to the disintegration of tonality. But it is these contrapuntal examples—and they are in the majority—which prove that the diminished fifth answer replaces the perfect answer of polyphonic structure (which Bartók did not renounce in other cases), and the *dux-comes* relationship also demonstrates that it is not a question of two equally important tonalities but a parallel between one dominating tonality and a secondary tonality which is complementary to the first, colouring it and veiling it over.

It also happens sometimes that the two tonal levels separated by a diminished fifth form an ostinato, either as a "background"—as, for example, in the Prima parte of the Third Quartet—or as a "non-thematic" transition section, as in the first movement of the Sixth Quartet.

Example 148.

In the second movement of the First Sonata for violin and piano, a violin melody which is unambiguously in the tonality of C unfolds above the deep F-sharp organ point of the piano. Coming very close to this detail even in intonation is an already mentioned part of the central movement of the Fourth Quartet, where the melodic material is likewise heard in the tonality of C above a G-flat pentatonic ostinato. This latter example, which was referred to earlier as being one of the finest examples of complementary chromaticism is also unequivocal proof of the complementary tendency of diminished fifth bitonality.

Finally, the third typical combination of tonalities in Bartók's music is semitone bitonality. The roots of this phenomenon go back as far as the consistent major seventh parallel of the 1908 Bagatelles (8, 10) and the new tonality conception which had already been evolved by the composition of the seventh piece, where B major is coloured by C major. József Ujfalussy has already pointed to the important role played by "semitone tension bitonality" in the musical idiom of Bartók in connection with the analyses of *Bluebeard's Castle* and the Dance Suite (Ujfalussy 1971:114, 203).

Similar phenomena can be observed in numerous chamber works dating from the twenties. For example, at the beginning of the First Sonata for violin and piano, which comes closest to the "free atonality" concept, the violin melody moves around a C centre above broken triads consistently based on C-sharp in the piano part.

Example 149.

Approaching this same method is the return of the first subject at the end of the Prima parte of the Third Quartet, where the melodic material, which belongs to the Key of C major, is supported by a C-sharp–G-sharp bass.

Example 150.

And in the Seconda parte the "revolving theme" centred on E-flat is accompanied by a harmonic basis formed by D Dorian triads which at the same time provide the thematic counterpoint (for the cello triad progression is actually the further development of the initial folksong theme).

Example 151.

This series of examples can be completed by a phenomenon already discussed: semitone bitonality is likewise concealed in the inner structure of the Fourth Quartet's "Arab theme" and the Fifth Quartet's scale themes.

In light of all this it may well be asked why, of all the many possibilities offered by bitonality, it was precisely these three tonality combinations, employing the tension of the semitone, the diminished fifth, and the augmented fifth, that Bartók favoured? This question may be approached from two angles. First it is necessary to examine what is individual in all three of these bitonal combinations, and secondly we must investigate what gives to these interval relationships the tension which is so characteristic of them.

By the first approach we once again arrive at the technique based on the complementary principle. We have already established that in Bartók's various methods it is chiefly the combination of unified systems which are ccmplete in themselves that is common. Of thc possible polymodal combinations, for example, it is the pairing of the Lydian and Phrygian which stands out because, related to a common base, without any artificial intervention whatsoever, this leads in a natural way to twelve-degree chromaticism. Now a virtually completely analogous method can be provided by the combination of two tonalities.

Firm believers in atonality consider bitonality a compromise between tonality and atonality. In certain cases this is undoubtedly true, mainly when the two contrasted tonalities do not lose their individual tonal character, and so it is as if the two tonal centres exist independently alongside each other within the piece. Such methods are to be met with in Bartók, too, principally in the form of combination of relative keys. The best example of this is the Marcia movement of the Sixth Quartet, where the major form of the theme is accompanied like a shadow by its relative minor version (B major–G-sharp minor). The two do not merge into each other: each retains its own independent modal and tonal character.

As opposed to this, we found in the case of bimodal methods that although the individual modes may appear as relatively self-contained, independent systems, they do lose their independence either partly or completely in the complex material of the musical fabric, and, producing a new quality, merge into one another. The typical examples of bitonality demonstrate essentially these same characteristics; Bartók selected and preferred the three tonality combinations analysed above because they contain the pentatonic complementary basis with the help of which the seven-degree system becomes twelve-degree. This means at the same time that with these tonality combinations the two tonalities no longer exist in parallel with each other but neutralize each other. The most "economic" use of this technique is represented by the detail already quoted several times from the Fourth Quartet where C major and G-flat pentatony are combined. In the other cases, however, when each tonality is represented by a complete seven-degree system, there are, apart from the five-degree complementary basic notes, two "superfluous" notes in each which are identical with two notes from the other tonality, or their enharmonic equivalents. That is the C major–A minor tonal plane can most easily be complemented into a twelve-degree system by the C-sharp major–A-sharp minor, F-sharp major–D-sharp-minor, and B-major–G-sharp-minor tonal planes since the F-sharp–C-sharp–G-sharp–D-sharp–A-sharp pentatonic group of notes is common to all three. The "superfluous" notes appear on one side or the other side or on both sides of the fifth column.

F C G D A E B							
	F♯	C♯	G♯	D♯	A♯	E♯	B♯
B	F♯	C♯	G♯	D♯	A♯	E♯	
E B	F♯	C♯	G♯	D♯	A♯		

The three complementary seven-degree systems contain three major and three minor tonalities. Combined with the C major–A minor tonality, these tonalities produce the relations which have crystallized as the most typical Bartók bitonalities. This is also why bitonality with the tension of a semitone, a diminished fifth and an augmented fifth dominates.

This explanation of Bartókian bitonality, based on the complementary principle shows the importance of adjacent chromatic note relationships as opposed to polar relationships. The polar relationship is also valid, but its content has an "adjacent note" quality it is a question of the mistuning by a semitone of the nearest, that is the fifth, relation (dominant) of an initial tonality. In the same way, the augmented fifth relationship is explained by this exact principle: this is the chromatic displacement of the dominant tonality in a different direction. With this we have arrived at another aspect of Bartók's mistuning technique, or to the recognition of a new system of relationships which is also connected with mistuning. As the perfect octave-fifth relations were replaced by mistuned relations in melodic and harmonic structures, so in the pairing and combining of tonalities it is likewise these non-perfect octave and non-perfect fifth relations which play the decisive role.

With this we have reached the other approach to the problem concerning why it is precisely these interval relationships which characterize Bartók's bitonal technique. The system of functional tonality is based on the most immediate and strongest relationships appearing in the acoustic overtone series: octave identity (numerical relationship: 2) and fifth relationship (numerically 3). Thus the natural relationship of all other notes to the fundamental note can be measured partly by reference to the overtone series (relating them acoustically) and partly by reference to fifth reiationship (relating them tonally). The chromatically adjacent notes to the fundamental note, however, can be regarded as the notes most alien to it, for they come in the uppermost section of the overtone series where the notes are, so to speak, indistinguishable, and taken on the basis of fifth relationship the chromatic adjacent note is separated from the fundamental note by seven fifths, and the diatonic semitone neighbour comes at a distance of five fifths from the fundamental. In this way the adjacent chromatic note relations really mean the negation, in the philosophical sense of the word, of the acoustic-tonal order, the greatest possible antithesis to the thesis of tonality. Bartók carried out the act of discontinued preservation by making the adjacent chromatic note relations, which "disrupt" these fifth relationships, a connecting link in the chain of tonalities connected on the fifth-relation basis, while at the same time alongside this he retained the fifth relationships of tonality.[8] In other words: his very particular tonal system is built on the coexistence of *perfect* and *non-perfect* fifth relationships.

This, therefore, is the other explanation of the matter: the "non-perfect" octave (that is, the octave mistuned in two directions) is actually the augmented or diminished octave which is the same as the two chromatically adjacent notes; and the "non-perfect" (that is, mistuned) fifth is none other than the diminished or augmented fifth. In other words, we are once more faced with the three basic forms of Bartókian bitonality, combining tonalities with semitone, diminished fifth or augmented fifth tension between them.

In Bartók's bitonal methods, however, it is not only the quantitative relationship between the two keys, or their distance from each other, that has to be examined but the inner qualitative structure of the relationship between these two tonalities. Indeed, it follows more or less naturally from what has been said so far that with Bartók bitonality is only an idiomatic process in the interests of enrichment of the tonality principle without its actually influencing the strictly "monotonal" unity of the works. That is, in the great majority of cases where bitonality is used, one of the tonalities has a dominating role in the tonality complex, and as a result the two tonalities which come together are not by any means equal: in comparison with the one which dominates and also has a structural role to play, the other fulfils a "mistuning" complementary function.

Valuable information is offered on this topic from the composer himself in a late study which dates from 1945 and was supposed to have been a foreword for the piano anthology planned for publication by the E. B. Marks Corporation. Referring to the early piano works

---

[8]This principle assumes a concrete form in the Coda of the Third Quartet: the structure of the chords is provided by a perfect fifth-column, their connection being strictly based on the principle of adjacent notes.

and the already familiar explanations of these, Bartók writes among other things: "The tonality of the first Bagatelle is, of course, not a mixture of C-sharp minor and F minor but simply a Phrygian coloured C major. In spite of this, it was quoted several times as an 'early example of bi-tonality' in the 1920's when it was fashionable to talk about bi- and polytonality" (*Bartók Essays* 1976:433).

This of course does not mean that with this one sentence Bartók dismissed once and for all the possibility of using polytonality in connection with his art. The quotation rather underlines that we are to notice in the occurrence of bitonality a special tonal relationship which is in the end, like polymodality, a means, a component in Bartók's complex conception of tonality.

As far as the Bagatelle referred to is concerned, the composer is undoubtedly right in stressing that the key to the tonality of the piece does not lie simply in the simultaneous presence of the tonalities indicated by the two different key-signatures. On the other hand it cannot be denied that the musical fabric of the piece is composed of two separate tonal and modal layers—C Phrygian and C-sharp minor. Thus in the whole complex two tonal levels, C and C-sharp, and also two modes, Phrygian and minor, confront one another. At the same time, through the different modes coming together in the different tonalities there arise even more modes, since the third of C-sharp minor appears to be major in relation to the likewise minor third of C Phrygian. Similarly the fourth degree of the minor scale is an augmented fourth when related to the Phrygian keynote, and thus represents a Lydian level, and the minor sixth of the minor scale is the alien major sixth alternative in the Phrygian scale. So it is easy to see that certain degrees of the C-sharp minor scale appear as the chromatically adjacent notes in the Phrygian scale on C, primarily the third, but also the fourth and sixth. Taking all this into consideration we can scarcely feel even Bartók's expression "Phrygian coloured C major" to be satisfactory from absolutely every point of view, for it might also be put the other way round: major coloured C Phrygian. But in place of using very categorical descriptions it would be more to the point to come to a thorough understanding of the principle behind the phenomenon—namely that here we are dealing with an unambiguous

C tonality, the polymodal character of which has been achieved by the composer through bitonality.

Example 152.

It is the combination of different keys that produces polymodality in the piece "Minor and Major" (no. 103 in *Mikrokosmos*). B major, which appears alongside the left hand's A minor part, obviously represents more than just another tonality: in relation to the minor third and perfect fourth of A minor, it brings a Lydian colour into the piece.

Example 153.

On the basis of all this it has perhaps become clear what is meant by saying that Bartók's bitonal methods are not tonal ambiguities but special structures in which the individual factors produce a new quality.

Having looked at some of the simpler examples we must now investigate the more complex phenomena, too. One typical bitonal structure with Bartók is a tonal divergence between the harmonic foundation and the melody belonging to it. The closing theme in the first movement of the Second Quartet, for example, may be divided tonally into two levels: the cello's fifths have without any doubt an F-sharp tonality, whereas the first violin's melody comes to rest on the note C-sharp and this C-sharp is further reinforced by a codetta.

Example 154.

While in the example just given there is a perfect fifth relationship between the tonality of the harmony and that of the melody, it is a mistuned relationship that binds harmony and melody in the majority of cases. It has already been possible to note this tendency in some of the examples of diminished fifth and semitone bitonality; confrontation of melody and harmony in a mistuned relationship. Or, put another way—bitonality comes about as a result of the mistuning of the perfect octave-fifth relationships. And with this we have reached a very important point in the argument: recognition of the special dialectics of *idiomatic polytonality and structural monotonality*. As Bartók himself stressed when explaining polymodality, in his works we should not look for instances where one part is constructed from one mode from the beginning of the piece to the end and the other part from another mode likewise throughout, it is in a similar way that we have to interpret the phenomenon of polytonality. It is not a matter of tonal duality or plurality extending over the whole work but of the breaking up of tonality in certain larger or smaller units within the musical fabric as a whole, which can be regarded as an idiomatic phenomenon, and this does not preclude tonal unity from reigning in the works from a structural point of view. Thus when we say that in Bartókian bitonality one of the tonalities has a dominating role, this does not refer to the given detail (in which it would be difficult to decide which of the tonalities used is the dominating one and which is the one with a colouring function) but to the whole work, movement or formal unit. Once again we can refer to the Fifth Quartet as being the best, but by no means the only, example. In the theme based on a G-flat–F tonal duality it would be senseless to regard either one tonality or the other as the dominating one, the decisive one. When at the end of the work, however, this same material meets on a tonal central note, approaching it from two different directions, there can no longer be any doubt as to the tonal unity of the movement and at the same time of the work.

This monotonality which is produced by way of polytonal material provides not only the structural unity of the work but also its structural differentiation. In other words the tonal unity of the work is secured not only by the framework tonality but also by the complex of different tonalities which appear in the various formal sections of the work. Here is further evidence that Bartók endeavoured to preserve the form-building principles of the tonal era, and it was only with extension and revaluation of concepts that he produced new qualities.

In the tonal plan of the works it is quite conspicuous how the perfect octave-fifth relations are replaced by their mistuned versions. This is, for example, how the peculiarly Bartókian structure is produced in which the second most important tonality is on a level a diminished fifth (augmented fourth) higher than the basic tonality of the work. What else could this be but the displacement of the dominant key in functional tonality—that is, the mistuning of the tonic-dominant relationship. In an unfinished draft Bartók analyses the Fifth Quartet and in connection with the B-flat–E–B-flat tonal structure of the first movement he actually states that in relation to the B-flat tonality the tonality of E "plays the role of dominant."[9] He also draws attention here to the fact that the themes of the movement come in ascending major second levels—that is, on the degrees of the whole-tone scale, the main theme being built on the B-flat–E–B-flat outline just mentioned. Striving in the direction of halving the octave can be seen here—that is, the possibility of "exact" halving offered by

---

[9]"Jouant le rôle de la dominante"—Bartók's unpublished draft analysis in French. The English translation in *Bartók Essays* (No. 54, 414) was made according to the German draft: "Etwa als Dominante" (dominant-like).

distance division, as opposed to the asymmetrical fifth-fourth division of diatony.

Another good example for this procedure is offered by the first movement of the Suite for piano. The scale of the melody here is a transformation of the so called "Bartókian scale," a differently cut version of the "heptatonia secunda," in which the fifth degree has now also been sharpened, leaving now no perfect fifth above the tonic B-flat.[10] To carry this idea to its logical conclusion, the chords accompanying the tune have no perfect fifth intervals either, so instead of the traditional alternation of tonic and dominant we have alternating B-flat major and E major (instead of F major) chords. E major is a mistuned or substitute dominant, exactly on the same pitches as in the Fifth Quartet composed eighteen years later. It is the sign of mastery and firm control on Bartók's part that, after this rather unorthodox initial harmonization, he has the tune played a second time and now presents the traditional harmonization with its alternations of B-flat major and F major chords.

This duality of the unorthodox and the traditional is revealed in another aspect, as well. In the structure of the melody there are certain terraces, arranged in such a way that they deliberately overlap with the alternating modes of harmonization; when we have a perfect fifth interval in the melody there is a mistuned fifth in the chords, and vice versa. Here is a diagram of this ingenious arrangement.

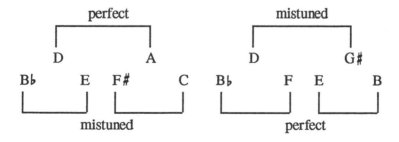

[10]See note 4 in chap. 5.

This figure suggests the following, consistently observed principle of Bartók: to preserve the acoustically perfect intervals (octave, fifth, fourth) and, at the same time, to mistune them by one semitone in order to create tension and bring about an entirely new type of sound. In this way he created a dual system in which the perfect and mistuned functions are in a logical and complementary relationship.

Besides the "mistuned dominant" the "mistuned tonic" also appears in the tonal plan of Bartókian forms. The best examples of this are provided chiefly by the Third Quartet, where the second part has D tonality and later E-flat tonality after the C-sharp tonality of the first part, obviously displaying an effort on the part of the composer to construct the tonal levels on the basis of the adjacent chromatic note principle.

We can now attempt to summarize the characteristics of the many aspects of Bartók's conception of tonality. Its starting point, its natural basis, is the European functional tonal tradition. Retaining the fundamental elements of this tonal tradition and developing them further, he supplements them with the modality of different kinds of folk music and the art music of the East. But by simultaneous combination of them he enriches both tonality and modality in particular directions so that the tonal system may in a complementary way reach, or at least approach, the twelve-degree tonal ideal produced as an inevitable development of the tonal tradition. This is polymodality and polytonality. The two are not separated from each other: the essence of polymodality is simultaneous use of different divisions of the octave right up to complete exhaustion of the whole chromatic range of the octave, and the essence of polytonality is the combination of different tonal levels, likewise in the interests of twelve-degree chromaticism. The two can appear separately, but polymodality is generally supplemented by polytonality. The resultant tonality or modality complex is bound together by a common centre-note or framework-note which includes the content and—chiefly—the structural function of the keynote of tonal significance and the final note of modal significance. Bartók's tonality, in the last analysis, can be summed up as *polymodal polytonality related to a common centre*.

A striving towards synthesis, as we have already noticed, is the most important and most firmly fixed feature of Bartók's creative activity. The presence of this can be observed not only in the new combination of tonality and modality and the re-establishment of tonal duality, freely extended and created anew, but also in the way that Bartók took over and transformed *all* the ready-made elements provided by tradition. His unlimited desire to assimilate and his ability to merge into on all useful results—the centuries of experience of European art music and the experiments of his contemporaries, the material and methods of primitive folk music and ancient art music of the East—is in itself something quite unique. It was only possible, however, for this large-scale reception to become the source of a large-scale synthesis because he transformed every element he took over; he took nothing over and used nothing in its original form, in its original capacity. Bartók's whole creative art is characterized by transformation and merging different factors into one. Its special quality and its greatness partly lie in that it exists on so many levels and can be explained from so many angles. It is a rich growth, the innumerable roots of which are nourished by the whole of human culture. It is not a simple continuation but a free re-creation of everything ancient, of everything preceding it.

PART TWO

ANALYSES

CHAPTER SEVEN

EARLY CHAMBER WORKS

A glance at the list of Béla Bartók's first youthful compositions immediately shows what a large number of chamber works he wrote, both for strings alone and chamber music with piano, alongside piano pieces and more simple vocal works. It supplies a characteristic picture of the developing young musician, whose artistic objectives were already shaped by practical considerations to compose mainly pieces which could actually be performed within the framework of domestic music-making, and do not call for large forces. Thus, virtually from the start chamber music became his mother tongue. That a tradition of domestic music-making was cultuvated in the Bartók family is borne out both by his mother being a piano teacher, and the activity of his father, who died at an early age. Béla Bartók Sr. the principal of an agricultural school, was a cultured amateur cellist, who organized and led an amateur orchestra at Nagyszentmiklós. Later, during his Pozsony years, the young Bartók also had the opportunity for intensive chamber-music playing. Although he was still scarcely acquainted with the technique of composition (László Erkcl mainly taught him the piano), he composed several chamber-music pieces for his company of young musicans. Some of these works have survived, the rest we only know of from various references. In any case, this active music playing in Pozsony went a long way towards ensuring that by the time the young Bartók enrolled at the Budapest Academy of Music in 1899, he had quite a few chamber compositions behind him.

Two of the relatively long list of pieces composed in Pozsony stand pre-eminent, clearly showing the tremendous development the young composer had made since his first Sonata for Piano and Violin (unpubl. op.5, 1895[?]), a work nothing more than capably arranged by a musician as yet inexperienced in the study of harmony. The path he traversed from that date onwards can be assessed already by the piece in the same form dating from 1897(?). The romantic tone of this second Sonata for Violin and Piano points to Brahms, and is continued in the Piano Quartet in C Minor, dating from the following year, which according to the manuscript was completed in about four to five months. The sequence of movements follows the typical Viennese tradition, in particular the trends leading to Romanticism. First movement: Allegro, $\frac{6}{4}$, C minor; second movement: (Scherzo) Allegro molto, $\frac{3}{4}$, E-flat major; third movement: Adagio espressivo, $\frac{4}{4}$, E-flat major; fourth movement: (Finale) Allegro vivace, $\frac{2}{2}$, C minor. The closing movement is marked by a gradual increase in tempo through Presto to the Coda's Prestissimo. In the second, Scherzo, movement the tone of Beethoven's dynamic, demonic scherzos can faintly be felt behind the romantic qualities.

The piano quartet in C minor was followed in the same year (1898) by a string quartet in F major. It is strange that this later work, although in a certain sense more mature and showing a few signs of the later development, is more rudimentary with regard to the handling of the material. Bartók was not yet as proficient in writing for strings as for the piano. The piano quartet was "carried" by the richly elaborated, imaginative piano part. Nevertheless, the string quartet is an interesting juvenile composition with the following structure: 1. Allegro, $\frac{2}{4}$, F major; 2. Adagio, $\frac{6}{4}$, A major; 3. Scherzo, Vivace, $\frac{3}{4}$, A major; 4. Adagio—Allegro, $\frac{3}{4}$, F-minor.

Although like the earlier two pieces, this work too shows the influence of Brahms, properly speaking it progresses "backwards" regarding its influences: a few Mendelssohnian elements appear, and even more strongly, the tone of the great Viennese Classical masters, primarily that of Beethoven. The Scherzo, the slow introductory section and the following dynamic, fast section in the closing movement, show the influence of Beethoven's middle period.

Signs of individuality and creativeness mainly appear in the Scherzo, whose sparkling, asymmetric rhythm foreshadows Bartók's later works with Bulgarian rhythm, and the tone as a whole presages his ironic, satirical caricatures from the type of his "Mephisto scherzos." All that, however, only refers to the Scherzo, as the trio section is in fact insignificant. The thematic pattern is permeated with the Classical concept of contrasts, but it is very typical that the stronger first subjects always come out better than the more gentle second subjects, which in places tend to be excessively sweet and sentimental.

During his years of study at the Academy of Music in Budapest, presumably due to Hans Koessler's strict methodical teaching, chamber music fell into the background in Bartók's workshop. Altogether two works, a quintet and a piece scored for violin and piano, have survived from his first academic term, and only the last term (1902/1903) yielded a relevant composition—a Sonata for Piano and Violin (1903). Even that work was not completed at this time, as the slow, middle movement was written sometime later, presumably after the *Kossuth Symphony*. But the third movement was premièred on 8 June 1903, at a concert of the Reading Circle of the Academy of Music, performed by the composer and one of his fellow stundents, Sándor Kőszegi.

If the string quartet in F major demonstrated significant progress over the first Pozsony compositions, we now witness even greater strides in the development between the quartet and the Sonata for Piano and Violin of 1903. The work has the following structure: 1. Allegro moderato (molto rubato), $\frac{4}{4}$, E minor; 2. Andante, $\frac{2}{4}$, A minor; 3. Vivace, $\frac{2}{4}$, E minor.[1] The harmonic emotional world strikes one immediately in the first movement, with typical Brahmsian parallel thirds and a melodic pattern with frequent auxiliary notes. This, together with the melodic steps of augmented seconds, already indicates an endeavour towards Hungarian style. As an interesting formal idea, Bartók inserts a fugato in the middle of the first movement, in all probability under Liszt's influence. The "Hungarian" elements appear only sporadically in the first movement, but are assigned a major role in the last movement. The most significant section is the second

[1]Published as score supplement in Documenta Baratókiana (1964, 1965).

movement, written afterwards, in a march rhythm; it moves around a single axis-note, referring to Beethoven. At the same time a characteristic triadic melody also appears in the movement (bar 183), which a few years later also appeared in Schoenberg's String Quartet No.2, clear evidence of the common Romantic sources of the two composers. The whole work, particularly the second movement, is dominated by the characteristic textural figures with runs and broken chords, that prevail in Bartók's piano works of the time.

The première of the Sonata's closing movement at the Academy of Music was covered by the press, some of whose more noteworthy opinions are worth quoting. "Béla Bartók's production brought the programme to an effective conclusion. This highly gifted student at our Academy of Music gave a marked proof of his rare genius, this time not only as a pianist but as a composer as well. He performed, with Sándor Kőszegi, the third movement of a sonata for violin and piano in *Hungarian* style, followed by a piano fantasia and the first movement of a sonata for left hand . . ."[2] "Béla Bartók, the 'second Dohnányi,' achieved resounding success with his fiery, demonic violin sonata, his piano fantasia imbued with Nietzsche, and a speciality performed with extreme virtuosity— his sonata for left hand only."[3]

The complete work received its première the following year, at a concert by the Hubay-Popper String Quartet on 25 January 1904. The violin part was played by Hubay. Meanwhile, on 13 January of the same year, the *Kossuth Symphony* also reached the concert platform, directing even greater attention to Bartók. However, the orchestral composition "dwarfed" to a certain extent the works that were premièred after it, which explains the reserved reception given to the sonata for violin and piano.

At today's chamber concert of the Hubay-Popper String Quartet, we heard a violin sonata by Béla Bartók, who recently made a successful début at the Philharmonic Society with his symphonic poem *Kossuth*. This turbulent young man obviously feels incomparably more comfortable in the free form of the symphonic poem, unrestricted by formal considerations, than in the narrower sphere of chamber music. His

[2]*Magyarország* (10 June 1903) in Demény 1954:387.
[3]*Zenelap* Vol. XVII (23 June 1903) in Demény 1954:388.

talent seems to lean much more towards the brilliant colours of the modern orchestra than towards the strict design and clear outlines required by the sonata. Being young and hot-blooded, he feels shackled by the form. He prefers to shake off these shackles in order to plunge into rhapsody, to make détours, and allow moods and ideas to flow in quick alternation. A nervous restlessness, one may even say fidgetiness runs through all three movements, destroying any lasting effect and allowing no deep impression to prevail. The first Allegro opens promisingly with an anxious query from the piano, answered with profound sorrow by the violin, soon to become lost in uncertain meditation and every form of brooding sophistry. The Andante opens most gracefully, with an elegiac theme of Hungarian colour from the violin, later surrounded as it were by the same instrument's free fantasies. The atmosphere is interrupted by pale, short-winded sections. Further on, the Finale is in the same vein: despite its gay, nationalistic first subject it does not develop into a livelier musical mood. Jenő Hubay performed the violin part with great distinction, and the composer gave of his whole temperament to ensure success for his work.[4]

We listened with great interest to Béla Bartók's violin sonata, but we found chamber music to be not his real terrain. The life-blood of his talent is the orchestra. His imagination can wander freely in the realm of the symphonic poem, where it is not confined to such a strict form as in chamber music, in which a primary requirement is to preserve the unity of style.[5]

A serious, modern work, rich in invention, Hungarian in its overall character and powerful in treatment. For our part we consider the Andante to be the most excellent, although the charming Finale with its sparkling rhythm outstrips it as far as external effect is concerned.[6]

An interesting work, but somewhat laboured; it recalls now Brahms, now Grieg, one might almost say a confused piece that obviously cost more trouble than it is worth. I liked the Andante most. The Hungarian finale is banal and of no interest.[7]

Soon afterwards, on 3 February 1904, Bartók performed his Sonata for Piano and Violon in Vienna, with Fitzner, at a concert of

[4]*Pester Lloyd* (26 January 1904) by August Beer in Demény 1954:437.

[5]*Magyarország* (27 January 1904) in Demény 1954:388.

[6]*Zenevilág* Vol. V (2 February 1904) in Demény 1954:388–89.

[7]*Egyetértés* (26 January 1904) in Demény 1954:389.

the famous Fitzner Chamber Orchestra. From the reviews of the Vienna performance let us quote a few lines from Dr. Theodor Helm in the *Pester Lloyd*: "Of the three movements I liked best the finale, which sweeps along fresh and defiant—a crowning achievement which only a few new chamber-music works can boast."[8]

It is interesting to note that the Budapest critics in general stand in opposition to the one from Vienna, all preferring the Andante movement. We would tend to agree with the Budapest critics, also considering the closing movement, which was written earlier, a more superficial and immature section than the slow movement.

The last, interesting stage in the career of the Sonata for Piano and Violin is connected with Bartók's first appearance in Paris. In 1905 Bartók entered the Rubinstein competition for pianists and composers. He achieved no success, partly due to a number of external circumstances. In a bitter letter he wrote: "And how they baited me! I was within an ace of being compelled to withdraw. They began by saying that the parts of the *Concertstück* were faulty, the piece was too difficult and could not be played because time was too short for rehearsals. I corrected the parts (there were 10 to 15 mistakes all told), and, after much wangling, it was finally played rather well, after all. As for the quintet, they declared flatly and categorically that it could not be learned, since there was not enough time. Luckily I happened to have the violin sonata handy (though actually, of course, it made no difference), and so we performed that. How long it took us to find a violinist!"[9]

The quintet mentioned in the letter is the Piano Quintet Bartók composed in 1904. This piece foreshadows the career of many later Bartók works: it was first performed abroad, not in Hungary. After the Vienna premire, the Grünfeld-Bürger String Quartet wanted to perform the work in Budapest, but due to its particular difficulty they were unable to learn it and played instead, with Bartók's participation, Schubert's "Trout" Quintet. The first Hungarian performance of the Piano Quintet on 21 November 1904, was finally undertaken by the

[8]*Pester Lloyd* (13 February 1904) by Theodor Helm in Demény 1954:389.
[9]To his mother, August 8th, 1905. *Bartók Letters* 1971:No.25.

Viennese Prill Quartet, but again this time the difficulty of the work almost ruined the concert. Bartók in a letter wrote, "the difficulty of my quintet gravely jeopardized the accomplishment of its first performance—but after all it still somehow came through. The audience liked it to the extent of 3 recalls. We twice in the last movement almost *umschmeiss*-ed."[10]

As far as the Viennese première is concerned, it is worth quoting Helm's review from the *Pester Lloyd*: "The eminent Viennese Prill String Quartet granted us a very interesting and impressive performance of a piano quintet, the latest chamber work by your talented compatriot Béla Bartók. The piano part was performed by the young composer himself, of course wonderfully. A consuming inner flame seems to burn in these notes, intense, bold, and demonic, which certainly sounded alien to some 'strictly conservative' ears. This genuine 'Sturm und Drang' work is by a real talent, which however still needs clarification, even so at no point does it repudiate its national origin, indeed, in the sobbing Adagio and the jubilating csárdás rhythm of the last movement, it vividly recalls the spirit of some of Liszt's rhapsodies."[11]

The Piano Quintet as a whole is a representative piece of Bartók's first creative period. Its more lasting value is also indicated by Bartók having included it in his composer's evening of 1910, alongside the *Bagatelles* and the String Quartet No.1. A large-scale composition, it consists of four movements: 1. Andante—Allegro, $\frac{4}{4}$, C major; 2. Vivace (Scherzando), $\frac{3}{4}$, F-sharp minor; 3. Adagio, $\frac{4}{4}$; 4. Vivace molto, $\frac{2}{4}$, C major. The four movements are not separate, nor are they linked *attaca*, but are composed organically in one. Here, as in several other features, one feels Liszt's influence stronger than even before. This is perhaps the first work in which Bartók's later general striving after formal unity becomes evident. Apart from the movements being joined together, this is shown in the use of a single, constantly recurring motto to act as a melodic frame marking the major formal sections. The whole work is introduced by this melody,

[10]To István Thomán, November 24th, 1904. Bartók Levelei 1976:no.82.
[11]*Pester Lloyd*, 26 November 1904 by Theodor Helm in Demény 1954:453.

with its characteriscally romantic, ascending gesture. These few bars do not serve to strengthen the tonality but rather to loosen it up, and only by the end of the introduction does it take on a definite form at the appearance of the movement's first subject.

From a thematic point of view the Piano Quintet is quite homogenous; the first and last movements are linked by their related Hungarian-style themes. A most important and typical feature is that in this early chamber work of Bartók we already catch sight of numerous formal concepts found in his later, great string quartets: the frame melody already mentioned, as well as the use of monothematic construction, linking the outer movements by varying the material. Another interesting feature similarly attests the unity of Bartók's oeuvre. As mentioned in connection with the String Quartet in F Major, the asymmetric rhythm of its Scherzos presages the later Bulgarian types of rhythm. This scherzo rhythm appears again here, in an almost unchanged form. It is worth quoting the two themes side by side (see Ex. 155 a, b). Their common characteristic is the juxtaposition of three even-numbered units and one odd-numbered unit (2+2+2+3). At that time Bartók had not yet arrived at the stage of writing down this rhythm as it really stands, using instead $\frac{3}{4}$ notation which is metrically the same but altered by the hemiola. All this however does not conceal the relationship of this rhythmic formula with No.5 of the "Six Dances in Bulgarian Rhythm" in *Mikrokosmos* (c).

Example 155.

It is therefore evident that specific novel asymmetric formulae were present in Bartók's rhythmic imagination very early on, whose development was later encouraged to a great extent by his discovery of similar occurrences in folk music.

The Piano Quintet is important chiefly in that it is the first piece to develop the national tone, a concept wholly relating to Liszt's national aspirations, and which thus binds the oeuvres of Liszt and Bartók into the closest continuity. In this the Piano Quintet does not stand alone, as the *Kossuth Symphony* shows a similar endeavour, not to mention the Rhapsody for piano op.1. But while the *Kossuth* is influenced predominantly by Richard Strauss, as evident from the orchestration, his chamber music with piano so far contains more directly the legacy of Liszt. No doubt this is the more superficial, brilliant side of Liszt, used on the surface to solve erroneously the problem of the music's Hungarian character. The young Bartók, however, who precisely in these years, 1903–4, arrived at the full development of his romantic patriotism (cf. his political statements, his ostentatious Hungarian national costume, and the writing-paper he used), inevitably identified with this more external, flamboyantly national tone. It was the road along which he had to travel so as to arrive at a recognition of Liszt's other, more profound side, and a more mature, intimate and true realization of his own national feeling.

CHAPTER EIGHT

THE FIRST STRING QUARTET

The compositional history of the writing of the First Quartet is closely connected with that of the posthumous Violin Concerto. Thus, although the year 1908 is generally stated in the literature as the quartet's date of composition, we can justifiably presume that various sketches for it dates back to 1907, and it assumed its final form in January of 1909. Clarification of these problems has chiefly been due to the work of Denijs Dille, who extracted the complete picture from various documents preserved in the Budapest Bartók Archives and from information obtained from Stefi Geyer.[1]

In the score of the Violin Concerto a note in Bartók's own hand shows that he began to compose the work on 1 July 1907, in Jászberény and finished it in Budapest on 5 February 1908; accompanying this information is yet another supplementary note in the score which indicates 28 June 1907, Jászberény, beside the humorous quotation of the children's song which begins "Der Esel ist ein dummes Tier." From Stefi Geyer we now know that this is a reference to the happy days spent in Jászberény when she and her brother entertained Bartók as a guest at the home of their Jászberény relatives. It was obviously at this time that the young composer fell in love with the young violinist and the two-movement Violin Concerto composed for Stefi Geyer became the direct expression of his feelings: the first movement is the portrait of the "young girl" and the second movement depicts the "violin virtuoso."

---

[1] Denijs Dille, "Angaben zum Violinkonzert 1906, den Deux Portraits, dem Quartett Op.7 und den zwei Rumänischen Tänzen," *Documenta Bartókiana* (1964), 92.

There is a manuscript preserved in the Budapest Bartók Archives on one side of which three themes from the Violin Concerto
are sketched in pencil, while on the other side there are four theme
sketches for the First Quartet, these latter written in ink. The violin
concerto sketches are accompanied by humorous drawings and notes
from which it can justifiably be concluded that they originated during
the happy time together in Jászberény. Although it is not certain, it
may nevertheless be supposed that the quartet sketches also date
from that time.

Actual composition of the work, however, began only in 1908,
presumably in February or March, at the time when the relationship
with Stefi Geyer came to an end. From the information obtained from
the violinist we know that Bartók wrote as follows in his last letter to
her: "I have begun a quartet; the first theme is the theme of the
second movement (that is, of the violin concerto): this is my funeral
dirge."

It is shown by the theme sketches mentioned above, which
presumably date from 1907, that at that time Bartók still intended to
construct the first movement from the introductory theme of the
second movement in the final form, and so the use of the Violin Concerto theme is a later idea which, according to the evidence in the letter, obviously finds its explanation in the breaking off of the
relationship. But from all this it does not follow that the second and
third movements of the final form were finished earlier than the first,
as Denijs Dille supposes. It is more probable that Bartók structured
the earlier theme sketches (which incidentally do not show that the
composer intended them for a string quartet) even in the course of
1908 into a conception in which the role of opening movement is
played by the slow polyphonic material with an altered version of the
theme taken from the Violin Concerto. Thus, this summarizes the
Violin Concerto since in its structure and character it related to the
first movement of the concerto, while its theme relates it to the
second movement. This was Bartók's first reaction to Stefi Geyer's
rejection and her finishing the relationship. (It should be noticed that
the second reaction, that is anger and caricature, became embodied
later in the "Grotesque" movement of the *Two Portraits*.)

Writing was interrupted in the summer of 1908 by lengthy tours abroad; in June he went to Germany, where he introduced the Fourteen Bagatelles to Busoni, and in July he went through Switzerland to the south of France. After the earlier visits to Paris in which his programme was very bound, this was now free roaming in the most beautiful parts of France, in the Haute Savoie and on the south coast. He wrote to Etelka Freund on 2 September 1908: "At last, via Lyon, Vienna, Valence and Avignon, I have reached the *non plus ultra* of my desires: the sea. It's only the little Mediterranean Sea, but a *sea* it is nevertheless. Now I'm in the village of Les Saintes Maries, not far from Arles. It's wonderful! I walked for 7 hours without meeting a soul. Here I have bathed in the sea for the first time, walked barefoot for the first time, and seen a mirage for the first time. For these three 'first time' it's been well worth making such a long detour" (*Bartók Letters* 1971:91).

A true complement to this tour was provided in the autumn of the same year by a trip to Transylvania and concerning the joyous discoveries he made there he wrote as follows to Irma Freund: "Yesterday I went along the Torda Gorge; today I'm making merry at Torockó below Székelykő. In some ways this famous Székelykő reminds me of the Grand Salève, except that there's no *funiculaire* here! Of all the villages in Hungary which I've visited so far, this one is certainly the most beautifully situated" (*Bartók Letters* 1971:92). It can be assumed, therefore, that he continued writing the string quartet when he returned from this journey at the end of 1908, and according to the note in his own hand in the "Stichvorlage" sent to the Rózsavölgyi company, he completed it on 27 January 1909. This is also supported by the postcard he wrote to Etelka Freund on 28 January 1909. "I am happy to announce that the quartet got itself finished yesterday and would be pleased to visit you on Saturday evening (in my company). Would you be kind enough to receive it. If not, then perhaps on Sunday, after lunch . . ." (*Bartók Letters* 1971:94).

This jocular announcement was thus probably followed by a performance before a close circle of friends—for the time being, only on the piano. It can be assumed that had an immediate success, for the

Waldbauer-Kerpely String Quartet, consisting of young artists, began
studying the work in that very year.

The "Stichvorlage" preserved in the Budapest Bartók Archives
offers a few important details concerning the gradual evolution of the
work's final form. The score is in an unknown hand, Bartók in all
probability having had it copied by someone, and later he introduced
some alterations to this copy. The central section of the first movement was originally five bars longer, but the composer erased the last
five bars and this is how the form evolved in which, after the colour
chords appearing at figure **10**, a caesura leads to the return of the
theme—now an octave higher.

Evidence of the gradual development of the special connection
between the first and second movements can be seen in that Bartók
had the copyist leave this part empty (the first fourteen bars of the
second movement) and only wrote in the final solution during correction of the finished copy. This detail is all the more interesting since
the material of this part, the "winding theme" moving in parallel
thirds, had already appeared among the very first thematic sketches. Is
it possible, therefore, that the composer originally imagined the join
between the two themes in a different way? Or is Denijs Dille's
hypothesis concerning the reversed order of writing true after all?

Another correction is also instructive: in the section between
figures **17** and **20** in the second movement Bartók erased an earlier
version which did not contain the great dramatic tension of the final
form. A further point which concerns the evolution of the final version of the First Quartet is that in 1931 Bartók adjusted the
metronome indications given in 1909 and printed in the first
Rózsavölgyi edition. For on 19 October 1931, Max Rostal, the English
violinist and quartet leader, wrote to Bartók concerning the correct
tempi of the work (*Documenta Bartókiana* 1968:164). Bartók replied
in his letter of 6 November. ". . . I am very sorry that I haven't been
able to reply earlier in order to be able to do so I had to study
thoroughly the tempo and MM signs, especially of the First Quartet,
and I've only now found the necessary time. Let's hope you will have
an opportunity to play the works in other places, too, so that when
you do so, you will be able to consider the contents of this letter, but

perhaps it won't reach you in time. Quartet I. In the first movement, the MM sign is indeed quite impossible and incomprehensible, and in the 3rd movement, too, I find many misplaced MM figures. I should add at this point that in my early works MM signs are very often inexact, or rather they do not correspond to the correct tempo. The only explanation I can think of is that I metronomized too hastily at the time, and perhaps my metronome was working imperfectly. I have phonogrammes made 20 years ago of some of my piano pieces played by myself and they show that I play them today in exactly the same tempo as I did then. Now I use a balance metronome which, of course, cannot show any considerable differences from the correct oscillation number. Let me give you all the tempi exactly" (*Bartók Letters* 1971:217–18).

After the work was completed more than a year passed before Bartók's First Quartet was given a performance. The première was given in the programme of Bartók's first composer's evening in the Royal concert hall on 19 March 1910. This was a memorable date in the history of Hungarian music: Bartók's composer's evening was preceded two days earlier by a similar introductory concert by Kodály. These two closely connected concerts were like the unfurling of the flag of new Hungarian music.

At his composer's evening Bartók himself played a series of his piano pieces, and alongside these the Piano Quintet dating from 1904 and the First Quartet were also performed. A large part in the success of the concert was played by the extraordinarily talented young Waldbauer Quartet, who from this time onwards became permanent and perhaps the most devoted interpreters of Bartók's chamber music.

To judge the significance of this introductory concert it is absolutely necessary for us to look into the contemporary criticism which, quite typically, contains the two basic ways of receiving Bartók: the rejection of conservatism, and approval and enthusiasm which does not yet fully "understand" but rather "feels" in advance and has favourable presentiments. Thanks to the investigations carried out by János Demény, we have before us today a virtually complete documentation of the criticism of both concerts (Demény 1955).

Those critics who, around 1903 and 1905, had celebrated the "true Hungarian national genius" in Bartók after the arrogant nationalism of the Millennium, now gave expression to their disappointment. For by this time the shouting emphatic Hungarian quality, the romantic way of being Hungarian, had disappeared from Bartók's music and was replaced by a more refined Hungarian tone which strove towards the essence of the matter. This, however, was naturally not noticed by the critics—*could* not have been noticed by them since the basis of it was the area of folk art which was just then being discovered in the course of Kodály's and Bartók's first journeys in the interests of investigating folk music.

Of the newspaper criticisms, perhaps it was only the opinion of the *Népszava* which approached Bartók's string quartet with sympathy and understanding. The article, although it is not signed, was probably written by Béla Reinitz, later to become Bartók's enthusiastic devotee and friend. The critic does not stand unequivocally beside Bartók; he has indeed numerous objections to the quartet, but his tone is free from all preconceived ideas, and what is most important, he makes no attempt to pit the earlier Piano Quintet against the new tone of the string quartet.

Two more lengthy essay-type pieces appeared on Bartók's quartet, both in periodicals. One was Sándor Kovács's study in the periodical *Renaissance* under the title "Socialist Music" (Demény 1955:373–74). With a somewhat simplifying method, it is true, the writer does, however, establish well-intentioned aesthetic and sociological parallels between the polyphony of Bartók's music and the democracy of the society of the future. The other large study, by Antal Molnár, was published in the columns of the *Zeneközlöny* (*Music Gazette*) about a year after the first performance.[2] Antal Molnár, who was at that time the viola player in the Waldbauer Quartet, wrote *from within* concerning the work, with more authority than any critic, uniting as he did in himself the active musician's ability to perceive with the professional knowledge and objective perspective of the scholarly composer-musicologist. At the same time, complete identity with the composer and the ability to enter a conceptual alliance with him can be read in the lines of his study.

[2]*Zeneközlöny* IX, 1911.

First movement: Lento

Before the analysis of the first movement, a very important motivic relationship between the Violin Concerto composed for Stefi Geyer and the string quartet should be taken into consideration. In the Bartók literature it is a commonplace that in the early compositions a broken seventh chord plays an important role. This is the so-called "Stefi Geyer Leitmotiv" mentioned in a letter of 11 September 1907 (*Bartók Letters* 1971:No. 42), used as a first subject in the first movement of the Violin Concerto (Portrait No. 1, "The Ideal"). It is not difficult to recognize that the second movement of the Concerto is based on the same pattern in a different order of notes; furthermore that this version is in close relationship with the beginning of the string quartet.

Example 156.

That is why we can assert that the very slow first movement of the First Quartet is the concentrate of the violin concerto in a dual sense. While the outline of its opening theme is clearly related to the theme of the concerto's second movement, the slow tempo, polyphonic texture and sensitively romantic harmonic construction link it to the first, "Ideal" movement of the concerto. These are the two slow movements in which the young Bartók came closest to a yearning and resigned musical tone, which was inspired by reading Nietzsche and Schopenhauer, and aptly expressed in the sensitive harmony and meandering melodic writing. Under such influence it was natural that the composer should express his passionate affection with the same musical character as his torment, resignation and longing for death. Musically, his direct model was Wagner; in fact, the beginning of the quartet's first movement can be taken as a kind of counterpart to the *Tristan* prelude (with an upward sixth in the latter and a downward sixth in the former). Bartók's youthful enthusiasm for Wagner had by this time found its way into his compositions.

The first movement also shows signs of other influences. Its imitative counterpoint echoes Beethoven, especially the fugue-like opening of his String Quartet in C-sharp Minor, Op. 131.[3] At first the slowly unfolding imitative structure suggests a fugue in Bartók's piece, too, but it later becomes clear that an individual solution has been found: the parts entwine in closely knit pairs. In this counterpoint both the Bachian archetype and the direct example of Beethoven fade into the background; the parts interlace like the winding ornaments best resembling the trailing plants typical of the new style in fine art. If anything exists that can be labelled musical *art nouveau*, then Bartók's first quartet is surely one of the best examples. In it ornamentation becomes content.

In examining the fugal technique of the First String Quartet we can take the fugue theme and fugal structure first: the question of form will in any case be discussed separately. A special technique is in evidence above all in that the four parts do not enter at equal distances from each other in time as in the majority of fugues, but two at a time in stretto.

The two pairs of parts correspond to one another in no more than a unit of five notes (that is, with minor deviations, to which we shall return later); the following part would thus—on the basis of strict fugal structure principles—be a codetta leading to the next entrance. This explanation, however, obviously does not work: at most it is possible to call the three bars before the entry of the third and fourth parts (cello-viola) a codetta, a tail-piece. The characteristic method of the fugue, therefore, lies in that the two upper and two lower parts are closely connected to each other—it is two parts together that provide the so-called "fugue theme." We might even simply call it a double fugue in which the countersubject is a transposed imitation of the subject (there are examples of this in Bach, too).

[3]See also chapter 1, "The Legacy of Beethoven," in Part One.

The two parts are so closely related, both melodically and har-
monically that to imagine them having independent lives is virtually
impossible. The motif consisting of a downward sixth and a fifth which
turns back on this is a melodic unit more or less complete in itself, a
characteristic type in Wagnerian and late Romantic melody, but it is
self-evident in connection with this late Romantic character that
without a harmonic context it is somewhat meagre. The mature art of
the young Bartók is characterized by the way in which he weaves the
two melodies into one another, and through the stretto entry constructs what amounts to another opening motif.

The tense seventh chord is, incidentally, an important element in
the theme: after the entry it appears three more times, on different
degrees, forming tonal islands in the wavering tonality. This interlinking of the component parts of the seventh chord, on the other hand,
draws attention to how much the two parts, with regard to their position, are composed in one; the "space" between the larger melodic
leaps is consistently filled out by the other voice. This is how Bartók's
inclination towards complementary structures makes an appearance
even here, in a late Romantic setting. And the "inexact" imitation of
the downward sixth is explained by the harmonic demands of the
structure: the first violin's F–A-flat motif is answered not by C–E-flat
but by C–E, which ensures principally the tension of the F minor
seventh chord, and also makes it possible for the ascending fifth G–D
to be answered not by the neutral fifth D–A but by the melodic leap E
flat–B flat which produces a new seventh chord.[4]

The fugue subject is thus a combined texture composed of the
two voices, over four bars; after the imitation of the first motif of five
notes the free counterpoint which follows also enters with thematic
claims: here the material consists of descending fifths and small cambiata figures. The contrapuntal character of the two parts ends in the
fifth bar and changes gradually over to parallel movement. This is
really a codetta; the two lower part take over only three bars without
any alteration, and then the movement of the parts becomes free,

---

[4]For the other explanation of the "inexact imitation" see chapter 6, "Tonality," in Part
One.

preparing the way for a new formal section. It should be noted that the roles of the two lower parts interchange in an interesting way: the cello plays the first violin's part, which means the cello moves in a higher register than the viola.

That Bartók was by no means striving after the revival of Baroque fugue form here is indicated by the small syncopated motif which comes into the foreground after the fuga exposition being made to appear as a secondary theme, and by the disappearance of the contrapuntal nature of the structure. The varied development of the small sighing syncopated motif makes a formal middle section which is followed at figure 5 by the reminiscent return of the fugue theme: neither the whole theme nor the accompanying contrapuntal texture returns, only the characteristic sixth leap bending downwards, embedded in harmonic blocks. Here the two important motifs join forces: the sigh motif gives a direct answer to the gesticular sixth-motif of the fugue theme.

A sharp formal cut is produced by the sudden break in the upward moving fabric of the three upper voices. A trio section follows which is evolved from the uniting of two motifs there in a passionate, occasionally interrupted rubato melody (viola, joined later by the second violin) which is developed from the rhythm of the sigh motif above a fifth organ point on C–G; meanwhile, above this there is a thin violin melody flying in a strongly contrasting high register. The trio itself is also in three parts; in the central section some typically French chordal sequences appear, strongly reminding one of Ravel's *Ma mère l'oye* (Stevens 1964:174), yet this possible model was only being composed at this time and Bartók could not have known it. Another surprising aspect is that these Ravelian chords are played above a typical cello melody *à la Kodály*.[5] The last two bars of the trio round off the section with a poetic sound effect and this leads back to the fugue theme; each component of the B-flat major triad is coloured by adjacent notes—the B flat by A, the D by C-sharp and the F by G-flat.[6]

---

[5]For further explanation see chapter 2, "Forerunners and Contemporaries," in Part One.

[6]See chapter 5, "Polymodal Chromaticism," in Part One.

The trio breaks off just as suddenly and remains as open as the section which introduced it. Leading note relationship is, however, present in both: in the former the lowest part moves from C sharp to C, the keynote of the trio, and in the latter the E in the highest part leads to F, the opening note of the returning fugue theme. Thus even here one characteristic method of Bartók's later form structuring is already present: the sharp cut which does nevertheless connect organically interrelated sections by invisible threads.

The recapitulation which starts at figure **11** recalls the two-part texture from the beginning of the movement an octave higher but note for note (only the codetta becomes shortened to one bar), but the entrance of the two lower parts is merely hinted at for a single bar. After that the central part of the first section is replaced by six bars of polyphonic texture with a rising tendency, and still later the rounding off motif is also presented in a condensed form: the four note downward sixth phrase returns in a harmonized form, alluding to the same chords as those after figure **5**—that is, A, F-sharp, E-flat, and C. There is, however, an essential transformation in that the downward sixth motif here takes a major form throughout (A–C-sharp, F-sharp–A-sharp, E-flat–G, C–E). This transformation to the major is nevertheless present only on the melodic level, for the chords below the individual notes are mostly minor in content. This minor character is reinforced by the five bar coda following it, which in both its tonality and in certain fragments of its melody recalls the opening of the movement; but instead of F minor it is A-flat minor which dominates.

The key to the deliberate tonal ambiguity of the movement is to be found in the augmented triad consisting of the notes E–A-flat–C. The two sixths heard at the beginning of the movement—as has already been pointed out—produce a chord which is the third inversion of F minor seventh. The E–A-flat–C augmented triad is present here, too, but the note F quite unequivocally determines its tonal affiliation. In the fifth bar before the end of the movement this characteristic augmented triad is heard once more (supplemented by the degrees of a whole-tone scale), but its tonal tendency is determined by the very next bar: it resolves onto A-flat minor. It is not insignificant that on this occasion Bartók writes the E as F-flat, by which he expresses the tendency to resolve onto E-flat.

Example 157.

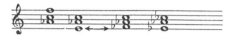

On the basis of all this it can be taken that the movement is tonally determined by F minor–A-flat minor duality, and not founded on the relative key relationship as later is the case with the D minor–F major of the Sixth Quartet, but through the centrality and tonal ambiguity of the augmented triad mentioned.[7]

Second movement: Allegretto

The attacca connection between the first two movements is a somewhat external point. If we are to believe Denijs Dille's assumption, maybe Bartók wished in some way to compensate for the fact that he added the first movement later to the already finished second and third movements. He brought about the combination with particular care, partly motivically and partly by the gradual acceleration of the tempo.

This writing of two movements as one, however, is likewise a reference to Beethoven's C-sharp Minor Quartet: there, too, the C-sharp minor first movement is closely connected to the D major second movement. This structuring of the movements in one is a typical romantic phenomenon which in fact disappears from Bartók's later string quartets, with the exception of the third. In the Piano Quintet preceding the First Quartet, however, we find similar form-building methods.

The structure of the whole movement is characterized by organic writing taken virtually to extremes, just like the majority of later

---

[7]Tonal ambiguity is largely discussed by Gow 1963:260. It is worth mentioning furthermore that one of Anton Webern's early work, the *Langsamer Satz* composed in 1905 for string quartet, similarly moves within a relative key framework: it begins in C minor and ends in E-flat major.

romantic works: the chamber works of César Franck, Reger's string quartets, or Schoenberg's First and Second String Quartets. And so, although the outlines of classical sonata form can clearly be recognized, every single detail of the movement is pervaded by one of the few thematic or motivic ideas which are taken as a basis.[8] In spite of even the functionally static exposition being more dynamic, more development-like, with Bartók than with earlier masters, orientation in the formal construction of the movement is provided clearly by the relative dynamics of the music.

At the beginning of the exposition a winding melody appears, arranged in consistent parallel thirds. It is only later that it becomes clear, however, that although this theme stands at the start of the first group of themes, it is to be regarded rather as a framework theme which has a smaller share in the movement's thematic work than those which follow it. The role of the first subject is thus filled by the motif which is heard after figure 1 in the second violin, accompanied by the first violin's ostinato figure. This drooping gesture, just like the majority of the melodic elements in the movement, represents the late-romantic amorphic melodic type: somewhat asymmetrical, tonally indecisive and open at almost every point, easy to break up into parts and fit in elsewhere.

At figure 3 transitional material begins which, with the help of a little rhythmic element, leads organically into the second subject at figure 6. As regards texture, this theme comes very close to the former; it is heard in the middle parts while the outer parts accompany with an ostinato motif. As opposed to the warm expressive theme, the closing theme consists of cold whole-tone scale motifs above knocking, drum-like pizzicato on the cello (9). The appearance of the closing theme, however, presents no barrier to the reappearance the earlier second subject (at 10), which is very typical of this late romantic structure. The return of the framework theme shows that the exposition reaches a conclusion at 11 and the development section begins.

---

[8]More detailed analysis see in chapter 4, "Monothematicism and Variation" in Part One.

After the considerably dynamic exposition the development holds even further dynamism. In the first part of the variational-dissecting development process the first subject and its accompanying motif play the leading role, while later (at **20**) the second subject becomes the centre of the thematic work. After an organically developed process of leading back, it is the framework theme which recapitulates first—indeed, it is displayed more broadly here than anywhere else in the movement. And after figure **28**, at the Poco sostenuto, the drooping gesture of the first subject also returns—accompanied by the scale motif familiar from the closing material. This dense combination of the first subject and second subject material is a typically Bartókian technique: a beautiful example of the abbreviated recapitulation later to become even more frequent. The recapitulation is also more concise on this occasion because the second subject, which played such a large part in the development, is now omitted. The coda gives the framework motif one further hearing but in augmented rhythm, in high position on the two violins, above a softly resonant accompaniment.

The tonality of the movement is not completely unambiguous here either, although the B major closing chord leaves one in less doubt than the A-flat minor ending of the first movement. The framework function of B major does in any case become clear from the fact that at the beginning of the movement the half closes of the framework theme, always remaining open—A-sharp–C-sharp, F-sharp–A-sharp, C-sharp–E- sharp—represent an unstated B tonality. This is later borne out by the framework theme's second appearance at the end of the exposition; the winding parallel thirds resolve in C-flat major (fifth bar after figure **11**), which is obviously the enharmonic notation of B major and is justified only by what precedes it. The third appearance of the framework theme presents a C-sharp minor resolution at the border between the development and the recapitulation, but this is obviously an interrupted cadence. Its fourth occurrence is once more unambiguous: the coda closing in the already mentioned B major.

It is understandable that it is only by the appearance of the framework theme that it is possible to expose the tonal structure of the movement. The other themes are indeed considerably uncertain as to their tonality. The drooping motif of the first subject contains no tonal character whatsoever—at most, the accompanying ostinato points towards F-sharp tonality. The second subject's tonality floats likewise; here, too, it is only the accompanying ostinato that forms a relatively firm framework (E-flat). And the closing theme is constructed from a whole-tone series, and it is only the repeated notes of the cello's pizzicato motif (D-sharp and C) which offer any tonal basis. In the recapitulation the first subject returns in C-sharp instead of F sharp, while the closing theme comes with F-sharp and D-sharp as points of support. Even though all this does not follow the customary arrangement of keys of the sonata strictly, it can be fitted into the B major framework of the movement.

Third movement: Introduzione — Allegro Vivace

The final movement of the quartet is preceded by an introduction, which forms a bridge in terms of both tone and character. The main source of its material is a solitary *recitativo* melody, again reminiscent of Beethoven's procedure in quartet writing (this time A minor, Op. 132) with a short recitative introduction to its final movement. Bartók's cello recitative melody, however, is of a typically Hungarian character, recalling the well-known nineteenth-century art song "Just a Fair Girl" by Elemér Szentirmai.[9] It might seem odd that here Bartók practically quotes a popular art song, especially as by this time he had embarked upon his folksong collecting tours in Transylvania. One possible explanation is a bent for programme-like references and travesty, techniques which were not alien to Bartók's compositional method.[10] But there is another explanation, too. If the quartet is the musical outcome of Bartók's "recovery" from the crisis of his love for Stefi Geyer, then it can be assumed that the reference to "Just a Fair Girl" in the strange dialogue of the Introduzione carries mocking, parodic overtones. Writing in 1918, Kodály described

[9]See chapter 3, "The Folk Music Influence," in Part One.

[10]Similar references to art song are found in the Violin Concerto ("Der Esel ist ein Dummes Tier") and Concerto for Orchestra ("You are beautiful, you are wonderful, Hungary").

this quartet as a *retour à la vie*.[11] He would hardly have been referring just to the gradually accelerating tempo of the three movements, but rather felt, or even knew, that they traced the road of recovery from the crisis of the "funeral dirge."

The cello monologue of the Introduzione is continued by a violin monologue, its lonely melody climbing up into the highest regions of the instrument and there fading out. After this the actual movement itself begins, with a decisive, energetic theme under repeated organ point. The theme consists of two parts which are organically connected and yet quite clearly separate: the first part is a closed, emblem-like motif heard twice, closly akin to the first subject of the second movement, and the second part, a melody in Hungarian folk rhythm, is developed from the first:

Example 158.

With the exception of one single episode-melody the thematic material of the whole movement is developed from these two elements of the principal theme. The first section—we can call it the first subject group—uses the first element, and indeed in two different characters: from figure **4** as a light, scherzo mood, and from **7** its hard, emblem-like nature emphasized. Here, in the shape of a small motif of willful character, some new material slipped in, which plays an important part in Bartók's oeuvre; it also appears in no. 83 *Mikrokosmos* and in the *Music for Strings, Percussion and Celesta*. Strictly speaking, not even this is "new" material since it is related to the first subject of the preceding movement, too.

---

[11]Zoltán Kodály, "Bartók Béla II. vonósnégyese" ["Béla Bartók's Second String Quartet"], *Nyugat* XI (1918).

Example 159.

The whole of the second half of the exposition is filled with the second subject, syncopated and in folk rhythm, developed from the second element of the theme, and here, too, some new material is slipped in—an Adagio melody with a strongly folk character (figure 11). This melody, coming close to pentatony, is incidentally one of the first signs that at this stage, the more ancient forms of Hungarian folk music had already exerted some influence over Bartók.[12] The syncopated fast theme and the adagio melody together form the movement's so-called second subject group. The closing subject is evolved from the syncopated rhythm.

The development section begins at figure **14** and mainly makes use of the first element of the first subject. After a calm, ironically commonplace variation, a scherzando-grazioso fugato is rolled off as the centre of gravity of the development, as it were. The carefree tone almost changes, as later so often with Bartók, to hard, deadly sarcasm. Attraction between similar characters is displayed in that the sarcastic tone of the fugato is followed by the likewise sarcastic tone of the "willful" theme, and it is only then that the recapitulation begins (at

[12]See chapter 3, "The Folk Music Influence," in Part One.

28). The basic tone of the recapitulation is now influenced by the tension of the development: the extreme tension extends into this section, too.

Like that of the preceding movement, the structure of this movement is also characterized by all the thematic material being, so to speak, on the surface all the time, and since all the elements are organically related to one another, their appearance is understandable at virtually every point in the musical development. It must nevertheless be added that this technique is later present in only the second of Bartók's quartets, and after that it almost completely disappears. Organic structuring later becomes associated with greater economy and stricter formal discipline.

On this occasion, too, it is the outer points which help to clarify the tonal structure. The repetition of E at the beginning of the movement and the banal A major cadence in the bar before figure 1 together with the A fifth-chord at the end of the movement ensure an unambiguous tonal framework. Within this, the first part of the first subject is considerably uncertain as to tonality; in the folksong theme it is at most the first note that provides the tonal point of support (B-flat in the exposition, A in the recapitulation), while the syncopated theme is ambiguous—melodically it moves around a C-sharp centre (at figure 12—that is, in the exposition), whereas on the basis of its harmony it represents an F-sharp minor tonality. This is transposed in the recapitulation to F-sharp and B minor respectively. The tonal accompaniment of the coda is very characteristic: the tonality of A has become more or less established when it is suddenly changed by the repetition of B-flat, generally speaking creating the same sort of impression as the weighty subdominant stretch at the end of baroque works, after which the return to the basic key is even more effective. But here this B-flat introduces a whole-tone scale which, extending from B-flat to G-sharp, has a sort of dominant effect and, like leading note steps progressing upwards and downwards simultaneously, prepares for resolution on to A.

Example 160.

The final chord places two fifths on top of one another which indicates on the one hand that the specificity of the tonality (major or minor) remains open, and on the other hand that the second fifth (E–B) does not detract from the determinative tonal strength of the fundamental note (A). This reveals that the *retour à la vie* symbolizes not only a personal recovery but also a compositional transformation: the post-Wagnerian Bartók of the first movement gives way to a colder, harder, "twentieth-century" Bartók by the end of the composition.

CHAPTER NINE

THE SECOND STRING QUARTET

There is little information concerning the origins of the work. Very wide limits are indicated by the composer's dating noted at the end of the score: "1915–1917." At this time Bartók lived in Rákoskeresztúry (a suburb of Budapest) and the general worries of the war-torn world made his life difficult. Perhaps these external circumstances also contributed to the writing being protracted over such a long period; during this long time Bartók was obviously compelled to stop working on several occasions.

There is evidence of this vexed life in a letter Bartók wrote to his mother on 16 September 1916. "The following 'official' announcement arrived yesterday (the 14th) about Márta in Szalonta: they have set out from Vásárhely together with three companies of soldiers, the soldiers on foot, with them in cars and on carts. One can imagine they are now progressing slowly but at least in safety, and that they are now on this side of Kolozsvár (this is also in the official news). In other words they are moving under permanent armed guard. Now that I know this I almost envy them; it might be quite an entertaining business taking an active part like that in one of the minor scenes of the war . . . But it's fortunate that with the help of the lieutenant general dignitary we can get news of the various stages of their 'flight'. It would be wretched to be in complete uncertainty for so long!"[1]

---

[1]János Demény, *Bartók Béla levelei. Szerk.* (Budapest: Zeneműkiadó, 1976), no. 338. "Lieutnant general dignitary" is a reference to his father-in-law, Károly Ziegler.

It is obviously to these vicissitudes that this remark refers in a later statement by Bartók: "I went through a great deal of excitement."[2] But we also know that in spite of everything he did work during the war years, indeed a surprising number of compositions came from his pen then. "I have even found the time—and ability—to do some composing: it seems that the Muses are not silent in modern war," he wrote in 1915 to his Transylvanian friend, János Busiţia (*Bartók Letters* No. 99). In this period, the Sonatina, the *Rumanian Folk Dances* for piano and the two series of *Rumanian Christmas Songs (Colindas)* were written, and then he began work on the Five Songs of op. 15, but by the spring of 1916 he finished not only these five but also a further Five Songs written to poems by Endre Ady (op. 16), and composed one of his most significant piano works, the Suite, op. 14. Besides all this, two large-scale works were also in preparation in parallel—the Second String Quartet and, from 1914 to 1916, *The Wooden Prince*.

In connection with the creation of the Second Quartet, important information is offered by an interesting document which is rare in Bartók research; from the estate of Zoltán Kodály the Budapest Bartók Archives obtained a two-page sketch in pen and pencil which contains, with the exception of the last seventeen bars, a rough draft of the third movement of the quartet. There is no date on it and it is impossible even to presume during which part of the known period of composition (1915–17) it was actually put to paper.[3] On another, fuller sketch preserved in the New York Bartók Archives the date of completion is given: "Oct. 1917."

The Budapest Bartók Archives' draft conceals valuable information concerning Bartók's method of composition: the draft contains the material of the third movement of the work virtually in its final form, and where it is incomplete, the composer left precisely the

---

[2]"A szerző a darabjáról" ["The Composer on His Piece, Béla Bartók's statement on *The Wooden Prince* on the occasion of the première], *Magyar Színpad* 12 May 1917. Published in Demény 1959:29–30.

[3]Vera Lampert, "Vázlat Bartók II. vonósnégyesének utolsó tételéhez" ["A Draft for the Last Movement of Bartók's Second String Quartet"], *Magyar Zene* XIII (1972) 252–63.

amount of space (bars 43–49) into which the appropriate part of the completed composition fits —that is, when he put the draft to paper Bartók already had the musical process of the whole movement in his mind. It can also be noticed that it is primarily the thematic sections which crystallized in his imagination, so it is chiefly the connecting material which is incomplete.

Just as with the First Quartet, the final tempo indications for the Second Quartet came only later. The history of the alteration of the tempo indications is briefly as follows. In 1935 André Gertler turned to Bartók requesting him to write a brief analysis of the Second Quartet and to re-examine the metronome indications in the work (*Documenta Bartókiana* 1968:183–84). In answer to Gertler's prompting letter, Bartók wrote on 31 January 1936: "Now at last I can send you a list of corrections to the metronome numbers. Unfortunately, however, I cannot undertake a detailed written analysis of the form; there is in any case nothing special in the form. The first movement is a normal sonata form; the second is a kind of rondo with a development-type section in the middle; the last movement is the most difficult to define—in the last analysis it is some kind of augmented ABA form" (*Bartók levelei* 1976:no.781) The list of corrections enclosed was published in 1948 by István Barna, with André Gertler's permission; in the more recent scores and parts from Universal Edition it is these corrected metronome indications which appear.

The first performance of the Second Quartet was given on 3 March 1918, at a concert by the Waldbauer-Kerpely Quartet. This ensemble, that had also introduced Bartók's First Quartet in 1910, also carried the Second Quartet to success, and from then onwards performed Bartók's chamber music all over the world more and more intensively. Bartók knew the talents of the group and he composed the Second Quartet expressly for them—it is also dedicated to them. Thus Bartók's compositional activity became interwoven with the activities of this excellent group; this relationship remained close in later years as well, although by then several other world-famous quartets had undertaken performances of Bartók's works.

Bartók's new string quartet was given a more unified reception than the first. Even the opposing or restrained critics were much more respectful than in 1910. János Hammerschlag's criticism in German in the columns of the *Pester Lloyd*, for example, doubts the genre characteristics of the quartet, meanwhile paying great respect (Demény 1959:76). A less technical and analytical but generally more enthusiastic account of the work was written by Béla Reinitz, who also remarked how Bartók's chamber music had become one with the group of talented young musicians (Demény 1959:75). But on this occasion the finest and most in-depth account was written by Zoltán Kodály in the periodical *Nyugat*, going beyond the limits of the simple concert criticism, making a comrade-in-arms statement, as it were.[4]

First movement: Moderato

The movement's first subject is heard above a harmonic accompaniment in a swaying rhythm. It is sensitive, a true violin melody, and the similarity of its character to some melodies of the two Sonatas for violin and piano written a few years later is very striking. The first two bars are a real foundation for the whole movement: the ornamental element running upwards in fourths appears as an important motif in the course of what follows (a); the three-note unit following this (b) provides the material for the development section; and the arching 1:5 model (D–C-sharp–G-sharp–G) takes on importance when the principal theme appears in the recapitulation (c).

Example 161.

Once the six-bar unit of the first subject is completed, motivic work commences immediately, using the first opening motif (a) : the "Auftakt" motif consisting of two fourths begins to expand, and indeed with great rapidity. At figure **2**, the first violin part is already moving over a range of three octaves. The first tension is followed by a quick calming: the "Auftakt" motif is tamed within the limits of an octave

[4]"Bartók Béla II. vonósnégyese" ["Béla Bartók's Second String Quartet"], *Nyugat* XI (1918). Quoted by Demény 1959:76.

and is extended in the course of imitative playing by a new descending element. It is typical of the organic writing of the movement that this triplet extension (it might also be called a variation) of the first subject later becomes joined to the secondary theme starting at figure **5**.

The second subject, formed from a single augmented triad, leads through a long chromatic transition to the calmingly closed final theme which is periodic in structure. Once again it is organic structure that is indicated by the fact that the minor trichord motif from which the final theme is formed has already appeared in the chromatic transition section.

The development section (at figure **10**) begins with a motivic transformation of the characteristic opening motif, but the real tension of this formal section is created when the three-note unit (b) from the first subject becomes an independent motif.

It is real virtuosity in Bartók's development technique that after this extraordinarily dynamic exposition he can increase this dynamism even further in the development. Accompanied by the dense parallel third movement of the inner parts, the two outer parts stretch out the motif in a varied form to its most expansive form. This dramatic climax is followed by a slower sostenuto section. The second violin rises above a block of augmented fourth chords with a repeated-note melody with a lament character, into the end of which is built the varied motif. This sort of passionate lament interpretation on repeated-note melody is borne out by several analogous melodies from *Bluebeard's Castle* and *The Wooden Prince*.

After the sostenuto section—although the volume diminishes— we come to another melodic climax; then the parts, closely intertwining, fall back and grow quiet. This line which calms down and becomes smoothed out is also emphasized by the clarification of chromaticism into pentatony.

The quieter, more relaxed tone is continued by the recapitulation: the opening motif returns unchanged but its continuation is somewhat modified. In place of the chromatic descending melodic line, outwardly calm but inwardly tense, comes a melody in a swaying rhythm, waving upwards and downwards in a 1:5 model. The gentle arches outlined by its melodic line—by a certain inner emotional in-

tensification—become more and more heated. The individual swelling
of the melodic arches reminds one of the quartet's most directly related compositions, the Suite for piano.

Example 162.

After an abbreviated recapitulation of the second subject it is surprising to find the first subject coming into the foreground once more—to
be precise, the motivic development of the "Auftakt" thematic motif,
but in a transitional function. After a general pause the final theme's
minor trichord appears—unisono—in a weighty, emblem-like form.
(Does this in some way replace the long transition developed from
the minor trichord in the exposition?) The whole final theme period
returns in a more relaxed, quieter character, also changed melodically,
the two violins playing the melody in parallel octaves while the cello
accompanies them with harp-like pizzicato chords.

In the coda of the movement there is a detail which is typical of
Bartók's instrumental "dramaturgy": it turns out that the first subject
and the final theme, which so far have been set in contrast with each
other, are actually related. Bartók "unmasks" the thematic work here
when he begins gradually to expand the dolce theme, which covers a
range of a minor third, and suddenly there it is before us—the opening motif of the first subject has developed from it.

Example 163.

The coda, however, not only unmasks but also summarizes: with Wagnerian technique all the thematic material of the movement is used on top of each other: initially the first subject and the second subject (five bars after figure **21**), then in the last seven bars the second subject and the final theme.

One may try to analyse the movement's considerably ambiguous tonal structure by considering the final theme, that being the only definite tonal focal point. But even this periodically closed theme conceals some tonal ambiguity, for its harmony does not coincide with the tonality which is naturally to be felt from its melody. The melody's keynote, which is reinforced by the period's imperfect cadence—perfect cadence relationship, is C-sharp in the exposition, and A in the recapitulation. But Bartók interpreted this melodic keynote as a fifth, and in the exposition he harmonized the C-sharp based melody in F-sharp minor.[5] This is modified to a certain extent in the recapitulation when the melody's A minor trichord is accompanied by A major harmonies; but in the last analysis the inner contradiction mentioned above evolves here, too, when a final D major chord is attached to the melody ending in A.

The phenomenon is naturally by no means extraordinary. Even among Bach's chorales we can find melodies given harmonies which can be interpreted in different ways. With Bartók this happens even more naturally since the modal principle stemming from the melody is

[5]See chapter 6, "Tonality" in Part One.

almost always obliged to join forces with the tonality systems originating in European traditions. There is no reason for us to lay emphasis in a mechanical way on either element in this tonal duality. We have to accept the ambiguity which goes with it: in the exposition the final theme is in C-sharp and F-sharp tonality, and in the recapitulation it is in A and D.

With the second subject the source of the ambiguity is the augmented triad. Here, however, the matter is settled more unequivocally by the chords used in conjunction with it: in the exposition F-sharp minor is built under the augmented triad as a tonal basis, and in the recapitulation this tonal basis is D major. The agreement between this and the harmonic level of the final theme is not to be neglected; it indicates that the movement's harmonic profile, coming close to late romanticism, is a homogeneous unit. But even though the tonal traditions of sonata structure would permit us to do so, we can scarcely conclude from this that we should regard the tonality of the second subject and final theme in the recapitulation—that is, D—as being the tonality of the whole movement.[6]

Nor is any help offered in the matter by the first subject. There can be no question here of tonality springing naturally from melody. In the exposition, melody and harmony together make one feel a vague B-flat minor tonality. In the recapitulation this same theme becomes even more doubtful tonally as a result of a peculiar circular movement in the chord progression which turns back on itself. The chord leading back to the recapitulation is the dominant seventh of the key. But instead of E, it resolves onto F, indeed onto a chord which is similarly dominant in structure, which would in turn demand resolution onto B-flat. Instead of B-flat it is again a tonality one semitone higher which appears—that is, once more a dominant seventh chord based on B. Just as with an interrupted cadence, as a result of the substitutional or "mistuned" resolution the two chords move in a "shortened" circuit until a "proper" resolution does in the end lead to B-flat. This suspended B-flat tonality, however—though it does in the

[6]That is why we cannot accept David Gow's interpretation, according to which the whole movement should be considered as D minor (Gow 1973:268).

last analysis agree with the opening tonality of the movement—can not be made valid for the whole movement. Or at most it can only be considered as one point of support.

So let us consider the end of the movement, being the principal tonal point of support. In the two bars before figure **23** the A-minor tonality of the cello part, taken in the melodic sense, is supported on the one hand by A minor VII_3^4, and after figure **23** the same inverted seventh chord from A minor is coloured by a B-flat minor seventh chord. This sort of semitone bitonality is no rare phenomenon in Bartók, but the two notes are never equal in importance—one dominates, the other provides colour: here it becomes clear from the double support of A minor that it is not A that colours B-flat, but the other way round.[7]

Example 164.

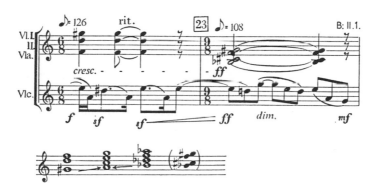

But the A tonality is reinforced by melodic phenomena as well. Before, the cello laid stress on the A–E fifth, and in the two penultimate bars—rhythmically rhyming with the former case—it increasingly comes to end on A. Before and after this, however, it repeats on no fewer than three occasions the little melodic fragment which unambiguously has its origins in the final theme. The melody does actually descend onto E, but this has a plagal or subfinal effect and does

[7]George Perle arrived at a similar conclusion, but following another reasoning, based on "symmetrical" interpretation. See Perle 1955:309.

not destroy the feeling of A-minor tonality which has already taken root in our minds.

Example 165.

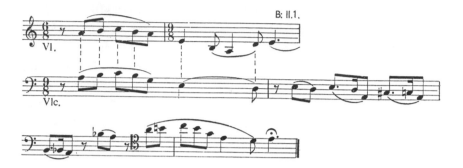

And finally, what does the second subject's augmented triad contribute to all this? As we know, this chord is in itself neutral but in association with some other element it can become unambiguous. And this is what happens here: the feeling of A tonality which has evolved melodically is reinforced by the notes A and C-sharp in the chord, especially when A comes in the uppermost part in the last chord. And in the cello part the final E comes as the fifth of A and the adjacent F from the augmented triad has only a colouring function. In other words, the augmented triad in the upper voices is coloured into A tonality by the little melody in the cello. The notes A and E dominate, and they are given colour by C, C-sharp and F without any feeling of the tonality disintegrating.

Example 166.

After all this, one still queries how the A tonality coda is to be reconciled with the B-flat tonality of the opening of the movement and with the tonality of the other themes. The B-flat tonality of the first subject, however, is not so strong or firmly established as to stand with any force as a contrast to the movement's A tonality. Furthermore, this sort of semitone duality is not alien to Bartók 's compositional technique, particularly in the creative period around the Second String Quartet, at which time the closed and, from a tonal point of view, decisive tonal system which he was to use later had not yet evolved. And as far as the tonal connections of the other themes are concerned, the tonalities of F-sharp, C-sharp and D can easily be fitted into the system of interrelationships belonging to A.

Second movement: Allegro molto capriccioso

This movement belongs to a garland-like formal type. Two traditional forms, a rondo and a variation series, are united in it: for the rondo theme produces more and more variations at its every appearance— that is, in place of a simple recapitulation we are faced with a higher level recapitulation on every occasion.

At the opening of the movement there is a hard barbaric tritone motif which has a kind of framework function. Its melodic character, consisting of upbeat quaver movement rhythm and the repetition of one single interval, paves the way for the rondo theme. The rondo theme belongs among Bartók's characteristic barbaric ostinatos and is a close relation of the minor third theme of the second movement in the Dance Suite. Arab folk music is evoked by both the drum-like accompaniment and the melody of the theme.[8] The structure of the theme is extraordinarily clear: it divides into two almost identical phrases which correspond to each other. The second phrase differs from the first only in that the melody darts higher than in the first phrase by a major second, which is a simple but effective means of extension. The inner phrase structure is three-part: it is opened by third repetition, in the centre there is a "revolving motif" which turns back upon itself, and the phrase is completed by a scale-like descent.

[8]See chapter 3, "The Folk Music Influence" in Part One.

Example 167.

The first appearance of the rondo theme is immediately followed by a variation: the theme moves from the first violin down into the two lowest instruments. The variation makes use of the first and third parts of the theme.

Example 168.

The framework motif is wedged in between the first and second variations, a fifth higher and in inversion. Then follows another variation of the rondo theme, more remote in comparison with the preceding one. Accordingly the ostinato accompaniment also changes: as well as the repetition of the single note, the upper auxiliary notes also appear.

Example 169.

At figure **9** the rondo theme moves over through organic texture into the framework motif, which is not in such a static form as in the two previous occasions: it is now broken up motivically. At figure **11** the cello plays a new motif with the rhythm of a folksong line and with this the first episode begins. After the new motif has been divided up, a big chromatic intensification leads to the other new material of the episode (**13**). The new motif consists of a downward seventh in restrained tempo (Sostenuto) and an "a tempo" ending added onto it immediately. These two elements in the motif are related to one another as question and answer. At **14** the rondo theme returns in a new guise in keeping with the variational process. On this occasion it is the first and second elements of the basic theme that form the centre of the variational work.

Example 170.

This is immediately followed by a new variation in which one of the theme's motifs is arranged as a small period:

Example 171.

Further variations of the framework motif introduce the second episode. The motif in folksong rhythm appears once more, and open motivic work is evolved from its three-note cadence and the semi-quaver figure of the framework motif (**21**). The whole episode is very dynamic in character just like the development section in a sonata movement. In the middle of this (**25**) we witness a peculiar dramatic detail: the minor third motif of the rondo theme collides as rhythmic element with the dolce melody developed from the motif in folksong rhythm. Dark rhythm blocks become wedged in between the individual sections of the melodic element. From this battle it is the melodic element that emerges victorious: at figure **27**—to a delicate pizzicato accompaniment—the melody is at last able to unfold in its entirety. (Its final element unmistakably refers to the augmented triad motif which has a second subject function in the first movement.) After figure **29**, the first four-note motif of the melody, after a gradual increase in speed, joins with the elements of the framework motif and a strepitoso ascent (**31**) leads to the question-answer motif, in a way which is analogous to the chromatic intensification before figure **13** in the previous episode. The amplitudinous question motif rises in terraces and reaches its climax in the third bar before figure **33**; after that the accelerating elements of the answer motif lead to the next big junction in the form, the return of the rondo theme.

This latest version of the rondo theme also contains metrical transformation: as opposed to the even metre ($\frac{2}{4}$) which has obtained so far, it now moves over to uneven ($\frac{3}{4}$) (Allegro molto, before figure **34**). On this occasion the variation makes use of spring-like expansion of the theme.

Example 172.

We are reminded of the so-called proportion of the old dance forms by this transformation of the rondo theme into an uneven metre. Here, too—as in the dances—the change from even to uneven is a method of intensification. This more tense variation of the rondo theme, on a higher level, leads to similar transformation of the episode elements. In the four-note chromatic figures beginning at figure **37** there is a return of the apparently disappeared framework motif, a further variation of the variation, when the two elements— original form and variation—are so remote from each other that their relationship is scarcely recognizable. The episode closes by evoking the rhythm-melody battle which took place in the earlier episode. What appeared there in the form of a third motif now returns in darkly snapping chords with an element from the lonely melody wedged in here and there.

At figure **14** a *ff* pizzicato chord introduces the last return of the rondo theme, and also the large-scale coda. Although it does include yet further variations of the rondo theme, the coda, as regards function, is nevertheless rather in the nature of a summary. The acceleration in tempo produces a transformation of the basic character of the rondo theme to a prestissimo which has the effect of a stretta: the fairly robust, angular dance character which has prevailed so far becomes replaced by a gliding-rushing tone. The metre changes from $\frac{3}{4}$ to $\frac{6}{4}$, which likewise has significance as a summary, as in this kind of metre duple and triple elements appear together. The horizontal summary in the metre is aided by the polymetrics evident vertically: for a large part of the coda the cello accompanies the upper parts in $\frac{4}{4}$, so that duple note-groups are heard simultaneously with the triple groups.

The coda is also a summary in the melodic sense: it travels once more the road of expansion covered by the other variations so far, and indeed the expansion is in this case even more extreme: the original minor third theme first assumes an even narrower form, and it is from that that the most spacious melodic arch evolves. The coda is a summary as regards the structure of its melody, too. In the rondo theme and in the first four variations of the rondo theme there was a dome-shaped melody and in the fifth a spring-like stretching melody. Now both occur at once: the various units produce a dome-shaped outline, but at the same time the repeated return to the D starting point and the gradual augmentation of the individual arches contain the spring movement principle. Naturally in the process the phrase structure of the theme disintegrates and is replaced by homogeneous connection of smaller units of one or two bars.

The harmonic and tonal character differ considerably from that of the first movement. In the latter it was the chromaticism characteristic of the post-Romantic tonal world that dominated, and it was possible to establish the tonality largely on the basis of criteria appropriate to that world. Here chromatically woven melody virtually completely disappears (traces of it are at most to be found in the episodes), and it is replaced by hard interval repetitions. The framework motif is characterized by a diminished fifth and the rondo theme by the initial minor third and its different extended variations. In keeping with this, the tonality of the formal sections is also determined by the "plane" of the drum-like note-repetitions and interval-repetitions. In this way the framework tonality of the movement evolves on the plane of D: the rondo theme opens out of the D–F minor third and comes to a close on this same minor third at the end of the movement. The fourth and fifth appearance of the rondo theme between figures **14** and **18** in the centre of the movement are also built on this tonal level of D.

The disappearance of the late romantic harmonic background does not, however, mean that functional attraction has been entirely eliminated from the tonal relationships. The survival and transformation of functional attraction appears very characteristically straight away in the movement's framework motif. The tense character and leading-note resolution of the diminished fifth and augmented fourth intervals is a phenomenon which has its roots in classical harmonic order. This is what Bartók uses and breaks down to a purely melodic level when he leads to the movement's basic tonality with a chain of diminished fifths and augmented fourths.

Example 173.

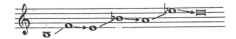

The essentially harmonic process appears in its purely melodic projection, so much so that the melodic elements take on an independent life of their own and an independent system of attractions with the adjacent semitones evolves—in both directions. For in the melodic projection the third of the resolving tonality comes as the root (for example: of the B-flat–D which resolves the tense A–E-flat dominant it is not the B-flat which remains as the root but D). This is how it comes about that the C-sharp–D dominant-tonic progression can also be replaced by E-flat–D, and yet with exactly the same dominant-tonic attraction content.

Third movement: Lento

The movement is introduced by mistily rolling dissonances coloured by sordino. The melodic event is provided by consistent augmentation of two-note downward curving melodic fragments. Starting out from an augmented second, the motif assumes the form of a major third, fourth, fifth and minor seventh. From figure 1, complementary rhythm polyphonic writing unfolds in the lower voices and above this there is a gesticular fourth motif(a). The melodic outline is unmistakably related to the opening of the first movement's first subject, but what was earlier a fast run upwards of an ornamental nature now appears as a weighty, gesticular character. This formal section is completed by a slow, rhythmically even emblem motif consisting of chord blocks. Its melodic line refers back to the fourth motif; its harmonic content on the other hand is reminiscent of the first movement's augmented triad motif (b).

Example 174.

In the formal section beginning at figure **2** it is an emphatic melody which has a descending line and an anapaestic rhythm that plays the most important role. It can be compared with a dirge collected by Kodály: its plaintive tone comes across very penetratingly here, too.[9] Disregarding its first two notes, a note for note quotation of the first movement's first subject is concealed within it.

Example 175.

[9]See chapter 3, "The Folk Music Influence" in Part One.

Lengthy motivic development work leads to the third theme in the movement (figure **4**), which melodically is characterized by movement in two directions round a steady axis-note. The melody is consistently heard with fourth-chord harmonies, sometimes with precise mirror-symmetry. Its subdued colours, with *pp* dynamics, lend it an awesome, mystic atmosphere. This formal section is separated by the emblem motif from the section which follows in the nature of a development. A real combat evolves between the emblem motif and a third-motif which has not played any part so far. After this dramatic clash, there begins a formidable intensification using pp dynamics and sotto voce colour, in which a minor third projection of the first fourth-motif and variations of the fourth theme moving round this axis come to be used simultaneously in counterpoint.[10] After the culmination at figure **8** the recapitulation begins, and this brings back the themes of the movement in abbreviated form and in a different order. The gesticular fourth-motif returns only in its third form. Immediately after that follows the fourth-chord theme on the steady axis, and the movement is ended by recalling the battle between the emblem motif and the exclamatory third-motif. Before the tragic close which falls back into *pianissimo* the dirge melody makes one more sorrowful appearance. This ending is just as dramatic and open as that of *The Miraculous Mandarin* or that of the Suite op. 14.

The closing chord, consisting of the third A–C, which is also the closing chord of the emblem motif which appears at the main formal junctions in the movement, determines quite unambiguously the tonality of the movement. In this light it then also becomes obvious that the A above the G-sharp–F motif in the rushing dissonance of the introduction is likewise a tonal framework. Apart from this in the tonally fairly indeterminate movement it is only the third theme moving on a steady axis which represents a definite tonality: E in the exposition and C in the recapitulation. It should be added that even though the steady axis note would in itself be enough to determine the tonality of the theme, the E is further supported here by the cadence of the theme which evokes a typical closing phrase in Hungarian folksongs.

[10]Quotation-like connection with Debussy's *Pelléas et Mélisande* is treated in chapter 2, "Forerunners and Contemporaries" in Part One.

The unambiguous A tonality of the closing movement incidentally bears out in retrospect our claim regarding the tonal position of the
first movement. Thus the three-movement symmetrical tempo structure of the work has a corresponding symmetrical tonal structure: A–
D–A. The point does arise that in the First String Quartet we did not
discover any such tonal unity, but there the tempo structure is also
open, not symmetrical, since it gradually progresses from slow to fast.

CHAPTER TEN

THE TWO SONATAS FOR VIOLIN AND PIANO

Bartók's two Sonatas for Violin and Piano were written in 1921 and 1922, after a few years' silence following the First World War—the period of the *Improvisations* and the *Dance Suite*. The genre presented new problems for the composer, as up to that time he had only employed this classical combination of instruments in a few juvenile works.

External factors played a part in renewing Bartók's interest in the genre in the early 1920s. When, after a few years' absence following the war, Bartók once again appeared on the concert platform (an explanation for which can be found in a letter he wrote to János Busiția: "... I have to spend all my free time earning money. I play the piano in concerts, and write articles for foreign periodicals ..."[1]), his concerts almost always included one or two compositions with violin. On 16 March 1921, he played Ravel's piano trio with Imre Waldbauer and Jenő Kerpely, and soon after, on 23 April, performed Debussy's Sonata in G Minor for Violin and Piano, with Zoltán Székely, at a concert mainly featuring contemporary works (Demény 1959: 153,159). The outstanding generation of Hungarian violonists of the time, Imre Waldbauer, Zoltán Székely, Ede Zathureczky and the Arányi sisters living in Britain, in all probability played a major part in Bartók considering it worthwhile to compose violin pieces. These highly gifted young musicians, whose development matched the increasing demands of music, were already capable of inspiring Bartók

---

[1]8 May 1921, *Bartók levelei* No. 382.

to explore new technical and musical ground. Just as the Rhapsodies and Violin Concerto were later born on József Szigeti's and Zoltán Székely's personal encouragement, so the two sonatas for violin and piano owe their existence to Jelly Arányi's inspiration.

Bartók's acquaintance with the Arányi family dated back to 1902; during his Music Academy days he met them for domestic chamber-music evenings. ". . . This Arányi family are very interesting: first because they are closely related to Joachim . . . secondly because German is never spoken in this family," Bartók wrote to his mother.[2] Of the three Arányi girls, Adila, Hortense and Jelly, two became violinists of European repute. The family later, before the war, settled in Britain, only returning to Hungary for a short visit in 1921, at which time Bartók renewed his friendship with the Arányi sisters, and as Jelly asserts in her recollections, composed the first Sonata expressly at her request.[3]

Closer connection with the Arányi family might probably also have been occasioned by the fact that Bartók's name had at the time become known in London musical circles. In November 1920 the distinguished journal *Sackbut* carried a lengthy study on Bartók's art by Cecil Gray, and his fortieth birthday was commemorated both in the *Revue Musicale* in Paris and the Viennese *Musikblätter des Anbruch*. In the autumn of 1921, Bartók corresponded with Michel Dimitri Calvocoressi about a concert tour to Britain, and it seemed natural to assign the Arányi family an important part in it. On 20 October 1921, Bartók wrote to Calvocoressi in London, "I wish to inform you that in the meantime I have had an opportunity to play chamber music with Miss Jelly Arányi. I found her to be an excellent violinist, with whom I would gladly play together in public anywhere and at any time . . . In fact, I am just now composing a sonata for violin and piano, which I would gladly perform first with Miss Arányi."[4] And later, when after the London performances of the First Sonata he was again invited for a concert tour to Britain, he wrote to Calvocoressi on 20 August 1922:

[2] 12 November 1902, *Bartók levelei* No. 19.
[3] Joseph Macleod, *The Sisters d'Arányi* (London, 1969), 136.
[4] Unpublished letter in German in the collection of the Budapest Bartók Archive.

"Should I be called upon to play violin and piano music in Britain, I would of course most willingly do so with Miss Arányi, as it would be difficult for me to find another adequate violinist."[5]

The question arises, however, whether Bartók really composed the First Sonata expressly at Jelly Arányi's request, and if they actually discussed this during the Arányi family's visit to Budapest in the summer or early autumn of 1921, why did Bartók not mention this fact to Calvocoressi in the letter quoted above? The question is justified even more by the fact that the premières of the two sonatas are not linked with Jelly Arányi's name, since the First Sonata was first performed by Mary Dickenson-Auner and Eduard Steuermann in Vienna on 8 February 1922, and the Second Sonata was premièred by Bartók himself, with Imre Waldbauer, one year later, on 7 February 1923 in Berlin, at one of the composers' evenings organized by the Melos Society.[6] Bartók thus played the pieces with Jelly Arányi only at their first London performances—the First Sonata on 14 March 1922 at a domestic concert in the home of the Hungarian chargé d'affaires, Hedry, and on 24 March at a public concert, and the Second Sonata on 7 May 1923, at a concert of the British Music Society. It is worth mentioning that this London performance of the Second Sonata was preceded by the first Budapest performance on 27 February 1923, with Ede Zathureczky, and the performance in Amsterdam and Rotterdam, on 27 and 28 April, when the violin part was played by Zoltán Székely.

All this seems to indicate that in the first stages the sonatas were not inseparable from the person of Jelly Arányi. Nevertheless, the score printed in 1923 already bears the inscription on the title page *"Deux Sonates / pour Violon et Piano / composées pour Mlle Jelly d'Arányi."* So it is possible that the early and perhaps vague idea to dedicate the work to her became a final decision only after Bartók's two concert tours to Britain, where he had been convinced by the then 29-year-old violinist's wonderful performance of the music. Bartók's delight is also shown in a letter he wrote to his mother after

---

[5]See note above.

[6]Printed programs of these concerts are preserved in the Budapest Bartók Archives.

the first Sonata's first performance in Paris. "My recital on the 8th [April 1922] went off well. Afterwards I was invited to a dinner at Prunières', which was attended by over half the 'leading composers of the world'—that is, Ravel, Szymanowski, Stravinksy—as well as a few young (notorious) Frenchmen whom you would not know. Most of them were very enthusiastic about the Sonata for violin, and not less so about Jelly's playing, for she 'excelled herself' that evening. N.B. the concert was at 5 p.m., and the Sonata was performed once again after dinner at Prunières' for the benefit of the select company I've just mentioned."[7]

During this ascending period of Bartók's international reputation, two masterworks like the First and Second Sonata for Violin and Piano naturally attracted the interest of supporters and cultivators of new music. Prunières devoted a long study to the First Sonata in the *Revue Musicale*, and similar reviews of a serious nature appeared after the London and Berlin performances, and the "young Frenchmen" whom Bartók encountered at Prunières' house, voiced their enthusiasm. It is worth quoting the letters Milhaud and Poulenc wrote to the composer about the First Sonata.

> My Dear Friend, I feel I must tell you once again how greatly I was moved by your sonata. It is a noble, pure and rugged piece [de race, pure et rude] . . . Please express my greatest admiration to Miss Arányi, too. She is worthy of the work she interprets. Yours faithfully, Milhaud.

> My Dear Bartók, . . . You gave great pleasure to all the young French musicians by coming to Paris to play us your wonderful sonata and piano pieces — thank you...Best wishes, your friend, Poulenc. (*Documenta Bartókiana* 1968:No. 66, 67)

The fact that Bartók's two Sonatas for Violin and Piano were written in such close chronological proximity, as the outcome of a single creative impetus, is not unique in the composer's output. A glance at the list of his works reveals how often works of the same genre, employing the same forces, feature as a pair: Suites nos. 1 and 2 (1905, 1907), *Two Portraits and Two Pictures* (1908, 1910), Five Songs op. 15 and op. 16 (1915, 1916), String Quartets nos. 3 and 4

[7]15 April 1922, *Bartók Letters* No. 119.

(1927, 1928) and Rhapsodies nos. 1 and 2 (1928). The First and Second Piano Concertos, even if not written in such close succession, were also written within a relatively short time (1926, 1930–31). Taking into account the internal structure and material of these works, it seems to indicate that Bartók very often approached one and the same assignment twice, finding different but not radically opposite solutions. In the case of the two Sonatas for Violin and Piano it would seem expedient to analyse them jointly, since many questions find more definite and detailed answers when placed in the context of the works than if applied separately. All this, however, does not exempt us from approaching separately certain aspects of the two compositions, in particular their structural outlines.

Sonata no. 1

The three-movement design of the First Sonata (Allegro appassionato, Adagio, Allegro molto) is fairly traditional in the sonata, yet it had hardly appeared in Bartók's work up until this time—he had last employed it in his early Sonata for Piano and Violin of 1903. The main characteristic of this design is not just how many movements there are, but the successive organization of tempos, the fast–slow–fast sequence of movements. Thus, although both the First and Second String Quartets consist of three movements, their design is actually different, as the tempo in the First Quartet quickens gradually, while in the Second a fast movement is flanked by two slow ones.

Hence we may say that in the First Violin-Piano Sonata the mature Bartók came face to face, in effect for the first time, with the "traditional" fast–slow–fast design.[8] The tempo structure is not the only new feature; so also is the originality of the material and the "dramaturgy" it incorporates. József Ujfalussy has constructively pointed out how the function of the framing movements is transformed and their interrelationship modified. "Even in the hovering texture of some of his early works there was the muscular quality of folk music...he had for the most part made use of the wild, throbbing quality of Arabic folk music to convey the note of defiance and rebellion, and to express the

[8]A good observation by András F. Wilhelm (unpublished?).

elemental forces of nature. These expressions of revolt, however, were preceded and followed by movements expressing anguish...In the finales of the two Sonatas for Violin and Piano, however, we find both contrasts and unity between the elements of East-Euorpean folk-dance music and the music which expressed the self-destructive torment of suffering" (Ujfalussy 1971:200–1).

Another significant change lies in the fact that the expressive, almost expressionistic character, which József Ujfalussy describes as "hovering texture" and "self-destructive torment of suffering," is here not linked exclusively with slow music. The expressive melodiousness, for example, which emerges in the slow movements of the Second String Quartet, is paralleled by the Allegro appassionato tempo and character of the first movement of the First Sonata. The Second Quartet is, incidentally, an important source and predecessor of the Sonatas, particularly as regards the use and melodic treatment of the violin. One might say that the violin parts in the Sonatas draw primarily on the Second Quartet, not merely in the formulation of the basic character of the melodies, but in the method of their development as well.

Since to outline the structural design entails separating the formal constituents, we must trace the various themes and their specific features, as seen both in the material and its development. It should be noted right away that the material for the two instruments is clearly separate. Bartók broke with the tradition of the form which considers the violin and the piano homogeneous, each being assigned essentially identical thematic material. In Bartók the themes do not wander from one instrument to the other as in classical and romantic sonatas for violin and piano; the various themes are inseparably linked to the specifically instrument-oriented structure and so, apart from a few exceptions, a theme heard first, for example, on the violin, remains in the violin part throughout. This does not exclude exchanging roles within the music itself: the lead is assigned now to the violin and now to the piano. But for this very reason the secondary, or one may say accompanying material, always remains important, as each instrument is not made to play accompaniment figures and passage work which are alien to it.

First movement: Allegro appassionato

The presentation of the first theme immediately illustrates the divergency of material for the two instruments, and the individual role of each part; the widely spread rippling broken chords from the piano are only conceivable on a keyboard instrument, while the melody heard above it is a typical violin melody.

As in the Second String Quartet, the melody progresses by expanding the intervals to quite an extreme.

Example 176.

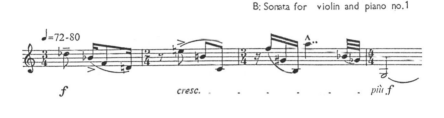

Wide, expansive intervals play an important part throughout the work, their appearance being of two kinds; the theme quoted above expands melodically and the wide leaps heighten the melodic tension. But occasionally, mainly in the piano part, the wide intervals and large leaps do not outline a melody, having instead merely a colouristic effect, expressing passionate gestures of flashes of restlessness.

Example 177.

The first subject up to figure **6**, has an A–B–A structure, as material of a different character is inserted between the two appearances of the characteristic outward pivoting violin-melody—not as an individual formal unit, but clearly separate, and of a different character. At this point the violin and the piano are not clearly separated as in the opening part, so the violin continues the widely expanding melody, supplemented by diminished and augmented octaves and fifths from the piano, which serve to underline the mood of friction.

Since in the first subject the leading role was taken by the violin and the melodic style natural to it, it seems logical and "fair" for the piano and the rhythmic style associated with it to take over in the second subject. For the second subject is virtually nothing more than the repetition and development of a sharply pointed iambic rhythmic figure. It is typical of Bartók's economic handling of form and his struggle for organic unity that this rhythmic figure already appeared in the first subject. When it comes to the fore in the second subject, it assumes two different yet clearly connected forms. It first appears moving mirror-fashion in wide leaps as part of a more varied rhythmic figure, and later is further developed, appearing as a repetitive rhythm, accentuating its agitato character. Here we witness the birth of a type of theme which later assumed great significance in Bartók; the first form can be compared with the closing subject of the first movement of the Sonata for Two Pianos and Percussion, the second with the analogous subject in the Third Piano Concerto.

Example 178.

While the piano has the leading role, the violin naturally remains in the background, acting as an accompaniment. Bartók modelled this accompanying material on the violin texture in Szymanowski's works. Before and also during the work's composition, Bartók came into close contact as a concert pianist with the eminent Polish composer's music; on 12 November 1921, for example, he accompanied the three-section violin piece *Myths* at Zoltán Székely's concert. In all probability Szymanowski's music interested Bartók further, since we know from a letter by Emil Hertzka, the director of Universal Publishers, that in 1921 Bartók ordered all of Szymanowski's work for piano, and violin and piano, that had been published up to that time.[9] In the First Sonata Szymanowski's influence is evident not in the music itself—as by that time Bartók had already formulated his own idiom and world of expression, which are rather remote from the Impressionistic world of the Polish composer's music with its gentle colours—but rather in his use of the characteristic lyricism, and especially the colour effects, inherent in the violin. It was surely Szymanowski's example that encouraged Bartók to accompany the piano subject in question with arpeggios crossing the strings for the sake of colour, tremolos and trills. Here mention sould be made of the frequent and consistent use of features characteristic of violin playing as *sul ponticello, con sordino, pizzicato.*

At figure **9** the second, agitato motif of the second subject leads into a slower, sostenuto theme, built upon a new, restrained variant of the iambic pulse, and which functions as a kind of closing subject, a "closing appendix." The dissolving connected thematic elements, the melodic contraction and the relaxing of the rhythm all point to the end of one of the movement's most important formal sections—the exposition. The development section, however, does not begin with a transformation of the already familiar material but with an isolated little transitional section, which with its consistent parallel thirds prepares as it were for the varied appearance of the violin theme. The exact mirror inversions, symmetrically opening and closing melodic curves and "graphic" design, which till now have emerged only periodically, now assume an exclusive role in the piano part.

[9]Unpublished letter, a photocopy of which is in the Budapest Bartók Archives.

Example 179.

An interesting feature in the bold change that takes place functionally: the excited, passionate violin theme, which in the exposition
was extremely tense and emotional, in the development section
returns with a tranquillo and dolce character, its smooth melodic line
broken at most by a few flageolets. The second subject material on
the other hand appears in a more tempestuous, excited and fierce
form, and only calms down when the ascending melody from the violin
leads back to the recapitulation (figure 20).

The recapitulation offers a fine example of Bartók's varied and
condensed recapitulations. Of the A–B–A structure of the first subject only A–B remains, the long transitions are shortened, and the
second theme of the second subject is transformed into an ascending
melody with syncopated rhythm, assuming the character of a conclusion. In the Coda, the violin theme is accompanied by the triplet
rhythm and mirror inversions from the development section, its last

espressivo appearance serving to sum up the whole movement, then dying away above quintuplet arpeggios from the piano.

Second movement: Adagio

Outwardly, the movement is in simple ternary form. Within this, however, the individual formal sections take into consideration the differing characters of the two instruments, each pursuing an A–B–A_v–B_v structure, containing further elaborate and sometimes complex structural refinements.

In the first section, there is a clear polarization of the material for each instrument: the violin plays the melody, the piano plays chords, both first playing alone. An ingenious device ensures that despite this the two instruments remain unseparated: the piano interrupts the end of the violin part, and conversely the violin, when the piano has presented its own material, before arriving at the cadence, joins in melodically at the same high pitch where it had left off.

Both in its soloistic character and in content, the violin melody is reminiscent of the beginning of the early Violin Concerto ("Ideal Portrait"). True, there the opening is an ascending melodic line, while here it is descending one, but the melodic fabric in both pursues the same late romantic chromaticism. Even more closely related to this slow, solo melody are the variation theme of the slow movement in the Violin Concerto of 1938 and the ritornello melody of the Sixth String Quartet. But while these latter melodies have a clearly defined four-section structure, the sonata's melody is free and asymmetrical despite its internal layout, relating to the type of upward-tending, romantic, yearning melodic line that appears at the end of the first movement of the early Violin Concerto and in the violin cadence introducing the third movement of the First Quartet.

The solo melody begins with a rhythmically balanced phrase that lies within the compass of an octave, becoming increasingly complex and chromatic as it progresses. This by no means contradicts the opening phrase, whose nine notes sound eight different pitches of the chromatic scale, with the opening note alone being repeated an octave higher. This procedure recalls Schoenberg, and is continued consistently during the further development of the melody. Indeed, at two points, a section each consisting of five different notes is repeated with a "row" character as it were; that is, in a different rhythmic and melodic presentation (x and y in the example below) in the centre of the melody presented as a sequence, in which the melodic line begins to climb consistently upwards, there unfolds a full twelve-tone "row" in which altogether only two notes are repeated. This "row" really conceals an ascending sequence, in which the earlier self-contained unit is transformed into an open chain of two major thirds and a perfect fourth (z).

Example 180.

The second appearance of the solo melody (figure **2**) confirms that Bartók deliberately used this concealed sequence construction. Here, too, the melody consists first of ascending sequences, but after the peak reached at B-flat″, the direction reverses, descending in three

long chains of thirds, thus also making a perfect twelve-tone "row."[10]
The compass of each unit of these descending sequences is an augmented octave, but now made up differently: the chain consists of
three minor thirds and a major third. At the first appearance therefore the intervals were of 4 and 5 semitones, while at the second the
intervals are of 3 and 4 semitones, thus everything having decreased in
order of magnitude. Accordingly, though the compass remains the
same, the augmented third gives the first an expansive character while
the diminished fourth gives the second one of contraction.

Example 181.

The chordal piano theme is built out of a variety of minor third
open harmony. Although the theme is piano and dolce, it is filled with
an inner tension by the minor triads clashing with the major Lydian
melody outlined by them. This tension is further intensified by the
directly opposing tonalities of the opening and closing chords of C
minor and F-sharp minor.

As previously mentioned, the violin and the piano present the
material separate of the first major formal unit of the movement side
by side like blocks. The asymmetric A–B–A–B form, however, is made
symmetric, even if only just by the recapitulation of the first phrase of
the violin theme, which brings to a close this section and at the same
time leads to the following central section.

The tempo slows down, first to Sostenuto ($\flat$=70–63), then to
Più adagio ($\flat$=from 60–56 to 48), but the emotional excitement
shows a contrary, increasing tendency. Tension is produced

---

[10]Stevens also detects a twelve-tone row, but he counts it from a later point of the
melody, disregarding the natural division (Cf. Stevens 1964:206, 320).

straightaway by the polar opposition of remote lying pitches: the piano's contra F-sharp and the violin's c'–c'' played pianissimo. But the violin melody, reminiscent of a descending phrase from folksong, is itself a source of tension, being staccato and rhythmically pointed. Bartók here employs an anapaestic rhythm beginning with an accent, drawn from Hungarian folksong, heightening its effect with extreme rhythmic contrast and a marcato mode of performance.

Example 182.

This is one of Bartók's favourite rhythmic elements, whose path can be traced from the "lament melody" of the Second String Quartet through the gesture motifs in *The Miraculous Mandarin* to the typical melodic patterns of the Fourth String Quartet and the Divertimento, to mention but a few examples.

At figure **5** the piano assumes the leading role and responds to the violin's broken melody with broadly flowing continuous phrases, though the tension is still not resolved, as the whole material is extremely animated both melodically and rhythmically. This middle formal section, incidentally, repeats exactly the A–B–A–B structure of the first major section, including the technique of variative development and the constantly changing tonality. At the end of the section the beginning of the first violin melody is quoted once again, referring back to the end of the previous section and at the same time preparing for the recapitulation.

The first section returns with its full four-part structure, but the violin part is masked beneath rich figuration, while the chords in the piano part are also richly embellished. The closing passage is most interesting; the opening violin melody reappears, but instead of the whole first phrase just its characteristic cadence (an economical procedure, as the full melody has already been heard many times), and the movement closes with a fragmentary recall of the rhythmically pointed material from the middle section. This four-bar excerpt is significant from the formal standpoint. Viewed in its entirety the movement can be said to show a struggle between two fundamental principles of form building: one being a symmetrical, three-part structure with recapitulation, which provides the overall form, the other an asymmetrical structure consisting of paired sections, with no recapitulation, and which governs the individual formal sections.

$$X \qquad\qquad Y \qquad\qquad X$$

$$\overline{|\,A\ \ B\ \ A\ \ B\,|} \qquad \overline{|\,C\ \ D\ \ C\ \ D\,|} \qquad \overline{|\,A\ \ B\ \ A\ \ B\,|}$$

As has already been pointed out, when by the end of the first unit (X) A returns, even though abbreviated, it slightly alters the pairing-principle form in the direction of the rounded, ternary form. When, however, at the end of the movement, in section X, one of the elements of the Y section is briefly hinted at, this slightly changes the odd numbered, three-part overall form into an even numbered structure, i.e., X Y X Y. This abbreviated, "even" form was to provide the basic formal idea of the Third String Quartet.

Third movement: Allegro

This movement is a sonata rondo of sweeping momentum and mostly of folk music inspiration. A four-bar introduction by way of a "curtain-raiser" is followed by the principal material of the movement on the violin, the rondo theme, one of Bartók's typical, dome-shaped, scale-like themes. Although no actual connection can be demonstrated, the origin of the theme can be felt behind its sound: Rumanian instrumental folk music, in which such lively, robust melodies with motor-rhythms linking pairs of notes are often found.[11] The perfect and diminished fifths piled upon each other in the accompanying piano part also imitate the type of accompaniment found in Rumanian peasant music. There is no question here, however, of just

[11]For example, Nos. 187b, 190 in Béla Bartók, *Volksmusik der Rumänen von Maramureş* (München: Drei Masken Verlag, 1923).

the natural influences and straightforward adaptation of folk music, since the whole extended formal section—the exposition of the rondo theme and its development—is also permeated by the single theme motor-rhythm of Baroque music, namely it would appear that here one of the important stylistic features of the year 1926 seems to appear in Bartók's music.

From the busy scale theme, the continuous musical material runs into the second thematic section almost without pause. This section functions as a kind of second subject or first episode, within the structure of the sonata rondo. But the theme does not contrast with the previous one, indeed it seems to be the organic continuation of it, as here the character of Rumanian folk music breaks through even more unequivocally. Bartók's folk music collection in Máramaros includes such melodies, which repeat and embellish a single note.[12]

Example 183.

Up until this point the leading role in both themes has been assigned to the violin, with the piano merely providing an accompaniment. In the third theme, beginning at figure 12, the lead is taken by the piano, with the accompaniment coming from the violin. The movement's leggierissimo, flowing theme grows out of a minor triad almost imperceptibly, representing a definite contrast to the foregoing material.

[12]On this Ruthenian tune type cf. László Somfai, "Sajátságos formastruktúra az 1920-as évek hangszeres kompozicióiban" ["A Specific Form Structure in the Instrumental Compositions of the 1920s"], Tizennyolc Bartók-tanulmány [Eighteen Bartók Studies] (Budapest: Zeneműkiadó, 1981), 265–69.

Significant from the formal point of view is the reappearance in this episode of the Ruthenian material, symetrically flanking the movement's theme of real contrast, the lowing material.

Before figure **22** a varied appearance of the "curtain" motif indicates the end of a significant formal section: the return of the rondo theme, and the beginning of the development section of the sonata rondo. First the rondo theme scarcely deviates from its original form, which is obviously required by the rondo principle, but further on there begins a free variation process; an augmented, slower version of the rondo theme is heard on the piano (this being the only instance where one of the instruments borrows from the other's material, and even here it goes hand in hand with fundamental inner changes), in a marcato, pesante manner. This is followed, by way of direct contrast, by a grazioso violin melody, which is nothing else than a very remote variation of the Ruthenian episode theme, with a different character.

Example 184.

These two theme variations are inseparably connected, and join alternately to form a five-part symmetrical section at the centre of the movement:

Violin:	grazioso		grazioso	
Piano: augmented		augmented		augmented
rondo theme		rondo theme		rondo theme

The return of the original form of the rondo theme at figure **33** marks the beginning of the recapitulation, in which the Ruthenian theme again flanks the flowing piano theme. The process is checked by the "curtain" motif at which point the Coda begins. At figure **44** the grazioso theme of the development section appears first, followed by its inseparable pair-theme, the augmented rondo theme, which accelerates to Presto (figure **46**) and turns into a stretto, thus closing the movement with a dashing tempestuous scale progression.

Sonata no. 2

The two-movement structure of the Second Sonata is, properly speaking, closer to Bartók than the three-movement form of the First Sonata, as from his early Violin Concerto onwards, he had often chosen this framework for his instrumental compositions, still returning repeatedly to the form after the Second Sonata. It should be pointed out, however, that these earlier two-movement forms are based on a different formal principle from the Sonata. Apart from the early Violin Concerto, which ultimately is a composition unresolved in form, the typical two-movement Bartók form—that of the *Two Portraits* and the *Two Pictures*—is not a structure that meets the requirements of the sonata. The dual structure of the *Two Portraits* is based on a single theme presented in two different, opposing ways, and that of the *Two Pictures* on two genre pictures; so that both lack the sonata's requirement for a more elaborate construction, going beyond a monothematic structure.

The main structural question of the Second Sonata, therefore, is whether Bartók succeeded in achieving a synthesis between the simpler structure of a pair of movements and that of the more complex sonata, and if so, how? The fact that soon after the First Sonata he began composing a similar work may also indicate that perhaps Bartók felt dissatisfied with the solution he found for the first piece. The composer himself mentioned repeatedly that he preferred the Second Sonata, and it is well worth noting that once when the question was raised of performing the First Sonata in an abbreviated form, he suggested playing the second and third movements.[13] Thus, he must have felt that if something had to be omitted, it should be the first movement, as the piece would still remain viable in the form of a pair of slow and fast movements.

The structure of the Second Sonata also rests on the opposition of slow and fast. Bartók scholars have written exhaustively on the subject of the background to this structural principle, showing it to be a

[13]Letter to Endre Gertler, 18 June 1936. *Bartók levelei* No. 790, pp. 265–69.

pairing of the "slow and fast" dances of the Hungarian *verbunkos* (Stevens 1964:210, Ujfalussy 1971:199). Bartók later made use of this simple structure in his two Rhapsodies, though it ought to be added that in the case of the *Constrasts*, he was no longer satisfied with this two-movement form, as the material and the content of the work both went beyond that of the *verbunkos* dances. It is all the more interesting that even in the 1920s Bartók wrote two more compositions, the Second Sonata for Violin and Piano and the Third String Quartet, in which he felt the two-movement structure, rooted in the popular slow–fast model, a sufficient and adequate basis for such large-scale serious musical works.

First Movement: Molto moderato

The tempo indication immediately tells us something important; on the one hand the moderate speed is really related to the slow dance of the *verbunkos* (this dance type being only relatively slow, having an internal dynamism), and on the other to the traditional sonata principle: it is not a real slow movement but a more moderate variant of the sonata's fast opening.

This tempo marking, however, serves merely as a starting point, since this incredibly sensitive, almost bar-for-bar changing tempo forms an organic part of the movement's character. The "slow" character is thus accompanied by another determining factor: the dominance of an uneven pulse, a "non giusto" rhythm. A "tempo map" of the first twenty bars can be outlined, telling us a great deal about the movement's inner material:

```
Bar: .      1            3           5          7
Tempó:   Molto mod. ... poco rall. ... a tempo... ritard. ...
M.M.: (♪) 116

            8                9                  10
         a tempo... ritard. .... a tempo (più vivo)... rallent. ....
                                      132                  80

                  12           13
         quasi a tempo... Poco rall. ... Meno mosso... Ritard. ...
            cca 96                        76

         14          16              17         18    20
         a tempo... poco stringendo... rallent. .... al... ritard.
         116                                         98
```

The frequent change in tempo is closely connected with the strongly improvisatory character of the first movement, and its first subject section. The two sustained notes of the four-bar introduction—contra F sharp from the piano and E from the violin—seem to suggest the performers's meditation and concentration of their energies, as if the melody were being born and formulated right there and then. When afterwards the resolute and characteristic opening motif—like an opening headline—is born, its further development equally gives rise to a sense of improvisation in the way it rambles freely, twisting and turning, trying out different ornaments like "hora lungá" melodies of Rumanian folk music.[14]

Example 185.

The two instruments have a different relationship from that in the First Sonata; in the first subject the leading role is clearly assigned to the violin, which is quite natural, as this improvisatory, searching music, behind which can be felt the example of folk music, is better suited to the string instrument than to the piano. It is very important, however, that here the piano, besides offering a chordal background to the violin's freely rambling melody, itself also tries to a certain extent to "go after" it with a few little, rhythmic snippets of melody.

Next comes a transitional section; the piano assumes the leading role with a motif consisting of very short note values, which refers partly back to the opening of the first subject and partly foreshadows a motivic element that is to assume great significance later in the movement. In both, the dominating feature is the joining of contrasting short- and long-note values in a further development of the iambic and anapaestic rhythm beginning with an accent, something we have

[14]Bartók's own characterization: ". . . it is performed like an improvisation, using a few standard patterns rather freely." Béla Bartók, *Rumanian Folk Music* Vol. Two: Vocal Melodies. Ed. by Benjamin Suchoff (The Hague: Martinus Nijhoff, 1967), 25.

already seen in the middle section of the slow movement of the First Sonata. A whole range of Bartók's themes and motifs can be classified on this basis, but for now let us confine ourselves to the sonata.

Example 186.

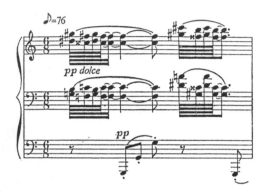

In this transitional section the violin remains in the background and only colours the piano part with flageolets. As in the first movement of the First Sonata, here too appear the successions of thirds in parallel and contrary motion, though they do not have such an important role. The first section of the transition (about eight bars) is still based upon the first subject, but in a considerably changed form. Towards the end, its transitory function is emphasized when it foreshadows the material of the following section, that of the second subject, by initiating a change into $\frac{5}{8}$ time.

The second subject, beginning at figure **5**, is in sharp contrast with the first subject: instead of the frequently changing metre and rhythm in the latter, here an even $\frac{5}{8}$ motion is maintained over a long period. The leading role returns to the violin which, however, is not "accompanied" by the piano, but counterpointed in both melodic and rhythmic sense. The metre of the piano part at first only halves the quintuple rhythm in the violin part, then later engages in even more complex polyrhythmic and polymetric play, at the same time taking over the lead.

After stating the second subject, the violin melody refers distinctly back to the first subject, without quoting it note for note; its characteristic, hesitating, improvisatory melody reappears, outlined in a few sustained notes. But it is far from being a recapitulation of the theme; the reference merely indicates a new formal section, as at figure 7 new material appears: long sustained melodic lines in the violin part above agitated rhythmic blocks of chords, broken by small note values. But these small notes—demisemiquavers—call attention to the fact that the material is not completely "new," since they have appeared in conjunction with the piano chords in the transitional section linking the first and second subjects. Their significance lies precisely in the contrast between the tiny rhythmic values and the sustained notes; but while in the transitional section the short notes formed the opening gesture of the first subject, here they have both an opening and a closing function. In fact, in their closing function the rapid notes have a more telling effect than in the opening, as the melodic unit with a demisemiquaver as a feminine ending suggests a sudden standstill.

Example 187.

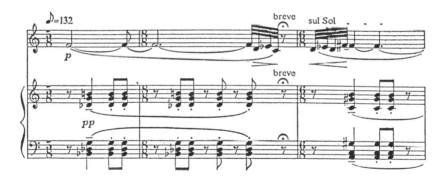

As regards its structural function, the material can be considered as another second subject, or a closing theme, but its motivic relationship with the first subject seems to indicate that within the framework of the sonata exposition, Bartók evolved a recapitulatory, rounding off subdivision which contains three thematic elements, but arranged in an even, four-section pattern: A–B–(A)–C_A.

Between figures 9 and 16 comes the development section, which subjects the three different themes presented in the exposition to free variation. Characteristically, only the opening motif—the head motif—of the first subject appears in an unchanged form, while the other thematic elements are so active and varied that their original form can only be inferred from the rhythmic patterns and shapes. The largest and most far-reaching development appears precisely in the seemingly most humble material, the supplementary theme that uses short rhythmic values. It becomes opposed to the "real" second subject, which mostly moves in $\frac{5}{8}$ time, and gains a growingly independent role, thereby drawing attention to the polarization of the thematic types, the "final distribution of roles": the second subject, moving in even quavers but in different metres, settles into the piano part, the recitative, excitable supplementary theme in exaggerated rhythm, into the violin part. The latter is lent extraordinary tension by dissonant double stops of parallel major sixths, major sevenths and fourths.

Example 188.

We have already encountered this type of music in the middle section of the First Sonata, where the same tenseness and expressiveness was prominent, albeit in a more static position, and not at the end of a process of development as here. The development section of this Sonata, particularly its final stage (figures **13–16**), with its grating sound, successions of inversions and extremely wide interval leaps, is one of Bartók's most exciting and explosive utterances, and bridges the gap between *The Miraculous Mandarin* and the Fourth String Quartet along a path of logical creative development.

The recapitulation restates only the first subject material, but broadly expounded in a richer form than all its previous appearances. It is an economical idea when one considers that in the development section the first subject was assigned the smallest role. In the recapitulation it also returns in a more complex form insofar as it is tonally extended: first it is heard a fourth lower, and only returns to its original pitch at the end of the movement, transposed an octave higher, the sliding upward being the outcome of a gradual, improvisatory melodic movement.

The characteristic head motif of the first subject is repeated at the end of the movement on three terraces, descending from its three-line octave to the one-line octave, then breaking off with a rest, though not a pause between movements, which leads into the second movement. The real connection between the two movements regarding the joint between them is even closer than at first appears from the external feature of their being composed without a break, since a variant of the head motif, with no upbeat, and at its third appearance even devoid of the characteristic anapaestic rhythm, foreshadows note for note the second movement's pizzicato first subject, only in retrograde motion (which, due to the scale structure of the theme, also has the effect of an inversion).

Example 189.

Second movement: Allegretto

The characteristic first subject built from a scale is stated by the solo violin and framed by the piano's accompaniment pattern typical of instrumental—mainly Rumanian—folk music. Already we see that of the two instruments it is the violin from which the theme draws its character.

Without further development or continuation this theme gives way at figure **3** to the piano's second subject contrasting with the first both in sound and structure; as against the former's scale movement, this is of a static character and resembles not Rumanian but Hungarian folksong. It is worth mentioning that its repetition of a single note recalls the theme of the *Allegro barbaro,* while its rhythm and articulation recall the second subject in the first movement of the First Piano Concerto.

Example 190.

With the exception of the middle section resembling a trio, the whole movement is built from these two themes, and with quite an individual structure which combines the sonata rondo with variation form. The first of the two themes—let us call it the Rumanian scale theme—is, on the basis of its periodical recurrence, a rondo theme, but similar to the procedure employed in the middle movement of the Second String Quartet, each of its returns is also a new variation, and this sequence of variations progresses successively from simple quaver motion to the final $\frac{3}{8}$, whirling, stretto variation. It is worth examining these variations side by side to see the variative "dramaturgy" of the movement.

Example 191.

The second theme—let us call it Hungarian folksong theme—on the other hand, acts as the episode or second subject of a sonata rondo; it maintains throughout its rhythmic and chordal character, only becoming expanded, richer and more complex, true to the development principle in sonata compositions.

The place of the development section in the middle of the movement is taken by a trio that brings new material: the violin plays a scherzando theme with a rather wry humour above clusters of whole-tone scales from the piano. This trio presents a veritable catalogue of Bartók's weirdly humourous, ironic and demonic moods, including elements of his early *Burlesques* and the dance of the Wooden Puppet in the *The Wooden Prince*, as well as foreshadowing the "Burletta" from the much later Sixth String Quartet. And in the "somersaulting" counterpart from the piano (at figure **30**) one can yet recognize the humorous fugato of the closing movement of the First String Quartet.

Example 192.

The special character and structural weight of this large-scale trio section is further enhanced by its being broken at three points to allow for the insertion of the first movement's material. The second subject and the violin melody in the first movement with double stops attached to it are recalled unmistakably, even if not note for note, from the development section (figure **13**), for six bars at figure **29**, and for five bars at figure **31**, while the third quotation—of the first subject of the first movement played by flageolet—appears at the end of the trio section to prepare for the recapitulation.

The recapiulation first recalls the slower, pizzicato variation of the Rumanian scale theme, and than brings a new variation of it above a motor-rhythm accompaniment in $\frac{5}{8}$ time (figure **36**). The Hungarian folksong theme returns first in its original form, secondly with scherzando character, and finally in a broad, maestoso form, $\frac{7}{8}$ Bulgarian rhythm. This, however, does not alter its Hungarian character at all, and moreover throws light onto another aspect—its relationship to the arrangement of "The Ballad of Angoli Borbála," no. 6 of the Fifteen Hungarian Peasant Songs for piano. The last appearance of the scale theme is stretto-like, as we have mentioned already, and could have the function of a Coda were it not superseded by a different structural principle. The tempo is a dashing Vivacissimo ($\bullet. = 112$), the peak so far of the tempo acceleration, and the theme darkens in tone, due mainly to the excited, ominously rumbling piano part, reminiscent of the first movement of the Piano Suite and the piece "Chase" in *Out-of-Doors*. All this, however, is not yet the close; as the continuous and unrelenting pace slackens at figure **53**, becoming improvisatory and irregular and ending in a violin cadence, which in turn gives way to the emergence of the first movement's first subject. For some time the tempo of the fast movement, as if inertia were temporary, encroaches upon the originally slow theme as well, but the slow tempo gradually becomes predominant. The theme disintegrates, climbs into the highest register of the violin, where it tapers off, and in ethereal purity over the piano's C–G fifth, dies away on four-line E, the major third of the key.

The quotation of the first subject of the first movement is doubtless an indication that the three-section, rounded off formal principle gains the upper hand over the even two-movement structure. Yet the question is by no means so simple, because the recapitulation in the first movement, which was left imperfect, or rather incomplete, is interestingly complemented by the three quotations worked into the trio in the second movement. Two of these quotations are nothing less than the material that was missing from the recapitulation—the second subject and the supplementary theme belonging to it. The third very short quotation recalls, like a motto, the first movement's first subject. It would be unreasonable for it to have a longer form, as it had already once been repeated at the end of the first movement and was to return once more at the end of the work. The quotations therefore mean that Bartók, by leaving the first movement suspended, then condensed into the second, and finally completed only after the second was over, was aiming at a greater organic unity than ever before. It is not a real three-section form, but rather a very special example of binary form, in which the struggle of the two different form principles can be seen and grasped. We have already encountered the same phenomenon in the slow movement of the First Sonata, but the real solution is only to come five years later, in the Third String Quartet, where, as we shall see, the real recapitulation of the two movements is shifted to the end of the work, thus creating in the highest-degree a unity out of the two-section binary form.

Bartók here reaches beyond the earlier and simpler two-section structures, and raises the work to the formal level called for by a sonata. The structure is achieved not by the juxtaposition of different material, but as a result of a complex organization, in which the shaping formal sections are linked by particular internal relationships. The creation of two different characters from the same material signifies an important result of Bartók's creative development, but it is notable that this principle is realized on a much higher plane in the Second Sonata than, for example, in the *Two Portraits*. Monothematicism is given a role here too since, as we have pointed out, the second movement's first subject is fashioned from the inversion of the first movement's first subject. But the system of relationships is much more complicated than this, since the second subject of the first movement is also akin to the first subject of the second movement, as is particularly evident in the theme's variation that appears in the recapitulation.

Example 193.

Here formal logic fails, for the two basic themes of contrasting character in the first movement are both related to the first subject of the second movement. This then means that the work realizes three different aspects of a single idea, the second movement being in fact none other than the organic development of the first movement, summarizing it on a higher level.

Points of Contact Between the Two Sonatas

In conclusion, attention should be drawn to some features common to the two sonatas, primarily to the consistent use of certain thematic types and characteristic content which emerge in them. As mentioned already, the middle section of the middle movement of the First Sonata introduces "micro-melodic units" in a particular rhythm—a contrast of very short and very long note values—a pattern which is again assigned a role in the first movement of the Second Sonata, as the additional element that accompanies the two basic themes. This material serves to express an extraordinary dynamism and inner tension, though its dramaturgical function is here not as unequivocally developed yet as in the great works of 1926 and 1927, the piano piece "The Night's Music" and the Third String Quartet.

Another feature of Bartók's musical style also emerges in these pieces: dome-structured scale-like melody as a thematic component. This is in essence the common cohesive element in the themes of the Second Sonata, but it should be noted that the first subject of the closing movement of the First Sonata also belongs to this type: it opens with an ascending melodic line resembling a scale, which then turns back and outlines an arch. This type of theme was to be given an extremely significant role in the Seconda parte of the Third Quartet, and even more so in almost all the movements of the Fourth Quartet, to mention just the nearest examples. It is one of the most significant types of theme in Bartók's music, which from this point onwards, runs virtually through his whole output, from the First Piano Concerto, through the Fifth String Quartet, *Music for Strings, Percussion and Celesta* and the Sonata for Two Pianos and Percussion, to the Third Piano Concerto.

But the closing movements of the two Sonatas are linked not only by the melodic outline of their themes consisting of scale elements but, beyond that, by common modal root as well. Placing the two themes side by side, it becomes evident that apart from the similar scale structures, both themes consistently avoid the perfect fifth above the scale's keynote, thus the fifth degree of the scale is a diminished fifth in the First Sonata and an augmented fifth in the

Second. Consequently, the First is dominated by a minor character with a diminished fifth, and the Second by a Lydian character, in fact a whole-tone scale with a minor sixth. This contrast, however, conceals a common root in the tonal system which is called "heptatonia secunda" by Lajos Bárdos, from the two different modes (offcuts) of which the hexachord framework of the two relevant themes was born.[15]

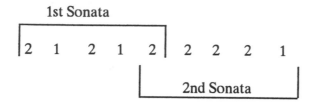

This conceptual, or one may say logical, relationship is borne out and reinforced by the relationship between the character of the two movements, both showing the undeniable influence of Rumanian instrumental folk music. Ernő Lendvai has observed a similar correlation in the opening and closing melodies of the *Cantata Profana*, which equally bears the mark of Rumanian folk music.[16]

Both closing movements employ the same typical device of Bartók's "instrumental dramaturgy": towards the middle of the structure, the dancing, "barbaric" rondo gives way to a grazioso-scherzando music. A similar phenomenon has been observed in the middle movement of the Second String Quartet, but only in the Fourth and Fifth Quartets does the type of movement developed in the sonatas, and the "dramaturgy" that goes with it, find its true continuation.

[15] See "Polymodal Chromaticism" in Part One, and Lajos Bárdos and József Ujfalussy, op. cit.

[16] Ernő Lendvai, *Bartók dramaturgiája* [*Bartók's Dramaturgy*] (Budapest: Zenemkiadó, 1964), 225.

CHAPTER ELEVEN

THE THIRD STRING QUARTET

In the summer of 1927, immediately before the time at which the Third Quartet was written, Bartók was in Germany on a concert tour. At the I.S.C.M. festival arranged in Frankfurt he introduced his First Piano Concerto under the baton of Furtwangler in July, and then on the sixteenth he introduced his Piano Sonata in Baden-Baden at a concert arranged as part of the *Deutsches Kammermusikfest*. At the same concert Alban Berg's *Lyric Suite* was also performed. That Bartók gained interesting impressions during this concert tour is shown by a letter dated 22 July, written from Davos to his mother: "...on the sixteenth there were three different concerts; at 11 in the morning was the one in which I also played; at 5 in the afternoon there was a performance introducing works written for mechanical piano and mechanical organ; and at 9 in the evening Lichtbild (film) performances with music recorded on film to go with it (this is a new invention, and it already sounds just as good as the better gramophones). Then on the screen appeared, separately, Schreker (composer), Kerr (critic), and finally Schoenberg. Each of them spoke about this new invention, their voices naturally being co-ordinated most precisely with the movement of their mouths" (*Bartók levelei* no. 502).

Bartók travelled from Davos in Switzerland to the performances and also returned there, where his wife was being treated in a sanatorium. On 7 August he wrote to József Szigeti : ". . . according to the doctor my wife's condition is so favourable that she will be able to come home to Pest at the end of September" (*Bartók levelei* no. 503) We do not know how long his wife actually did remain there, but it is certain that Bartók returned earlier to compose. He wrote a letter from Budapest to Universal as early as 10 September, and on the 13th he gave a radio concert in Budapest. At the end of the Third Quartet score the composer indicates September of 1927 as the date of the work's composition.

Bartók entered the work for the Philadelphia Musical Fund Society's competition. We have no information as to precisely when this happened and what the events leading up to it were, but we can presume that it was connected in some way with the two-and-a-half-month concert tour he began in America in December of 1927. Either his attention was drawn to the competition in the United States, or the friends and concert organizers who arranged the tour urged him to take part in the competition. Thus, we do not know whether he composed the quartet expressly for the competition or whether he sent in the already written work, making good use of the opportunity offered. For almost a whole year there was no news at all about the result of the competition. This may explain why Bartók sent the "Druckvorlage" of the quartet score to Universal on 13 September 1928, and began to make enquiries by letter concerning whether the Wiener Streichquartett—Rudolf Kolisch's quartet—might like to play it. But not much later, on 27 September, he sent a pressing letter to the publishers to say that he needed the parts, for the time being only written out by hand, since the Hungarian Quartet (the Waldbauer Quartet) wanted to give the first performance of it in Budapest.[1] After this, on 2 October, news arrived from the United States that the work, along with the Serenata op. 46 by Casella, had won first prize in the competition.[2] Bartók then wrote another letter to Universal Edition: "Yesterday morning I sent you the original manuscript of my third string quartet instead of the photocopy, since the making of the reproduction would have taken some more time. Then in the afternoon I heard—for the moment just from the Budapest newspapers and Reiner and Murray's cable from New York—that I have won the

[1]Bartók's correspondence with Universal Edition has so far remained unpublished. A photocopy was placed at my disposal by the Budapest Bartók Archives.

[2]*The Monthly Musical Record*, London (29 April 1929).

Philadelphia Musical Fund Society's prize with the work. As a result (that is, in accordance with the Prize specification) the manuscript is the property of the Society mentioned."[3]

In his letter to Frigyes Reiner, dated 29 October, we learn in more detail how he received the news of his winning the prize. "My Dear Friend! Many thanks for the congratulations cabled jointly by you and Murray. Don't think, however, that you were the first with the news: you were outstripped by the paper *Az Est* which, on the afternoon of Oct. 2, reported that I had won 6,000 dollars! I read this with suspicion and calmed down a little only when I got your cable in the evening and was able to say to myself that, after all, I really had won something. Within a few days I had learned from foreign newspapers that at least four of us had won something; who had won how much we couldn't discover from the many conflicting reports. So I waited patiently until at last, a few days ago, the letter from Philadelphia arrived, telling me exactly what had happened (and including the cheque of course). There is no need for me to stress the fact that the money "came in handy"; we are able to breathe more freely now, to say nothing of the publicity we've had . . . It had been such a long drawn-out affair that I didn't count on winning anything and only the day before I received the news I had sent the *Druckvorlage* to Universal Edition in order that they might get it printed" (*Bartók Letters* No. 139).

Universal—obviously under the influence of the international prize—set to work on the quartet very quickly, which did not please the composer very much, as became clear from his letter of 12 October. "When I got back from Prague I learned from your letter of 6 October that you wish to put my third quartet to press—or may even have already done so. This was not my intention when I sent you the photocopy four weeks ago. For the fact of the matter is that I have first of all to hear the work since it is possible that various smaller details (bowing, too difficult chords and such like) will have to be changed. In any event I think that these possible alterations will be of very little sig-

[3] October 1928, Budapest, from the original German. See note 1.

nificance. So if the score is now being engraved you must know that such alterations to the block may have to be carried out later. If you wish to avoid this, the engraving should be discontinued . . ."[4] From this it can be seen that Bartók only felt the composition to be complete once he had also tried it out in performance. For this reason, too, he pressed for the first performance. In his letter of 16 October to Universal he acknowledged receipt of the parts, and then forwarded them to the Waldbauer Quartet; also connected with this is the fact that the Wiener Streichquartett also received the parts for study purposes in spite of the Philadelphia Musical Fund Society, that had arranged the competition, having exclusive performing rights on the work for three months. In the end it was the Waldbauer-Kerpely Quartet that gave the first performance of the Third Quartet on 19 February 1929, in the Wigmore Hall in London. But two days later it was performed by the Vienna Quartet in Frankfurt as one of the I.S.C.M. concert series. From then onwards the excellent Vienna Quartet (Rudolf Kolisch, Felix Khuner, Jenő Lehner and Benar Heifetz) became, like the Waldbauer ensemble, enthusiastic propagandists of Bartók's chamber music. The group led by Kolisch made even greater and more consistent efforts than the Waldbauer group to play the new chamber music as widely as possible. It is with their name that the premières of most of the chamber works of the new Viennese school are connected, and it is very typical that alongside the works of Schoenberg, Berg and Webern, Bartók's quartets also frequently appeared in their programmes. At the Frankfurt performance mentioned above along with the Bartók quartet, Schoenberg's Third Quartet and Berg's *Lyric Suite* were also performed.

The first performance in Hungary took place in the Music Academy's main hall on 6 March 1929, at the concert given by the Waldbauer-Kerpely Quartet. Bartók was not present since he had a BBC concert in England on the previous day. Two pieces, which

---

[4]The photocopy mentioned in the letter was the "Druckvorlage" sent on 13 September. Why Bartók meanwhile—on 2 October—sent the original manuscript as well we do not know, but that copy certainly cannot have remained long with the publishers since the manuscript was required by the Society announcing the competition.

might also be called studies, stand out from among the criticisms: that of Sándor Jemnitz (*Népszava*) and that of Aladár Tóth (*Pesti Napló*). These two—they can justifiably be called the greatest—figures in the history of music criticism in Hungary warmly received Bartók's new work in the spirit of progressive aesthetics.[5] Both pieces are characterized by critical courage, confidence and a sense of responsibility. To take a stand right at the outset beside this truly new composition, which was difficult to understand, and to explain it with depth—this required a truly great spirit and courage, coming close to that of the composer himself.

The formal plan of this work is even more individual than that of the Second String Quartet. The external division presents two basic formal units with the inscriptions *Prima parte* and *Seconda parte*. To these movements, fundamentally different in both their material and their character, are added two other smaller sections—the *Ricapitulazione della prima parte*, that is an abbreviated recalling of the first movement, and then the *Coda*, which, as far as its material is concerned, is really the "Ricapitulazione" of the "Seconda parte." The four formal units are written completely as one, to be played without any break—in the manner of Romantic sonatas written as one movement. Here, however, all this can scarcely be said to contain any Romantic features, especially considering that this work by Bartók—together with the piano works dating from the year 1926—displays a decidedly anti-Romantic attitude.

Prima parte: Moderato

Above static harmony a sensitively unfolding violin melody starts the movement. Functionally it is rather a framework theme than a first subject, but virtually every important motivic element of the movement is contained within it. It is a rhythmic and melodic "primordial figure" sufficient for the development of a complete organism. The most striking point is the continuance of the two kinds of rhythm pattern:

---

[5]Quoted by Demény 1962:325–27.

Example 194.

It is from the extension of the first melodic motif that the first theme develops—the three part motif consisting of an upward fourth and a third which turns back. It is not difficult to recognize in this one of the characteristic cadence types of pentatonic Hungarian folk songs.[6]

Example 195.

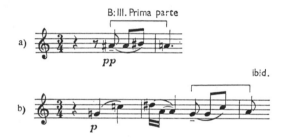

It is from the extension of the second phrase that one of the most important parts of the development section material in the movement is constructed: the melodic element set against harmony blocks.

Example 196.

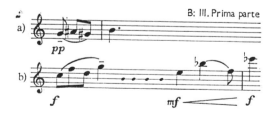

[6]See chapter 3, "The Folk Music Influence."

The theme's third, melodically arching phrase assumes importance in the development process of the movement, and not merely in the parts which continue the writing in close relation to the theme but also in the development section where it has a considerable independent setting.

Example 197.

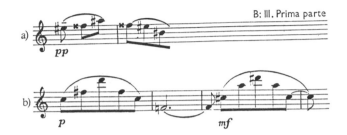

Finally the little three-note scale which completes the melody is the embryo from which the scale motifs of the development section grow. At first sight this system of interrelationships may appear exaggerated, but it will be justified in the analysis which follows, for all the elements in the movement can be fitted into a closed organism.

After the framework theme, a contrapuntal section begins with more or less precise imitation of the opening motifs of the themes. The fugue-like entries are somewhat obscured by the cello playing a supporting part—even before its own thematic entry—to the two violins' counterpoint. This is the plan of the entries:

Example 198.

From the entry of the two lower instruments onwards the rhythmically moving motifs increasingly expand, and at figure **2** there is a return of relative calm with the narrower elements of the framework theme being recalled. At figure **3** the imitation work is continued on a *forte* dynamic level right up to the summarizing of the theme's opening motif, harmonized with fifth-chords. Further proof of organic development is that the bitonal ostinato of the new formal section beginning at figure **4** stems from the opening motif of the first theme. The ostinato serves as a background for the new thematic element, which is composed of capricious little melodic gestures. Bartók had already experimented with this effect, reminiscent of natural sounds and noises, in the First and Second Sonata for piano and violin, and then later, just before this string quartet, he also found it justified in a programme music way in the piano work "The Night's Music."

At figure **6** the flexible, intertwining polyphonic writing once more comes into the foreground. Behind the four-note motif, tensed out spaciously, we can recognize a variation of the first part of the framework theme, which appeared at figure **2** (a). The imitational development of the motif brings the opening movement of the First Quartet to mind; in both, the intervals of the theme's opening motif combine to make seventh chords (b).

Example 199.

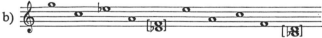

In the looser development-like section beginning at figure **7,** melodic and harmonic elements confront each other. It has already been mentioned that the melodic motif is a broad variation of the second phrase of the framework motif. If we take into consideration the fact that the theme's third, arching element also appears here, we come to the conclusion that the hard chord blocks are really breaking up a related melody into pieces. We have already encountered this kind of Bartókian dramatic development technique, based on a contrast between melody and chord, in the middle of the central movement of the Second Quartet, in a similar development-like episode.

The chord sequence also displays individual features. Already mentioned was a part where the three-note motif was outlined by fifth-chords. Triads outline the melody here, too—indeed, two of them in counter-movement. This polyphony between two chord layers is naturally scarcely successful in actual sound since the two simultaneously sounding triads merge into a single dissonant mass. This is not a rare phenomenon in Bartók's works dating from between 1926 and 1931, especially in piano works. It must be added, however, that this sort of polyphonic use of chords comes over much more plastically on the piano than on string instruments.

After the hard triad-blocks—a peculiar paradox—an enormous chord piling eight fourths on top of each other takes shape with pleasing gentleness from the melodic motifs. The three last notes of the four-note motifs produce this fourth-chain using nine different notes, and the first notes of the motifs give another fourth-chain which supplements the figure into twelve-tone chromaticism.

Example 200.

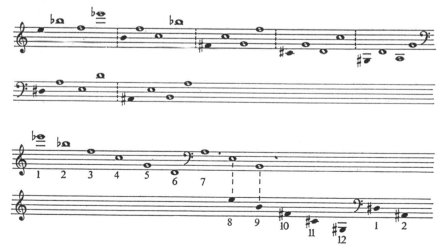

At figure **9** a three-note motif with a diminished octave compass unfolds from the fourth chords. The motif presents apparently new
material but it is actually no more than the further extended closing
section of the broad four-note motif which appeared at figure **6**.
Through dynamic intensification the diminished octave motif leads to
the little scale motif which is heard in a framework similar to the earlier chord blocks, and while from one angle it refers back to the dome
arch of the framework theme from another angle it anticipates one of
the principal ideas of the Seconda parte.

Example 201.

In place of a real recapitulation it is only the first theme which returns
with that kind of reminding function. The other themes familiar from
the exposition are missing: only the first two phrases of the framework
motif appear—inevitably, since we have arrived at an important formal junction: the Seconda parte is to begin.

   The tonal framework for the Prima parte is provided by C-sharp.
This is the basis for the second-pile in the introduction and the organ
point in the return of the theme. The C-sharp tonality first appears
melodically at figure **2** unambiguously on the stressed notes of the
framework theme. Otherwise long stretches are dominated by the ambiguity of semitone or polar bitonality. Thus, even in the recapitulation indicated the C-sharp–G-sharp basis is coloured by G–D–A, and
indeed this is more than colouring here, for the melody itself fits into
this tonal layer. On the border between the Prima parte and the
Seconda parte there is a process which is interesting from the tonal
point of view: a simple slide from the keynote C sharp leads to the
keynote D of the Seconda parte—completely like Beethoven's
method (even the notes are the same) between the first and second
movements of his op. 131 quartet.

Seconda parte: Allegro

The movement begins with projecting the colouring "background" into the foreground: above an organ point trill on D–E-flat a glissando-like melodic fragment appears which here and there enriches the music like a pinpoint. This technique was later to play an important role in the fourth movement of the Fifth Quartet. The first theme, divided into folksong-like phrases, is built into the triad mixture of the cello's pizzicatos; the top part shapes the melody in the D Dorian mode. It is worth comparing it with the central theme of the piano piece "With Drums and Pipes"; it would appear that the series *Out of Doors* (from which "The Night's Music" also comes) has strong threads connecting it to the compositional world of the Third Quartet.

Example 202.

At figure **3** a polymetric, barbaric folk dance theme with a rolling character appears. On account of its being composed of scale-arches it may also be compared with the first subject, but whereas in the latter the keynote is the lowest point in the scale-arch, here the theme has firm axis lying on E-flat, around which the melody weaves a winding line upwards and downwards. From the melodic structure aspect the theme reminds one of the theme of the Second Quartet's last movement, based on the E axis; but in character—if only because of the difference in tempo and rhythm—they are very different. As regards rhythm the theme may be compared with the first subject in the first movement of the Second Sonata for Violin and Piano. Both are characterized by a combination of $\frac{5}{8}$ and $\frac{3}{8}$ units. Here, however, there is a very considerable difference in melodic line.

Example 203.

This second theme's accompanying material—as in the first movement—is connected with the preceding theme, and in this way the musical structure is made even more organic: unbroken ascending scales evolve from the triad mixtures of the theme. The trill organ point is also heard—its basic note, D, supports the tonality of the accompaniment, while its adjacent note, E-flat, supports the central note of the movement. The second theme continues dynamically straight away: it appears in inversion and many rhythmic variations.

At figure **10** the cello and viola give a third theme which makes a rather sharp contrast to the preceding one in rhythm and melodic line, but at the same time it displays close relationship to the first theme of the movement. Bartókian organic structure is once more eloquently proved by the transitional section between the second and third themes (between figures **7** and **11**); the elements of the former theme are gradually broken up and at the same time the rhythmic conception of the new theme appears and with it one or two fragments of the melody. While in character it reverts to the first subject, the third subject follows the dynamic pattern of the second subject in its development. Its melodic and rhythmic disintegration flows into a section which is even more open and relaxed than what has preceded it, a true development. At figure **23** large-scale, lengthy thematic development of the second subject begins, and at the beginning of this the third theme is also woven in.

At figure **31** a fughetta starts from a more distant variation of the second theme. The fast semiquaver theme, leggerissimo in character, is accompanied by a simplified outline of itself in quavers, by way of a countersubject as it were. The sparkling fughetta rolls off *piano* and *pianissimo* throughout, coloured at its climax by *sul ponticello*. This is a splendid example of Bartók's flitting-scintillating scherzo-atmosphere; it is the descendant of the coda of the Second Quartet's second movement and the forerunner of the glistening scherzo in the Fourth Quartet.

After the fughetta the return of the first theme (at figure **36**) suggests the beginning of a recapitulation, but this is merely a pseudo-recapitulation, since the development work is now continued even more dynamically. At figure **40** the third subject appears contracted into a completely chromatic projection, structured in canon and mirror-canon, and after **41** the composer's "scalpel" continues to strip off the thematic and motivic layers—penetrating right down to the "skeleton" of the themes. Of the scale-like melodic arch—the melodic material common to all three themes—no more remains than the basic gesture divested of all concrete melody and rhythm: the glissando. After this complete—and, it may safely be said, dramatic—demolition of the material used in the music, we expect a static point of rest, a recapitulation, but surprisingly it is not the movement's own recapitulation which appears but that of the first movement.

Ricapitulazione della prima parte

In the *Ricapitulazione* there are two structural principles at work—actually striving in contrasting directions. One stems from the nature of the recapitulation: the task of rounding off the material exposed, arranging things reassuringly, to make things stop statically. The tempo is actually faster here since the composer here prescribes Moderato with $\quad \downarrow = 96$ as opposed to the first part's Moderato with $\downarrow = 88$; in reality, however, it is still a deceleration which takes place because the rhythmic values are increased; the first subject, for example, returns in a rhythm augmented to three times the original values. The other trend shows Bartók's tendency as a composer (he himself made a statement concerning this) never to make anything reappear in an unaltered form. This recapitulation is an extreme example of a transformed recapitulation because it is necessary to carry out real detective work in order to in any way identify the returning themes.

Example 204.

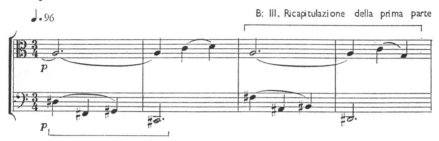

The first surprise: from the slow counterpoint of the two lower parts unfold the outlines of the first and third subjects together. The cello brings back the four-note third theme. Above this the viola plays the first theme with augmented rhythmic values and in crab.

The downward bending three-note motif which comes into the foreground at figure **1** may be the crab of the opening melody just heard on the viola, but at the same time it also refers back to the final element of the dome motif in the first part. The micro-melodics of the second theme, evoking nocturnal sounds, returns relatively briefly— only one melodic detail is given a larger role in a mirror inversion variation. It is only after this (at figure **3**) that the true recapitulation of the first theme follows—that is, the crab quotation concealed in the counterpoint to the third theme proves to have been no more than a vague reference. But the three-note opening motif does not come in its original form here, either, but in a so-called permutational variation (giving numbers to the notes of the original motif, in the order 2-1-3):

Example 205.

Thus the thematic material of the first part returns in essentially reversed order, which is significant from the formal construction point of view, since it conceals within it the basic principle behind Bartók's symmetrical, palyndromic sonata movement which later became firmly established.[7] After all this the recapitulation briefly evokes the second part of the development section, and then brings back in a virtually unaltered form the small Lento codetta which in the first part prepared the way for the recapitulation of the theme, and here for the transition to the *Coda*.

Coda: Allegro molto

The *Coda* is in its entirety constructed from the material of the *Seconda parte* and for this reason it, too, is really a recapitulation, like the part which precedes it. In the middle of it comes the second, E-flat centred theme of the *Seconda parte* which also played such a large part in the development. Of the three themes this is obviously the most suitable for varied motivic development. Apart from this the whole Coda is like a stretta; its fast tempo (Allegro molto), much changing of the metre, and accumulation of motifs make it extraordinarily animated. In the first part of the Coda the scale elements of the theme are in the foreground. Then rolling evolves between the various motifs of the theme. The climax of the stretta's rushing excitement comes at figure **10** where a version of the theme which is straightened out into scale form is played by the two violins in second canon using extreme diminution (displaced by a quaver), while the two lower instruments provide a counterpoint, likewise in canon form, in the shape of enormous glissandos over a range of two octaves. At figure **11** the third theme also returns and then the work is closed by excited series of trills and roughly snapping chords.

The two movements of the work display a considerably individual structure, both separately and together. The *Ricapitulazione* and *Coda* at the end of the work have undoubtedly a closing function: they do not by any means make the form three-part as some analysts have interpreted it. In the case of the Second Sonata for Violin and

---

[7]In the Second Piano Concerto and in the Fourth and Fifth String Quartets.

Piano the two movements really do become a three-part structure as a result of the material of the first movement being recalled at the end. Here, however, it is not of secondary importance that it is the material of *both* parts that returns in the closing section: the two-part form is thus not completed by *one* third part but by a complex consisting of *two* parts—that is, the binary structure remains binary.

The little section which has a finishing function really has the purpose of inwardly welding the two movements together. For if we consider that neither movement has a real recapitulation (in the first the first theme does return but just as an indication, and in the second the first theme makes only a pseudo-return), then it is obvious that the *Ricapitulazione* is the real recapitulation of the first part and the *Coda* that of the second.

Prima parte			Seconda parte		Ricapit.	Coda
Expos	Develop	Abbrev recap	Expos	Develop	Recap	Recap

The amazing economy of the composer is also evident in this in-dividual construction. Since the first theme of the first part has al-ready made a signal return in the first part itself, it is given a relatively small role in the recapitulation. And the first theme of the second part can be omitted from the coda because it has likewise already been used in the pseudo-recapitulation.

Reference has already been made to the fact that it is a slide from the C-sharp tonality of the first part that leads to the D tonality of the beginning of the second part. This D tonality, however, which is also borne out melodically by the D Dorian theme, is soon replaced by a new, chromatically raised level: the E-flat axis-note of the second theme suggests an E-flat tonality, especially since the melody—similarly to the first—is likewise in the Dorian mode. But this second theme really represents a tonal accumulation: the E-flat tonality melody—as a continuation of the first part—is accompanied by D tonality chords. This D–E-flat duality can be observed at the end of the exposition as well: the bass, establishing the D tonal level at figure **21**, slides up to E-flat once more by the beginning of the development. At figure **26** there is a repeat of the exposition's semitone-bitonality: the E-flat centred melody is accompanied by D tonality chords. The Seconda parte is ended by this D tonality when the cello part, resolving from C-sharp, settles for a considerable time on D, so as later to move on from there and gradually lead over into the ensuing formal section. There can naturally be no question of a firmly established final effect here (the analysis of the form has emphasized precisely its open character), but it can be no accident that the movement set out on a D tonal level and breaks off on a D level.

From a tonal point of view the *Ricapitulazione* is even more loose than the main section itself, since here the basic points are missing which earlier were pointers in determining the tonality. The Lento codetta, however, which returns unaltered, is very characteristic. The bass changes precisely at the point where, because of the consequences, it resolves not onto C-sharp but onto C. "In theory" it ought to have led to C-sharp here, too—this should determine the tonality retrospectively—but because of the coda's E-flat centre the melody finally goes to C.

Since the coda's thematic material is provided by the E-flat centred second theme it is quite regular that its tonality should evolve according to the original tonality of the theme. But E-flat is only one component of the tonality of the movement, for alongside it an important role was also played by D tonality in the main section. At the same time, the coda is the closing section of the whole work and so it is necessary to bring back the C-sharp tonality of the *Prima parte* in some form—at least according to the compositional technique which had evolved with Bartók by this time and which makes for unity tonally, too. Whether this C-sharp tonality does in fact return can be decided by a glance at the closing chord of the work. But the genius of the composition is seen in the way in which this closing C-sharp tonality is added earlier to the E-flat tonality of the coda's material.

The aforementioned climax of the excitement in this formal section is prepared by accumulated repetition of tetrachords in the framework of a diminished fourth. Notice the target-notes of the two outer parts:

Example 206.

Between the E-flat and C-sharp which have been reached melodically there lies the static D, which played such an important part together with E-flat in the *Seconda parte*. The exciting final moments thus really combine three tonalities. Then in the stretta intensification beginning at figure **10** these tonalities also appear separately. The upward striving scale developed from the E-flat centred theme sets out from E-flat and at **11** arrives at D-sharp (which is of course equal to E-flat). The second violin part, moving in canon in diminution with that of the first violin, starts from D, and so the accustomed D tonality once more joins E-flat. To all this the glissandos on the two lower instruments contribute by preparing C-sharp tonality, which finally and emphatically enters the scene with a relatively new theme, the third theme, which has not been heard for so long. This theme, which originally remained considerably open from the aspect of tonality and always changed its position, now emphasizes the C-sharp tonality both in its ascending form with fifth-mixtures and also in its descending form with fourth-mixtures. This accumulating of tonalities and the final selection of one single tonality from among them shows how great a part is played by tonality in Bartók with regard to formal structure.

CHAPTER TWELVE

THE FOURTH STRING QUARTET

According to the date written at the end of the score by the composer, Bartók started to write the Fourth Quartet in July of 1928 and completed it in September. As we know, during this period there was still no news of the Third Quartet, which the composer had submitted to the Philadelphia Musical Fund Society's competition. Then when the prize did finally arrive, attention was directed toward the Third Quartet, and it was chiefly in that connection that Bartók corresponded with Universal Edition in the interests of publication and the first performance. And so there is scarcely any trace of the birth of the new quartet, except the following reference which appears in a letter written on 22 December. "Some time ago I brought to the notice of Mr. Hertzka, director, the fact that I have also a fourth quartet which is now finished in manuscript. I think it would be wise to publish this latter a little later (perhaps only early in the autumn)."[1]

Bartók was patient because on this occasion, as with that of the Third, he wanted the work to be performed before it would be printed. And so it happened that not long after the first performance in Hungary of the Third Quartet, the Waldbauer Quartet performed the Fourth Quartet on 20 March 1929, in the course of Bartók's composer's evening, in a programme which also contained the Third Quartet, some pieces from *Out of Doors*, the cello version of the First Rhapsody and the vocal solo version of *Village Scenes*. Aladar Tóth

[1]See note 1 in the preceding chapter.

and Sándor Jemnitz again wrote about this truly important musical event—the first performance of a new Bartók composition—in splendid studies.[2]

In addition to the Hungarian string quartet group, a foreign quartet also played a serious role in gaining international recognition for the Fourth Quartet—this time not the Kolisch Quartet but the Pro Arte ensemble from Brussels. Their impresario, Gaston Verhuyck-Coulon, with whom Bartók was already in contact in connection with the Prevost arrangement of *Allegro barbaro* for wind orchestra, introduced the young group, who were nevertheless already world famous, to Bartók in his letter of 22 February 1929, and, referring to information obtained from André Gertler, requested the parts for the Third and Fourth Quartets.[3] The Pro Arte Quartet had already played the First and Second Quartets on several occasions— the first, for example, in July of 1927 in Frankfurt, just after Bartók's appearance there. Whether Bartók heard the Quartet's performance at that time we do not know. In any event, he quickly complied with Verhuyck-Coulon's request, thus the group performed the work early in October of 1929 in Berlin and on 21 October in Vienna.[4] The performance in Vienna was preceded by an interesting exchange of letters. Paul Bechert, director of the I.T.H.M.A. theatrical and musical agency, wrote to Bartók forwarding the Pro Arte's request that the master should dedicate the Fourth Quartet to them (*Documenta Bartókiana* 1968:148). Bartók complied with the request, although he scarcely knew the ensemble personally. In all probability it was Paul Bechert's emphatic request and the international reputation of the Quartet which prompted him in this decision and possibly also the hope that in this way an even wide international audience might be secured for his work. And so on 14 October he wrote the following letter to Universal. "I do not know what stage the publication of the

[2]*Pesti Napló* (22 March 1929); *Népszava* (22 March 1929). Quoted by Demény 1962:329–32.

[3]Gaston Verhuyck-Coulon's letter is in the possession of the Budapest Bartók Archives, and has not yet been published.

[4]Press documentation concerning the Berlin performance is published in Demény 1962:344–45.

Fourth Quartet score is at. If, however, it is at all possible I would ask you to add the following dedication: Au Quatuor Pro Arte, and after that the names of the gentlemen concerned (which I cannot give you exactly but which you can certainly find out). . ." On the same day he wrote a favourable reply to Paul Bechert. Thus when it came to the first Viennese performance on 21 October, the Pro Arte ensemble played the work as "their own."

It must be added straight away that the ensemble proved truly worthy of Bartók's apparent trust and confidence. In their letter of 23 October, Universal Edition discusses a "particularly great success," and this is further underlined by the criticism. The Brussels impresario, Verhuyck-Coulon, thanks Bartók for the dedication on 15 November and writes, among other things: "The Pro Arte Quartet like your work very much indeed and consider it one of the fundamental pieces [une des pièces capitales] of modern chamber music literature." The draft of Bartók's reply to this letter, presumably written at the beginning of December, is preserved in the Budapest Bartók Archives: in it he expressed his delight that the ensemble liked his work so much and writes that he would like to hear the interpretation. With this, and later actions, the Pro Arte Quartet rendered imperishable services in introducing Bartók's quartet art internationally.

Another detail which belongs to the history of the Fourth Quartet is that the publisher, as in the case of the Third Quartet, asked Bartók whether he would undertake the preparation of the formal analysis usual in the Philharmonia miniature score series. At first Bartók refused and trusted the publishers with the writing of the analysis. But with the Fourth Quartet—it would appear—he was not satisfied with the introduction printed at first although it is known that it, too, appeared with his consent, and in the end he himself wrote a short analysis of the individually structured work.[5] This analysis—which incidentally is to be found in the scores put out more recently—is nicely complemented by what he wrote to Max Rostal concerning the work's tempi in his letter of 6 November 1931. "While

[5]Published without title or signature as the introduction to the Universal Edition Score (UE 98788, W.Ph.166), in English, French, and German.

in Quartet I the tempo should be very elastic all through, in Quartet IV it is much more even and machine-like (except in the 3rd movement). But even here the chords, for instance, in the 37th bar of the 1st movement can, and, indeed, should be played more forcefully, making the tempo, of course, rather drawn out. To indicate the change of tempo at this point (and in similar places) would be confusing; the tempo changes of itself, so to speak, or correctly grasps and interprets the character of these 'pesante' chords. All the MM figures are correct here. In the 2nd movement the main tempo should, if possible, be ♩. = 98 or even quicker, not slower (of course with legato bowing . . . and *on no account spiccato!*) ; from bar 78 to 101 (of the middle section)   ♩. = 88 is better; from 102 on, the main tempo again. The 5th movement can perhaps be played somewhat quicker than indicated by the MM figures."[6]

First movement: Allegro

The formal construction of the work has been outlined by the composer himself in the foreword to the pocket score (Universal). This truly authentic explanation is also followed in this analysis, but further clarification has been put forward with reference to one or two points. Bartók does use the customary terms of analysis somewhat mechanically in a few cases, and, strictly speaking, he himself is not aware of the new elements in his own formal construction.

The first 13-bar unit undoubtedly has the function of a first subject: Bartók calls it a "first subject group." This is really a multi-layered first subject section, actually composed of three different kinds of material. The first is a vigorous opening gesture of two bars which is then answered by a second gesture of similar length. In the period-like relationship between the two elements the special point is that in the first the parts close in together while in the second they open out. This opening outwards naturally serves the dynamism of formal construction, for it is very difficult to continue a thematic unit which is closed within a period. In Bartók's theme-development and

[6]In the place of the "middle movement" translation of the Demény publication, we have used the word "middle section" (*Bartók Letters* No. 162).

form-building technique, however, an essential role is played by the organic continuation of the parts and building them into each other, even when the material is apparently broken up. Here, too, in the first 13-bar unit of the Fourth Quartet the continuity is interrupted by five caesuras. These interruptions, however, influence only the atmosphere, for from a purely musical point of view there is an organic inner relationship between the parts which are separated from one another. In the first four bars, as has been mentioned above, the first gesture is answered by the second gesture.

After the first "period" with its broad gestures there appears material which is narrower in movement. Its motivic basic element, however, is none other than the closing trichord just heard. The parts enter in a terraced way and a characteristic "note-cluster" is produced by their being closely built upon each other. The layers of the first cluster are built from below upwards and those of the second from above downwards, in a close minor second pile. The end of the second cluster—corresponding with the second gesture of the beginning of the work—opens out and the parts, crossing each other, become rearranged into a major second pile.

At the end of the first cluster, hidden away as it were in the cello part, a little rhythmic motif with a chromatic melodic arch appears. This motif—we may anticipate—is the basic element, the proto-motif of the movement, and indeed of the whole work. Its importance soon becomes evident: after the opening out of the second cluster the first subject is brought to a close with it. Now the emblem-like, terse motif appears in a mirror canon arrangement. A new trend in Bartók's development technique is already in evidence in these first thirteen bars. In the earlier string quartets after the exposition of a theme or motif, dynamic thematic development work began, which was, however, essentially writing which continued according to traditional principles. The material of the first subject in the Fourth Quartet is fundamentally different from this: the continuity is divided into relatively static blocks, and it is within these blocks, almost in micro-structures, that dynamism develops. The music is more concise and compact than anything preceding it and can really only be compared to the development technique of Webern.

The formal section from bars 14 to 29 is a transition according to Bartók's analysis. Its material is a wave-line motif consisting of four notes which unfolds polyphonically three levels above a bitonal basic texture. This motif is so characteristic and plays such an important role in the movement—and even more so in the work's final movement—that we might be better advised to regard it as a second first subject and not a transition. This is also supported after it by the reappearance of the proto-motif's mirror canon that the two similar blocks firmly surround the section regarded by Bartók as a transition, but as a result of this it scarcely possesses any transitional character. It is rather proto-motif canon which may be regarded as transitional material, for here it leads to a new formal unit beginning in bar 30.

Concerning the four-note motif, it has been shown elsewhere that it is a mistuned tetratonic melody, a form of an imaginary fifth framework which has been distorted into a diminished fifth. This is best proved in the last movement when it becomes clear that the motif is the central "section" of a mistuned pentatonic system. Thus the motif is in itself bitonal in an individual linear form of bitonality (see Example 121). But the motif's accompaniment, already referred to, is likewise bitonal: a C-major trichord level is heard in the viola's ostinato while the cello accompanies this with G-sharp minor second inversion chords. These two tonal levels are not alien to the bitonality of the melodic levels above them, the notes they use can also be separated and divided into two pentatonic systems at a distance of a diminished fifth from each other.

Example 207.

This stratum, which from the tonal point of view is double (C–F-sharp) is, however, divided by Bartók into three layers in the texture: for the motif sets out from C-sharp and is then continued by a canon on a level one fifth higher, and then a new part joins in on a level which is in a diminished fifth relationship to this latter. This third and uppermost part produces a double tension in the texture because it progresses in a tense, anti-acoustic relationship not only with the part immediately below it but also with the lowest part.

The most characteristic melodic element of the second subject, beginning in bar 30, is derived from the proto-motif. The whole- tone scale motifs along with it make the theme group considerably vague from the tonal aspect. On the basis of the beginning and the stronger cadence of one of the scale motifs a feeling of A-flat tonality evolves—even if only faintly. Seen from this angle Bartók's analysis becomes more understandable with regard to the function of the preceding section. The part which shows C–G-sharp bitonality is "transitional" in function because one of its levels points back to the C tonality of the first subject and its other level (G-sharp) forward to the A-flat tonality of the second subject which agrees with it enharmonically. This aspect, however, does not diminish the particularly important role played by the motif in question.

The downward chromatic gesture at the beginning of the second subject later turns round—just as it has the same value both upwards and downwards in the proto-motif—and in this way a folksong-like, more closed theme of fifth-structure evolves from it. But the melody is only relatively closed, since there is no natural feeling of cadence because of the double fifth-answer, and so the cadence—mistuned in relation to the fifth levels—is only created by recalling the chromatic opening motif. This theme section starts from A-flat and arrives at E—that is, its mistuned dominant.

The six-bar final theme beginning in bar 44 is born from an extension of the proto-motif. The broad downward arch of the motif is accompanied by straightforward melody-axes repeating the same note. This type of theme plays an especially important part in Bartók's works which display neo-Baroque aspirations. Its closest relation from the First Piano Concerto can be seen in Example 30.

The tonal position of the final theme is likewise not unambiguous. Since it is directly connected to the second subject ending on E, it is possible to regard E as the tonal centre here, too. There can, however, be no question of a "keynote" since this E axis is placed at the uppermost point in the texture. The exposition is concluded by a minor second cluster. Its tonal definition is provided solely by the chromatic tetrachords moving towards E in the two lower parts.

Example 208.

The development section begins with a combination of the second subject's chromatic gesture and the trichord of the note clusters. From the auxiliary note motif originate demi-semiquaver trills, the same kind of musical picture as in the Musette from the suite *Out of Doors* dating from 1926. The repetition of the trills, starting with a sforzando, has a shivering effect. To this "shivering" background large-scale development of the four-note mistuned motif begins; the small motif, which at its first appearance (bars 14–24) continually turned back upon itself, here comes in a broadly arching melodic form. Behind its melodic development it is, however, quite apparent that its roots reach back into the development of the diminished fifth canon.

Together with the unfolding of the melody there also starts a variation process the tendency of which is to structurally expand the motif. It should be noticed that it goes through a similar expanding process in the last movement. In bar 75, as the final result of the motivic dissecting work which has taken place up to this point, the musical texture disintegrates into its most basic elements: every melodic element disappears and only broad glissandos and trill motifs remain. This part is very similar to the end of the Third Quartet's *Seconda parte.*

But after this great "demolition" we can also witness the reconstruction process: struggle begins between the shivering trills and the proto-motif, which once more steps in the foreground. The two different kinds of material are almost "brutally" confronted with each other: the proto-motif or an occasional fragment of it breaks open and wedges its way into the closed blocks of the trill motif.

The end of the development section and at the same time the beginning of the recapitulation is indicated by the basic motif appearing unisono. From the recent battle this was the motif which emerged triumphant, so it is logical for it to come now not as a secondary element as at the beginning of the exposition but to be given greater emphasis. For this reason it is also wedged in between three appearances of the returning opening motif using three different instrumentations.

The recapitulation continues in a perfectly regular manner, although each individual theme and motif is transformed more or less. This transformation is also accompanied by certain condensing: as opposed to the 48 bars of the exposition, the recapitulation has 42, and within these there is a significant decrease in the first and second theme groups, the final theme being the only one to grow and that only because the coda of the movement develops from it.

Interrelationship between the development section and the coda is a phenomenon already familiar from formal structure in Beethoven. We meet the same thing in this Bartók movement, but it is characteristic of Bartók's economic structure that only the dynamic closing and returning section from the development is used for the coda— that is, the battle between the two contrasting motifs. The melodic element is represented here, too, by the basic motif, but contrasted with it on this occasion is not the trill motif but rising and augmenting melodic blocks unfolding out of a mysterious *piano.* Their victory appears inevitable at first, but after a climax (bar 152) the basic motif appears again and now comes out triumphant. This triumph is reinforced by a canon in diminution and a melodic extension which lends an even more closed character to the motif.

Example 209.

The position within the recapitulation of the section which we have called the second first subject group also proves that it is more than transitional material: it returns on the same tonal level, only transposed down an octave—that is, it belongs unequivocally to the first subject group. On the other hand, the other themes, in keeping with the sonata principle, appear in a different tonality. The second subject ends in C, and this same C tonality is then continued by the final theme. In the dramatic struggle of the coda, the melody—climbing higher and higher out of the depths—contrasting with the proto-motif, rests consistently on F-sharp and G-sharp—that is, on the Bartókian (mistuned) dominants of C; in other words, on the adjacent chromatic notes of the acoustic dominant. This same melodic preparation precedes the motif which ends the movement; the contrapuntal game breaks off on A-flat—that is, the augmented fifth of C. From there it "resolves" into C; in the summarizing emblem motif the melody's minor third is coloured by a major third, and indeed in a structure which is different from that of the alpha chord: the minor third is underneath and the major third is above.

Example 210.

Second movement: Prestissimo, con sordino

It has already been mentioned that the direct antecedents of this movement can be found in the Second and Third Quartets. An extension of this kind of tone to cover a whole movement is presented with particular emphasis in Berg's *Lyric Suite*—the composition which inspired Bartók in other respects as well. The connection with Berg is indeed strengthened by yet another element: in the fifth movement of the *Lyric Suite* (Presto delirando) there are the same kinds of light, flitting glissando effects as in this movement by Bartók (bars 136–145, and at the end of the movement). There are, of course, glissandos in the Third Quartet as well, and also in the first movement of the Fourth, but there they have a weighty "clinging" character. Here these light glissandos, stemming from the tone of the movement which is in any case light and fleeting, are the final variations of the chromatic upward and downward melodic lines.

"The second movement has a scherzo character and is in three sections," writes Bartók in his outline of the form. Its theme is an arching melody which rises and falls back chromatically—within the framework of a perfect fifth, in the tonality of E. It is first heard on the two lower instruments and then on a level a fifth higher on the two violins. The theme is accompanied by point-like chords on the two other instruments, each joining on two adjacent notes of the chromatic theme. By the time the melody arrives back at the starting note, E, the accompaniment rises as far as A-sharp and, by means of a direct leading-note step, reaches the basic note of the level beginning a fifth higher.

The harmonic profile of the movement is also determined by the superimposition of two perfect fifths in a chordal form, however, semitone displacement makes the sound tense.

Example 211.

In the scherzo theme the first fifth wave-arch has really been answered by a wave measuring a fourth. This fourth also has some influence on the chords in the movement—fourth chords become constructed from it.

The first part of the scherzo form is also tripartite within itself. The theme returns in bar 54 in a four-part canon at the octave in diminution, and at bar 62 a sixteen-bar transitional section begins which prepares for the trio. A motif using complementary writing and weavering two major seconds into each other, anticipates the second-piles of the trio.

In the trio section a large part is played by the clusters composed of various melodic repetitions. Bartók's organic and economic structuring is characterized by the melody and the accompanying background fabric being built from the same material; the parts—filling each other out, that is in a complementary way—add up to second-piles. At the same time the theme starting in bar 78 also refers back to the first movement's note clusters. In the centre of the trio section the cluster remains alone and its moving parts fill out two fifth chromatically. We will meet with a similar cluster effect in the trio of the Scherzo movement in the Fifth Quartet, too.

Example 212.

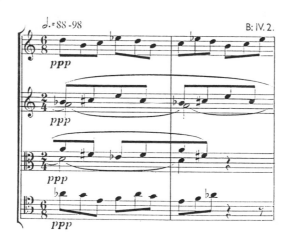

The colour technique of the clusters suddenly changes in bar 136 to light glissandos, an then *sul ponticello* playing lends an even more individual and even more colourful sound to the end of the trio.

As a result of the tonally neutral character of the clusters and other note piles, it is not possible to determine the tonality of the trio. The tonal character is gradually restored in the closing section, however, when the fifth-chords are brought back. Chromatic raising of the fifth-chords leads back to the tonality of E which on this occasion comes only at the melodic level, for the other parts add colour to this with adjacent notes and fifth-chords on other foundations (bar 189). This recapitulation, however, is anticipated by a clever pseudo-recapitulation: from bar 175 the parts throw the scherzo theme's opening motif to each other in its original form and in inversion. Adjacent chromatic notes already appear here to mistune and colour the tonality.

In the middle of the scherzo recapitulation an interesting combination of the theme and the complementary transitional motif appears as new thematic material. This is accompanied by the cello's pizzicato-glissando fifth-chords.

Example 213.

The animated movement is ended by an even more animated coda. The glissando motifs come into the foreground once more, and to these a colourful background is provided by fast scale motifs, chains of trills, pizzicato and *sul ponticello* playing. The musical material, completely dissolved as it were, quietens down to *ppp* and then on the wings of major ninth glissandos really does fly off. The closing harmony rounds off the movement tonally: airy E harmonics join an E–B–F-sharp fifth- chord.[7]

[7]András Mihály published a penetrating analysis of the metrics of this movement in *Muzsika* Nos. 9, 10, 12 (1967).

Third movement: Non troppo lento

In the movement which occupies the central position in the symmetrical construction of the work it is principally the change in texture that is conspicuous; up to this point counterpoint has dominated, or at least been mixed in with homophonic elements. Here it is homophony that reigns supreme; the whole movement is characterized by static harmonic blocks with melodies unfolding under them, above them, or among them. The key to the movement lies in the structure of the chords and their relationships to the melodic elements.

The opening chord and the closing chord, containing the same notes but not structured in the same way, offer very important guidance in the analysis of the harmony of the movement. In the opening structure major seconds dominate, and in the closing structure the same is heard but laid out in fifths.

Example 214.

The opening out of this closer structure into something wider shows that both have an imaginary common basis, the chord consisting of five interrelated fifths.

Example 215.

Harmonic movement between the outer points is generally of a slower nature; each chord block is spread out over a lengthy area as the static basis behind the melodic action. This slow melodic action is essentially no more than a variation of the fifth-structure basic chord—coloured with adjacent chromatic notes. Thus the second chord beginning in bar 13, for example, has two notes from the perfect fifth-structure surrounded by chromatic colouring notes.

Example 216.

Tension grows in proportion to the disintegration of the fifth-structure and the enrichment of the melodic elements. In the third formal unit, starting in bar 22, the fifth-structure already incomplete, the missing notes being replaced by chromatically adjacent notes.

Example 217.

When the melody calms down, the harmonic structure rests on a perfect fifth-chain in bar 33 and then similar "alien" notes again make the musical texture tense.

We reach a point of rest in bar 41: the perfect fifth- structure changes over to a perfect fourth-structure. After this comes a climax in the excitement (the tempo also changes Agitato), and the chord structure is once more coloured by "alien" notes. In bars 47–51 wave motion of the two outer parts seems to introduce a new harmonic element into movement, but this, too, is actually a continuation of the earlier chord forming principle the two-phase chord change uses a complete pentatonic system—but of course pentatonic systems form a chain consisting of four interrelated fifths.

In the harmonic action of the movement, therefore, quite independently of the melodic process, a special tension wave can be observed. This is made even more interesting and complex by the
combined movement of the two dimensions. For the melody consistently complements the chords. The first chord, still arranged in
seconds, is filled out in the middle by the melody.

Similarly the second melodic unit beginning in bar 14 is built into
the chord block. And the third, in the highest register of the cello,
even rises above the harmonic block. By the time it comes to rest, its
final note, A, becomes an organic part of the fifth-structure sounding
above it.

Example 218.

This complementary process is finally tensely extended by the violin
melody which appears at the climax in the movement's excitement in
such a way that the notes of the melody are fitted in among the notes
of the chord virtually like cog-wheels.

Example 219.

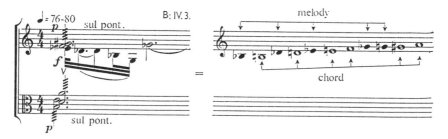

This is the climax in the tension curve of the movement, but the complementary process reaches its peak on yet a higher level in the most complete complement possible: G-flat pentatony and C diatony (the black and white keys on the piano) are fitted into one another and this produces a complete chromatic scale. After this there is nothing surprising in the fact that the final chord of the movement is supplemented by the note D, with which the whole process began.

All this combined harmonic and melodic action encloses within a firm formal framework a gradual unfolding of a single melody with a Hungarian folk character, and its variation. The closed eight-bar theme is divided into two equal parts: the first is considerably improvisational in character, consisting of movement around a single centre note; the second part is a parlando-rubato monologue, with a more expansive melodic arch. The first part is chromatic, the second diatonic. The repeated notes of the first part create tension not only through their excited rhythm but also through their complementary relationship with the accompanying chords. On the other hand, the second part is related to the harmonic accompaniment in a similar way when it comes to rest: the final note is no longer a complementary note but a component part of the harmony.

Example 220.

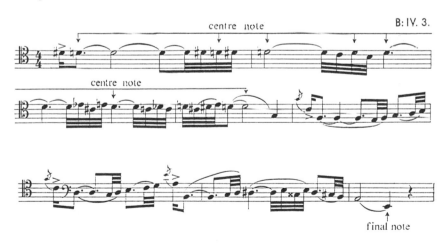

The central section of the movement evolves in a different way; here, when the melody reaches the extreme point of the variational process, it breaks up into tiny fragments almost like bird-twittering (bars 35–40). Then at the Agitato climax the melodic character reciting on a single note (first part of the theme) returns, in relation to which the following eight bars make a variation of the calming (second) part of the theme. In bar 55 a tranquil summary begins; the diatonic monologue melody returns to the cello while the violin accompanies it with a counterpart which has a mirror canon effect. (This can only be called an effect because it cannot be regarded as an exact mirror, nor an exact canon.)

The tonal structure of the movement can be outlined by the movement of two different factors. One is the chordal process which provides the real foundation of the tonality. Th other is the terraced structure composed of the first parts of the varied melody, which is rather just a modal projection of the tonality.

Example 221.

theme	var. 1.	var. 2	central section	vars. 3-4	diat.monologue	var. 5 (Coda)
bar 6	bar 14	bar 22	bar 34	bar 42	bar 55	bar 64

B _____
F _____ 6
D _____ ↕3

G♭ _____
6 ↓____ _ _ _ _ _ _ ₃↕ A _____
C

Fourth movement: Allegretto pizzicato

This second scherzo-like movement is strongly related to the Prestissimo which corresponds to it in the symmetrical order of the work. In the Prestissimo it is the muted tone-colour that gives a special tonal character to the music, and here this is provided by pizzicato. The relationship, however, is even deeper than this; Bartók himself draws attention to the fact that the movement's "theme being identical with that of the second movement; there it moved within the

narrow realm of the chromatic scale—here it is extended over the
diatonic scale; accordingly its range in the former is a fifth, while here
it is an octave."[8] It is characteristic of Bartók's primarily musical thinking that he does not carry out the extension of the chromatic arch-
melody mechanically, and thus, as opposed to the chromatic melody
moving in minor seconds, he does not apply the whole-tone scale
moving in nothing but major seconds, but the augmented fourth-
minor seventh so-called acoustic scale of Rumanian origin. The basic
unit's tendency towards logical extension, however, is apparent in the
Lydian opening of the theme, which uses a group of major seconds,
and in its last part, which comes nearer to the whole-tone scale:

Example 222.

The movement is also characterized by expansion in the tonal sense.
The theme of the second movement was played in two fifth layers;
here the theme is heard in a four-part fugato arrangement, and on
four different fifth levels. This sort of fugato arrangement, which later
assumes an even more consistent form in the *Music for Strings, Percussion and Celesta*, obviously produces greater tonal breadth than the
two-level answer at the fifth.

It is worth following the relationship of the theme entries to the
accompanying harmonic basis. The tonality of the movement is A flat,
which in the fugato arrangement agrees with the first entry of the
theme. It is, however, very characteristic of Bartók's harmonic world
that the melody based on A-flat has an accompanying chord based on
G—to be precise, a chord which, along with a G–D–G perfect octave
layer, contains another A-flat–E-flat layer which in relation to the first
is mistuned. It is out of this mistuned level that the melody appears. The

---

[8] Bartók erroneously calls the scale in question diatonic, for the notes it contains do not
form a related fifth chain. This mode of "heptatonia secunda" (see Lajos Bárdos's
study in *Magyar Zene* 1962/63) does, however, create a "diatonic impression" since its
tetrachords taken singly are diatonic in structure.

entry of the second part—on a level a fifth higher, that is starting from E-flat—is accompanied by similar tonal ambiguity. Here the melody does appear out of the fifth- chord based on E-flat, but the chord's fifth and octave are coloured by adjacent chromatic notes here, too: A is heard beside B-flat, and E beside E-flat. And the E also chromatically colours the second fifth of the E-flat basic note, that is F.

The third part enters from the same background as that which preceded it, but a fifth higher—that is on the B-flat level. The B-flat–F–B-flat octave framework is coloured in the same way here by A and E, but their functions are different: the A colours the basic note and the E colours the fifth. From the tonal point of view, the fourth entry is the clearest of all: the melody's F level is supported by an F major triad, but the third and fifth are alternately coloured by adjacent chromatic notes—B-flat and B.

There is a peculiar polymetric relationship between melody and accompaniment. The eight-bar melody, regular in construction, is accompanied by "guitar-like" chords which are asymmetrically divided. The asymmetry of this accompaniment appears even within the $\frac{3}{4}$ metre, but there are even more complicated metrical displacements to notice than this. The *sforzato* accents of the individual chords produce larger metrical units, and the peculiar thing is that these larger metrical units are different and continually alternate. In the first nine bars, for example, $\frac{5}{4}$, $\frac{6}{4}$, $\frac{7}{4}$ and $\frac{8}{4}$ divisions appear in a consistently increasing order within the $\frac{3}{4}$ notation.

The relationship between melody and accompaniment is thus characterized not only by simple polymetrics but by complete metrical independence, for which it is primarily Arab folk music that may have served as an example to Bartók. It will suffice to document the metrical contrasts of a single line. (Notice that only in one case does the accent of melody and accompaniment coincide, and this merely increases the strange feeling of deviation in the other accents.)

Example 223.

The thirty-six bar formal section structured as a four-part fugato—the first part of the three part scherzo form—ends in A-flat tonality at the end of the significantly augmented fourth entry. From this close, however, by means of further motivic use of the theme, a transitional section begins without caesura, providing a continuous bridge over to the trio, which begins in bar 45.

The theme is a close variant of the trio theme in the second movement. The hard pizzicato effect of banging on the fingerboard prescribed by the composer lends it an individual colour. The background is provided here, too, by cluster-like colour-chords.

A free recapitulation of the scherzo theme begins in bar 88. The fugato structure is here replaced by a two-part octave canon in diminution, in the first violin and the cello, the guitar effects of the two parts between them continuing the character of the trio. The thematic material, closed to start with, is broken up as in a development by means of inversions and rhythmic imitations, and then closes like a fan (bars 102–112) and, settling into the A-flat major level, moves into a small coda (bar 113). The material, broken into scale motifs which mirror one another and into rhythm imitation, is very closely related to the pizzicato episode in the second movement of the *Music for Strings, Percussion and Celesta* (from bar 242). The motivic material of the coda on the other hand, which has derived from the last part of the scherzo theme and taken on an independent life, anticipates no. 124 of *Mikrokosmos*—"Staccato." After a momentary suspension of the rhythmic progress another fan-like closing gesture leads to the final chord of the movement. Only the A-flat at the top and bottom of the chord represents tonality, for the "area" between them is filled out by the notes of the theme's scale, further coloured by two adjacent chromatic notes.

Example 224.

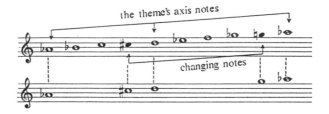

Fifth movement: Allegretto molto

While the relationship between the second and fourth movements rested on the principle of variation, the first and last movements of the work—that is, its pillar movements—are connected by the cyclic principle. What played a relatively subsidiary role in the first movement (Bartók describing it as no more than transitional material) here appears as a first subject and plays a dominating role in the whole movement's thematic work.

The whole movement is a sort of "Allegro barbaro." The four-note motif appearing as first subject bore certain traces of Arab folk music even in the first movement; these come forward now even more unambiguously as a result of the transformation of the rhythmic character and the drum-beat accompaniment.

The appearance of the theme—to quote the composer once more—is introduced by "chord beats (chords of fifths obscured by seconds)." We have already seen how important fifth-chords are in the work's harmonic system. It is, therefore, to be expected that the fifth movement should summarize and condense from this aspect as well. In keeping with the movement's C tonality the central layer of the fifth-chord is the fifth C–G, to the basic note of which D-flat is added as an adjacent chromatic note, and to its fifth F-sharp is added. The tonally decisive C–G plane is, however, veiled by the cello's F–C–G fifth-chord broken in a downward direction which sounds, precisely because of its being broken downwards, a little like a G–C–F fourth-chord. As a new note the F also clashes with the adjacent chromatic note F sharp, thus intensifying the hard, raw quality of the chord.

Example 225.

It is out of this introductory chord repetition that the theme's drum-like ostinato accompaniment develops. Here the C–G fifth becomes the sole basis of the music, but the number of adjacent chromatic notes increases, for the D-flat and F-sharp which create tension from within the fifth are now joined by A-flat in the form of an acciaccatura. From the metrical point of view it is very important that the even quavers of the viola are divided by several interrupting chords on the cello—reinforced by *sf*-s—into metrical units of three and two. The groups of three and two combine consistently into larger 3 + 3 + 2 units—that is, into a kind of asymmetrical accompaniment form which is a very frequent phenomenon in Arab folk music. Note that

Bartók modified the even quaver accompaniment of the piece "Os-tinato" from the series *Mikrokosmos* when he transcribed it for two pianos, in such a way that similar 3 + 3 + 2 metrical units are produced (see Example 55).

The short barbaric theme develops with the help of inversion, expansion and changes in register. After its first appearance, it is heard two octaves higher in bar 23 in mirror inversion. It must be stressed that this is not a note-for-note mirror inversion, but a version in which the melody progresses along an unaltered interval structure in the opposite direction.

Example 226.

In the other variations (bars 31 and 37) the interval structure is also expanded; this is how, for example, a perfect fourth model evolves from the mistuned tetratonic melody. It is, however, characteristic of all the various versions that they fit perfectly into the ostinato chord of the accompaniment.

Example 227.

In the course of further development of the theme when more remote motivic combinations also appear, the accompanying chord slips down to the A–E fifth level (into which fits the form of the theme which has an A-sharp–D framework fits) and then, as the most important modulatory section, the F-sharp–C-sharp fifth level as-sumes supremacy and this, the other hand, is now coloured by the ad-jacent chromatic notes C and G. Although the set of notes used is in itself virtually unchanged, its application indicates that the musical process has arrived at a higher tonal plane, to a "Bartók dominant" level, as it were/, while the theme returns in its original form. This is no static recapitulation with any settling tendency, but a bridge to another dynamic turning point when the first three notes of the theme break away from it and carry on as an independent motif with a scherzando character. The fifth-structure which has so far reigned is now supplemented by fourth-structure:

Example 228.

As a result of the gradual break up of the melodic elements, the bare fifth-chords once more come into the foreground—even rhyming with the introductory section, only in a different tonality. An interesting point is the confrontation of fourth-chord and fifth-chord: in the upper parts there is an E-flat–A-flat–D-flat fourth chord, to which the cello plays a D–A–E fifth chord. As in the introduction, the breaking of the chord in a downward direction also gives the impression of a fourth-chord on this occasion as a result of which the upper and lower chord levels clash in semitone bitonality. But the tonal withdrawal is only temporary, for after the parts move chromatically in different directions, a unisono leads the C cadence of bar 148.

The border between two large formal units is indicated by the sharp cut of a general pause. The new section is not a development section but a central section like a trio, which has completely new material. This "new" material, however, is an undisguised reference to the first movement. For the light grazioso theme beginning in bar 156 is none other than the folksong structured closing melody of the second subject in the first movement. There the melody was played in three fifth layers and here it is heard on three fourth levels and finished with a mistuned cadence.

Example 229.

The emblem-like proto-motif also returns from the first movement, setting a hard marcato character against the grazioso theme. The whole central part of the movement is taken up with these two materials and rich development of them, and then in bar 238 the beginning of the recapitulation of the first part arrives with the appearance of the Arab theme. The drumming accompaniment is now omitted, though the hard grating fifth-chords play a part here, too, but just between the various appearances of the theme. Instead of simultaneity, placing things side by side now dominates. Here also the contrasting keys, displaced by a semitone, appear side by side laid out in a linear way. The placing of the C-sharp and C tonalities alongside one another chordally is followed by linear spreading out of the whole melody's bitonality (see Example 121).

After the scherzando motif is recalled in G-sharp tonality, the coda begins in bar 365 and this ascends, through building up the Arab theme, to the resurrection of the first movement's emblem-motif. A contrapuntal accumulation of the emblem-like proto-motif—almost identical note for note with the end of the first movement—closes the movement, and at the same time the whole work, with a *ff* marcato character.

CHAPTER THIRTEEN

THE FIFTH STRING QUARTET

Bartók wrote this work as a commission from Elizabeth Sprague-Coolidge. This American patroness, famous for her support of contemporary music, commissioned works from numerous significant composers of the period; among them, Schoenberg's Fourth Quartet written in 1936 as the result of a request from her. When and how she came to be in contact with Bartók is not known, but since Bartók was permanently represented at the I.S.C.M. festivals from the 1920s onwards, he was obviously held to be one of the leading European composers in the United States as well, at least in more expert professional circles.

Interesting information on this question is provided by a letter dated November 1935, from Gaston Verhuyck-Coulon, the Brussels impresario, in which he tells Bartók that Mrs. Coolidge had handed over the parts of the Fifth Quartet to the Pro Arte Quartet and entrusted the group with a few performances. "It will probably be of interest to you," Verhuyck-Coulon adds, "that this work was ordered on the recommendation of our friends the Pro Arte Quartet."[1]

The composition was completed extremely quickly on this occasion, too: Bartók began work on it on 6 August 1934, and finished it precisely a month later, as is shown by the usual note at the end of the score. It must be added that this was the sole composition written in

---

[1] This letter, in French, is in possession of the Budapest Bartók Archives, and has not yet been published.

that year, and the preceding year yielded no more than orchestral ar-
rangment (*Hungarian Peasant Songs* from the *15 Hungarian Peasant
Songs* written originally for piano and the *Hungarian Folksongs* from
the series of *Twenty Hungarian Folksongs*). Thus the Fifth Quartet is
the first great creative achievement after a short period of "silence,"
the "first chord" in the great works of the 1930s.

The first performance of the Fifth Quartet, in accordance with
the wishes of the commissioner, took place in Washington on 8 April
1935, at the Viennese Kolisch Quartet's concert. The other works in
the programme were Beethoven's great B-flat Major Quartet op. 130,
and Alban Berg's *Lyric Suite*."[2]

Mrs. Coolidge, to whom the work is dedicated and who, as the
commissioner, possessed exclusive performing rights on the work for
almost nine months, also asked for a performance from the Pro Arte
Quartet, as mentioned above. From Verhuyck-Coulon's letter we
know that the group performed the work in Marseille on 13 December 1935, and the impresario asked Bartók for a short introduction
and formal analysis for this concert. It is not known for certain
whether Bartók actually sent what was requested to the Pro Arte
Quartet, but some evidence is offered by an incomplete draft
preserved in the Budapest Bartók Archives and first published by
László Somfai.[3] This is also a document as valuable as the analysis of
the Fourth Quartet published later in Universal Edition, and in certain respects it is even more valuable since it affords a glimpse of the
new individual conception of Bartók's tonal thinking.[4]

After the first performance in Washington almost a whole year
passed before the work was first performed in Hungary. The interpretation on this occasion was given by the successors to the
Waldbauer Quartet—the New Hungarian Quartet.[5] They first played

[2]János Demény offers documentation of the reception of the concert (Demény
1962:504)

[3]For a critical publication in Hungarian, supplemented by the French and German language draft, see *Bartók Béla Írásai 1* (1989) Nos. 19, 19a, 19b.

[4]See chapter 6, "Tonality" in Part One.

[5]The members: Sándor Végh, László Halmos, Dénes Koromzay and Vilmos Palotai.

it in Vienna at the concert of the I.S.C.M. Austrian section on 18 February 1936, and it was then heard in the main hall in the Music Academy in Budapest. It is typical that the *Pester Lloyd*, whose Viennese correspondent had received Bartók's new work in February with rapturous adjectives (it is true that the critic was none other than Ernst Křenek), reported on the Hungarian performance almost sourly.[6] The paper's home staff obviously represented the conservative upper middle class attitude which did actually "bow" before Bartók's greatness on the basis of his success abroad, but they were unable to understand it.

The finest critical study was Sándor Jemnitz's piece in the *Népszava*. Jemnitz, who not much later published a long and penetrating study on the Fifth Quartet in German in the periodical *Musica Viva*, gave a shorter account of the musical event in the Budapest paper, but with great enthusiasm and expert understanding, and also stressed on the progressive political significance of the performance.[7]

First movement: Allegro

The first subject evolves before us through a hard hammering, almost clattering, note repetition, just as in the first movement of the First Piano Concerto, except that the directions of the two melodies are different.

Example 230.

---

[6]*Pester Lloyd* (25 February 1936). See Demény 1962.

[7]*Népszava* 4 March 1936. See Demény 1962:531. It becomes clear, however, from Sándor Jemnitz's correspondence that on 17 February 1936, Bartók sent Jemnitz the formal analyses prepared for Gaston Verhuyck-Coulon. (*Jemnitz Sándor válogatott zenekritikái* [*Selected Music Criticism of Sándor Jemnitz*] (Budapest: Zeneműkiadó, 1973), 484.

Example 230 (continued)

The theme started by the two lower parts is answered in octave canon by the two upper parts. As has been explained earlier, the theme itself has a mistuned octave structure—that is, it is built on a B-flat–E–A framework, in which the E–A level is produced by downward displacement of F–B-flat by a semitone. When the two upper parts enter an octave higher, the lowest part is already moving in the mistuned plane, so that the combined sound made tense by semitone bitonality. And when the upper parts also reach the E–A level, the lowest part's tetratonic motif slides down another semitone, and thus the bitonal tension is not relieved. The two parts woven in a contrapuntal texture eventually meet and with leading-note type of semitone step this leads to a playful transitional section. At the end of this short transition the clattering motif which opened the movement reappears. It can already be sensed that this clattering motif is to fulfill the function of framework motif in the movement; it appears at almost all the junctions in the form. Here it is heard in a grating mass of D and C-sharp notes, which already secures the tonal transition as well: C-sharp resolves like a leading-note on to C, and D on to E-flat, and in this way the succeeding formal section evolves, the C minor tonal plane of the second subject.

This second subject is characterized by melodic leaps over wide intervals and by polymetric displacement. The theme is played by the two violins, while the two lower parts accompany with a rhythmic counterpoint.

An important melodic feature of the second subject is that it moves in the two-line octave and continually jumps back to the one-line C as a steady support note. This characteristic Bartókian melodic type—with one side fixed and steady and the other expanding—might also be called a "spring melody," indicating in this way the inner dynamism of the melodic type.

Example 231.

The melody, which is written in $\frac{4}{4}$ but actually moves in units of $\frac{3}{8}$ $\frac{4}{8}$ $\frac{5}{8}$ $\frac{6}{8}$ and $\frac{7}{8}$, stretches higher and higher, and when it reaches its climax it suddenly breaks off—interrupted by the clattering framework motif. This is a marvellous moment in Bartók's instrumental dramaturgy, when the two materials struggle dramatically: the melody interrupted on A-flat (G-sharp)–B still cries out repeatedly, but it is the framework theme, appearing on the C tonal plane, that is victorious (bars 36–44).

This appearance of the clattering framework theme signifies the start of a new formal section. But from the tonal point of view it is the G-sharp–B surviving traces of the preceding theme that prepare the tonality of the new theme, and indeed by means of the leading note method of the preceding formal boundary, except that whereas in the earlier case the second opened out into a minor third, here the minor third closes in, the G sharp leads the melody's A tonality, and the B prepares the steady B-flat bass.

The formal function of the new dolce character theme is a final section. The soft, waving melody represents a significant contrast to the hard energetic tone which has dominated so far. Its structure is an inversion of the first subject: the latter rose from B-flat through E to A, but here there is a descent from A to B-flat. The mistuned octave framework is reinforced by the pedal notes, squeezing the melodic movement between B-flat and A.

The texture of the final theme is also different in character; the first two themes were treated contrapuntally and drawn with considerably broad "brush-strokes." As opposed to these, the new theme is homophonic, and the melody always appears in only one part, above or below a thin harmonic support. The whole thematic section is characterized by a fine texture almost like a spider's web and by "durchbrochene Arbeit."

The B-flat–A tension is gradually relaxed with the lower level leading chromatically through B, C, C-sharp and then settling in a D–A–D perfect fifth-octave compass. The perfect octave compass is, however, filled in by two tetrachords of which the lower is tuned up a semitone. This is the first appearance of the mistuned major and Phrygian scales to play such a large role in the final movement. The two tetrachord layers together exhaust the whole twelve-note range (see Ex. 102).

The final theme ends on an F major second inversion chord; we might almost think that in this way the dominant level of the development section is being prepared on the basis of the regular modulation design of the classical sonata structure. This is indeed an important formal turning point; the appearance of the clattering framework motif also indicates that the development section is beginning. The F plane just reached is, however, suddenly slipped by the composer down to E; just like the themes, the whole movement has a mistuned fifth-structure. Thus the development section begins in E—that is, on the level of the characteristically mistuned dominant.

The two elements of the first subject take on independent life: an ostinato evolves from the first expanding motif, and above this what was originally its melodic continuation, the pentatonic fourth-motif, sounds as a counterpart. The virtuosity of the first section of the development can be seen in the way in which three different motifs become fitted together in the characteristic common rhythm pattern of the movement. The fourth-motif becomes traced onto the clattering framework motif, and then with the same beat the "upbeat" part of the final theme also takes part as an independent motif in the musical process and leads organically to the second development section beginning at figure E.

In this section the second subject's characteristic accompanying element assumes importance, but above it is not its own melodic material that is heard but the tetratonic motif broken off from the end of the first subject. In bar 97 the two pairs of parts exchange roles: the syncopated chords move up into the two violins and the tetratonic motif is continued in the two lower instruments. In bar 104 exciting intensification begins: the parts throw the tetratonic motif to each other in a stretto, slipping increasingly higher and higher chromatically. At the climax of the development section—in keeping with the beginning—in the tonal plane of E a rhythmic variation of the clattering theme and an ascending form of the tetratonic motif are placed together (bars 111–114) and then the tetratonic motif, supplemented so as to become pentatonic, settles into a consistent wave-line in parallel octaves. Here it is easy to see the mistuning of the octave in two directions: the E plane of the upper part is imitated by the lower parts in the E-sharp and D-sharp planes.

The wave-line pentatonic theme is finally transformed into scales which rear upward and this leads to the recapitulation of the framework motif, which signifies the form boundary of the development section. This is the point where, according to the traditional sonata principle, the first subject ought to return. But Bartók chooses a special method whereby the first subject returns only fragmentarily—only hinted at, as it were, building it into the material of the framework motif (to be precise, that is what it developed from at the beginning of the movement), and then, to our surprise, it is the final theme which returns first.

It is worth devoting special attention to the ingenious tonal methods. Since the first subject is not really brought back yet, it would be premature to bring back the B-flat tonality. The development ends with the tonality of E, but we should remember that at the beginning of the development, before the framework motif, the final theme ended in F. It signifies the symmetrical rounding off of the development that it is now the tonality of F that appears first in the framework motif and the fragment of the first subject. In the clattering framework motif, however, E is also present alongside F for a time, as a memory of the key of the development just finished.

It is of great importance that the signal first subject's direction is altered: it does not come out of the framework motif's note repetition by arching upwards, but downwards. This same change in direction also characterized the final theme and—to anticipate—the return of all the other themes as well.

The final theme is prepared by the same material on this occasion as in the exposition, only its direction and tonality are changing. Earlier the melody moved downwards in a major seventh framework bounded by A and B-flat, and here it moves upwards within an F-sharp–E-sharp framework.

After the final theme it is the second subject which returns, and only after that does the first subject appear in its complete form—that is, the themes, in keeping with certain symmetrical structural principle, return in a precisely reversed order. The inverse technique is thus valid in both "time" and "space," the only reservation being that the "crab progression" does not refer to the themes themselves but only to their order. The spatial inversion of the themes, however, is consistent: in the recapitulation all melodic movement appears in its mirror form, in the same way as may be observed in the outer movements of the Second Piano Concerto.

It is typical of Bartók's structural economy that the pentatonic fourth-motif is omitted from the recapitulation of the first subject, obviously because it played a particularly large role in the first part of the development section.

In the coda, which has the effect of a stretta, the main role is played by the tetrachord motif at the end of the final theme. The composer uses with incredible richness the tetrachord's "upbeat" character which seems to be "leading to something." These tetrachords leading upwards and downwards, point like so many arrows at different tonal planes—some transitional, some final. In bar 209 they once more lead, in a summarizing way, to the framework motif, which appears in the B-flat plane. But one further little diversion leads out of the tonality of B-flat to D-flat in the upper parts, and to the plane of E in the lower parts. This is an increase in tension before the cadence, a sort of dominant (mistuned dominant) detour, so that the feeling of having arrived at the closing tonality may be all the stronger.

The parts, closing fan-wise from two directions, clearly the summarizing nature of the major and Phrygian tetrachords playing such an important role in the coda, and at the same time they already create the foundations of the close relationship with the final movement.

Example 232.

Second movement: adagio molto

The movement is introduced by amorphous, almost pointillist material. Its tonality, too, solidifies only in the fifth bar on the basis of the cello's held D. The first closed formal unit is prepared by major second motifs which fit into one another chromatically and then by augmented fourth motifs.

Above consonant triad blocks little five-note melodies open out which are obviously extensions of the melodic fragments in the introductory section. In this part special attention is called for by the individual complementary technique which Bartók—among others—already used in the second movement of the First Sonata for Violin and Piano. The melody above the chords never fits into the chord but uses primarily the adjacent chromatic notes of the notes in the chord. The melody above the C major triad consists of the upper adjacent chromatic note of the root, and the lower adjacent notes of the third and fifth. And the A minor seventh chord in bar 15 is complemented by the root's upper and lower, the fifth's upper, the third's lower and the seventh's lower and upper adjacent chromatic notes.

Example 233.

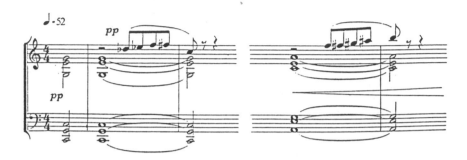

At figure **B** a new formal section begins in the tonality of G: a "background fabric" is evolved from a tremolo organ point, pizzicato glissandos and fast scale fragments, behind a folk character melody structured on a mistuned fourth. Considering the melodic material of the movement so far it can be established that this melody, which settles into an interrelated, clear, four-line structure, has evolved through gradual organization of the fragmentary melodic world. This melodic world is then once more broken up: beginning at figure **C** melodies consisting of fourth-chains rise up and lead with increasing expressiveness to the largo climax in bar 43, from which the melody winds downwards, with the tension of continual parallel diminished octaves (major sevenths), to the calming tonal plane of D. Consonant chord blocks appear once more, evoking, as it were, the movement's first closed formal section, but the five-note little melodic units are now replaced by a mere complementary note here and there. In bar 50 the introductory material also returns—actually in inverse order, in keeping with bridge form, and in this way the movement ends with the same trill motifs as it began. The last trill is extended by a little "quasi glissando" scale motif and the movement ends "perdendosi" with the deep D on the cello. (We shall return to this movement in connection with the analysis of the fourth movement.)

Third movement: Scherzo alla bulgarese (vivace)

This movement forms the symmetry-axis of the five-movement work, and for this reason it naturally has no counterpart, no corresponding movement, as the other movements in the work have. The use of the word "bulgarese" is somewhat misleading, and refers exclusively to the metrical character of the movement, since the melodic world displays principally Hungarian and, to a lesser extent, Rumanian folk elements.

The first scherzo theme is built on the dome-arch, fifth-layer strophic structure of the new-style Hungarian folksongs. Bartók uses an individual technique here in that the fifth-structure is complemented by third-structure in the melody, and, as a result of this, in the verse as well. This combined third-structure and fifth-structure is clearly shown in the diagram below. The individual lines are indicated by their first and last notes. It is interesting to compare this scherzo melody with the main theme, likewise of folksong structure, in the second movement of the *Music for Strings, Percussion and Celesta*, and its close relative, no. 130 from *Mikrokosmos*: "Village Joke." Apart from the aforementioned dome structure, the breaking up of the third line into two smaller units characterizes all three pieces alike.

Line	I	II	III	IV
Fifth Quartet	1-1	3-5	9-7/5-3	9-1
Music	1-1	5-4	7-10-4/3-7-2	1-1
Mikrokosmos no. 130	1-1	5-5	10-6/6-2	2-1

The third lines broken into two parts are further characterized by the fact that they represent the climax of the melody, and the second half line is always placed one level lower, as if it were an organic return to the fourth line.

Bartók evolves the diatonic set of notes in the Dorian scherzo
theme from a chain of minor and major thirds, or viewed from
another angle, from two parallel fifth-chains. This is no new
phenomenon in Bartók, since the leitmotif of his early works also contains a similar melody forming principle. The theme here is an extreme development of this. Comparison with Alban Berg's Violin
Concerto presents itself almost involuntarily: there the abstract note-
row and the theme formed from it are both produced by the towering
of thirds upon each other. There is a characteristic difference,
however, in that while Berg uses this method to extend diatony (the
third-chain uses up nine degrees of the twelve-tone scale), Bartók
forms a Dorian-mode diatonic scale from it.

Example 234.

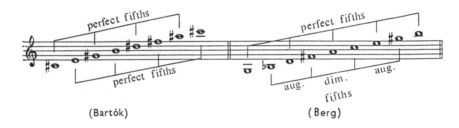

(Bartók)   (Berg)

The harmonies accompanying the C-sharp Dorian theme appear in a
D-sharp layer, which displays a surprising bitonality. The solution to
the chords based on D-sharp, however, is to be found in the melodic
third-structure of the theme: C-sharp is here not a keynote, but a
centre-note, and the harmonies are no more than the downward mirror reflections of the thirds towering upwards. This is also proved
melodically in the closing part of the movement.

Example 235.

Example 235 (continued)

Another point in the structure of the scherzo theme is that each of its lines is followed by an imitating line—like a somewhat distorted shadow. From these "shadow parts" grows a three-bar transition after which a verse is heard again. Its structure resembles that of the earlier one, only the melody of the single lines is changed: each line comes in a mirror inversion, but there is no question of precise inversion, merely the "contours" of the melodic lines are inverted.

In bar 24 (fig. A) a new theme appears in the first violin, with a sharper and more differentiated rhythmic profile. Its structure is likewise strophic, but as opposed to the earlier four lines, this is divided into three lines. To this structural difference is added a contrast in tone, too: as opposed to the first theme's light rolling character, this one is harder, more energetic, more angular. But the inner relationship between the two themes soon becomes apparent. With the appearance of the second theme the first does not disappear—it merely becomes an accompaniment. Its subsidiary role does not last long, however; very soon, in bar 30, a new thematic form appears which is a characteristic combination of the two earlier themes. It is related to the third-structure theme by its rhythm pattern which has an unstressed beginning, but the semiquaver revolving motif in the middle and the ending joined on to it stem from the second theme. A close relative of this theme is to be found among the "Dances in Bulgarian Rhythm" from *Mikrokosmos* (no. 148), not only the obvious $\frac{4}{8} + \frac{2}{8} + \frac{3}{8}$ but the melodic outline and the three-level structure also displaying close relationship·

Example 236.

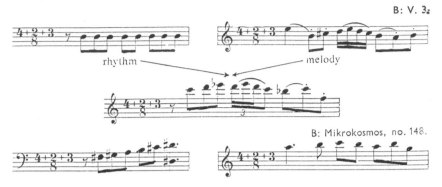

From use of one little motif (a minor trichord) of the theme which has come about from this combination, a longer and more relaxed section results (bars 36–49). After the climax in dynamics and in tension (bars 42–44) a gradual abatement and calming leads to the return of the first scherzo theme (bar 50). But the theme does not return unaltered: the first and third lines of the melody arch upwards, and the second and fourth lines downwards—that is, the recapitulation summarizes, as it were, the two strophic structures at the beginning of the movement.

The trio is connected to the scherzo by a sustained third pedal on the viola. This thin organ point is joined by an ostinato motif repeated every bar (first violin), securing a colouring background, so to speak, for the theme to be heard later. In the fifth bar it becomes clear that the metrically stressed principal notes of the ostinato motif, which has a chromatic character and narrows like a cone-shaped funnel, support a melodic tetratonic motif. The trio's eight introductory bars, together with the presentation of the colouring background, also form a bridge over the difference in tempo between the scherzo and the trio: the tempo gradually accelerates to vivacissimo. The hitherto asymmetric pattern is replaced here by a symmetrical $\frac{3}{8} + \frac{2}{8} + \frac{2}{8} + \frac{3}{8}$ metre.

The theme of the trio begins in bar 9. Its structure—like that of the scherzo themes—is strophic; indeed the folk character is even more conspicuous and unequivocal. On this occasion there is a perfectly simple Hungarian bagpipe tune hidden behind the guise of the complicated Bulgarian metre. The even rhythm of the bagpipe tune is made infinitely alive and interesting by the refined alternation of the proportions between the notes corresponding with the individual syllables. The skeleton of the pattern, consisting of even crotchets, appears in choriambic and antispastic version, similar to the adaptable rhythm of the Hungarian folksong. A particularly interesting point in this rhythm is that the ratio between the long and the short notes is not the ordinary 3:1 or 2:1 , but 3:2.

After the first verse, generally choriambic, another verse starts immediately which is similar in character but antispastic in rhythm and different in structure (bars 17–24); the first verse is closely related to the descending structure of the old style of folksong, and the second to the dome-shaped structure of the new style.

After the introduction of the two folksong verses, a real battle begins between another similar folksong-like motif and a dissonant "choking" motif. In bar 41, the dissonant "choking" motif (which is none other than the ostinato which has been accompanying up to this point) becomes victorious, is joined by a precise mirror reflection counterpart, and for nine bars the texture of the music contains a colour effect devoid of any melodic element. We encountered a similar effect in the second movement of the Fourth Quartet (bar 113), where there was similar parallel movement between several chromatically filled-in fifth-layers. The relationship between the colour effect of the two sections is further reinforced by *con sordino* playing, and also by the pedal technique supporting the moving parts.

After the *fortissimo* colour effect quietens down, the melodic elements begin to appear "shyly," uncertainly, like people creeping out of their hiding places when a storm moves away (from bar 50). The two elements continue to struggle with each other for a time, but the folk motif more and more decisively regains supremacy. It is a striking point in Bartók's organic structural technique when the trio's bagpipe theme returns in third progressions which refer to the Scherzo and, without any obstacles, lead directly back to it.

The Scherzo's first theme appears in the recapitulation doubly extended: that is, the two verses are here actually built into one another, and in such a way that every single line's basic and mirror inversion and the "shadow imitation" of each of them all stand alongside one another. Thus here the summarizing technique which characterized the return before the trio is used even more consistently.

The second theme returns in bar 30 of the scherzo da capo, in a significantly extended form: the individual phrases are given cadences, and the descending verse consisting previously of three lines is now supplemented into a four-line dome-shaped folksong structure. The scherzo recapitulation then continues in accordance with its first appearance but enriched with numerous further alterations. The central section, based on the development of the minor trichord motif, is here even more dynamic: it switches into an Agitato stretto in bar 58. This tempo then remains to the end, except that two bars in a somewhat restrained tempo are wedged in between the question-answer kind of recalling of the first scherzo theme (after bar 85)—an intensification of the tension before the resolution, as it were.

Fourth movement: Andante

The key to the symmetrical construction of the whole composition is that the movements which correspond to each other are related not only in their tone and atmosphere but also by a concrete thematic link. In the case of the second and fourth movements this interrelationship is more than mere thematic reference: every element in the two movements is common; and the formal application of them also follows the same principles. For precisely this reason the fourth movement can justifiably be regarded as a fuller and more developed variation of the second movement.

The fourth movement is introduced by the same sort of open pointillist material as the second movement. Here a pizzicato motif corresponds to the earlier trill motif, and the interconnected major seconds grow into a slow rhythmic trill.

Example 237.

The extending, broadening tendency is shown by the increase in the extent of the introductory section: the second movement's nine bars are answered by twenty-two in the fourth movement. It must be added, however, that this increase is present only in the quantity of the material, for the time taken up by the two formal units is virtually identical, since the tempo of the second movement is Adagio molto ($\downarrow$=40-38), that is almost twice as slow as the Andante. The consonant harmonic blocks are also responded to by static harmonic blocks in the fourth movement, although the way they are played is different; these take on a special colour by means of saltato note repetition in sextuplet rhythm.

Whereas in the second movement the complementary melodic fragments appeared above the held chords, here they are wedged in between the chord blocks. The descending monologue melody unfolding from them is also a close relative.

Example 238.

In the centre of the movement it is the broadly arching theme of folksong structure that appears here, too. It is developed—as is generally the case with all the variations in the fourth movement—more richly and more melodically, but this cannot conceal the completely consistent relationship between the two melodies. If the difference in tonality is disregarded, the precise note-for-note agreement between the themes becomes obvious by appropriately placing one above the other.

Example 239.

Example 239 (continued)

Incidental to the richer development of the melody is the fact that it is heard in an octave canon between the first violin and the cello (strictly speaking, at a distance of two octaves). It is particularly worthy of attention that the effects accompanying the melody are also related: the second movement's tremolo organ point is here responded to by the viola's held notes coloured with dissonances, whereas the little scale fragments are replaced by little wave motifs. It is from the chromatic scale fragment of the "colouring background" in the second movement that Bartók has developed the next formal section in the fourth movement, which has a transitional nature (bars 55–63). The last three bars of this transitional section, however, introduce an apparently new motif into the musical process. But the iambic minor third motif embedded in the chord blocks does have its own antecedent in the twenty-second bar of the movement, immediately before the sextuplet chord blocks.

Example 240.

This minor third motif then becomes connected to the long fourth-
chains already familiar from the second movement. The fourth-chain
broadens into an exciting formal section here, too; above the ominous
murmuring of the chromatic "wave motifs" in the two lower parts, the
fourth-chains produce real storm music. An occasional natural scene
was by no means alien to Bartók's apparently abstract musical thinking. Listening to the great celesta-harp-piano waves in the third movement of the *Music for Strings, Percussion and Celesta*, Bartók once
whispered to his neighbour: "Listen, the sea!"[8] The "storm" abates
from bar 80, and the calm after the storm, the quietening of the tor-
mented soul, is depicted by a peaceful series of harmonies—quite
reminiscent of Beethoven's Sixth Symphony.

This is where the fourth movement essentially differs from the
second; in the earlier movement the musical process does bring back
the amorphous material from the beginning of the movement, even
though in a significantly abbreviated form, and at the same time the
broken, tragic tone. Here in bars 95–97 only the chord blocks return,
in a very abbreviated form, only as a token as it were, and instead of
the introductory material it is the hushed calm after the storm which
puts the final full stop to the movement. Underneath the sustained B
on the first violin the cello arrives, by pizzicato glissandos and rising
by thirds, at the closing chord of the movement's tonality, the G minor
triad. Its minor character, however, is coloured with major by the
violin's held B.

Thus Bartók does not use symmetrical bridge form at every point
and "at all costs." The symmetrical structure becomes healthily
relaxed in the fourth movement, thus becoming more organically connected with the final movement. But there is something else which
precluded the use of the recapitulating symmetrical form. As has already been mentioned, the fourth movement really differs from the
second and moves beyond being a simple variation in that whereas the
atmosphere of the second movement returns to the amorphousness,
the darkness, the fragmentation of the beginning, the fourth move-

[8]Bence Szabolcsi, "Mensch und Natur in Bartóks Geisteswelt," *Studia Musicologica*
Tom.V (1963), 526.

ment becomes smoothly continuous—it opens out and moves through a large and passionate crisis to a harmonic calm and catharsis.

Fifth movement: Allegro vivace — Presto

In the complicated structure of the movement the framework motif, the new Bartókian formal element, serves as an important guide, just as it did in the first movement. Its triplet, upbeat rhythm and tetrachord structure is often a guiding principle with regard to tonality. This function appears straight away in the introduction as it leads, after some diversions, to the dominant of the movement's B-flat tonality.

Example 241.

But the Presto theme, the first thematic material in the movement, does not start from this F just reached, but from a mistuned dominant—that is, from E. The repeating note first section of the theme refers on the one hand back to the beginning of the opening movement, and on the other hand it rather reminds one of the start of the First Quartet's finale. From the repeated E the melody slides down by means of a Phrygian tetrachord to the first melodic terrace of the theme, and from there it descends further in a similar way to the terrace below that. The characteristic fifth-structure of Hungarian folksongs can be found here in a mistuned form; the B-flat level is answered by an E level. When the lower layer is finished (the descending tetrachord is not only an opening element but also a closing element), we would expect a B-flat cadence, but this comes only after a suspension and not even in the soprano melody but in the bass, and then the long continuation of the melody leads to the tonal plane of F, and it is only a somewhat forceful "appendix" which restores the feeling of B-flat tonality (bars 50–54).

After this junction in the form, as a contrast to the hitherto descending theme, an ascending theme starts. This ascending theme, however, can scarcely be regarded as new material; although it is not a precise inversion of the earlier theme, it is nevertheless closely related to it on the basis of its tetrachord units and its structure: it is an inverted variation of it.

Example 242.

After this, Bartók makes thorough use of the possibilities offered by precise inversion and varied inversion. In the first 149 bars of the movement he forms a closed unit from the two related themes thus presented, and in such a way that he brings back the two themes so far introduced in precise mirror inversion, too, and in inverted order. In this way evolves this individual formal unit considerably rare in sonatas:

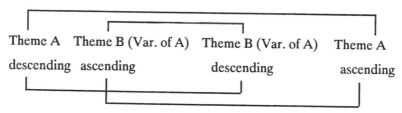

It is also worth observing the structure of the themes. The first has already been mentioned: mistuned fifth-levels above and below each other. Mistuning plays an important role in the second, too: the two tetrachords of the major scale are slipped close to one another, and so, for example, in the ascending form it sets out from G-flat and arrives in G. On the basis of this the tonal plan of the four-part formal unit can also be outlined :

Framework	Theme A		Theme B		Theme B		Theme A	
	E-B♭ -E-B♭		G♭ -C-F		G-D♭ -A♭		B-F-B-F	
B♭ -F		F		A♭		C		B♭

The upper line shows the inner tonal structure of the closed thematic units, and the lower line the tonality of the material wedged in between them. It is noticeable that each new beginning of a theme is combined with displacement by a semitone; just as within the themes, the technique of mistuning is always present between the themes as well.

This first large formal unit in the exposition, as well as introducing the two basic themes—or to be precise by doing exactly that—clearly throws light on the melodic and rhythmic proto-motifs of the whole movement. The melodic proto-motif is, as has been mentioned, the tetrachord, which is built into the musical material mirror-wise; in its ascending form it is major in structure, and in its descending form it is Phrygian (see Exs. 102–103).

In the rhythmic variation process two motifs move into the foreground conspicuously; one stems from further development of the first theme (a), while the other is a fundamental gesture of both the first and second themes (b). The upbeat motif produced by the two, which was introduced in a triplet form in the framework motif, lies at the heart of all the rhythmic movement, and so we can see in it the rhythmic proto-motif corresponding to the melodic proto-motif (c).

Example 243.

After the appearance of the framework motif (**D**), indicating a formal boundary, new material appears which has a "quasi-second subject" function. It has no special melodic character, although the tetrachord motif has a role here, too, even if only temporarily. From a melodic extension of it alpha chords appear opening upwards, there is a dynamic intensification reaching *fff*, and then the four instruments construct homogeneous minor second piles one upon the other, each consisting of ten chromatic degrees. This is a good example of Bartók's individual cluster technique (bars 183–200).

From **E** a freely written contrapuntal section begins which has the function of a final theme, and which takes its motivic material from the tetrachord elements and rhythm motifs of the first two themes. The changing note opening motif of the imitational section does, however, create the impression of new material. A very similar start and way of writing can be seen in no. 128 of *Mikrokosmos*.

With regard to tempo, too, Bartók tried to make the character of a faster section (più presto, ♩ = 144) even more unambiguous for the performers by the indications "scorrevole" and "leggerissimo." As a result of the incredible animation and contrapuntal complication of the musical material, a flitting, scintillating musical picture evolves. At one point the chromatic "durchbrochene Arbeit" of the tetrachord motif refers back to similar development of the tetratonic motif in the first movement.

Example 244.

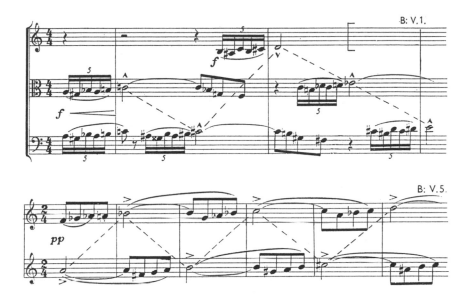

From the multicoloured whirling of the tetrachords a two-direction scale motif eventualty evolves, as a kind of summary; the two violins move upwards scale-wise and the two lower instruments downwards, broadening the music out like a fan, rushing forward into the appearance of the framework motif in the tonality of F-sharp.

The scale motif summarizes the most important elements in the exposition's material with classical conciseness. It consists of two tetrachcrds—indeed, two mistuned tetrachord layers; the upward moving one starts from F-sharp and arrives at F, and the downward one goes from A to A-sharp. These eight-degree scales are not just summaries in principle, for both can be extracted from the fundamental form of the two first subject themes. It can be seen that the descending form builds Phrygian tetrachords upon each other, and the ascending does it with major tetrachords.

The mistuning technique is most brilliantly proved when the repeating scales, which have a diminished octave compass, open out

at the end and lead in a form which is now mistuned to the tonality of
F-sharp.

Example 245.

The framework motif appears at this point in a significantly altered
form: it takes on the melodic profile of the opening motif in the
recent contrapuntal section. Its dynamics suggest the beginning of a
development section.

In place of a development section—obviously because the
material presented has already been through abundant elaboration
and development earlier—new material appears: new, that is, in relation to this movement—it is the first subject of the first movement.
The tempo is increased to prestissimo ($\downarrow$ = 152), and to an excited,
ominous "background texture" (*col legno* drumming in the two violins
and mistuned glissandos in the cello) a fugato starts with the first
movement theme just mentioned. In keeping with the spirit of the
whole work, the theme entries are built not on a perfect but on a mistuned fifth structure (on the E–B-flat–E–B-flat tonal levels).

From the continuation of the first movement theme it is eventually the tetrachord motif that crystallizes here, too, and the material
thus flows organically into the latest appearance of the framework
motif. But it seems that on this occasion the framework motif is not
used to indicate any formal division, but becomes itself the object of
development work. Moving through different metamorphoses, a
humorous, capriccioso variation is evolved from it. From the auxiliary
note opening motif are born bald glissandos; the largely motory
rhythm also relaxes, and the melodies appear in capriciously changing
tempi until in the end the framework motif, now in its original form,

pulls together the virtually disintegrating material. And so we come to the important formal division: the beginning of the recapitulation.

As is general with Bartók, the recapitulation is abbreviated. Thus the double first subject appears without repetition, the first theme returning only in a descending form, and the second theme only in an ascending form. But between the cluster material, which has the function of a secondary theme, and the tetrachord counterpoint, which has a closing function, is now wedged a strange section. A banal melody is played in A major on the second violin, and this is accompanied on the other instruments by stereotyped I–V harmonies. When the melody reaches the top finishing note, the same melody is heard a semitone higher, slipped into B-flat major. Meanwhile, however, the accompanying chords remain in A major. The "out of tune" barrel-organ effect produced by this bitonality indicates that here we are faced with one of Bartók's bitter jokes (Winrow 1971). We are reminded of Mozart's *Dorfmusikanten Sextett*, or Stravinsky's accumulation of functions in the fair in *Petrushka*.

The solution to this quotation-like detail, however, lies hidden in the work itself. For the A major melody is no more than a non-mistuned, diatonic version of the second principal theme. It is as if Bartók wants to point out that this melody would be so very banal and flat in a perfect octave-fifth compass without mistuning. And then when he displaces it bitonally—this is also mistuning—the unaltered accompaniment makes it ridiculous. This is the difference between organic mistuning, the inner transformation of material, and external manipulation.

The quotation cannot last for long; the original form of the theme sweeps it away "con slancio," and the tetrachord motif rushes into the same scales, having a closing function, as we encountered at the end of the exposition. There this led to the tonality of F-sharp, but here it races into the imaginary E tonality of the coda, which is marked "stretto"that is, into the mistuned dominant of B-flat.

Example 246.

The accelerated ostinato repetition of the tetrachords piling on top of
each other—above the E organ point coloured by D-sharp—increases
the tension so much that in the end the approach, opening out fan-
wise, to the final B-flat represents a calming solution, with one last accented summary of the tetrachord motif.

CHAPTER FOURTEEN

SONATA FOR TWO PIANOS AND PERCUSSION

The history of this work's origins can be traced with fair accuracy from Bartók's correspondence with Paul Sacher, the leader of the Basle Chamber Orchestra (Schuh 1952). The première of the *Music for Strings, Percussion and Celesta* on 21 January 1937 scored such a success that by May Sacher commissioned Bartók to compose a new work, this time not for Sacher's own ensemble but for the Basle ISCM group. The commission called for an unspecified chamber ensemble, and so Bartók himself had to select the medium best suiting his intentions. In his first reply of 24 May, Bartók wrote, "I would agree with the matter in principle, but on the one hand the time limit seems much too short and on the other I cannot yet definitely commit myself; hence I would accept the commission only with the proviso that the performing of it (the realization) should depend on how much time I shall have in the summer for this work. This then means that a definite answer on my part can only be expected in early September." In the same letter Bartók asked for further details on the nature of the commission: "What kind of chamber music can it be? How would a quartet for two pianos and two percussion groups be? Or a piano trio? Do you or don't you consider a work for voice and piano chamber music?" (Schuh 1952:72).

Sacher's answer seems to have encouraged Bartók, as on 30 June he already made more concrete proposals, during his summer holidays in Carynthia: "The quartet for two pianos and two percussion groups would naturally be scored for four performers, two of whom could naturally play side drums and other similar instruments. Of course, as I have already written to you, I should only be able to tell by

393

the end of August whether the work can be taken into consideration and whether it can be dispatched around the first half of October, or whether I choose one of the other two possibilities (a little trio or songs) instead" (Schuh 1952:73).

It seems, therefore, that Bartók had the work already in view, but, perhaps precisely because of the unusual selection of instruments, did not venture to give a final answer before considering the work in detail. According to his working method of many years, in 1937, too, he used the time after his summer holiday for intensive work. It is not exactly known how long he stayed in Heiligenblut, but we know that by the end of June he was already there with his wife. The note at the end of the score marks July and August as the time of composition, and so it seems possible that the first ideas for the work were born during his holiday in Austria. On the other hand we know that, contrary to the composer's dating, the piece was not ready by the end of August, as on 2 September he wrote to Sacher, "I am pleased to tell you that I have been able to nearly finish the planned work—my choice fell on a quartet for 2 pianos and 2 percussion groups—and so you may count on it. It consists of three movements, the 1st and 2nd of which are ready, and the 3rd halfway through. Its duration will be presumably somewhat more that 20 minutes. Now of course there still comes the wearisome work of making the final copy of which copies can be made. I hope to be able to send you the 1st and 2nd movements by the end of September, and the 3rd by mid-October. I shall send you copies, one for each performer. The piano part is by no means more difficult than those in my sonatas for piano and violin; the timpani part is approximately like that in last year's piece (i.e., *Music for Strings, Percussion and Celesta*), but the xylophone is somewhat more difficult, although it is not particularly difficult either . . .The pianist must naturally be very good; and of course the xylophone player also has to practise the part diligently" (Schuh 1952:73).

This shows that originally Bartók did not compose the work for himself and his wife. But at Sacher's suggestion he immediately undertook to play at the première; the suggestion obviously met with his—perhaps unspoken—wishes.

In his letter of 18 October, Bartók even gave the final title: "The title of my work should be 'Sonata for 2 Pianos and Percussion', because if two percussionists are not enough, a third performer may perhaps also be needed, so that the 'quartet' may turn into a 'quintet' " (Schuh 1952:73).

This worry proved unfounded, but the title still remained "sonata" instead of "quartet." We know from Bartók's letter of 11 November that by that time he was certain of the quartet solution: "Recently I had the opportunity to take a thorough look at a percussion group: it will be easy to solve the performance of the work with only two percussionists, according to my original idea" (Schuh 1952:73).

A constantly recurring subject in the letters is the question of the performability of the works, the difficulty of their performance. In connection with his previous work, composed for Sacher, he repeatedly expressed his opinion on the question, as for instance in a letter of 26 June 1936: "But it is more delicate to fulfil the request that the work should not be too difficult. I shall be able as far as possible to avoid technical difficulties. If one writes something new, the performer encounters difficulties from the unusualness alone" (Schuh 1952:71). The same subject recurs in connection with this work. In a letter of 11 November 1937, Bartók forewarned Sacher: "There are plenty of rhythmic difficulties (in the 1st movement)":

Example 247.

The other difficulty lies in apportioning the right volume; several grades are needed within a *f* of *mf* or *p* *(pp)*" (Schuh 1952:73).

The same day, Bartók replied to Annie Müller-Widmann who, after having learned from Sacher about the prospective appearance of the Bartóks, again offered her hospitality. "Both of us thank you most sincerely for your kind invitation," writes Bartók. "We shall arrive in Basle some 4 to 5 days before January 16, for the rehearsals and lectures. Now we are engaged in studying my new work, which—in particular the first movement—includes a great many difficulties; so it took quite some time for me to learn my part (first piano). I hope there will be no difficulty with the percussionists. Mr Sacher is being kind enough to rehearse with them before our arrival" (*Bartók levelei* no. 853).

Owing to the careful preparations, the première on 16 January 1938 was a great success; the percussion parts were played by two eminent Basle musicians, Fritz Schiesser and Philipp Rühlig. Their accomplishment can only be fully appreciated if one knows that in October of that year Bartók wanted to cancel the first performance in Budapest precisely because of the failure of the players to keep together, and it was only due to Ernest Ansermet that the work was finally still performed, as he undertook the uniquely unusual task of conducting a piece which was in essence a chamber work. In performing the work, a similar solution has often been applied since that time, but in our opinion this always means a compromise, as a basic condition for a really good performance is that the four musicians are acquainted with the work as a piece of chamber music and so keep together of their own accord.

At the first performance in Basle, the audience received Bartók's work with great enthusiasm, and the most noted critic Wilhelm Merian, who has written a virtual study when reviewing *Music for Strings, Percussion and Celesta*, had this to say: "This composition seems to be the most powerful and valuable produced by Bartók so far and indeed by modern music."[1]

Before the première, the Basle *National Zeitung* carried Bartók's article on the work, on 13 January 1938. In the knowledge that Bartók's analyses of his own works are usually reticent and highly

[1]Werner Fuchss, *Béla Bartók und die Schweiz* (Bern: Hallwag), 1973, 74.

"objective" it is a pleasure to see that his statement was more extensive on this occasion, not restricted to a mere analysis of form.[2]

The ensemble of two pianos and percussion, which with the four performers may really be considered a quartet, is undeniably an unusual combination not only in Bartók's output but in the whole history of music up to that date. Nevertheless, it cannot be considered entirely without precedent. As far as the piano is concerned, Bartók himself wrote that he had originally planned the work for one piano; the final composition, however, seems to indicate that the doubling of the piano in fact served not only to balance volume, but grew into a fundamental factor. As William W. Austin has pointed out, the Baroque practice of contrast and response, providing a spatial effect, assumed a significant role in Bartók's work in the 1930s.[3] In *Cantata Profana* there are two choruses opposed to each other, and in *Music for Strings, Percussion and Celesta*, two groups of string orchestras are contrasted, and so it seems scarcely surprising that Bartók also tried to apply his favourite instrument, the piano, to a similar response technique. He may also have drawn direct inspiration for employing two pianos from Stravinsky's Concerto for two pianos. We know that Bartók first played this Stravinsky piece with his wife at a concert in March 1939, but it is not known when he first got to know the work. Nevertheless, it may be supposed that Bartók, who in those years was constantly travelling and following with great interest the musical scene in Europe, could at the time he composed his sonata have known Stravinsky's work for two pianos, which was premièred on 21 November 1935 in Paris.

But apart from all this, Bartók may have been influenced in designing the work for two pianos by a subjective factor as well, the wish to lead his wife, the pianist Ditta Pásztory, smoothly to the concert podium. Ditta Pásztory had given no solo concerts, and Bartók seems never to have insisted on it, but the idea of joint performance must have been attractive to him, and indeed, the Basle première in January 1938 was followed by a growing number of joint concerts,

[2]For an English translation see *Bartók Essays* no.56.
[3]William W. Austin, *Music in the 20th Century* (New York: Norton, 1966), 323.

with a repertoire ranging from Mozart to Stravinsky. This also seems justified by László Somfai's interesting observation, according to which Bartók formulated the first piano part, which he intended for himself, in such a way that it should lead the performance, setting an example for the second piano part.

As far as the soloistic use of the percussion instruments is concerned, here too Bartók may have drawn one of his main stimuli from Stravinsky. Bartók was closely familiar with the Russian composer's vocal piece orchestrated for four pianos and percussion, *Les Noces*; his cycle *Village Scenes* of 1924 shows the direct influence of the piece. It was in Bartók's First Piano Concerto that percussion was first assigned a particularly significant role, presaging a great many exciting possibilities for the inherent colour grouping of the piano and percussion instruments. The next step in this field was taken in the *Music for Strings, Percussion and Celesta*, which followed the piano concerto by a decade, and where Bartók placed a huge percussion apparatus beside the great block of strings and the trio of piano, harp, and celesta.

In heightening the role of percussion instruments, Bartók may also have found a model in another composer, Edgar Varèse, who scored his *Hypersprism* (1923) and *Intégrales* (1925) for wind instruments and percussion, and *Ionisation* (1931) for percussion instruments only. It is not known whether Bartók was acquainted with Varèse's work, but the two composers are known to have been in contact with each other, as Varèse conducted the first New York performance of *Two Pictures* in 1919, and as the chairman of the International Composer's Guild between 1924 and 1931, he encouraged the performance of Bartók's works and his personal appearance in the United States (*Documenta Bartókiana* 1968:120–21, 164–65). This makes probable that Bartók became acquainted with some of Varèse's compositions, or at least was aware of the French-born avant-garde composer's particular aims, which may have encouraged him towards an increasingly independent use of the percussion.[4]

[4]In one of his Harvard Lectures, Bartók later spoke unfavorably about works exclusively employing percussion, and about concert programmes featuring only such works. See *Bartók Essays* no.46.

The growing prominence of percussion instruments in the first decades of the twentieth century was closely related to those extreme attempts at enriching and "modernizing" music by the addition of natural sound and noises, or even their exclusive employment. But alongside these attempts of the Futurists and the Bruitists, percussion effects had another, more important and more profound source in the music of primitive peoples of Africa and the musical traditions of the great Far Eastern cultures. It goes without saying that for Bartók this latter provided the real inspiration, as we have already pointed out in connection with his scales and the modality of his music.

Bartók's percussion apparatus in *Music* and in the *Sonata* does not serve to imitate "noise," but as a reconstruction of African and Asian colours in music. The membranophone instruments (drums) at that time usual in European music are richly complemented by idiophone instruments with their particular manifold colours, such as xylophone, cymbals, tam-tam and triangle. But it is of great significance that among them Bartók assigned a different role to even those instruments even which had already appeared in Europe, mainly in music of a military style or in so-called "Janissary music." For instance, alongside the traditional cymbal use, he assigned a major role to playing the *suspended* cymbal with different sticks, thus attaining a high-pitched sounding "gong effect" instead of the hard military effect, and in this way his apparatus approaches the sonority of Balinese gamelan ensembles.

Although during the work of composition Bartók used the term "quartet" on several occasions, the formal basis of the work is far removed from that of his string quartets. It is true that quite different models are invented in the string quartets from the three accelerating movements in the First through the symmetrical three-movement form in the Second and the highly irregular two-movement form in the Third, to the symmetrical five-movement form in the Fourth and Fifth, but the Sonata, at least in its structural principle, is still more closely related to the First Sonata for Violin and Piano and the Piano Sonata. It is linked to them primarily by its traditional sonata model of a fast–slow–fast order of movements. In all probability this is expressed in the fact that Bartók, after having found that the work could be designated a "quartet," still retained the term "sonata," originally used to ensure freedom for the work. And indeed we may be justified in thinking that he opted for this title not merely to evade the terms "quartet" or "quintet," but to legitimate the internal organizational principle of the work, which had already taken its final shape.

This picture is somewhat modified by the slow introduction, which points to a relationship with the *Music*, whose slow contrapuntal first movement is here reduced to a short introduction. The baroque sonata model thus shows through the classical; and the fact that this supposition is not completely unfounded is also borne out by the Sonata for Solo Violin, which has an unambiguously Baroque structure. Slow opening sections assumed a growing role in Bartók's form conception from the late 1930s onwards, as affirmed also by the Sixth String Quartet.

As in the Third Quartet and the Second Sonata for Violin and Piano, we find in the Sonata a kind of model synthesis. It is not ready-made forms of models but structural principles that interact with each other and join in a lasting synthesis. In the first two works a struggle between the principles of binary and ternary form resulted in a singular, unique model, while here the struggle between three-movement and four-movement forms results in a peerless structure, wonderfully proportioned and crystal clear in its organization.

First movement: Assai lento — Allegro molto

In Bartók the formal idea of a slow, fugal introduction goes back through the *Music for Strings, Percussion and Celesta*, to the First String Quartet, taking as its model in form, structure and melodic pattern Beethoven's String Quartet in C-sharp Minor. During the discussion of the cambiata motif we have already pointed to internal relationships between a number of themes.[5] But the cambiata motif is only one component of this phenomenon, which should not be allowed to conceal another major connection. In the theme of the slow introduction, three-note melodic germs are born alongside the densely woven four-note cambiata motifs.

[5]See chapter 4, "Monothematicism and Variation," in Part One.

Example 248.

As clearly indicated by the metre of the theme, the real pulse divides the melody into three-note units, in fact exploring all three possible divisions:

Example 249.

Melodically too, the three-note units divide up in logical succession, each consisting of a contracting and an expanding element, and furthermore linked by progression in a variety of directions. Such three-note melodic germs can be observed in the monothematic system of interrelations in the Third and Sixth Quartets. The thoroughly logical process this time takes place concentrated within a single bar; as compared with the first stated motif, the second is its retrograde inversion, and the third opens out the melodic line which until now was closed, allowing the possibility of continuation. At the same time, a consistent expansion can be obeserved in the interval structure.

Example 250.

Measured in semitones, the expansion is simply one from 4 to 5 to 6, but from a musical point of view it means a line with diminished fourth, a perfect fourth and a diminished fifth—that is, a dynamic action of tension, resolution and subsequent tension.

It is also worth considering the three-note motifs individually, for example the first immediately exhibits a familiar formula: its diminished fourth refers to Bach's and Beethoven's themes in the minor, passing directly from the leading note to the third degree. This type of theme can be traced from Beethoven through Liszt, but similarities between the various stages are not necessarily a result of borrowing or quotation, and it is much more probable that appearances of this type of theme and motif stem from the strength of a great, common tradition.

Here the question of the oft-mentioned Liszt Étude, *La leggierezza*, should be dealt with. Morphologically there are certainly some similiraties and even parallels between Liszt's theme and that of Bartók, in particular Bartók's use of parallel sixths.[6] Still, one can hardly call it "quotation," since the term implies a quite deliberate and moreover obvious procedure, and furthermore calls for the "quoting" composer to take over the melody or fragment not only morphologically but in character as well. Bartók's theme, however, with its Lento tempo, serious convolutions and almost forbidding character, is quite remote, both in technique and character, from the *leggiero* character of Liszt's piece. The possibility remains a satirical, deliberately distorted quotation, but here such an explanation seems totally unjus-

---

[6]Ferenc Bónis, "Quotations in Bartók's Music," *Studia Musicologica* Tom. 5 (1963).

tified and senseless. What possible reason could Bartók have had for composing a counterpart of *La leggierezza*, a kind of "pesantezza," in the Sonata? The memory of Liszt's piece might possibly have been present in Bartók's mind when he formulated the theme, but in all probability the leading role was assumed not by that, but by the particular tradition of melodic construction whose influence has already been referred to on many occasions.

The three small units are furthermore interestingly linked together by concealed principles of organization. First and foremost, the whole melody is presented in retardation; before it, as if by way of an introduction, just the first two melodic units are heard twice, and, as a closing note, are joined by the first note of the third member. By the time the full melodic line is heard, the self-contained quality of the theme can already be felt. The reason for this lies in the logic of the micro-structure: the first two units are so close in their melodic content that they may almost be considered a repeat, a small A–A form. The third, entirely different melodic motif, provides a satisfying close melodically since it rounds off the melodic line into a tiny bar form: A–A–B. By way of an interesting internal contradiction—the dialectic of formal development—the third unit actually "closes" by "opening" the melody, so that what from the melodic point of view is an opening, within the micro-form functions as a close.

The tonal structure of the theme is equally interesting. The melody, consisting of nine notes, is built upon nine adjacent degrees of the chromatic scale, without repeating a single note. Its chromatic character is realized primarily from two-note melodic germs, in a clear division of lower and upper layers. Here the lower layer is especially interesting, since the use of the cambiata can be seen separately when detached from the upper layer. Considered from this aspect, one again encounters the survival of the Bach tradition, where polyphony concealed within one part is a frequent characteristic. And if we were to interchange the two middle notes of the lower layer, the part would outline a descending chromatic scale, a common type of passacaglia theme in Baroque music. This character of the theme becomes evident mainly in its ostinato form, particularly in the development section.

Example 251.

In the Introduction Bartók makes consistent use of the complementary chromaticism of the theme: while the first piano covers
the chromatic route already discussed, starting from F-sharp to C-
sharp, the second piano outlines the same nine-note chromatic line
above the first, which means that the two parts use up the complete
twelve-tone scale with six notes in common.

Example 252.

This presentation conceals the tonal bases outlined within the full
chromaticism, whereby one part starts from F-sharp and closes on C-
sharp, and the other starts from C and closes on G, the joint compass
of the theme fitting precisely the 1:5 model, or as has been noted, the
mistuned fifth-fourth structure.

Example 253.

In the course of this analysis we have passed almost imperceptibly from an analysis of the monophonic theme to an analysis of its
polyphonic structure. This is obviously due to the fact that polyphonic
treatment is inherent in the theme itself. In other words, the theme
and its imitation heard a diminished fifth together form the complete
material.

When we examined Bartók's canon and fugue technique, we found that at certain points perfect fifth imitation gives way to diminished or augmented, that is *mistuned* fifth imitation. In chapter 6, "Tonality and Polytonality", we explained that perhaps the primary reason for this is to substitute for the flat and empty sound of the perfect fifth. Therefore, *instead of C-sharp* the second part (the answer), entering above the first part beginning on *F-sharp*, starts from *C,* also proved by the fact that the timpani, which introduced the melody beginning on *F-sharp* by a roll on *F-sharp*, accompanies the entry of the second part by playing the real dominant, i.e., *C-sharp.*

Thus the question arises: what may be the reason for this fluctuation between the use of a perfect fifth and a diminished fifth in canon technique? Although by no means an unbroken law, the following examples justify the statement that Bartók mostly uses perfect fifth imitation when he mistunes the structural framework of the theme, and employs mistuned, mostly diminished fifth imitation when the theme has a traditional—perfect fifth or fourth—framework. In the *Music* the fugue movement is built with entries of strictly perfect fifth, but the theme itself, although its extreme notes form a perfect fifth, is in its actual framework of a mistuned, compressed character. Very similar to this is the fugato in the Third String Quartet, where the theme consistently avoids the perfect fifth and thus the second part entering a perfect fifth higher makes for a satisfying effect. In the fourth, Andante movement of the Fifth Quartet, a little canon unfolds at figure **B** between the first violin and the cello. The theme is a classic example of the mistuning of the fifth-fourth framework stemming from folksong, and it is natural therefore that the canon proceeds at the distance of a perfect octave (precisely two octaves).

Let us now take a reverse case. In the development section of the first movement of the Fifth Quartet, a canon on a pentatonic melody with a perfect octave framework begins at bar 119; its imitation occurs in the bass parts with a shift of a semitone. The closing movement in the same quartet shows a similar phenomenon, although here the layers of diminished fifths show, not in a canon relationship between two parts but within a single theme, in its horizontal structure. The two corresponding layers are each built on a triad; this

makes the stretched structure necessary and to mistune the perfect
fifth stratification based on folk-melody principle.

Example 254.

Mention should be made of an exception to show that the
phenomenon in question is not a law to be generally applied. In the
centre of the closing movement of the Fifth Quartet the first subject
of the first movement returns as a fugato, and both the theme and its
imitation rely on a mistuned structure of B-flat–E natural.

To return to the canon technique of the introduction to the
Sonata, we find that although the theme itself is fairly chromatic, it
clearly overlies the second inversion of a minor triad. So nothing
could be more natural than that in the canon woven out of it the harmonic tension is provided by a diminished fifth—justifying the logic of
a "chromatic tonality."

Example 255.

The canon technique of a diminished fifth relationship leaves its
mark on the whole first largo section of the Introduction; nevertheless

this is not the only device Bartók employs to gradually unfold the restrained, tense material, organizing it in a logically expanding manner.

Although this slow introductory section has been compared in function to the fugue movement of *Music for Strings, Percussion and Celesta*, it should be stressed that there is no question here of fugue, nor even fugato, but canon at most, and even that only over minor stretches, and rhythmically not always with note-for-note exactness. The first 17-bar section brings four such canon-like sections, the first of which is closely related to the three-bar introductory exposition of the theme, the second standing isolated between two sparkling, explosive passages, and the third being closely linked to the fourth, out which a strong intensification of dynamics and tempo, maintaining the onward progress, leads to the second major formal unit of the Introduction.

The succession of four canon sections brings a purposeful and consistent development in more than one aspect. The theme, in whose internal structure the technique of retrograde inversion assumed a significant role, appears in the third and fourth canon sections in mirror inversion. At the same time, the texture becomes increasingly compact and polyphonic, as the first consecutive octaves are joined by further consecutives: first minor sixth and then diminished fifths. Viewed from the side of diminished fifths, it seems logical and justified that here the minor sixth really equals an *augmented fifth*, thus after the perfect octave the material gains tension from these kinds of mistuned fifth. Finally, the tonal position of the canon sections is also varied: the F-sharp–C level in the first section slides upwards in the second and third sections, each by a semitone. Considering the development of these three factors, it can be seen how economically Bartók almost "worms his way" into developing the material; always one of the three factors remains unchanged, while the other two continue to proceed.

A change occurs at the climactic point reached after a huge increase in intensity (bar 18): in place of the legato, convoluted, creeping motion there begins a motion that is almost hammering. Complementary to this, the closing two minor third phrases in the first piano's chromatic new motivic material makes a strong impression on the listener.

	1st section (bars 4-5)	2nd section (bars 8-9)	3rd section (bars 12-13)	4th section (bars 14-15)
Theme's position:	original	original	mirror	mirror
Texture:	parallel octaves	parallel octaves and augm. fifth	parallel octave and augm. fifth	parallel double dim. fifth
Tonal plane:	C F sharp	D flat F G B	A flat C D F sharp	D A flat A flat D

Example 256.

The clash of the two closing notes, B-flat and B-natural, creates a tension that leaves its mark on the whole last section of the introduction, which gradually prepares for the explosive energy of the fast movement. First a tapping rhythm begins on the notes B-flat and B-natural, and then this is joined by a melodic gesture—the mirror inversion of the former two minor thirds: B-flat stepping down to G, and B-natural stepping up to D. At this point it turns out that the B-flat–B-natural clash is in fact the clash of the minor and major thirds of a G-rooted chord. A specific Bartókian dominant chord of the fast movement's clear C major tonality is here being assembled right before us, out of which an unpward-piercing ostinato motif develops like a sword. As a matter of fact, this is none other than a further development of a "traditional" dominant chord, filled with new tension. It should not be overlooked that the F–B ostinato from the timpani runs through the whole section, which supplemented by G and A-flat (bars 23–25) is still merely a dominant ninth chord of a key of C. This chord is coloured, extended and individualized by the B-flat as a mistuning of the third. In bar 26, G is omitted from the chord, only to reappear in the C major resolution. But in the last bar of the ostinato section, directly before it bursts into Allegro molto, the F from the timpani rises to F-sharp while in the other parts it remains F. This gives rise to a specific Bartókian dominant chord which does not anticipate a single note from the subsequent chord, the resolution. The F-sharp therefore substitutes for G and resolves in the manner of a leading note to the G of the C major triad, while in the upper parts A-flat does the same from the other side. B and F resolve similarly in the manner of leading notes to C–E, D being relatively neutral as in the traditional dominant chord, while B-flat increases the friction and tension of the leading note, B-natural.

Example 257.

The same is also true of the closing chord at the end of the third movement, the only difference between the two chord progressions being that in the latter the root of the traditional dominant, G, is also heard alongside F-sharp. In addition, the arpeggio directions marked by the composer show that the movement upward and downward *jointly* creates Bartók's specific dominant chord, which in fact unites the functions of a traditional dominant and subdominant, and so exhibits, instead of the old three-phase functional cadence, a two-phase "tonic–non-tonic" progression.

Example 258.

By the end of the Introduction, the rhythmic profile of the Al-legro molto movement's first subject has been prepared. This is one of the finest examples of Bartók's ingenious rhythmic combinations—the way the metric division of $3 \times \frac{3}{8}$ switches into a "limping" even time, clearly justifying the term *aksak* used by Brăiloiu.[7] The transformation of metre can be explained in two ways. In part by the partial application of the hemiola, which means that out of the $\frac{6}{8}$ part of the bar, $\frac{3}{4}$ can be formed by joining quavers in pairs, making $2 \times 3 = 3 \times 2$. The same cannot be done with a complete $\frac{9}{8}$ bar, as $4 \times \frac{2}{8} = \frac{8}{8}$, leaving $\frac{1}{8}$ pairless, thus the metric structure of the whole bar becomes heterogeneous, an uneven $\frac{3}{8}$ unit being added before or after the hemiola. The other ex-planation lies closer to the *aksak* principle, namely that simply in an even, $\frac{4}{4}$ metre every fourth value grows longer, heavier, and stumbles, giving rise to the so-called "limping" (= *aksak*) feeling. This is par-ticularly so if the surplus half-value, the $\frac{1}{8}$ is not included in the rhyth-mic pattern actually sounded, but falls on a pause. The actual sounding rhythmic pattern will seem to fit into a symmetrical $\frac{4}{4}$ metre:

[7]Brăiloiu, *Le rhythme aksak* (Abbeville, 1952).

Example 259.

Bartók bridged the change from the symmetrical metre of the foregoing to an asymmetrical metre via the ambiguity of the timpani part. In bar 18 the two pianos still move in a $\frac{9}{8}$ metre, and the timpani moves along with them, seemingly with the same distribution of accent, but the alternation of the two notes inevitably alters this distribution; two notes can be repeated in a triple division only if every third beat is given an accent. This, however, is not indicated by Bartók, who in fact "smuggles" the dual division into the triple one.

Example 260.

After this it seems quite natural that in the section *poco a poco accelerendo e sempre più agitato*, beginning at bar 21, the metric pattern of the fast movement's first subject is now outlined in another ostinato motif, above the ostinato from the timpani, also foreshadowing the "interference" that results from the two kinds of paired division of $\frac{9}{8}$

Example 261.

The relationship of the four-phrase isorhythmic first subject with the theme of the *Allegro barbaro* has many times been pointed out by Bartók scholars. We should now support this well-known melodic relationship with a metric one. It is characteristic of both melodies, taken by themselves, that they are very simple and symmetrical. But just as we have proved of the Sonata's theme that this seeming symmetry is built into the accompanying timpani part by a cleverly executed rhythmic alteration, it should be noted as well that in the *Allegro barbaro* the composer builds the melody into the pounding quavers of the accompanying part by a shift of a half bar, so that the theme heard after the introduction of four and a half bars there, too, stands at odds with the even pounding of the accompanying rhythm. The effect of a metric "upset" is further enhanced by the fact that in the bare accompaniment heard first, the third always sounds on the second quaver, but when this third becomes a melody, it is brought forward to the accentuated parts of the bar.

Example 262.

The parallel with the *Allegro barbaro* offers great help in the melodic analysis of the first subject in the Sonata, particularly in explaining the pentatonic melodic framework occasionally concealed by passing notes. The pentatonic three-note basis of the first two phrases of the piano piece here becomes extended to four notes (a pentatonic tetrachord).

Example 263.

The third and fourth phrases of the theme are still more unambiguously pentatonic, with the closing alone not belonging to the pentatonic system of the preceding bar; this, though unexpected, is a necessary sliding back into the tonal framework of the theme.

Example 264.

Although the individual phrases are more or less perfectly pentatonic within themselves, the three different pentatonic scales which thus emerge, if considered as a unit, bring about a ten-note chromatic scale, while the two missing notes can be found in the first two phrases in the form unaccented passing notes not belonging to a scale.

Example 265.

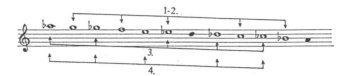

The aforementioned three different five-tone scales are in fact three transpositions at different levels of a single pentatonic system, which can also be expressed by saying that in the first system *la*=C, in the second *la*=A-flat, and in the third *la*=C-sharp. Thinking in terms of tonalities, this also means that alongside the opening and closing tonality of C, two of its mistuned variants have temporarily appeared: the tonic and the dominant (C and G) shifted a semitone higher (C-sharp and A-flat). This therefore offers a fine example of polytonality extended linearly.

This four-phrase melody, strengthened by double parallel octaves, is played by the two pianos. But within the octaves appear chords of different structures, which modify the linear relationship vertically. This means that the linear content of the notes of a phrase is not identical with the vertical, but together the two again add up to eleven-note chromaticism. It is very important, however, that the chords made from thirds and fourths which appear here do not *harmonize* the melody, they only colour it. The main reason for their differentiation, in all probability, is that Bartók wished to avoid the effect of a mixture. More exactly, he wished to use the mixture for a different purpose and so he excluded it from the formulation of the first subject. For in bar 61 the four-phrase melody reappears, but here played by only one of the pianos, the other accompanying with a mixtured scale.

The two appearances of the first subject flank a varied appearance of one of the motifs from the introduction, which also brings back the regular, symmetrical $\frac{9}{8}$ metre. However, the percussion instruments, in alternation still continuing to repeat the even rhythmic pattern, thereby ensure a complete unity to this first major section of the form.

The returning first subject has the dual function of closing down and leading on. It leads on both by repeating the closing phrase several times and by the mixtured scale progression concealed behind it. This scale melody organically anticipates the second subject which consists of scale melodies, and the mixture itself is in fact also such an anticipation, as the consistent parallel minor sixth in the theme are turned by appoggiaturas into perfect triads, and so the theme itself also appears in a mixtured texture. The scale melody, tinged by mixtures and appoggiaturas, is reminiscent of the slow movement of the First Sonata for violin and piano. Here, too, the tempo slows down, this time to *Un poco tranquillo* (♩.=104), and indeed, even the metre becomes calmer. True, it remains asymmetrical, but Bartók varies its presentation with inexhaustible invention, emphasizing its smoothly rolling character. As in the Scherzo movement of the Fifth String Quartet, where he contrasts trochaic with iambic metre, here he contrasts dactilic and anapaestic metre in gently proportioned 2–3–4 values. The musical example below shows that while the melody moves in new, asymmetrical subdivisions, the throbbing organ point of the second piano covertly recalls the subdivisons familiar from the first subject, and is only seemingly symmetrical.

Example 266.

The second subject is a good example of linearly extended bitonal ambiguity, and at the same time of the real asymmetry of a seemingly symmetrical, four-phrase melodic structure resembling a folksong. The descending scale in the first phrase is repeated in the second half of the theme, shifted a semitone lower, which means that a theme starting from G-sharp minor ends in G minor, or rather on its seventh degree. The asymmetry of the structure is caused by the material of the first phrase being repeated over two phrases, and so the dimensions of a quadruple division become a triple one, as the material of the second phrase is not repeated.

Example 267.

The tonal ambiguity clearly indicates the function of the D organ point that runs through the section: it is the common dominant of the two keys, being the mistuned dominant of G-sharp and the real dominant of G. To have a common note belonging to two keys is not a rare phenomenon in Bartók: József Ujfalussy has pointed to the duality of the F-sharp minor and F major tonality with a common third in the *Allegro barbaro* (Ujfalussy:1969). At the same time, the tonal duality of G–G-sharp has an important function in the tonal plan of the whole movement: in the traditional manner, the second subject appears in the dominant level as compared to the first subject, and to the key of the whole movement. But this "traditional" G tonality arrives through the less traditional, mistuned dominant, G-sharp, to which it returns in the second half of the second subject, only notated as A-flat (bar 95).

The closing theme again presents a new aspect of the $\frac{9}{8}$ metre: the $3\times\frac{3}{8}$ symmetrical subdivision returns, but the inner content is changed—as in place of even quavers a iambic pulse runs through the whole section.

Alongside the consistent variation of the metric character, the melodic character shows a similarly consistent change. It is almost a law with Bartók that after a first subject in a horizontal plane and a second subject moving stepwise in a scale, to have the closing theme represented by capriciously leaping melodic line. A similar arrangement can be observed in the tonal layout of the three themes: in the first subject pentatonicism assumes a major role, the second subject is of a diatonic character with consistent major triad harmony, while the closing subject draws upon a tonality of spatial division when its double third chord extends into a full octatonic scale (bar 123).

In Bartók's spirit of dynamic construction, the closing subject already undergoes profound transformation in the exposition: retaining its iambic pulse, it straightens into a scale melody, thus in fact building a bridge "backwards" to the second subject. Later on it turns out that this bridge leads not only backwards but forwards too, as, following a quite irregular idea, the second subject returns once again at the end of the exposition notably diminished in form, and with a melodic pattern which was to reappear, in a more developed and rounded form, in the second subject of the first movement of the Sixth String Quartet.

Example 268.

This unusual recapitulation has a thoroughly justified psychological function: the calm dolce melody is inserted between the fairly agitated closing subject and the tense, almost explosive development section by way of a "rest." But the E trill above it already prepares for the development section, by both dismantling the material, and acting as the foundation for the succeeding plane of tonality.

The development section is built upon a bold and dramatic confrontation of the introduction and the first subject. First the chromatic "hammering" motif of the middle section of the introduction appears, with a fast, light staccato character and chromatic imitations, at points with parallel progressions of five fourths piled upon each other. All this, however, is only a preparation for the real "drama" that begins in bar 195.

Out of the nine-note theme of the introduction an ostinato develops in the bass of the second piano, with fragments of the first subject heard above it from the first piano, which mainly underlines the tense rhythmic character and the asymmetrical shifts of metre. In an extremely interesting way, Bartók brilliantly blends the rhythmic character of the first subject with the contrasting iambic movement of the closing subject. This rhythmic contrast brings about a pronounced jazz effect, to some extent foreshadowing certain phrases in the *Contrasts*.

Example 269.

This jazz-like, or elemental emotional character is further enhanced by the fact that the regular triplet beats of the ostinato theme are reinforced by "leaping" figures in the left hand, also reminiscent of the technique of jazz pianists. One is amazed at this basic change of character in the theme which, as we have pointed out, has links with great traditions in music history from Bach through Beethoven to Liszt. First Bartók employs only notes in this "scattered" version, but later the whole theme appears in this dismantled fashion, occasionally also a fourth below the original, starting from E.

Example 270.

In the central episode containing the climax of the development section (bars 217–231), the ostinato comes to a sudden end and the lead is assigned to the two main percussion instruments, the timpani and the xylophone, which, above and below the dense, mostly contrasting motion of the two pianos, play the characteristic "leading rhythm" developed out of the first subject.

After this climax, which functions as a symmetrical apex, the ostinato returns, now in the first piano part and in mirror inversion (bar 232). Here appears the boldest dismantling of the theme: while so far one of the parts always retained the original melodic line, now only the pitches correspond to the original theme. With this, Bartók to all intents and purposes approaches the principle of twelve-tone technique.

Example 271.

The substitutions of fourths and fifths, which Bartók applies in
the two ostinato sections, actually rest on the same principle. While in
the first, as mentioned already, he build layers of fourths *below* the
theme in the original position, in the second he piles fifths *above* the
theme in mirror inversion, the only difference being that while
downwards he extends the E level of the theme by two levels, upwards
he only adds one D-sharp level to the G-sharp level of the theme. The
reason for this lies in the sound, as two layers of parallel fourths are
more distinct than two layers of fifths. Yet the logically necessary
plane of the A-sharp tonality is not missing, it merely appears in a very
concealed manner. In bar 243, the theme opens apart in mirror
fashion, an obvious reference to bar 23 of the introduction. Out of
this develops a three-note motif in bars 248 and 252, also in a mirror-
like motion, the true contents of which, despite the notation used at
the relevant points, are a D-sharp and a G-sharp triad with two thirds,
in other words a five-tone scale. The tonal planes of D-sharp and G-
sharp correspond exactly to the tonal planes of the ostinato theme.

Example 272.

This leaves no doubt that the chromatic mirror motif which forms the
root of the three-note motif is in bar 243 the centre of a similar triad
with double thirds which, were it complete, would represent an A-
sharp plane. Thus appears in a concealed, virtually imaginary form the
logically necessary second layer of fifths.

Example 273.

The following illustrated succession in which the imaginary A-sharp layer appears first, followed by the D-sharp and later by the G-sharp layers, shows that even here Bartók uses a symmetrical construction, because while in the first ostinato section the layers of fourths are constantly growing in number, here, after the presentation of the reverse form in the G-sharp plane, the layers are piled suddenly upon one another, and, progressing in reverse order, they gradually decrease in number, until the G-sharp layer again remains alone.

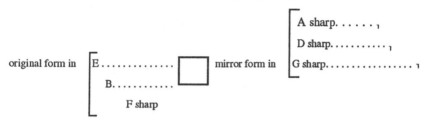

The symmetrical structure of the development section has an interesting effect on the basically asymmetrical sonata form; the second subject returns in mirror inversion in the recapitulation, corresponding to the inversion of the introduction's theme in the development section. This symmetry does not include the order of themes as it does in the Fifth String Quartet, but the tendency is still absolutely clear: an original combination of the traditional sonata principle with the new symmetry principle.

The question arises why the first subject and the closing subject are omitted from the theme inversion. But if one takes a closer look at the first subject's folksong-like four-line structure, it immediately becomes clear that it is in fact irreversible. What actually can be inverted, some minor melodic fragments, have already been assigned an ample role in the unusually dynamic development section. This gave rise to Bartók's extremely economic procedure, according to which at the beginning of the recapitulation, in the strongly accentuated moment of return, the first subject is initially only substituted for, by sounding the C tonality, abandoning or completely transforming its original melodic profile. In the third or fourth bar of the recapitulation the condensed melodic elements of the first and second phrases of the first subject are already distinctly heard, and this continues in a similar way throughout the whole recapitulation of the first subject. It should be added that this varying and substituting recapitulation is relatively short compared with the dimensions of the exposition, but this is called for to ensure the balance of form, since the first subject has taken up the whole development section and is to fill the Coda as well.

The closing subject cannot be inverted either, or more exactly, it can be inverted, but an inversion would be ineffective as the leaping melodic phrases alternated constantly at its first appearance. This material returns with an almost developmental dynamism, extending over a large surface, and contrasting even more clearly the two kinds of melodic motion derived from the same rhythmic type: the capricious, leaping form progressing for the most part in sixths and the form progressing like a scale. The second large unit of the recapitulation can be compared to the exciting ostinato sections of the development section: the first piano "gallops" for 22 bars over the ostinato motif developed from the theme, with the second piano and the two side-drums alternately interrupting it with agitated scale fragments and rhythmic motifs. Regarding the ostinato motif, Ernő Lendvai has pointed out that it uses up the complete chromatic scale in the broken minor-sixth inversions of its four augmented triads, which "dramaturgically" means that the leading part heard above it becomes a murmuring background, completely neutral tonality.[8]

Example 274.

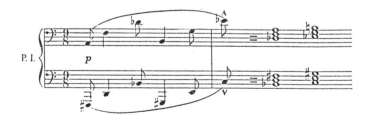

---

[8]Lendvai 1955: 53–54.

As was mentioned, the leading role in the Coda is again assumed by the first subject, first augmented and raised to a tonal plane a minor third higher. Its effect closely resembles the same formal passage in the first movement of the Fifth String Quartet.

The theme raised to the plane of E-flat is joined by way of a "dominant shadow" by its polarizing partner, the plane of A. To speak of such a "dominant shadow" is justified by the formal unit that directly follows, where the first subject returns in its original tempo, only slightly varied in rhythm and at the original pitch, meanwhile being shadowed in imitation by its real dominant equivalent. This verifies the interchangeability of the real dominant and the mistuned dominant, as does the role of the timpani in the last bars of the Coda. While the first piano repeats the first subject in its tonic position, and the second piano in its real dominant position, the timpani play alternately C and F-sharp, so that the real dominant is tinged by its mistuned variant. At the end the timpani underpins the last moment before the close with G, so that Bartók's aim at a kind of dominant function can be clearly observed: the closing chord without a third is approached from both sides by all the parts, with the exception of the bass-like leading note.

Second movement: Lento, ma non troppo

Of all Bartók's slow movements this one stands closest to "The Night's Music" of 1926. Although a small role is assigned here to what are termed sound effects, the rustlings of nature and the micromelodics and reduced rhythmic formulae expressing them, the melody at the centre of the movement is closely related to the solitary, meditative, introverted monologue in the piano piece. The relationship can be seen straightaway from the two opening phrases.

Example 275.

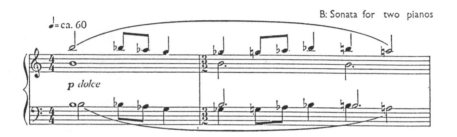

However, the structure of the movement as a whole shows a marked difference; while in "The Night's Music" the sounds of nature unfold over a long section before the melody of the solitary monologue appears, in the second movement of the Sonata the melody is heard straightaway after a short introduction by the percussion. One may say that here the percussion instruments, by their very nature, are sound effects, so there is no need for the piano's clusters and micro-melodics to suggest them; in fact, Bartók uses the percussion instruments to foreshadow the metric profile. In other words, the aim in the piano piece was precisely to conceal and disintegrate the metre, while here it is to deliberately suggest the pulse of the melody, to establish it in the subconscious as it were.

As in the first movement, the leading role is assigned to a four-phrase, essentially isometric and isorhythmic melody, rooted in folksong. Let us add right away that the fourth phrase is a little different from the first three, both in metre and rhythm, but this slight difference makes an effective close. The opening basic phrase is quite individual: $\frac{4}{4}$ and $\frac{3}{2}$ bars are linked to each other, disguising a phrase structure of five main beats. Bartók further enhances its special character by presenting the basic formula — ∪ ∪ —, which provides the rhythmic content of the phrase, in two different forms, which in fact helps to reveal the real structure. The simple form concealed behind it would be:

Example 276.

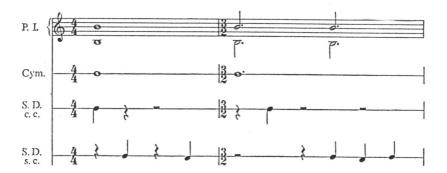

Bartók lengthens the first crotchet into twice its value, and this gives the theme its individual outline. But the metric structure this gives rise to does not conceal an even pulse, but a division of 4–3–3, in keeping with the asymmetric theme character of the previous movement. This is borne out by the version of the theme which appears in bar 14, and by the percussion accompaniment which accents the $\frac{3}{2}$ bar as 2x3 and 3x2, as well as by the repeating of the pedal notes.

Example 277.

This explains why extending the final phrase by two crotchets does not upset the internal balance of the four-phrase structure: it is this expansion which turns what have thus far been feminine endings of the phrases into a masculine one:

Example 278.

The same internal law can be discovered in the recapitulation of the melody in bars 21–25; here only the first two of the four phrases return, leaving the formal section open (as is necessary for the continuation), but Bartók changes the second phrase, originally with a feminine ending, into a masculine ending, intensifying the accent further with a special performance indication.

The folk music roots of the melodic structure are evident in the traces of a changing fifth structure; these traces can be observed in the relationship between the first and third phrases, more or less offset by the different dispositions of the four phrases, the scheme being:

Example 279.

Bartók's own reticent analysis, according to which the second movement is in an A–B–A ternary song form, masks a somewhat more complicated structure.[9] On the one hand the middle section B includes several separate sections, and on the other, which is more important, the quintuplet motif—the most important element in section B—reappears at the end of the movement, thus to a certain extent changing the ternary, full circle form. This phenomenon of form construction is similar to the one evident in the basically ternary slow movement of the First Sonata for Violin and Piano.

In connection with the return of section A, one should again refer to "The Night's Music," the source of the recapitulation technique, whereby the slowly progressing melodic line is accompanied by parallel layers of differentiated movement. Here, in the Sonata, the chromatic, undulating motion which accompanies the returning theme throughout, reaches back to the middle section. More important, however, is the accompanying layer of the theme: a counter-melody in a dotted, differentiated rhythm, which with its agitated gestures and capricious turns affords a marked contrast to the calmly progressing melody.

Due to the division of section B into three internal parts, the whole movement expands into five sections, which is the second basic tendency shaping the form. The slowly progressing melody, almost resembling a chorale, flanks agitated material, as in the similarly divided middle movement of the Third Piano Concerto. This middle section is often compared with Bartók's nature music, but here there are two different types. One is the quintuplet motif, which can be traced back to the tiny stirrings in "The Night's Music." Yet this is more than just an effect imitating nature or a bird-call. It is more individual and subjective, in part because its quintuplet rhythm is not merely one of the various differentiated "rhythmic gestures" but a permanent, crystallized form, and in part because its melodic content, the minor third, is one of Bartók's most subjective melodic features.

The salient features and individual character of this motif, its emotional content and psychological function, are indicated by the important role it is assigned in the formal section that forms the symmetrical axis of the movement—it divides the two outer parts of section B, the presentation of the quintuplet motif and the "undulation"

[9]See note 2.

that prepares for the recapitulation. The first piano discant part outlines a mistuned four-phrase changing fifth, sectionalized melody,
reinforced by the xylophone and accompanied by mixture chords,
while the timpani stubbornly repeats the quintuplet motif. The section is lent a particular tension by the confrontation of the menacing,
rumbling timpani ostinato and the *molto espressivo* melody.

It is worth taking a special look at the structure of the mixtures
connected with the melody. The four-note chord outlined by one of
the layers is joined in the other layer by chromatic adjacent notes with
a colouring function, a redoubled colour effect, since the mixture is itself a colour effect.

Example 280.

The colour-effect character of these "quasi clusters" is also proved by
the fact that at the end of the melody the last chord is turned into a
chromatic run from the second piano, which also in essence takes
place in the first piano part.

Example 281.

Third movement: Allegro non troppo

The first subject of the third movement is often connected by analysts to one of Beethoven's *contredanse* melodies, putting forward that here too we are faced with a musical quotation.[10] A similarity certainly exists between the two melodies, yet there is no reason not to approach the theme from the side of Bartók's *own* melodic world. Melodies with a "straight" line, spread out like a scale, are not at all rare in Bartók, indeed they represent one of his basic theme-types. Scale themes built from the characteristic scale with augmented fourth and minor seventh form an even more closely related family of melodies. Let us add that the fourth quaver at the opening of the theme is no novelty either, nor is the phrase structure in which the first ascending phrase is answered by a descending second phrase, and after a segmented, dissolving third phrase, an ending with an expanded, far-reaching fourth phrase.

As usual in Bartók, particularly in his scale subjects, the principal means of variation is a many-sided exploration of the modal character of the theme. Mirror inversion suits this extremely well, though surprisingly Bartók here only inverts the main contours instead of using an exact, note-for-note inversion. Although the descending version in the inverted first subject of the development section of the sonata rondo maintains its opening quaver leap of a fourth, Bartók then changes the structure of the theme so that the final note should ease the tonality. By retaining the structure of a fourth and a minor seventh, the inversion remains faithful, yet the character of the theme becomes changed.

Example 282.

Only the first phrase of the four-phrase melody returns at such a key point as this, while the material of the second phrase is simplified into an accompaniment figure that runs through the section like an ostinato.

Example 283.

Further on in the development section this breakdown of the elements prevails even more consistently: the scale motif and the motif of fourths are each given an individual existence, and along with them the playful rhythmic figures also display many different aspects.

The first subject or rondo theme next appears not at the beginning of the recapitulation—this would be too close to its presentation in the development section—but only in the Coda (bar 351). The ascending and descending forms are directly contrasted, in a mixtured harmonization of major triads, and are further enriched by a new variation, in the course of which the theme's phrases in order undergo a great many changes and finally regain their structure, this time in isorhythmic form. This recapitulation be a fuller and more static formulation of the theme (bars 387–395) has the function of closing and rounding off the form. Afterwards a breaking down of the material proceeds until the first phrase is emphasized separating chords, melody and rhythm.

The sonata-principle shaping of the movement can be best observed in the two episodes: the quasi second subject and the quasi closing theme. As against the dynamism of the former, the latter is relatively static, thus exhibiting even more clearly the role of formal units in the tonal plan of the movement, as well as the constructive strength within the form, which makes irreversible the rondo structure's tendency toward symmetry. The rhythmically organic winding melody coalesces into a "patch" of tension, against the hammering background of an alternative rhythmic pattern. Although the rhythm itself radiates an agitated atmosphere, the real tension comes from the mirror-like, winding melodic lines, which consistently outline, together with adjacent chromatic degrees, the G major triad that also determines the key of the formal section. The adjacent notes surrounding the main ones colour the central key with A-flat major and F-sharp major.

Example 284.

The complementary phenomenon appears in the recapitulation in a more complex form, piling eleven layers of fifths upon one another. The complex of notes, which superimposes different keys represented by layers of fifths, and colours them by adjacent degrees, is returned to the tonal plane by pedal notes: the F trill from the timpani prepares, as the dominant of the dominant, the E-flat key of the Coda, while the G-sharp chord with two thirds crystallized above it resolves onto A, the third of F, thus we arrive back to the level of "monotonality" from two directions.

Example 285.

CHAPTER FIFTEEN

CONTRASTS FOR VIOLIN, CLARINET AND PIANO

The history of how this work originated has so far been most accurately described by József Ujfalussy, in a lecture given at the International Bartók Seminar in Budapest in 1968 (Ujfalussy 1968: 342–44). Besides using available correspondence, he was able to complete and authenticate his researches with information from József Szigeti himself.

In his book, József Szigeti writes: "I have never commissioned any work for my own exclusive use; I somehow always managed to have my hands full without that. The nearest I came to commissioning a work was when I had a brainwave about suggesting to Benny Goodman that he authorize me to ask Bartók to write a work for three of us—Goodman, Bartók, and myself."[1] So the idea came from Szigeti, but the commission was actually given by Goodman. The main document concerning the history of the work's origin is Szigeti's letter to Bartók dated 11 August 1938.

> . . . what at the time, in the Pagani Restaurant seemed just an idea, has meanwhile become concrete reality, and that because Benny Goodman (the world-famous jazz clarinetist 'idol' mentioned at the time) came to see me on the Riviera during the few days of his European 'joy-ride'! I

---

[1] József Szigeti, *With Strings Attached: Reminiscences and Reflections* (New York: A. Knopf, 1953), 129.

took this opportunity to secure the 'commission' I've mentioned, under conditions which he gladly agreed to and which amount to *treble* the amount (a hundred dollars) you'd mentioned at the time! (i.e., my clever wife, whom I consulted on the matter, did not find the 100 dollars enough and said, let Benny pay three-hundred, and now I see she was right!) So please write to Benny Goodman . . . a registered letter in which you agree to write within a given time a 6–7 minute clarinet-violin duo with piano accompaniment, the ownership of which remains yours, but granting him the performance rights for three years, so that you will only have it printed after that time. You also reserve the gramophone recording rights for him and myself for three years. The royalties from performances, radio and his recordings of course pertain to you. If possible, it would be very good if the composition were to consist of two independent sections (which could perhaps be played separately, as in the Rhapsody no.1 for Violin), and of course we hope it will include a brilliant clarinet and violin cadenza! . . . In any case I can safely say that Benny brings out from the instrument whatever the clarinet is physically able to perform at all, and quite wonderfully—in regions *much* higher than the high note in "Eulenspiegel"! . . . (*Documenta Bartókiana* 1968:226).

Considering the date of the letter and the date when the work was completed—24 September 1938, which Bartók, as usual, marked on the closing bar of the manuscript—it becomes clear that the piece was composed in essence in September 1938, within scarcely a month. For quite some time it remained questionable whether the third movement, which Bartók added in between the two movements originally commissioned, was also written during that time. This seems to be indicated, although not unambiguously settled, by a letter Bartók wrote to Madam Müller-Widmann on 9 October: "As for me, I have been working hard this summer. I have finished the Violin Concerto and two pieces (commissioned) for Szigeti end the American jazz clarinetist Benny Goodman (3 pieces, to be exact, 16 minutes altogether) . . ." (*Bartók Letters* 1971:no.212).

We know from the information Ujfalussy was given by József Szigeti that Bartók composed the third, middle piece also in September, but at first kept to the request, and sent Benny Goodman only the two movements which had been asked for. Only later did he "dare" admit the third piece to his commissioner. József Szigeti quotes the humorous letter Bartók enclosed with the work: "Salesmen usually deliver less than what is expected from them. But there are exceptions, though I know people are not likely to be pleased with the contractor's largesse if he delivers a suit for an adult instead of the dress ordered for a two-year-old baby."[2]

This is why at the première on 9 January 1939, only the two-movement version of *Contrasts* was performed by Szigeti, Goodman and Endre Petri, under the title *Rhapsody—Two Dances*. The complete, final version of the work was first performed at the Columbia Recording Company in April 1940, with Bartók himself at the piano. That was when Bartók gave the work its final title, after lengthy deliberation, as we know from Szigeti. In his letter of 1 December 1938, Bartók wrote, "I don't really like the term Rhapsody . . . I even would rather prefer the title 'Two Dances' . . . " (Ujfalussy 1968:344).

The complete, three-movement version obviously excluded these titles, and Bartók sought a title that would be more concrete and programme-like than "trio," yet at the same time more general and perhaps more abstract than the customary titles for dance and genre pieces.

The history of the work's origin also throws a sharp light onto the composer's dilemma of using a two-section structure or a three-section one. József Szigeti explains the final form of the work as the self-determining law of genius when he writes, "Bartók was prompted by his unerring sense of form, sense of balance, or whatever we may call this sense, to add this, as it later turned out so highly necessary, 'night piece' with its wonderfully calm and free air" (Ujfalussy 1968:344). This approach, however, does not provide a full and unequivocal explanation, because the word "to add" reveals an involuntary assumption of the original concept of the commissioners. Although Bartók's exact process of composition is not known to us, the short time it took seems to indicate that the work burst from the composer's imagination almost in one piece, immediately implying the necessary creative concept of a three-movement structure. So the second movement, bearing the inscription "Pihenő" (Rest) is only

[2]See note 1.

seemingly "added" between the first, "Verbunkos" and the third "Sebes" (Rapid).

The question should by no means be reduced to some more or less simplified postulate according to which the two-movement form, due its folk-music roots, is of a lower order than the three- movement structure rooted in the classical tradition. What is true here is that in most of Bartók's binary structures, primarily in those resembling the sonata, the simple two-movement principle is broken through by need for a different form principle, one rounding off and summing up. In connection with the Second Sonata for Violin and Piano and the Third String Quartet, we have already attempted to prove that in these compositions the dual and treble structural principles virtually wrestle with each other in a struggle in which neither of the two gains an unambiguous victory. In any case it is worth noting that the two Rhapsodies for Violin of 1928 show no trace of this struggle, and this seems to indicate that the sonata-like structure represents a higher level in Bartók's scale of values, being closely linked with the traditional art forms. The reason for this lies not in the composer's traditionalism or a conservative approach to structure, but in his creative method of organic development, shaping and variation, which Bartók adopted as part of the Beethoven heritage and which became his most personal device.

Here then lies the explanation for why the trio *had* to become a three-movement piece. The slow recruiting dance and the fast dance in themselves call for no "bridge" or "rest." But for the Bartók of 1938 this traditional rhapsody form had self-evidently "outgrown its clothes" and become the vehicle for a higher musical message. Despite the commission, Bartók composed not what is known as a concert piece, but a *chamber-music work*, a worthy cousin of the string quartets and sonatas, which in both its material and structure follows the laws of chamber-music form.

The demands of chamber music are not only evident in the three-movement structure, but also in the internal structure of the individual movements. That is why it can be said that the three-movement form is not an external stylistic feature but an internal law, being not an addition but a quality intrinsic to the work from the outset.

Decisive evidence in this respect is the structure, which contains definite sonata form as compared to the simpler form of the rhapsodies.

I. *Verbunkos* — Moderato, ben ritmato

The movement is founded upon two subjects of contrasting character. The first, with an anacrusis-like subject-head of dotted rhythm and limpid melodic turns associated with it, expresses a characteristic historic Hungarian tone. József Ujfalussy points out its relationship to a number of themes in the Third Piano Concerto and the Divertimento, emphasizing their common, major mode, elegant society tone (Ujfalussy 1968:346–47).

Example 286.

In bar 30 the second subject appears with an entirely different rhythmic and melodic profile, related to others found in the two Rhapsodies for Violin, and in their common source, Rumanian folk music.

As a first approximation, according also to József Ujfalussy's analysis, this second theme functions as a middle section in the movement, between the two differing presentations of the first subject. The scheme can thus be depicted: A–B–A$_v$.

The organic development of the first theme, however, and the way in which it passes over into the second theme, point to a sonata-like construction. This is supported also by the perfectly balanced position of the two themes—the first consisting of 29 bars, the second of 28 bars, the first opening with the clarinet and continuing with the violin, the second opening with the violin and continuing with the clarinet. But it is the third formal section, starting in bar 58, which unambiguously determines the character of the structure. In material it consists of a return of the first theme, but in such a dynamic and re-cast form that it goes beyond the framework of a true recapitulation, and in fact can only be considered as a development. This whole formal unit before the final cadenza is filled by different variations on a single motif of the first subject, more precisely its incipit. Only the material that begins at bar 85 has the feeling of a more complete and more static—i.e., real—recapitulation, but it proves to be merely a hinted one, as after three bars it leads into a clarinet cadenza. After the cadenza only the opening "curtain" material of the movement returns, clearly functioning as a close. The above depicted scheme, now modified, may be interpreted as follows:

A B	A_V	A
Exposition	Development	Hinted Recap.

A singular feature of the structure, of which we have already seen examples in Bartók (for example, in the Third String Quartet), is that the composer attaches importance only to the exposition and development of the sonata form, but as for the recapitulation, he either omits it, merely hints at it, or substitutes for it.

II. *PIHENŐ* (REST) — LENTO

Here, too, the recapitulatory, rounded-out form can be clearly sensed, and furthermore in a reduced form, confined to brief hints evoking the opening material. Within this framework the procedures can be related to the technique Bartók employed in a number of pieces in *Mikrokosmos*—gradual transformation and free treatment of the opening material according to a chosen principle of development.

Although not unique, the regular folksong structure of the first major formal unit, following the A–A^5–A^5_V–A type of Hungarian folksong structure is worth noting.[3] This formal process is closely akin to the Bulgarian scherzo in the Fifth String Quartet and the second movement's first subject of the *Music for Strings, Percussion and Celesta*. Another singularity common to these structures within the above scheme is that the third phrase repeats the basic melody on sequential levels, and then leads on to the fourth phrase without a

---

[3] A^5 = A in a fifth higher position, A^5v = its variant.

cadential pause. In this movement the material is heard in duet on the violin and clarinet, the parts moving more or less in mirror. To give a clear presentation of the actual structure, we quote only the violin part.

Example 287.

The parallel with the Bulgarian scherzo of the Fifth Quartet is further strengthened by the melodic material itself: there, too, a dome-shaped melody of thirds forms the centre, and Bartók also exploits the variation possibilities inherent in the mirror inversion of the melody. For example, it is particularly characteristic of both works that the first, ascending phrase becomes a descending one by the fourth phrase.

Melodically the second formal section (bars 19–28) consists of new elements, though the duo of violin and clarinet continue the two-part counterpoint of the first section, emphasizing further its complementary rhythm. The new melodic element, the diminished fifth, soon turns out therefore to be an organic continuation of the melody presented in the first section, where the steps of thirds and seconds were also mostly built within the compass of a diminished fifth.

The third section (bars 29–43) seemingly leads still further away from the opening, but is actually an even closer variation than the second section, since the first phrase of the clarinet part is clearly recognizable in the melodic line compressed within the compass of a fourth.

Example 288.

Nevertheless, this formal section cannot be considered a recapitulation, as it is quite dynamic in character; its rhythm accelerates to quavers and triplets, while the middle interval becomes an augmented fourth, giving a particular tension to the melody (bar 41).

The question of tonality forms an organic part of the movement's structural problem. Compared to the unambiguous A tonality of the first movement, here we encounter a fairly ambivalent tonality. It is usually referred to as being in the tonality of B, which is actually true if one compares the B–F-sharp closing chord of the first phrase to the B major seventh chord which closes the movement. But it should not be forgotten that the first phrase of the violin-clarinet duo outlines an A major-minor triad and the piano trills in bar 5 also come to rest on A. This A–B ambiguity is also reinforced by the closing chord of the movement, and the violin's pizzicatos run through the whole closing section like an organ point. An interesting change-over takes place: at the beginning the final melodic A is heard *below* the chordal B–F-sharp, while at the end A is heard *above* the B major triad. This seems to indicate that this tonal ambivalence does not simply mean bitonality, but also a tonal contrasting of the chordal and melodic structures. In other words, B is the fundemantal note in a chordal sense, and A in a melodic sense. Similar procedures have already been encountered in Bartók's chamber music: in the slow movement of the Fourth Quartet, for example, the fundamental note of the chordal figures is A, whereas the melodic structure centres around D.[4]

This dual tonality of the second movement is given a deeper significance by the third movement, as the closing movement is in an unambiguous tonality of B-flat, but in the final chord this B-flat is surrounded, above and below, by colouring adjacent notes: A and C flat. This is none other than a condensation of the three tonalities of the three movements, since the tonality of the first is A, that of the second B (C-flat) and that of the third B-flat (Ujfalussy 1968:353).

On the basis of this analysis we would venture to state further that the organic concept and structure of the work are borne out by the consistent superposition of keys; that is, the second movement, while *retaining* the A tonality of the first movement, *adds* a layer of B tonality, and the third movement *adds* still a third plane onto this dual plane, making the work's tonal unity of A–B–B flat. Examples of such a procedure can also be found in earlier works. The same piling of keys by semitones was to be seen in the Third Quartet, where the Seconda parte adds the tonalities of D and E-flat to the C-sharp tonality of the Prima parte, with all three tonalities prevalent simultaneously in the Coda.

III. *Sebes (Rapid)* — Allegro vivace

The B-flat tonality of the closing movement naturally calls for a change of instrument: the place of the A clarinet is taken by a B-flat clarinet. It should be noted here that this time the violinist also has to change his instrument, as for the first thirty bars Bartók prescribes a specially tuned violin: the E string has to be retuned to E-flat and the G string to G-sharp. (As there is no time to retune and tune back, the practical procedure is to use another instrument which has been mistuned in advance.)

The phenomenon of mistuning—*scordatura*—and its role and increased significance in Bartók's oeuvre have already been discussed in

---

[4]See J. Kárpáti, "Tonal Divergences of Melody and Harmony: A Characteristic Device in Bartók's Musical Language," *Studia Musicologica* Tom.XXIV, 373–80.

detail in Part One. The dimished and perfect fifth in the introduction, played on open strings, give rise in any case to a very strange effect. But it is characteristic of the composer's well considered and thoroughly logical construction that here it is not merely a question of a simple effect; the chain of diminished and perfect fifths forms a special set of notes, a tonal system which is embodied in the first theme of the movement (Ujfalussy 1968:352–53). This also thoroughly justifies the view expressed earlier on the significance of the mistuning phenomena in connection with the musical idiom and tonal system. The chain of perfect fifths, which lays bare the genesis of our diatonic tone system, is here modified into a chain of partially mistuned fifths, with yet the same role.

Example 289.

The theme presented by the clarinet is joined by a second theme from the piano, which can be considered the direct continuation of the previous theme. Although the two themes together create the rondo theme of the movement, they represent, despite their obvious relationship, two different melodic profiles. The first is of a closed, chromatic character, opened only by a few perfect fourths, while the second, due to its prominent Lydian fourth, is from the outset open, and seemingly diatonic, consisting as it does of Lydian and minor tetrachords (heptatonia secunda).

Example 290.

At the entry of the second rondo theme, the mistuned violin accompaniment also changes—one may say turns around—the place of the perfect fifth being taken by a perfect fourth, and that of the diminished fifths by augmented fourths. The difference between enharmonically identical intervals almost becomes audible: the diminished fifth that so far closed inwardly (E-flat–A) slides a semitone upwards, and changes into a fourth (E–B-flat) with a prominent Lydian character.

Example 291.

The two rondo themes separately and together form the whole movement's pillared structure, complementing and contrasting one another. Among their relatively unchanged appearances there emerge individual transitional and episodic elements, whose individuality lies in that they develop the material of the episodes—except for two new motifs—out of one or another of the rondo themes. The rhythm of the first theme allows for polyphonic treatment of which Bartók makes use in the short sections beginning at bars 36 and 59, respectively. The development after bar 59 well exemplifies the consistent organic nature of the development—the dotted rhythm of the first rondo theme assumes an independent existence, transforming the second rondo theme into its own form, producing a *grazioso* version.

Another typical example of organic development appears in the section after bar 110, where a new motif, resembling a small episode, is born out of the scale-like "straightened" continuation of the second rondo theme, and this motif is to be assigned a role again in a few bars from bar 266 onwards.

The two real episode motifs of the rondo theme draw attention to significant connections. The large leaps in the first (from bar 52) reveal a close relationship with the *grazioso* themes of the Soanatas for Violin and Piano, and also to the "Burletta" movement of the Sixth String Quartet. This latter link throws light on further relationships; it explains the appearance of the rhythmically pointed motif with an appoggiatura which assumes a growing role in the second half of the rondo theme after the trio, and which is clearly the first formulation of the "Burletta" theme of the Sixth Quartet composed a year later.

Example 292.

Example 292 (continued)

The lengthy trio section in the middle of the movement also has close links with the trio section of the "Burletta." In the *Constrasts* the Hungarian folk-music character of the melody is interspersed with a bold complex Bulgarian metre, of which one can find hardly any examples in Hungarian folk music. Bartók links the $\frac{8}{8}$ metre of 3+2+3 subdivision with a $\frac{5}{8}$ metre of 2+3, resulting in an unusual symmetrical metre. This framework is filled with the strophic theme's isorhythmic phrases in complementary fashion. Behind this quite unique rhythmic pattern lies a repeated half Asclepiad metre, forming an inherent contrast to the typical melodic patterns of Hungarian folksong. This is another splendid example of Bartók's art of synthesis: while on the one hand he turns the asymmetrical "limping" Bulgarian metre into a symmetrical one, on the other hand he combines an unmistakably Hungarian melody with a classical Greek metre.

In the second half of the trio section, the folksong character falls into the background. The rhythmic pattern is joined by a simple scale melody, which in different manners is played by the instruments, in parallel and in mirror motion. The octaves, fifths and fourths, moving in parallel, have a colouring function, as have the whole-tone clusters starting at bar 164, which outline the scale melody in a mixture-like way. As against the strongly tonal character of the folksong melody, this section is of a rather unstable, indefinite tonality. As in the First Piano Concerto, the scale melodies extend the compass of a perfect octave to an augmented octave.

Example 293.

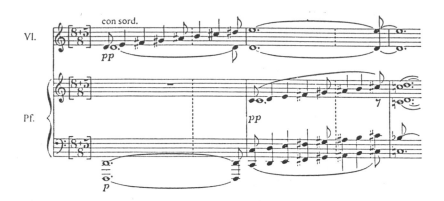

Having examined the material of the movement, an attempt can now be made to outline the structure, which looked at as a whole provides the answer to the dual character of the movement. For it should not be overlooked that while on the one hand definite links can be discerned with the "Burletta" music in the Sixth Quartet, the basic material of the movement, as presented in the two rondo themes, unambiguously recalls the Rumanian-like dance fantasy finales which we encountered in the two Sonatas for Violin and Piano. A common charactersitic of the musical material in these movements is a regular semiquaver motor rhythm, here not against the traditional background of the baroque prelude or toccata, but of Rumanian instrumental dance music. Bartók's collection of Rumanian folk music offers many examples both of this type of move-ment and of modal characters, richly combined.[5] The following ex-amples are supplemented by Bartók's most important uses of it in his First Sonata for Violin and Piano, in *Contrasts*, the Violin Concerto and the Concerto for Orchestra. In his short analysis of the Concerto, the author himself described this type of movement as *"perpetuum mobile*-like passages" (*Bartók Essays* 1976:no.80).

[5]Béla Bartók, *Rumanian Folk Music* Vols. I–III, ed. by Benjamin Suchoff (The Hague: Martinus Nijhof, 1967). Our example quotes melody no. 374b from Vol.I.

Example 294.

The wild, folk-dance character associated with the rondo theme is counterbalanced by a definite burlesque character, though not so much in the episodic sense as in the Sonatas for Violin and Piano; in the course of the movement the wild, *perpetuum mobile* material tends to decrease while the burlesque material increases so that eventually the Coda is dominated by the burlesque alone.

What may explain this shift of balance, which leads to the burlesque material gaining the upper hand by the end of the movement? The explanation is to be found in the Sixth Quartet, for whose closing movement Bartók originally planned a dance fantasy with a similar *perpetuum mobile* character. In the case of the quartet it is not known exactly what caused a change in the original plan, but I have already conjectured a reason. It is highly probable that Bartók was occupied with similar problems when composing the trio, which predates the quartet, and the same inner forces which led to the total abandonment of the folk-dance material in the Sixth Quartet may also have swung the weight from folk dance to burlesque in the closing movement of *Contrasts*.

This supposition is not contradicted by the fact that in between Bartók composed the closing movements of the Violin Concerto and the Divertimento—two finales which include dance fantasy "life-assertion" material.[6] But it should not be forgotten that both compositions are built on firm, traditional models, as against the quite individual trio, and the string quartet, which also turned into an individual work. Another explanation lies in the fact that we do not have here a "folk-dance finale" in the general sense of the term, but one of its specific types, which was only to find its real, mature form in the Concerto, some five years after the composition of *Constrasts*.

Chapter 4, "Monothematicism and Variation," gave a number of examples showing Bartók's different methods of composition in creating the internal unity of his works. In the case of *Contrasts* one can hardly speak of an expressly monothematic process, nevertheless it can be observed here, too, that the thematic material is lent unity by motivic links. Even between some of the themes of the outer movements a thematic relationship can be discovered, and they can be put together with the "homesickness" second subject in the first move-

---

[6]The term "life-assertion" was used by Bartók himself in his analysis of the Concerto (*Bartók Essays* 1976:no.80).

ment of the Sixth Quartet (Ujfalussy 1968:348). In other words, the middle section of the first movement—one may say its second subject, contrasting with the first subject—is related not only to the folk-music based second theme of the First Rhapsody, but to the trio section of the closing movement as well. The links are specifically melodic in character, though at the same time the rhythmic relationships are well to the fore. In any case, it is noticeable how the simpler accentuated iambic rhythm develops into a more complicated rhythmic formula. The theme of the Sixth Quartet, already mentioned, may be a connecting link as it were between the simpler and the more complex types: there the two mirror-like metric patterns consisting of an iambic and a trochaeic element, the choriamb and the antispast stand side-by-side (c). The trio melody of the closing movement of *Contrasts*, which we have already mentioned, conceals a half Asclepiad metre, where we can see the internal expansion of the antispast (d).

Example 295.

By comparison, a more disguised, but in fact more concrete motivic relationship exists between all the other themes of the three-movement composition. The main element of motivic relationship is the augmented fourth, which stands out as a characteristic interval both in the first subject of the first movement and the second rondo theme of the closing movement. To this should be added the similarity of mode, which also links the texture following the Lydian fourth incipits: in both an important melodic motif is the appearance of the minor seventh which, with the Lydian fourth, is Bartók's favourite scale. The same interval of an augmented fourth, sometimes in the form of a diminished fifth, assumes a significant role in the middle movement, too. In the first two melodic lines of the theme it is still heard in a concealed way, but the development, starting from bar 19, already distinctly reveals that the tension of the interval acts as a veritable enzyme in the melodic process. After this it is not surprising that the last variation is built upon it, unmistakably related to the gamelan effect in "From the Island of Bali" in *Mikrokosmos* (Stevens 1964:219).

This more or less overt system of thematic and motivic relationships provides a firm structural framework for the whole composition, following this symmetrical scheme.

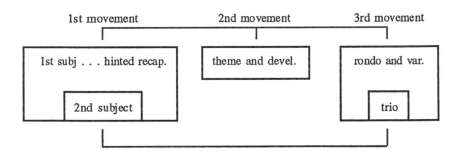

This in itself would suffice to prove that the composition is a worthy companion of the great chamber works, whose three-movement structure is not the result of a subsequent "addition" but an inevitable formulation of the qualities inherent in the relevant musical material. But these motivic contacts in themselves are merely external appearances of a much deeper system of relationships, which, while providing a key for the understanding of the work's perfect unity, also throws light on certain important laws in Bartók's composing technique and creative method.

The first movement's Lydian fourth incipit is first developed by the typical melodic turns of the *verbunkos*, in the clarinet part. This aspect of the theme has been elucidated in all its contexts by József Ujfalussy (Ujfalussy 1968:347), so let us rather turn to the violin part in which the incipit is followed by its motivic elaboration. The Lydian fourth motif turns into a triad with two thirds, in which the ponderous Lydian fourth melodic phrases pattern contains always the major third contrasted with the minor third. Let us immediately place it beside a close relative of the incipit, from the Sixth Quartet, where almost the same thing happens, only in a different order: the major third is heard first and the minor third after it (it should be noted that the former process also occurs).

Example 296.

The triad with two thirds is in itself nothing new in Bartók's music; we have already encountered a number of examples, and the subject has been treated in great detail by Bartók analysts. But it should not go unnoticed that here the use of the alternative third appears as a natural counterpart to the use of the alternative fifth, as the augmented fourth can also be thought of as the diminished alternative to the perfect fifth. This is reinforced by examining the four-note motif when it occurs. The first three notes in every case outline a major or minor triad, after which the fourth, rhythmically accentuated note, takes a surprising turn, drawing the chromatic adjacent note—a mistuned, shifted equivalent of one of the notes already heard—into the process. In the following example we see first the minor third beside the major (a), then the major third beside the minor (b), and finally the diminished fifth (augmented fourth) beside the perfect one (c).

Example 297.

This duality of the third and the fifth appears *in nucleo* in the "frame" or "curtain" motif of the first movement, introducing as it were imperceptibly these two sensitive degrees of the movement's scale and their alternation. It should be observed that Bartók scores the minor third, whose notation is indecisive, first as B-sharp and then as C, but in both cases he consistently writes a diminished fifth (E-flat) beside the perfect fifth. The same note always features in the melody as an augmented fourth (D-sharp), partly because this is clearer for the instrumentalist, and partly because the Rumanian modality of the melody dominates.

Before examining the further consequence of the two fifths, let us first take a look at the appearances of the triads with two thirds. The superimposed entry of the incipit in the development section, beginning at bar 58, brings together the entries of the clarinet and the violin which in the exposition were at a greater distance from one another, and at the same time it also exemplifies a whole structure of double thirds: the fundamental note of the C major triad relates as a minor third to A major, whereas for C major the minor third is provided by the clarinet part's augmented fourth (diminished fifth). It is worthwhile comparing it with a section from the "Marcia" in the Sixth Quartet, where the same device takes place in four parts.

Example 298.

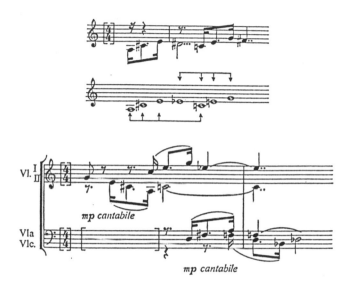

As we have mentioned, the incipit contained the possibility of the two thirds already at its first appearance, and it is thus logical that it is developed further in the same direction. More strange is that the movement's second subject, with its basically contrasting character, also shows a dual third structure, both in its purely melodic format and its chordal structure. From a modal aspect, it is nothing less than a hexachord with the unique structure of a Lydian fourth, minor sixth and variable third; but from the full context it becomes clear that C–B means the same alternative third on the G-sharp plane (the D-sharp perfect fifth being there above G-sharp) as G-sharp–G on the E plane (see Ex. 295b).

This so far is the same kind of play with dual thirds in the context of keys related by a third which we have already encountered in the previous example. In fact, however, here the structure is even more complex, as alongside the alternative thirds the alternative fundamental notes also appear: hence G is not merely the minor third of E but also the alternative fundamental note of G-sharp, from which it follows that the minor third of G-sharp, B, is at the same time the major third of G as well. So what are apparently colouring notes from the piano are in fact fundamental notes appearing in juxtaposition, related to a common third.

Example 299.

József Ujfalussy was the first to discover the great role and significance of chordal and tonal relationships with a common third in Bartók's music, starting with the tonal duality of F-sharp minor—F major built around the melodic A axis note in *Allegro barbaro* (Ujfalussy 1969). The closed system and logic of Bartók's creative method is clearly demonstrated by his traversal of all three natural paths of simultaneous use of the major and the minor: from the parallel relationship, through the dual-third relationship with a common root, to the relationship of common thirds with dual roots and dual fifths. One might add that the dual elements of the third can each be the centre of alternative structures. The minor third of a triad is at the same time the major third of a triad a half note lower. However, it should be stressed that this is not a chronological but a logical line. For example, he achieved a consistent pairing of parallel keys only in the Sixth Quartet, while the relationship of common thirds had already been accomplished in 1911 in *Allegro barbaro*.

In the case of *Contrasts*, its simultaneous technical bravura and its poetic versatility stems from Bartók's application of the dual-third solution *together* with the dual-root and dual-fifth solution. A clear example of this appears in the development section of the first movement (bar 65) and in one of the episodes in the third movement (bar 53). The conceptual identity of the two sections also shows the close relationship that can exist between externally different musical structures containing no motivic links.

Example 300.

uo. 3. tétel

By condensing the common and essential motifs in these two clear examples, an abstract musical idea can be formulated which stands behind the whole composition, and explains nearly all its thematic and motivic features. It is neither a monothematic basic idea nor a series, but a kind of transition between the two. In a schematic depiction, one has to start out from the alternating triad with two thirds. This structure constitutes the "basic cell":

The relationship of a common third is arrived at if, while retaining the third, another cell is linked to the basic cell on one side or the other, both sides being possible:

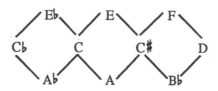

The two excerpts presented in the previous music example in fact represent a fragment of an even longer chain. But for the phenomenon itself, two cells linked to a single common third also suffice: both the incipit of the first movement's first subject and the second rondo theme of the closing movement fit such a double-cell contact.

Example 301.

The mirror-progression of the instrumental duet in the middle movement, however, draws upon the notes of a longer chain: nevertheless the structure of dual thirds and the shifting of the framing fifth clearly prove that the same structural principle prevails in this movement, too.

Example 302.

This relationship has already been demonstrated in the second rondo theme of the closing movement: the first rondo theme, on the other hand, exhibits a structure from which the dual thirds and variable fifths seem to be missing. A more detailed examination, however, shows that this theme is also built on the above structural principle, and perhaps even more consistently than the second theme. For the mistuned chain of fifths fits note for note into the system of a chain of fifths with a common third, consisting of four cells. The relationship becomes clearer still if we omit the thirds and arrange the fifths into two columns. Thus we arrive at the 1:6 model, which is another way of notating the chain of mistuned fifths and which immediately reveals the relationship with the "gamelan motif" of the second movement as well.

Example 303.

Finally, let us add a comment: although we have emphasized that the structural principle or structural "model" discussed here cannot be considered a twelve-tone series, the chain consisting of five cells, with two repeated notes each on both ends, fills out the whole twelve-tone system. This means that Bartók, although not intending to follow serial technique, arrived via the logical arrangement of the musical material at a structure which in principle is not far removed from the technique of twelve-tone organization. The "chain of cells" with a common third extends into the twelve notes. It cannot be overlooked that this chain also contains the tonalities of the three movements of the work (marked bold), and indeed in a close relationship.

After all this it is perhaps unnecessary to raise once again the question of whether the middle movement is a subsequent addition or a preconceived, organic part of the composition. The answer which has been rendered probable by recently revealed data is unequivocally confirmed by every little moment in the work.

CHAPTER SIXTEEN

THE SIXTH STRING QUARTET

Bartók began writing the Sixth Quartet in August 1939, immediately after completing the Divertimento. As is well known, Paul Sacher, who commissioned the Divertimento, put his wooden house in the Swiss Saanen at Bartók's disposal. Completely alone and withdrawn from the world, he completed the Divertimento in a brief two weeks, and might have finished the quartet as well had he not been forced back to Hungary by the tension of war and his mother's illness. It is not possible with any of the other quartets to see into Bartók's thoughts at the time of composition so well as in the Sixth. This is principally due to correspondence. In the letter written on 18 August 1939, to greet his son Béla on his birthday, we can read what follows.

> Somehow I feel like a musician of olden time the invited guest of a patron of the arts. For here I am, as you know, entirely the guest the Sachers; they see to everything—from a distance. In a word, I am living alone—in an ethnographic object: a genuine peasant cottage. The furnishings are not in character, but so much the better, because they are the last word in comfort. They even had a piano brought from Berne for me . . . Recently, even the weather has been favouring me—this is the 9th day that we've had beautifully clear skies, and not a drop of rain has fallen since the 9th. However, I can't take advantage of the weather to make excursions: I have to work. And for Sacher himself—on a commission (something for a string orchestra); in this respect also my position is like that of the old-time musician. Luckily the work went well, and I finished it in 15 days (a piece of about 25 minutes), I just finished it yesterday. Now I have another commission to fulfil, this time a string quartet for Z. Székely (that is, the "New Hungarian Quartet"). Since 1934, virtually everything I have done has been commissioned. The

poor, peaceful, honest Swiss are being compelled to burn with war-fever. The newspapers are full of military articles, they have taken defence measures on the more important passes etc.—military preparedness. I saw this for myself on the Julier Pass; for example, boulders have been made into road-blocks against tanks, and such like attractions. It's the same in Holland—even in Scheveningen.—I do not like your going to Rumania—in such uncertain times it is unwise to go anywhere so unsafe. I am also worried about whether I shall be able to get home from here if this or that happens. Fortunately I can put this worry out of my mind if I have to—it does not disturb my work . . . I hadn't read a newspaper for 2 weeks until I picked one up yesterday; the lapse of time was not perceptible, it was just as if I was reading one 2 weeks old. Nothing had happened in between. (Thank God!) . . ." (*Bartók Letters* 1971:no.219).

Thus Bartók broke off work on the quartet at the end of August, travelled home to Hungary, and as is indicated by the date on the manuscript, finished the work in November. Another important document from the period in which the quartet was written is his letter of 29 September to Géza Frid, which offers evidence that the relationship with Zoltán Székely, who had commissioned the work, had broken off. ". . . Would you be kind enough to ask Zoltán Székely why he has not replied to my letter of August 24th and why he is not making any arrangements in connection with the matter mentioned in it. Meanwhile the first, second and third movements of the Sixth Quartet, which is being written for them, have been completed (a fourth movement has still to be added to these); so I would like to hear from them as soon as possible as to whether they want the quartet or not. I asked them this, too, in my August letter . . ." (*Bartók levelei* 1976:no.963).

Information even more important than these letters is offered, however, by the sketches preserved in the New York Bartók Archives and which have been discussed by two researchers, John Vinton and Benjamin Suchoff."[1] These sketches not only show how one or two details evolved, but allow us a glance into the development of the

[1]John Vinton, "New Light on Bartók's Sixth Quartet," *The Music Review* XXV (1964); Benjamin Suchoff, "Structure and Concept in Bartók's Sixth Quartet," *Tempo* No.83 (1967/68).

conception of the work and the refining of the work's most important thematic material. As far as the conception is concerned, it has become clear from these sketches that Bartók originally intended to end the work with a fast finale in folk character. And the other point of unimaginably great value is that the ritornello theme which stands at the opening of each movement and finally grows into an independent movement, arrived at its final form after going through many transitional forms. On this occasion this gradual refining work not only shows the path along which a theme has developed—and at the same time that Bartók also belonged to the Beethoven type of "drilling-chiselling" creative artist family—but draws attention also to another change in conception: the theme did not simply assume a better and better form; its significance also grew, and eventually it became so important, so essential, that it came to exclude the fast finale originally planned. That is, the two basic pieces of information to be gained from the sketches are in the last analysis closely interrelated, for they are both manifestations of the same creative aspiration.

Whether the reason for the change in the conception of the work during composition lies exclusively in the musical structure, or whether external events induced Bartók to abandon the fast, folk character finale, can scarcely be determined today. In any event, the change can be explained by both together: on the one hand, the lonely monologue melody which was so refined rose increasingly to the foreground and was woven into a many-sided system of relationships with the other material in the movement. On the other hand, this was where the resignation and despair of the composer was expressed more authentically and sincerely than in any other musical material. We must not forget how uncertain and doubtful he became during the few months when the work was being written. War broke out. His mother's condition became increasingly critical and she died in December. Relations with Zoltán Székely were broken. Bartók became more and more possessed by the difficult dilemma of whether to remain at home in Hungary or to emigrate.

How symbolic is the fate of this work! Bartók wrote it while he was still in Europe, for the group of his compatriots who were working in Europe at that time, but events intervened and the artist, being forced to emigrate, eventually bade farewell to Europe with it. He took the score with him to the United States, and since performance of a new work became a question of life or death (in the first years of emigration—as is well known—he was unable to compose), he was compelled to offer the work written for Zoltán Székely to another quartet so that it would be performed. Fortunately that other ensemble was the Kolisch Quartet, who eventually gave the work its first performance in New York on 20 January 1941. It is for this reason that the work is dedicated to them.

Ritornello

The individual structure of the composition lies in that each of its movements is introduced by the same melody. Analytical literature sometimes calls this introductory material a motto, sometimes a ritornello, indicating in this way that the melody stands thematically apart, and at the same time that it has a function which holds the work together cyclically. I consider the term "ritornello" to be more precise, as a motto in its original sense stands apart from the work itself, but here, on the other hand, the connection is indeed very organic—so much so that by the end of the work this standing apart disappears in the fourth movement, and the whole movement unfolds from the ritornello itself.

The ritornello melody first appears on the viola alone, as a lonely monologue. The basic idea of this monologue beginning can, strictly speaking, be traced right back to the early *Two Portraits*. Here in the violin solo of the "Ideal Portrait," beginning with a Bartókian leitmotif, there already appears this melancholy contemplative kind of melody with its characteristic $\frac{6}{8}$ metre and broken seventh chords. This idea appears again considerably later in the second movement of the First Sonata for Violin and Piano. The melody comes a good deal closer to the ritornello theme in the string quartet. Not only the metre but, for example, the rhythm pattern in the whole of the first melodic line stems from the same basis.

Example 304.

The structure of the whole melody also displays similar features: after a gently falling first phrase, an ascent (second phrase), then sequences (third phrase), and finally a big arched ascent in one (the sonata), and a descent in the other (the quartet).

Example 305.

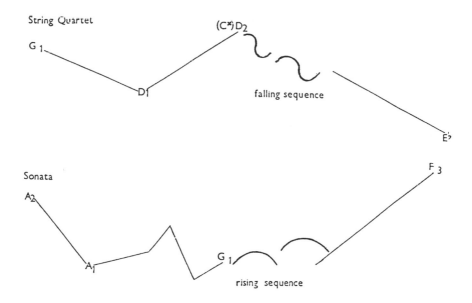

It was to be seen in the *Two Portraits* that the melody outlines seventh chords with the tension of a major seventh. This same tendency can be noticed in the melody of the sonata and finally in the descending sequences of the ritornello theme. A further common feature is the simultaneous appearance of the perfect fifth and its chromatic adjacent note. Like the leitmotif, the other broken chords related to it also radiate the atmosphere of the late Romantic harmonic world. Thus, from this point of view the Sixth Quartet is a kind of turning back to the early "romantic" compositions, to the world of the First and Second Quartets.

All this refers to the antecedents of the finished ritornello melody. But now let us look at the melody itself, taking into consideration the information offered by the sketches in existence and already published in connection with the evolving of the melody. The ritornello theme first appears in the following two forms—after the completion of the Divertimento, and on the same sheet of manuscript paper. All this indicates that the ritornello theme, in this simpler and shorter form, was already present among the first ideas of the string quartet, together with the first subject of the first movement, the theme of the Marcia and an important thematic idea for the fast finale which remained unwritten.[2]

Example 306.

---

[2]We have corrected the melody written wrongly by Vinton (op. cit., Ex. 10a, p.232) on the basis of the facsimile (Suchoff, op. cit., Facsimile I, p.3).

These two first sketches, very closely related to each other, are both characterized by a perfect octave compass. In the third version, still in a two-phrase structure but already augmented, it is not the first and last notes that are at a distance of an octave from one another but the last notes of the two phrases(a). It seems that Bartók threw this version out immediately, for without rewriting the first phrase he outlined a new and significantly longer continuation in place of the erased second phrase, and indicated the relationship with the first phrase by an arrow. In the development of the melody this was the moment—the *punctum saliens*, we might call it—when the two-phrase melody became an organically constructed four-phrase structure with a definite phrase (b) :

Example 307.

It can be seen that the second phrase's ascent to the climax is already present here, as are also the determined, sequence-like descent of the third phrase and the closing formula of the fourth phrase with the descending fourth. On the same page of the sketch can be found the almost final form of the ritornello melody. To the first three phrases of the melody, written down only once, are added two different fourth phrases (a, b).

Example 308.

a)

b)

c)

It is strange that the first phrase, which has firmly preserved its form from the first version onwards, and has changed at most only in tonal position, here gains the final form of its close, but this is a visibly later correction—that is, it is written in the line above the appropriate part of the melody (c). Thus we are here faced with the final form of the melody, except for the end of the fourth phrase. The final form of the last phrase, which has clearly evolved with some difficulty, draws our attention to important interrelationships. In the penultimate version it can be seen that Bartók immediately writes in the fitting in of the other instruments and the first motif of the unisono melody, which is none other than an inversion of the close.

Example 309.

Here the notes G–A-flat–E-flat are still directly connected to each other. In the final form this obvious connection is somewhat veiled by the note F flat being inserted, and the four-note motif thus produced clearly better suited Bartók's intentions, for it gives greater inner tension to the A-flat–E-flat cadence (a). It is worth noticing, incidentally, that we have already met this same motif in Bartók's First Quartet, and, perhaps not accidentally, at this same pitch (b). Yet another motif suggests itself here which is surprisingly placed again at this same absolute pitch: the questioning melody with the inscription "Muss es sein" in Beethoven's F major Quartet op. 135 (c).

Example 310.

In connection with the revival of the Romantic harmonic world the First Quartet was mentioned above, but this newer connection reveals even deeper conformity: it does not simply refer to the world of the early works, but to the new topicality of the great "ancestral source." In the way the Beethoven legacy was important to Bartók at the time of the First Quartet, it now becomes important to him once more, only in another sense. Around 1908 the return to Beethoven was synonymous with opposition to Romanticism, with the affirmation of the Classical and contrapuntal tradition. But here, at the time of the Sixth Quartet, it is in the shadow of the impending war that Bartók turns to Beethoven in his search for simplicity and humanity. Let me anticipate by mentioning the other details in the Sixth Quartet which refer to Beethoven, so that we can examine all the interrelationships in the matter. At the end of the ritornello the other instruments in the ensemble join the viola, and in broad parallel octaves they build a "bridge" between the lonely monologue just finished and the fast movement which follows. Part of the melody therefore refers back to the close of the ritornello theme, and it is out of an inversion of this that the first subject of the fast movement takes shape. Before this rolling theme is heard in its final form, it is played in this partly augmented form which has the function of a "bridge" and is rhythmically halting, disjointed—without any rhythmic profile at all, we might say-in the very same way as Beethoven introduces the theme of the Great Fugue.

We can see that whereas the young Bartók, when he was composing the First Quartet, saw an ideal in Beethoven's counterpoint, now it is principally a thematic example that he sees in him; either he again writes a definite type of theme or motif, or he borrows from the classical master his way of introducing the theme, and even the "dramaturgy" in the use of the theme. For as well as the introduction of the theme referring to the Great Fugue, the solution to the tension also comes about in a way which is reminiscent of Beethoven; the dramaturgical detail of the "schwer gefasster Entschluss" is repeated in the transformation into relaxed diatony of the tense chromatic theme.

This relaxation also reveals a great deal concerning the tonal relationship between the introductory ritornello and the movement. As has been mentioned already in the course of describing the way the melody evolved, the tonal character was originally expressed in a closed octave form. In the course of later alterations the perfect octave and fifth were replaced by mistuned relationships, and so alongside the tonality of D the adjacent chromatic notes also became important, chiefly G-sharp (the adjacent chromatic note of A). Then at the end of the ritornello it becomes clear that these chromatic adjacent notes have also a leading-note function: the A-flat–E-flat fourth opens out into the D–A fifth in the same way as the A-flat–E-flat fourth is prepared by the augmented second G–F-flat.

It is easier to examine the role and inner development of the ritornello melody if we extract it from the actual structure of the work and trace the path it follows separately. Most important of all is the systematic increase in the number of parts. Thus the melody, which first appears in a monologue form, returns before the second movement with a two-part texture. On this occasion the cello plays the melody and the first violin accompanies it with a counterpoint part. This counterpart is coloured by the tremolo in the second violin and the viola in double parallel octaves. The tonal balance of this counterpoint, written like this for 1+3 parts, but two-part in reality, is ensured by the three subsidiary parts which move parallel to one another, being veiled by sordino. The ritornello melody appears with smaller alterations which are worthy of attention. The nuances in the modification of the rhythm show Bartók's organic rhythm very clearly. As an extension of the preceding movement's first subject, the end of the first phrase changes to a duple rhythm.

Example 311.

The theme's third, descending phrase is extended from a binary to a trinary sequence which in turn causes a tonal change: the theme, which started out from E-flat, slips down to an F–C cadence instead of an E-flat–B-flat cadence. From a tonal point of view this alteration is of great significance, for the movement which follows in the tonality of B is prepared in the same kind of leading-note way by this cadence as happened in the first movement.

The third appearance of the ritornello brings new elements as an introduction to the Burletta movement. The number of parts is now raised to three: the first violin plays the melody, the second violin and the cello play the accompaniment, and the viola, from the point where the dynamic intensification begins (bar 10), reinforces the first violin part at the octave. A more important change is represented by the breaking up and extension of the ritornello melody. In the first six bars—starting from B-flat—the melody is identical with its preceding form, but when it reaches the climax of E, it breaks off, and in place of the descending third phrase the opening figure of the first phrase reappears to carry the melody upwards to a climax on B (bar 13) by an ascending sequence. Here the descending sequence of the third phrase begins and then progresses in three sections through two octaves to a B cadence. There is an interesting modification to be seen in the sequence motif itself: its melodic gesture is extended, and in this way it anticipates one of the important themes in the movement which follows.

Example 312.

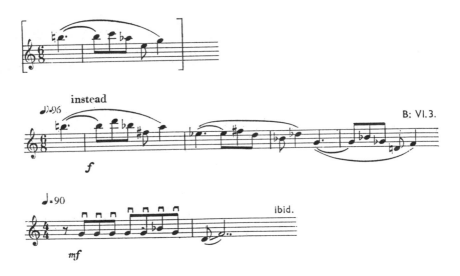

A further detail in the transformation of the ritornello theme is that the fourth and final phrase is replaced by a held note, and only the second violin's contrapuntal part provides a substitute for it with broadening melodic movement.

Example 313.

The tonal connection between the ritornello and the movement is arranged in a way similar to that in the other movements: the tonality of F is prepared in a leading-note way by the sustained B and then the E cadence, which is left open, of the broadening melody quoted above. And just as in the preceding movement one of the component parts of B major, the fifth, was already present at the end of the ritornello, here, too, the fundamental note of the tonality of F is firmly built into the end of the ritornello (in the viola part).

The fourth appearance of the ritornello, since it is the fourth movement itself, will not be discussed now but in the appropriate part of the analysis. In advance, this much can be said: the tendency towards a variational process which has been apparent so far dominates here as well; the texture becomes four- part, and the melodic material goes through further breaking up and extension.

First movement: Più mosso, pesante-vivace

In the analysis of the ritornello theme it has already been mentioned how the first subject, that is, the basic motif of this first subject, in the Vivace movement is born from the end of the ritornello. More minute examination then draws attention to the fact that the whole theme is no more than three forms of this three-note basic motif strung together. In the Più mosso, pesante section, which has a "bridging" function, this basic motif is emphasized by a fortissimo unisono block. Its melodic essence consists of a larger interval and a smaller conclusion in the opposite direction.

Example 314.

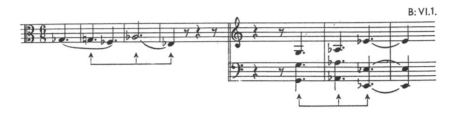

This same "bridge" also emphatically presents the whole theme, the three sections of which are none other than the basic motif and two variations of it; the second is a permutational variation in which the second and third notes of the motif exchange places, and the third is a contracted mirror-crab (a minor third instead of a fourth).

Example 315.

Many further variations of the theme, which shoots up quickly and is fairly small in extent, make up the first formal unit in the movement, the first subject section of sonata form. In this variational process the theme assumes many forms equally in its nine-note interrelationship and its basic elements of three or four notes. Not long after it is first heard, an inverted form of it also appears. It must be added that there it is not a question of a precise, note-for-note inversion, but a form which, with regard to no more than its direction, gives the "impression" of being a mirror inversion.

Each of these two basic forms of the first subject represents a firm area in the otherwise extraordinarily dynamic texture, in the process of the varied transformation of the motifs. It is worth looking at the five bars after the first appearance of the vivace theme, for example. With its expansion of the first fourth interval the second violin scarcely alters the theme at all, only making it tense, "mistuning" it, since the perfect fourth is replaced by an augmented fourth, and accordingly the theme's perfect octave framework becomes retuned to an augmented octave. This variation of the complete theme is immediately followed by variation of the details, the motifs. Besides the motif with the augmented fourth compass, its mirror inversion also appears (first violin), then a contracted form of the original fourth also appears in both an ascending form (viola) and a descending form (cello).

From bar 36 development work begins, using the same kind of technique, now over a longer stretch, right up to bar 53, where the complete theme is heard again in its descending form. In this dynamic developing section we can follow the break-up of the theme in detail, on the one hand in the gradual diminishing of the proportions of the theme, and on the other hand in the contraction of the intervals. The nine-note theme first reduces to seven notes (two three-note motifs and a final note) and then to four notes (one three-note motif and final note). The shortening of the rhythm also belongs to this reduction in proportions; the originally long first note gradually disappears. The interval contraction is similarly consistent: the opening gesture, expanded to an augmented fourth, is now contracted to the extreme limit of a major second. This is the smallest interval into which a smaller interval moving in the opposite direction—that is, the semitone—can be fitted.

Example 316.

In the interests of formal balance this dynamic breaking apart of the material is followed by a more static section in which the complete and original form of the theme returns in its descending and ascending versions alike. This steady part, however, is only temporary, since it is followed by a new development section. But this time the variation work is directed at the end of the theme, and from bar 68 it is once more the three-note basic motif that comes into the foreground. Although with regard to its material, this section is broken up, and dynamic in its effect—because of the motif becoming fixed into an ostinato—it does nevertheless have a definitely static and completing character. With regard to the intervals, contraction can be seen here, too, just as in the part between bars 36 and 53, but whereas there the original fourth compass became contracted to a major second, here the motif contracts from a wider, minor sixth version into its original fourth form. This static ostinato version of the first subject is functionally a transition to the second subject which appears in bar 81.

As opposed to the differentiated texture of the first subject, this second subject is simpler and has a smoother line. It radiates a folk atmosphere on account of the characteristic rhythm of the Máramaros Rumanian folk music, although there is no melodic relationship. After its first hearing two figurative variations follow immediately in the second violin and viola respectively. This kind of elaboration—figurative variation—rarely occurs in Bartók's works.

Example 317.

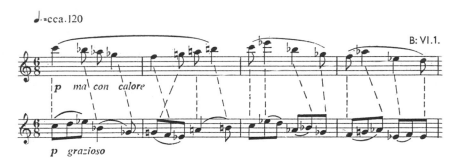

Although the second subject is placed very firmly in the tonal area, it is nevertheless ambiguous with regard to tonality. In the first moment the theme, in the C–F–C compass, appears to be in the tonality of F, in which it is not the keynote that is reinforced by pedal notes but the fifth. This tonality of F would be quite regular in the order of keys in a traditional sonata movement. The theme itself, however, suggests the tonality of C, particularly as a result of the fifth levels of its second half; the last C of the melody fits smoothly above the static C pedal. The tonality of C is also strengthened by the melody arching from C to C which is the counterpart in the first violin.

From the resting point in bar 93 in the tonality of C, a surprisingly traditional chain of keys, in the authentic mode sequence leads to the excited (Vivacissimo agitato) transitional section beginning in bar 99.

C–F–B flat–E flat–(A flat)
G sharp–C sharp–F sharp

This transitional section, which as far as its material is concerned, derives from the opening gesture in the ritornello theme, is a fine example of organic development of new material from old. Here, side by side, are the source material from which it stems (x), the process itself, showing how it evolves, and the final result which is the third most important thematic material in the movement—the closing subject (y).

Example 318.

And then further development of the final theme shows how it is a combination of the rhythmic profiles of the first and second subjects.

Example 319.

The end of the exposition contains a refined tonal ambiguity, al-though it is a pure F major triad that is actually heard. That is, the melodic motif of the final theme causes some tonal wavering by en-ding now with F, now with C, and finally, when the movement in the musical texture settles down, the F major harmony merges into the final C of the melody; that is, we feel the C melodically to be a tonal final note.

The development section beginning in bar 158 brings back the augmented introductory form of the first subject on a tonal level a diminished fifth higher. The three-note opening motif enters in the various parts with canon-like displacement, but here it is only a pseudo-canon since it is only the top part which plays the theme's melody. After the fourth-chord cadence the vivace form of the theme also appears, but in the two lowest parts on this occasion and in a key further displaced by one semitone. This return of the theme repre-sents the double start in the exposition—that is, the fact that the pesante version is immediately followed by the rolling vivace version. Thus the order of the two forms remains the same, but their correla-tion has changed, for the fast version is played a semitone lower, and its original octave compass is expanded to a major ninth. All this, however, is still quite static in comparison with the developmental dynamism of the part which now follows. The three-note basic motif, having been sometimes expanded, sometimes contracted even in the exposition, now expands to a minor ninth and in the ostinato beginning in bar 180, to minor seventh. We are faced here with the same sort of development method as in the first movement of the Fifth Quartet; in the two outer parts an ostinato accompaniment evolves from the first motif of the first subject, and from the closing motif of the theme is derived a melodic part which moves in mirror imitation in the two middle parts. A very interesting tonal method is used in this section in that the F–B tonality outlined by the ostinato part is taken over by the melodic parts as well. The "target note," which functions as a final note, is either F or B.

The first part of the development section broke the first subject up into its elements. On the other hand, the second part, which begins in bar 194, sets it back into its original form and even extends it further: the theme, originally two bars long, now grows to four or five bars, and this is quite naturally accompanied by spatial growth as well—to two or two and a half octaves. Another point in the extension of the theme is that in the part between bars 209 and 217 a descending version of it is immediately added to it. In this way a perfect wave-shaped melody has grown out of the theme which has so far been heard in only an ascending or a descending form.

The version which has a rising line emphasizes the scale-like or complementary writing of the theme. As opposed to this, the further variations which are developed from the descending version are based on the fourth-fifth chain which strictly speaking, was already present in the first form of the descending version.

Example 320.

Now it is the fourth as a melodic structural element that steps into the foreground, and together with this comes semitone friction. The correlations between these two elements can be seen clearly in the theme variant just quoted: while the first violin descends in fourth chains, the cello progresses in a descending chromatic scale. Here we witness an individual reinterpretation of the classical functional system. In some Baroque sequences, by means of repeating the perfect cadence in a continuous way, a harmonic sequence can be produced, in which the projection of a fourth-chain in one part (usually the bass) is a chromatic scale in another part. But this is also possible the other way round: the chromatic descent in the bass conceals within itself an authentic functional chain (this is what makes chromatically descending Baroque passacaglia variations so natural).

This parallel is naturally intended to indicate only indirect relationships, particularly since with Bartók authentic and plagal trends alternate in the fourth-fifth chain. This underlines all the more strongly the opposition of the two elements, that is the contrast between chromaticism and the acoustic relationship between the pure intervals which produce diatony. Then from bar 237 the relationship between these two elements becomes even clearer. Within the framework of the outer parts, which has major seventh tension, a swaying fourth-motif unfolds from the last part of the theme. One fourth-structure clashes with another fourth-structure displaced by a semitone; while the G-flat of the bass fits into one, the F of the first violin fits into the other.

Example 321.

Here the role of the fourth as structural element can be seen clearly. When the melody tries to increase the amplitude of the wave motion by greater impetus, a minor seventh appears instead of the fourth— that is, the fourth's double. We have already experienced this same phenomenon in the mystic fourth-theme of the Second Quartet's last movement. In this same place there is another phenomenon which reminds one of the Second Quartet, namely the swaying fourth-motif connected with the theme, which in the earlier work was connected with the recapitulation form of the first subject in the first movement. The friction between the trill motif and the three-note ostinato motif lend an extraordinary degree of tension to the last phase of the development section (bars 276–286). The three-note motif is this time not identical with the basic motif of the first subject but is produced by the final "appendix" to it (bars 274–275). This three-note motif moves in four different tonal planes in such a way that they are separated by either a diminished fifth or a diminished octave. Once again it becomes apparent that the diminished fifth is really the closest relative of the diminished octave and both are connected by the mistuning of the perfect octave or perfect fifth.

In the recapitulation, which begins in bar 287, only the vivace form of the first subject returns, and even that only as a symbol; the dynamic development within the exposition is not repeated, obviously because this theme has already been subjected to an abundance of variation, breaking up and expansion in the development section. This part in the formal structure is thus taken up with work on relatively new material. This "new material" is a minor third motif which has derived from the three-note motif just developed. The minor third motif creates a fresh impression after the fourth interval which has dominated so far. The way in which it is developed does, however, remind one very much of the earlier use of the fourth. In place of the semitone displacement of the fourth-chains we now have third-chains in semitone displacement. Earlier a 1:5 model was produced; here there is a 1:3 model. The second subject returns in bar 312, now in the tonality of C-sharp—that is, a semitone higher than in the exposition and lengthened by a new variation. This new version brings out more definitely the folk character concealed in the theme, for whereas the original form referred to folk music only in its rhythm and structure, it now comes close to it melodically as well.

Example 322.

After the material of the final theme has been brought back in a variation which does nevertheless agree essentially with its exposition form (bars 342–362), the first subject returns, with the function of a coda, in a pure G major triad block coloured only by pizzicato chords. Its tonality is first of all G major, which represents a traditional sub-dominant area before the movement's D major ending. The first violin climbs right up to A^3, but here we do not feel the fifth as a final note as at the end of the exposition because, after it has been reached, the second violin descends to D^2. This ending is a beautiful example of the coordination of polymodality and "monotonality," where the unambiguous D major cadence is preceded by going through the complete chromatic range melodically.

Second movement: Marcia

During the analysis of the ritornello theme reference has already been made to the way in which the cadence of the ritornello prepares the B major tonality of the movement. Throughout the movement, however, the tonality of B major is consistently accompanied by its own relative key, G-sharp minor. Even the little motif which appears between the movement and the ritornello is also a preparation for this. The parallel use of B major and G-sharp minor is a characteristic combination of bitonality and bimodality. Naturally it does not lead to chromaticism, since the two keys belong to the very same diatonic system, but it diffuses refracted light into the texture of the music. It might even be said that the two keys are not completely equal in importance; even if only because of its major character, B major

dominates, and G-sharp minor fits smoothly alongside it as a subsidiary. The individual relationship between the two tonalities can be
felt clearly in the character of the parts and the relationship between
them. The Marcia theme, major in character by virtue of its very nature, is accompanied by a minor variant of itself like a shadow.

Example 323.

This same major-minor relationship reigns in the ostinato accompaniment to the lament beginning in bar 55: the cello moves in the B
major tonal plane while the viola moves in the G- sharp minor plane.
This B major–G-sharp minor duality, which is present throughout the
whole movement, is also in evidence in the closing chord. If we examine this harmony in isolation we see that it is obviously no more
than a B major ninth chord with a *sixte ajoutée*. But if we take the consistent duality of the movement's tonal character into consideration,
then we have to regard the G-sharp in the final chord as a representative of the subsidiary, shadow tonality. And the melodic action
also supports this. Thus Bartók's compositional technique provides an
opportunity for us to separate out different structures from the accumulation of notes sounding at one time, and indeed not merely on a
theoretical basis but in the music as it is actually heard, too.

Several interrelationships are suddenly brought to our notice by
the movement's already quoted march theme. On the one hand, this
dotted broken triad appeared earlier, in an elegant *verbunkos* style, in
another Bartók work, the trio *Contrasts*, which was written not long
before the Sixth Quartet. József Ujfalussy further indicates that, although it is not based on a broken triad, the beginning of the Third

Piano Concerto also belongs to this thematic family (Ujfalussy 1968:347).

Example 324.

This kind of hard, angular, dotted rhythm theme can, on the other hand, be traced back, without any sense of forcing the issue, to Beethoven's march music in the French style. This sort of dotted rhythm melody in Beethoven either radiates a military, heroic attitude or becomes a demonic scherzo. It is sufficient to mention the C Minor Sonata for violin and piano or the Kreutzer Sonata, or the Scherzando of the E-flat Quartet op. 127.[3] Whereas in Beethoven's scherzando the military rhythm tends to move into the jocular-demonic sphere, with Bartók it begins with a wry, ironic tone and moves into stubborn rebellion especially with the lament beginning in bar 55.

In the development process, on the one hand, two elements of the theme assume independence. One is the dotted rhythm scale motif, the other the pointed, iambic third-motif. The organic quality of the thematic work is shown by the fact that the third important motif is evolved from the trill ending of the dotted scale motif (bars 24–25). Also instructive is the interesting section beginning in bar 33 in which the basis of the variation is provided by the triad motif from the opening motif. At the beginning of the movement, alongside the B major–G-sharp minor duality another major-minor duality became apparent in the triad in the opening of the theme, namely that B major is accompanied by a regular major dominant (F-sharp major)

[3]Ferenc Bónis regards this last as a quotation. Cf. Ferenc Bónis, "Qutotations in Bartók's Music," *Studia Musicologica* Tom.V (1963): 369.

while G-sharp minor is joined by a minor form of the degree (D-sharp minor). In the section which begins in bar 33 the major-minor duality divided out between the various instruments enters the triad motif itself, and now the clash between the two modes is present even within the limits of a single melody (see ex. 298). With a clear view of these fundamental elements, it is now possible to give an outline of the formal structure. Bars 17–25 are the presentation of the theme in its entirety; bars 25–32, the third-motif independently; 33–42, the triad motif together with the scale motif; 43–49, the closing trill motif together with the scale motif; 49–54, the third-motif as transition to the larger unit of bars 54–76 in which a crying and sorrowful lament melody unfolds above an ostinato developed from the triad motif. Then it needs only a little four-bar coda to complete the first large formal unit in the trio form.

The trio, with its soft, improvisational, rubato character, represents a strong contrast to the march. In spite of this, both melody and accompanying chords are related by strong connecting threads to the triad motifs of the first part and, within this, to the simultaneous use of major and minor thirds. The melody which appears in the high register of the cello is a good example not only of the double third but of the "double fifth" as well; we have already encountered this interval structure in the descending sequence of the Mesto ritornello, and a relative of this is the violin solo in the slow movement of the First Sonata for Violin and Piano, and finally one of the second movement themes in the Divertimento resembles it closely in its melodic line.

Example 325.

Apart from that, an interesting correlation can be noticed between the Sixth Quartet and the Divertimento. In the movement quoted from the Divertimento this theme is joined by the same kind of ascending and then descending lament melody as here in the quartet. And the high register of the cello also creates the naturalistic effect of weeping, as do the glissandos which go with it.

The trio, which so far has been improvisational and soloistic in character, is closed by an impressionistic sound picture. By fast repetition of the semiquaver motif formed from the opening motif of the march theme, four layers are built up on each other, and then a decelerating, augmented form of it prepares the way for the return of the Marcia. The recapitulation is characterized by two important modifications. First the previously one-part major theme is now heard in major triad mixtures composed of fifth and sixth mixtures and the minor theme which follows it like a shadow is coloured by harmonic notes. Both these effects intensify the painfully sarcastic character of the march. Secondly, the lament theme now rises even higher, complaining even more passionately, almost shrieking. Thus the recapitulation intensifies the earlier atmospheres to an even more extreme degree. Also in the recapitulation a role is played by Bartók's familiar varying method—mirror inversion. Thus the third-motif and scale theme which moved in an ascending direction in the first part turns downwards in the recapitulation.

Third movement: Burletta (moderato)

As might be deduced from its title, the mood of this movement can be traced right back to the early Burlesques for piano. Its first theme consists of two elements: a grotesque leaping motif in which gesticular mime elements dominate, and a repeated-note motif which is lent a fairly harsh character by interval friction and grace-notes. Close relatives of the grotesque leaping motif can be found in abundance among Bartók's works from the early scherzos, through the second Burlesque ("A Little Tipsy") to the musical portrayal of the Wooden Doll in *The Wooden Prince* or the Old Gallant in *The Miraculous Mandarin*.

Example 326.

Then from the second repeated-note motif in the theme (bar 25) is born a new theme which has, however, been anticipated in the ritornello—an indolent "bear-dance" kind of melody, the rough, folk tone of which is increased by quartertone dissonances.

The episodic material which appears in bar 33 is an individual summary of the Burletta's first theme: the rhythm pattern refers to the first motif while the repeated-note melody refers to the second motif.

After a longer transitional section (bars 35–45), in which "narrow" melodic writing, complementary in texture, alternates with fourth-melody, another new grotesque theme appears in the top part above a fourth ostinato accompaniment in the two lowest parts. The narrow-range, alternating melody, which is asymmetric in rhythm, is accompanied by the sound of various open strings, like a pedal, and this lends a certain primitive folk character to the whole theme. We encountered a similar type of theme in the first movement of the Fourth Quartet (closing subject, bars 44–46), and as a result of the double stopping and asymmetric rhythm relationship, the violin solos in Stravinsky's *The Soldier's Tale* also come to mind. In bar 55 the parts moving in pairs exchange roles, the fourth ostinato moving up into the two violins and the melody being taken over by the two lower instruments. This sort of treatment and exchanging of parts was also present in the development of the first movement of the Fifth Quartet (bars 86–103).

The first large formal unit in the Burletta is completed by the return of the first theme (bar 60), but the two motifs of which it is composed exchange places: first it is the repeated-note motif that is heard, and only then does the grotesque leaping motif appear, in a considerably free variation.

In bar 70 a double bar-line and the indication "Andantino" introduce the trio which, as regards character, is an even sharper contrast to the main section than the corresponding part in the preceding movement. In the trio's gentle, nostalgic melody the $\frac{6}{8}$ metre of the first movement returns—now alternating with $\frac{9}{8}$—and together with this comes the tonality of D. Its contrast with the main part of the movement lies primarily in its smooth, almost swaying melodic writing and its periodic closedness. This character is also reinforced by the accompaniment with its rocking movement.

The theme's first four-bar period is completed by a hemiola rhythm motif, and after this is repeated in a varied form, a second theme appears. Its dome-shaped arch and characteristic rhythms, in which there is the typical choriambic-antispastic combination of Rumanian folksongs, brings to mind one of the lyrical choral parts in *Cantata Profana*.

Example 327.

Volt né-ki volt né - ki ki-lenc szép szál fi - a volt__

(Nine in number were his sons)

Reference to the first movement is even more strongly in evidence if we consider that the trio has an individually intercrossed melodic and rhythmic relationship with the two most important themes in the first movement: the rhythm of the trio's first theme is derived from the first subject of the first movement, and its melody is derived from the second subject. In the second theme, on the other hand, the positions are reversed: here the rhythm points unmistakably back to the second subject of the first movement, while the melody has a remote connection with the first subject.

Example 328.

Attention must be drawn to two more important transformations in connection with the Burletta's recapitulation. With Bartók the recapitulation usually means an intensification combined with reinterpretation, in a line similar to the spiral. Here the expansion of the "bear dance" theme (bar 102), the breaking of the octave in the episode material formed from the repeated-note motif (bar 110), and the flitting variation, enriched with colour effects, of the ostinato deriving from the fourth-motif (bar 131) all have this kind of intensification effect. The tension of the intensfication is also increased by the "dramaturgy" of the movement: the *Cantata Profana* melody from the trio also returns, but it is split into pieces by weighty chord blocks (bars 135–144).

The framework tonality of the movement is F major, but at the beginning this remains considerably in the background within the complicated texture of adjacent chromatic notes. As opposed to this, the final chord is perfectly unambiguous, only the fifth being coloured by the augmented fourth. The tonality of F fits well into the tonal plan of the whole work, since in comparison with the D tonality of the first and last movements, the two inner movements are removed in either direction by a minor third—the Marcia downwards, and the Burletta upwards.

Fourth movement: Mesto

From the preparatory sketches it is known that the ritornello, now increased to four parts, was written to be an introduction here, too, and the point is precisely known where the slow introduction was to have flowed into the planned fast finale: after bar 45 where, in the final form, the Molto tranquillo section begins. Thus, these forty-five bars have to be considered as a ritornello even in the present form, for it appears as the logical continuation of the preceding ritornellos, and it has an introductory function here, too. It becomes clear, however, from the sudden increase in its extent that even at the time of composition, even within the framework of the fast movement conception, the ritornello had already begun to discard its original introductory role. At the beginning of the first movement it was thirteen bars long, at the beginning of the second it was sixteen, and at the beginning of the third it was twenty—that is, even the longest version is still less than half the length of the version now before us. It must be added that the tempo has also become slower, for instead of the earlier metronome values of 96, the composer now dictates only 88. All this shows that the gradual extension of the ritornello—almost against Bartók's intentions—led it to outgrow its own limits and, expanding in both measurement and significance, demanded the "rights" of an independent movement.

Rounding off the number of actual parts to four inevitably produced canon technique, which was represented in the earlier ritornellos at most by imitation of an occasional smaller part. The theme starts off in the first violin, and two bars later the cello enters with the same material in a diminished fifth transposition (from C, and from F-sharp). After the first phrase, however, it is not the second phrase that follows: the first violin starts from the octave of the last note and plays the whole of the first phrase again. In relation to this new tonality the cello enters displaced by an augmented fifth (F-sharp–B-flat). Thus Bartók's efforts to mistune the fifth canon by plus or minus one semitone become clearly evident.

The two-part canon is filled out by the middle parts with free contrapuntal material, and after the canon of the double appearance of the first phrase all the parts move in free counterpoint. In a sequential way, the first violin weaves the motif of the first half phrase higher and higher to the E-flat climax in bar 13, while the cello descends with the mirror inversion of the opening motif down to the lowest point at C in the same bar. After this formal division, similar expanding writing begins as an echo of the preceding process, as it were, becoming strengthened from *pp* only to *mf*, with colourless restraint ("senza colore"). The leading part is now the cello's, which once more moves downwards with the mirror inversion of the first half phrase, while the original ascending version of it is played by the three upper parts up to the formal division in bar 22.

It has been possible to notice that so far the material of the whole first phrase has been broken up into half-phrase units and opening motif units. This analytical work penetrates into the material even more deeply from bar 22 onwards. From the four-note ascending close of the first half phrase—as a result of breaking the octave—a broad cambiata motif is developed, and this same breadth breaks up the natural continuation of the melody, making it virtually unrecognizable. This disintegration of the material is balanced, on the other hand by the re-establishment of the original tonality. Thus after the F–E–D ending the ritornello melody is continued in bar 31 at the original pitch, with the second line being recalled on this occasion in a related way but accompanied by counterparts. The adjoining third phrase likewise comes at the same pitch, but instead of a descending sequence it is now repeated three times at the same level and then suddenly breaks off in bar 39 with an ending which is left open. In a slightly faster tempo (Più andante, $\downarrow$ = 116) the first line returns once more in the tonality of the beginning of the movement (descending from C to F-sharp) but it is treated in a significantly different way here: it is harmonized in a chorale style. This is an ominous, almost mystic moment in the work; dynamically it diminishes from *pp* to *ppp* and the tone again becomes numbed into colourlessness ("senza colore").

And this was to have been the end of the introduction and the material of the fast finale—which as regards its character is not far removed from the last movement thematics of *Contrasts*, the Divertimento or the Concerto—was to have been attached to it by means of a somewhat strained transition.

Example 329.

But is it not possible that the inner tension and strength of this forty-five bar slow movement, its resigned sadness and depth, would have frittered away into nothing if it had been followed at this point by a fast finale in folk character? Perhaps it might have been possible to fit another kind of material in here, but it must be confessed that the fast piece known from the sketch could only have been given room in Bartók's earliest works. It is therefore perfectly understandable that the elderly master changed his intentions and allowed the noble material being born under his hands to continue living its own life. In place of the fast finale, a quotation from the first movement follows. Is this a rounding off, the contrived creation of unity in the piece? Or some sort of necessary procedure which in spite of everything proved better than the folk dance of the first version? Not at all. A profound, almost programme-like dramaturgy manifests itself in this quotation. The first movement has largely a bright and balanced atmosphere which produced some relief after the tension of the introductory ritornello, and which gave a cheerful, confident *"Es muss sein"* answer to the anxious *"Muss es sein?"* question. In the course of the work, however, after a harrowing march and devilishly laughing burlesque, the growing feeling of anxiety and desperation has become dominant. This world of experience which clouds everything over could only have been relieved in an artificial self mutilating way without any organic antecedent by a folk-style finale. For this reason, here in the fourth movement, in the course of the fulfilment of the sorrowful ritornello, there is no longer any solution or relief, only the memory of it, a nostalgic reminiscence. For this reason, after the nadir of bars 40–45, there is a slightly varied nine-bar quotation from the first subject of the first movement, likewise one of nine bars from the second subject, and an eight-bar quotation from the first subject descending form.

After this, the ritornello once more takes the leading role. Similar to what happened in the first part of the movement, it develops here, too, in its ascending sequence form with the material of the first half of the first phrase, in two imitative parts which are coloured by the other two with a harmonic accompaniment. The "triumphant" ritornello theme, however, falls apart more and more; now

only the melancholy closing part of it remains on the surface (bars 75–
78) and then—as a farewell, as it were—the viola recalls the whole
first phrase of the ritornello melody. It is played in the same tonality
and in the same register as at the beginning of the work, but how very
different its significance is now. Even its final note has slipped up
from D to E-flat, mainly so that this phrase-end should not yet be a
tonal final note. In this way—as at the beginning of the first movement—the final D–A fifth preceded by the tension of the notes E-flat
and G-sharp. Under the ethereal sound of the D–A fifth, the cello's
pizzicato chords—the upper notes once more outlining the first half
phrase of the ritornello—give, with nostalgic renunciation, a sorrowful, painful, resigned final tone to the work.

Example 330.

SOURCE LIST OF THE WORKS QUOTED

Boosey & Hawkes Music Publisher Limited, London
Béla Bartók:
Contrasts
Divertimento
On the Island of Bali
Six Dances in Bulgarian Rhythm
Sonata for Two Pianos and Percussion
String Quartet no. 6
Viola Concerto
Violin Concerto (1907/1908)
Violin Concerto (1938)

Editio Musica, Budapest
Béla Bartók:
14 Bagatelles
Trois Burlesques
String Quartet no. 1

Wilhelm Hansen Musik-Forlag, Copenhagen
Arnold Schoenberg:
Piano Pieces op.23

C. F. Peters, New York
Arnold Schoenberg:
Five Pieces for Orchestra

G. Schirmer, New York

Arnold Schoenberg:
Ode to Napoleon Buonaparte
String Quartet no.4

Schott's Söhne, Mainz

Arnold Schoenberg:
Moses und Aron

Universal Edition A. G., Wien

Béla Bartók:
44 Duos For Two Violins
Bluebeard's Castle
Four Pieces for Orchestra
Music for Strings, Percussion and Celesta
Sonata for Violin and Piano no. 1
Sonata for Violin and Piano no. 2
String Quartets nos. 2, 3, 4, 5
Suite for Piano
The Miraculous Mandarin
The Night's Music
The Wooden Prince

Alban Berg:
Lyric Suite

Arnold Schoenberg:
Erwartung
Piano Pieces op.11
Piano Pieces op.19
15 Stefan George Songs
String Quartets nos. 2 and 3

BIBLIOGRAPHY

ANTOKOLETZ, Elliott

   1982   "Pitch-Set Derivations from the Folk Modes in Bartók's
          Music," *Studia Musicologica* XXIV:265–74.

   1984   *The Music of Béla Bartók: A Study of Tonality and Progression
          in Twentieth-Century Music*. Berkeley/Los Angeles: Univer-
          sity of California Press.

BABBITT, Milton

   1949   "The String Quartets of Bartók." *The Musical Quarterly*
          XXV:377–85.

BARTÓK Collected Writings

   1966   *Bartók Béla összegyűjtött írásai I* [Collected Writings of Béla
          Bartók I]. Edited by András Szőllősy. Budapest:
          Zeneműkiadó.

BARTÓK Essays

   1976   *Béla Bartók Essays*. Selected and edited by Benjamin Suchoff.
          London: Faber & Faber.

BARTÓK Írásai

   1989   *Bartók Béla írásai 1: Bartók Béla önmagáról, műveiről, az új
          magyar zenéről, műzene és népzene viszonyáról* [Béla Bartók's
          Writing 1: Béla Bartók on himself, on own compositions, on
          new Hungarian music, on the relationship of art music and

folk music]. Közreadja [ed. by] Tallián Tibor. Budapest: Zeneműkiadó.

BARTÓK Letters

1971   *Béla Bartók Letters*. Collected, selected, edited and annotated by János Demény. Budapest: Corvina Press.

BARTÓK levelei

1976   *Bartók Béla levelei*. Szerkesztette Demény János. Budapest: Zeneműkiadó.

CHAPMAN, Roger E.

1951   "The Fifth Quartet of Béla Bartók." *The Music Review* XII:296–303.

DEMÉNY, János

1954   "Bartók Béla tanulóévei és romantikus korszaka (1899–1905)" "[Béla Bartók's Student Years and Romantic Period"]. In *Zenetudományi Tanulmányok* II [ed. by] B. Szabolcsi, D. Bartha. Budapest: Akadémiai Kiadó.

1955   "Bartók Béla művészi kibontakozásának évei I (1906–1914)" ["The Years of Bartók's Artistic Evolution I"]. In *Zenetudományi Tanulmányok* III [ed. by] B. Szabolcsi, D. Bartha. Budapest: Akadémiai Kiadó.

1959   "Bartók Béla művészi kibontakozásának évei II (1914–1926)" ["The Years of Bartók's Artistic Evolution II"]. In *Zenetudományi Tanulmányok* VII [ed. by] B. Szabolcsi, D. Bartha. Budapest: Akadémiai Kiadó.

1962   "Bartók Béla pályája delelőjén . . . (1927–1940)" ["Béla Bartók at the Height of His Career . . ."]. In *Zenetudományi Tanulmányok* VII [ed. by] B. Szabolcsi, D.Bartha. Budapest: Akadémiai Kiadó.

DILLE, Denijs

1965   "Angaben zum Violinkonzert 1907, den Deux Portraits, dem Quartett Op.7 und den zwei Rumänischen Tänzen." In *Documenta Bartókiana* 1965:91–102.

Documenta Bartókiana. Published by D. Dille

1964   Vol. I. Mainz: B. Schott's Söhne–Budapest: Akadémiai Kiadó.

1965   Vol. II. Mainz: B. Schott's Söhne–Budapest: Akadémiai Kiadó.

1968   Vol. III. Mainz: B. Schott's Söhne–Budapest: Akadémiai Kiadó.

1970   Vol. IV. Mainz: B. Schott's Söhne–Budapest: Akadémiai Kiadó.

FORTE, Allen

1960   "Bartók's Serial Composition." *The Musical Quarterly* XLVI:233–45.

GOW, David

1973   "Tonality and Structure in Bartók's First Two String Quartets." *The Music Review* XXXIV: 259–71.

LENDVAI, Ernő

1955   *Bartók stilusa a "sszonáta két zongorára és ütőhangszerekre" és a "Zene húros-, ütő-hangszerekre és celestára" tükrében"* ["Bartók's style as reflected in Sonata for Two Pianos and Percussion and Music for Strings, Percussion and Celesta]. Budapest: Zeneműkiadó.

1971   *Béla Bartók. An Analysis of his Music*. London: Kahn & Averill.

1983   *The Workshop of Bartók and Kodály*. Budapest: Zeneműkiadó.

MASON, Colin

1950   "Bartók Through His Quartets." *Monthly Musical Record* 80.

1957   "An Essay in Analysis: Tonality, symmetry and latent serialism in Bartók's fourth Quartet." *The Music Review* XVIII:189–201.

NÜLL, Edwin von der

1930   *Béla Bartók: Ein Beitrag zur Morphologie der neuen Musik*. Halle/Saale: Mitteldeutsche Verlags-Aktiengesellschaft.

PERLE, George

1955   "Symmetrical Formations in the String Quartets of Béla
        Bartók." *The Music Review* XVI, 300–12.

1967   "The String Quartets of Béla Bartók." [Program notes for the
        recordings performed by the Tátrai String Quartet.] New
        York: Dover Publications Inc. Reprinted in *A Musical Offer-
        ing: Essays in Honor of Martin Bernstein*. Ed. by E. H.
        Clinkscale and C. Brook. New York: Pendragon Press, 1977,
        pp. 193–210.

SCHUH, Willi

1952   "Kompositionsaufträge." In *Alte und neue Musik: Das Basler
        Kammerorchester unter Leitung von Paul Sacher 1926–1951*.
        Zürich: Atlantis Verlag.

SOMFAI, László

1969   "'Per finire'. Some Aspects of the Finale in Bartók's Cyclic
        Form." *Studia Musicologica* XI:391–408.

1981   *Tizennyolc Bartók-tanulmány. [Eighteen Bartók Studies]*.
        Budapest: Zeneműkiadó. Includes among others: "Bartók 2.
        rapszódiájának rutén epizódja" ["Ruthenian episode in
        Bartók's 2nd Rhapsody"]. *Muzsika* 1971:XIV. (Study No.17)

STEVENS, Halsey

1964   *The Life and Music of Béla Bartók*. Rev. ed. New York: New
        York University Press.

SZABOLCSI, Bence

1961   *Béla Bartók: Leben und Werk*. Leipzig: Reclam Verlag.

UJFALUSSY, József

1968   "Bartók Béla: Kontrasztok hegedűre, klarinétra és zongorára
        (1938)" "[Béla Bartók: Contrasts for Violin, Clarinet and
        Piano (1938)"]. *Magyar Zene* IX:342–53.

1969   "Az Allegro barbaro harmóniai alapgondolata és Bartók
        hangsorai" ["Basic Harmonic Idea of the Allegro barbaro
        and Bartók's scales"]. *Magyar Zenetörténeti Tanulmányok*

Szabolcsi Bence 70. születésnapjára. Szerk. Bónis Ferenc. Budapest:Zeneműkiadó. 323–31.

1971   *Béla Bartók*. Budapest: Corvina Press.

WHITTALL, Arnold

1971   "Bartók's Second String Quartet." *The Music Review* XXXII:265–70.

WINROW, Barbara

1971   "Allegretto con indifferenza. A Study of the 'Barrel organ' Episode in Bartók's Fifth Quartet." *The Music Review* XXXII:102–6.

INDEX